Communism in Indian Politics

Communism in Indian Politics

BHABANI SEN GUPTA

COLUMBIA UNIVERSITY PRESS
NEW YORK AND LONDON · 1972

This study was prepared under the auspices
of the Southern Asian Institute,
Columbia University, New York.

To Shivaji

FROM HIS FATHER

FOREWORD

The Southern Asian Institute of Columbia University seeks a deeper knowledge of that vast and tumultuous area stretching from Pakistan in the West to Indonesia and the Philippines in the East. To understand the problems facing its leaders and diverse peoples requires sustained study and research. Our publications are intended to contribute to that better understanding.

Bhabani Sen Gupta analyzes the problems facing India's Communist parties and the ways in which those parties sought to deal with them. When he proposed his study to the Southern Asian Institute, it appeared to be a bold and complex venture. But we believe he has done a penetrating and wide-ranging piece of work, encompassing an important period in Indian political history, from the last years of the Nehru era through the early years of Mrs. Gandhi's premiership.

Howard Wriggins
Director, Southern Asian Institute

PREFACE AND
ACKNOWLEDGMENTS

This volume offers a *political* study of Communism in India since 1964. In that year, the CPI split into two groups under pressure of traumatic internal and external events. Paradoxically, the split strengthened rather than weakened the Communist movement in India. In the following four years, the movement, despite a second split, made impressive gains. Its most significant new thrust is toward mobilization of the poorer sections of the peasantry for militant, sometimes armed, protest.

There exist several scholarly studies of Indian Communism. None, however, spans the period covered here. Further, unlike the existing studies, this volume is an attempt to treat Communism primarily as an *Indian* political force, and to look at its operation in the context of the operations of the Indian political system. This, of course, is no innovation. Sidney Tarrow has studied Italian Communism in the context of the predominantly agrarian society of southern Italy. There have been attempts to look at Communism in Finland in relation to Finnish society and the

Finnish political system. Donald Zagoria has been doing interesting work on ecological studies of Communism in India and other Asian societies. In recent years, scholars have been shifting their focus from the "international" to the "national" content of the Communist movements and parties. Impetus for this shift of emphasis derives from the passing of the national Communist movements from the ideological and tactical control of the Soviet Union.

Even when Moscow wielded control of the international Communist movement, it had little effective control of those Communist parties that succeeded in making their own revolutions. In other words, there were two categories of Communist movements and parties: those that remained in what Lenin called the "primary class," and those that passed out of the "primary class" and tended to become "sovereign" movements. On the basis of empirical evidence, it is possible to suggest that when a Communist movement passes the "primary class" and enters the amphitheater of a political system, so to speak, as a serious contender for power, it must work out its own strategies and tactics in the context of the society in which it operates. "Sovereign" revolutions, as distinguished from "satellite" revolutions, chart their own course within the general framework of Marxism or Marxism-Leninism. Marxism, Lenin said, is not a dogma, but a "guide to action." This has been proved by each of the Communist revolutions that relied for success largely on the resources of the indigenous movement and its leadership. Marxism as a guide to political action has given birth to what can be called the general "pool" of applied Communism.

The great conflict between Moscow and Peking has sharply reduced, if not eliminated, either power's ability to control even the satellite Communist movements and parties. If a Communist party is loyal to Moscow or Peking, the loyalty is mostly self-chosen, and a matter of calculated convenience or advantage. "Independence" does not mean excommunication; rather it confers distinction and respectability. This does not mean that there is no such thing as international Communism. There is, and there will be, for as long as one can foresee. However, its character has been changing rather rapidly from that of a disciplined movement controlled and guided from Moscow to one of an international body of national Communist movements, each insisting on being treated with the dignity of an equal. This major development has weakened Soviet power to some extent, but it would seem to have strengthened several national Communist movements and, therefore, world Communism.

In any case, it has clarified and brought into the open what has always been known to perceptive observers of Communist movements: revolutions are made not by satellite parties, but by "sovereign" parties; revolutions are not the result of conspiracies hatched in the darkness of night, nor are they an act of subversion and sabotage wrought by foreign-trained or inspired agents. Revolutions are massive, convulsive social upheavals. They occur only when a political system dies after it has weakened, and when revolutionaries have succeeded in enlisting the support and sympathy of the vast majority of the population. If revolutions are to be studied in the context of social institutions and political systems, so should be revolutionary movements and parties.

In the wake of the Bolshevik revolution, Communist parties were formed in many countries, including India, by groups of revolutionaries under the inspiration and direction of the Comintern. However, no Comintern-controlled Communist movement succeeded in making a revolution. During and after World War II, the victors imposed their own political and social systems on the vanquished—the USSR on the East European countries, and the Western allies on Italy, Western Germany, and Japan.

Meanwhile, Tito carried out his own little "sovereign" revolution in Yugoslavia, whose impact was immediately felt on the satellite revolutions in the Balkans. In China, Mao Tse-tung, who had established the undeclared sovereignty of the Chinese Com-

munist movement and party in the late 1930s, overpowered the
forces of Chiang Kai-shek, defying Stalin's "advice." Stalin, who
had boasted, quite mistakenly, that he would "move his little
finger" and "nothing would be left of Tito or Titoism," now
bowed before the triumphant Chinese revolution, confessing that
"we were wrong and our Chinese comrades were right." Then
came the other "sovereign" revolutions in North Vietnam and
Cuba. Little now remained of the "monolith" of international
Communism except certain forms, and these also withered in no
time.

The pages of history are, however, strewn with repetitions of
human folly. And so, in his confrontation with the USSR, Mao
also tried in the 1960s to put together his own brand of international Communism. The result was the emergence of two world
Communist "systems," each only nominally and formally "directed" by Moscow or Peking. In reality, independence was thrust
upon the national movements and parties. If many of these still
chose to cling to one or the other of the fountainheads, it was because of the concrete advantages derived from the relationship.
Where the national Communist movements failed to assert their
independence to the extent desired, the deterrant lay in Soviet
military power rather than in the ideological leadership of the
CPSU.

In his polemical war with the Russians, however, Mao won a
major point. His perception of the principal contradiction of the
epoch differed fundamentally from Moscow's. While Moscow perceived the principal contradiction as between imperialism and socialism, thereby confirming the Soviet Union's leadership of the
global Communist and anti-imperialist movements, for Mao, the
chief confrontation of our time was between imperialism and the
national liberation movements. We do not have to look at this
contradiction merely in terms of Marxist-Leninist dialectics.
Shorn of the Marxian lexicon, it is the contradiction between the
increasing wealth of the rich nations and the growing poverty of

the poor. The Soviet Union and the East European countries belong, willingly or unwillingly, to the former category; China, North Vietnam, and Cuba belong to the latter. Between them is the distance of machine technology, which ideological affinity is not enough to close. Adam Smith and Marx were both impressed by the "wealth of nations." The bulkiest study of the new societies of our time bears the subtitle of a "study of the poverty of nations."

It is these new nations of poverty and the poor that have compelled scholars in recent years to develop a new perspective on Communism and Communist-led revolutions. The sociopolitical experiments in China, North Vietnam, and Cuba have a relevance to the new societies whose leaders, in their bid for development and modernization, have to accomplish in years what the Western societies did in decades. In the scholarly community, the old tendency to regard Communism as an alien conspiracy committed to the destruction of cherished values of civilization gradually yielded to a more objective, less value-laden approach. For the new societies, capitalist democracy, liberal-socialism, and Communism are all "foreign" ideologies, concepts, and institutions. If the central challenge is of development and modernization, Communism can be perceived objectively only as one of the two tested methods that have worked. The causes for success or failure of Communist movements have therefore to be sought in given political and social systems rather than in imported ideologies and techniques of insurrection. Roots of revolution have to be traced to destabilizing forces reacting on given social systems.

It is in this context of current academic enterprise to look at Communism as an internal challenge to a hard-pressed political system that the theoretical framework of the present study has been laid. My indebtedness to the theoretical achievements of scholars like Samuel P. Huntington, Chalmers Johnson, Barrington Moore Jr., Cyril E. Black, Harry Eckstein, Lucian W. Pye, Dankwart A. Rustow, Everett E. Hagen, Seymour M. Lipsett,

Fred W. Riggs, Edward Shils, Daniel Lerner, and others is freely and gratefully acknowledged. However, drawing upon the increasingly sophisticated literature on developing societies and on problems of development and modernization, and analyzing the experience of the various Communist movements and parties, I have attempted to devise a rather simple and hopefully valid theoretical framework for the study of Communist movements and parties in nations recently liberated from colonial rule.

For a Communist party in these societies to pass the "primary class" stage, three major problems must be resolved. These are the problems of legitimacy, independence, and identification. *Legitimacy* implies acceptance or recognition by the political system and by a major portion of the power elite, and is achieved through a complex, and often costly, process of socialization. *Independence,* which is linked with legitimacy, enables a Communist party to make its own decisions or judgments, to gain control of the domestic situation and to formulate its own strategy and tactics, without having to obey the voice of an outside master. Without this independence it can hardly move toward the threshold of power. *Identification,* the ability to determine which elements of the social strata are allies and which are enemies, assumes increasing importance as the social classes become differentiated in the process of development and modernization. Only when these three problems have been more or less resolved does a Communist party and movement become a major contender for power. There is nothing new in this theoretical construct except that it is simple and, as such, may be used more easily to measure the maturity, strength, promises, and problems of particular Communist movements in the developing societies passing through the dynamics of modernization.

Lenin, in one of his polemical essays, approvingly quoted the observation of Kautsky that "The revolutionary center is shifting from the West to the East." The first Communist revolution occurred in Russia. From Russia, the revolutionary center has shifted to China. The welfare-capitalist societies of Europe have probably resolved, or brought under control, the major contradictions in their social systems. While change, even radical change, cannot be ruled out, it is unlikely that, except under conditions of another global war in which Soviet armies overrun the whole of Europe, these societies will go through Communist-led revolutions. The United States of America is a universe unto itself. It evidently is yet to resolve many contradictions in the social and political system, some of which appear to be mutually antagonistic. However, it is inconceivable that America will face the threat of a revolution led by Communist revolutionaries. If these premises are correct, Communism's relevance to the future of the newly modernizing, predominantly agrarian societies of Asia, Africa, and Latin America assumes considerable importance. The relevance comes from a variety of factors which the scholars named earlier and others have discussed at length and with perspicacity. For the last decade and more, the focus of global tension and conflict has shifted from Europe to Asia. Asian tensions and conflicts can only be partially attributed to external intervention. Basically their causes and roots are to be found within the social and political systems. These systems are under tremendous and still-increasing pressure for radical structural change. The instability created by this swelling pressure builds up a situation favorable for Communism.

At the forefront of the non-Communist developing societies stands India, with its teeming millions, strategic location, vast size, and its exciting experiment in democracy tempered by a mild, state-directed, consent-oriented socialism. The next ten to twenty years will be crucial for the Indian system. It is already under strong pressure and severe strain, not all of this evident on the surface of politics. During this period of strain, the Communist movement in India has expanded its support base and varied its tactical assault on the system. Though still by and large a regional force, Communism can be said to have registered its bid for power. The movement as a whole appears to have resolved the problems of legitimacy and independence. It has begun seriously to grapple with the problem of identification.

This evidently is the time when the Communist movement in India should engage the attention of students of politics and comparative Communism. The movement is now facing problems peculiar to its own growth in India. The manner in which it succeeds or fails in resolving these problems will determine its future shape, content, and prospects. Each political society is a distinct entity. Some practitioners of comparative politics at times tend to overemphasize the similarities of political systems, institutions, and processes. While similarities certainly deserve careful scrutiny and scientific analysis, the mysteries of politics lie hidden in the depths of the social system and, even more unpredictably, in the minds of human beings. These mysteries confound political actors as much as they do political scientists. They confound Communists even though Marxism claims to be a scientific guide to social change and transformation. That is why the applied dimensions of Communism happen to be more interesting than the theoretical.

As Communism becomes more and more socialized within the Indian context, its applied characteristics emerge with greater clarity. These characteristics provoke many questions. If Communists succeed in capturing power in India, either for themselves or in partnership with others, what kind of social engineering will they employ? In other words, what kind of Communism will they try in India? In what peculiar ways will it be different from Soviet and Chinese Communism? What will be the impact on Communism of Indian society, its diverse cultures, demography, social institutions, political experience, value systems, and historical traditions? Will the long-cherished elite preference for representative government and the post-independence experience of democratic politics impart to Indian Communism an openness that the political experience of neither Russia nor China could possibly permit? How much coercion will the Indian Communists use and in what forms and for what purposes?

Will it be possible for the divided Communists to unite or is it likely that there will be for a long time to come more than one major Communist party in India? What are the possibilities of a strongly centralized, disciplined Communist movement developing in India in the foreseeable future? Or will there be not only more than one major party, but also each party developing on a federal basis, the state units enjoying autonomy within a loose and lenient centralized leadership?

How are the linguistic-nationalist cultures of India likely to shape and influence the Communist movement as it spreads to more of the linguistic areas? Will the weight of the great diversity of India tend to make Communism mellower than some of the Communists might like to see it? Will peasant mobilization lead to violence and, finally, to civil war? Is the Indian terrain suitable for armed peasant revolution? Will the Indian revolution travel the Chinese path? Or will the Communists still make it a more or less peaceful transition through the parliamentary way?

Some of these questions have been raised in this book more extensively than others, and tentative answers suggested. These will call for further, closer study as the Communist movement grows.

The methodology of this study may be briefly explained. It is not a chronological narrative of Communist politics in India since 1964. The first chapter focuses on the fundamental problems that the CPI grappled with for a decade and a half—the problems of legitimacy and independence. The party split resolved the problems for each of the two Communist groups. After offering a comparative picture of the tactical lines and strategic objectives of the two CPIs, I have explored the sociological base of Communist strength in West Bengal and Kerala. An entire chapter has been devoted to the gains Communism has made through the electoral process and the problems the process has created for the Communists. In two chapters of case studies of

Communist rule in West Bengal and Kerala, the emphasis has been on the emergence of the applied characteristics of Communism in India. Considerable attention has been given to peasant mobilization and to its various applied techniques including limited attempts at guerrilla warfare. Of the last three chapters, two deal with the prospects of Maoism in India, while the third speculates on how the Communist movement is likely to develop through the 1970s. In such a methodological treatment, a limited overlapping of narrative material is unavoidable. However, this has been kept to the minimum.

Apart from published books, monographs, articles by many writers, Indian as well as foreign, the primary reference resource for this study is the literature of the Communist parties themselves. I have interviewed and discussed problems and issues with a number of Communist leaders, none of whom, however, wanted to be directly quoted—a reluctance that can be explained by the fact that the interviews and discussions took place on the eve of the mid-term election of March 1971, when interparty bitterness was at its height, and most of the leaders said their views were tentative, given in a hurry.

I toured the West Bengal countryside on the eve of the election to observe aspects of peasant mobilization by the Communists; I was able to converse with peasant and trade-union front cadres in Bengal and Bihar. These people, mostly young, many of them from a rural background, were remarkably candid and forthcoming. Talking to them one would get the impression that the Communist movement in India is, by and large, an astonishingly "open" movement. Only the Maoist groups were secretive and difficult to reach. This was partly because the CPI(ML) had chosen to function as an underground party.

It now remains to record the genesis of this study. I was still working on *The Fulcrum of Asia* (New York, Pegasus, 1970) as a senior fellow of the East Asia Institute and the Research Institute

on Communist Affairs, Columbia University, when the idea occurred to me that there should be a study of Indian Communism
in the context of Indian politics. I mentioned this to a group of
friends and colleagues, among whom were Donald S. Zagoria, a
noted scholar on Sino-Soviet relations and on Communism, and
Roderick MacFarquhar, former editor of *China Quarterly*. They
asked me to draw up an outline of study. Zagoria and MacFarquhar sent copies of the outline to several persons. One of those
to show an immediate interest was A. Doak Barnett, of the Brook-
ings Institute. A few days later, I received a call from Howard
Wriggins, Director, Southern Asia Institute, Columbia University. Professor Wriggins invited me to undertake the study as a senior fellow of the Southern Asia Institute. As the work pro-
gressed, I was able to discuss it with several scholars at Columbia
and at Hunter College of the City University of New York, where
I was teaching. Zagoria and Wriggins read several chapters and
gave valuable comment. The former enabled me to present the
general theoretical framework of the study at seminars at Columbia University as well as Hunter College. Returning to India toward the end of 1970, I exchanged notes with several journalists
knowledgeable on Communist affairs. I gained from reading political literature published in India during the last three years
and from discussions with some of my colleagues at the School of
International Studies, Delhi.

I am grateful to Howard Wriggins for making this study possible. During the progression of this study, I came to know Howard
Wriggins not only as an astute and rigorous scholar, but also as a
man of quiet but rich humanism, of many silent acts of kindness
which are unforgettable. I am grateful to Don Zagoria and Rod
MacFarquhar, dear friends, in ways too numerous to mention.
What I appreciated most during my work on this study at Columbia was the complete freedom from political censure that I was
allowed. For errors of judgment and lapses in scholarship, I alone
am to blame.

I record my appreciation of the help rendered toward this study by Ashoke Mahadevan, a graduate student of Columbia University, who worked for a year as my research assistant; by K. P. Chatterji, of Calcutta, S. Pillai, of Kerala, and S. C. Sharma, of New Delhi, who also helped with research; and to S. L. Kaushik who typed the final manuscript under tremendous pressure of time. I enjoyed and benefited from the many criticisms offered, often quite forcefully, by my nephew, Partha Majumdar, a young talented journalist and an articulate Marxist, with whom I frequently discussed issues arising from the study. Finally, I am mindful of the numerous ways I was helped and sustained during the writing of the manuscript by one too dear and close to me to be mentioned in print.

B.S.G.

School of International Studies
Jawaharlal Nehru University, New Delhi
January, 1972

CONTENTS

Communism in Indian Politics

Abbreviations Used in Text and Notes

AICCR	All-India Coordination Committee of Communist Revolutionaries
AIKS	All-India Kisan Sabha
AITUC	All-India Trade Union Congress
BKD	Bharatiya Kranti Dal
CCP	Communist Party of China
CDSP	*Current Digest of Soviet Press*
CEC	central executive committee
CPR	Chinese People's Republic
CPSU	Communist Party of the Soviet Union
CSP	Congress Socialist Party
CTUC	Central Trade Union Congress
DMK	Dravida Munnetra Khazagham
ISP	Independent Socialist Party
KCP	Kerala Congress Party
ML	Muslim League
NLF	National Liberation Front
PCI	Communist Party of Italy
PKI	Communist Party of Indonesia
PSP	Praja Socialist Party
RSP	Revolutionary Socialist Party
SSP	Samyukta Socialist Party
SUC	Socialist Unity Center

1

THE LONG QUEST
FOR LEGITIMACY AND
INDEPENDENCE

The Indian Communist Party (CPI) split in two on April 11, 1964. Challenging the parent party, a second party emerged which decided to call itself the Communist Party of India (Marxist). Five years later, on May 1, 1969, this second party's extreme left, which had been expelled some sixteen months earlier, formally announced the inauguration of a third party, and named it the Communist Party of India (Marxist-Leninist). This triple division of the Indian Communist movement coincided with similar schisms in Communist parties of Indonesia, Burma, Malaysia, and Ceylon.

The global scenario was provided by the Sino-Soviet conflict, more particularly the decision of the CCP to project the Chinese revolution as the model for social revolutions in all of the newly liberated countries, and to organize an international Communist movement anchored on Marxism-Leninism and Mao Tse-tung thought. The internal ambience was no less significant. In India, as in other Asian countries, the old nationalist leadership had passed or was passing. It had lost much of its revolutionary elan and became a defender of the status quo built in the first years of independence. In some cases, it was the status quo of what Frantz Fanon has termed as "VC-10 socialism"—the accumulation of wealth by a small number at a high speed.

In India, the first Communist split occurred about two months before Nehru's death. At the time of the second split, the Congress party lost control of local government in a majority of the Indian states. The splintering of the Indian Communist movement was paralleled by deep schisms in almost all of the other political groups. Within a few months of the formation of the third Communist party, the Congress party itself broke into two warring factions, thereby heralding the end of the first phase of post-independence Indian politics. It had been a phase of by-and-large orderly, though not entirely unpainful, transition from the colonial period to independent national reconstruction under the leadership of a political elite that provided a bridge between empire and nation.

The CPI split in 1964 went unnoticed in Soviet mass media. When the parent CPI held its seventh congress in Bombay in December, Moscow Radio and Tass carried a brief report: "The seventh congress of the Indian Communit party has adopted a resolution on the ideological question. The resolution notes the historical significance of the decisions adopted by the twentieth and twenty-second congress of the CPSU for the world Communist movement." Then followed a precis of the resolution. Soviet mass media ignored the rival congress, also the seventh, held in Calcutta by the CPI(M).[1]

In contrast, Chinese mass media played up the news of the split, and hailed the birth of the new Communist party as "the

[1] Moscow Radio, Tass international service (in English), December 23, 1964 .

end of the first stage of the struggle against the bourgeois-reformist policies and disruptive organizational practices adopted by the Dange group." It was a clear victory of the Maoist challenge to Khrushchev's revisionism. "Adhering to Marxism-Leninism and expelling the renegade Dange group," reported *Peking Review,* "the congress issued a declaration calling on Communists to oppose revisionism and lead the people in the struggle against imperialism, safeguard national independence, and strive for people's democracy." Chinese media reported the CPI congress also. "Attended by delegations of the Communist parties of the Soviet Union, France, and Italy, and of the Tito clique of Yugoslavia," the congress "loudly prated about revisionist ideas, poured venom on China, and boosted the Lal Bahadur Shastri government." [2]

Students of international Communism have sometimes been inclined to look at the CPI split from the focal point of the Sino-Soviet conflict. Thus, Harry Gelman perceives the CPI as a "Sino-Soviet battleground," and offers the following explanation for the split:

The repeated efforts of the Soviet and Chinese Communist parties to pressure other parties in the world Communist movement into committing themselves in the struggle against the fraternal antagonist have fostered evident dissension, recrimination, and factional struggle in the ranks of many Communist parties, but nowhere more than in the Communist Party of India (CPI). As a result of numerous factors— geography, the importance of India, and the Indian Party's own history—the CPI was destined to become a sort of borderline region in the Communist internecine conflict, an arena where the opposing influences of the CPSU and the CCP have clashed more openly and on more equal terms than in almost any other Communist party of comparable importance. [3]

While the Sino-Soviet conflict certainly exercised a powerful impact on the internal tensions and dissensions of the CPI, the party

[2] *Peking Review,* January 22, 1965, pp. 17–18.

[3] Harry Gelman, "The Communist Party of India: Sino-Soviet Battleground," in A. Doak Barnett, ed., *Communist Strategies in Asia* (New York, 1966), p. 101.

did not break merely under the pressure of the ideological divide between Moscow and Peking. As John B. Wood has observed, it is unwise to dismiss the split "as a simple alignment of the party into a pro-Russian and a pro-Chinese faction." The profounder reasons of the break are "peculiar to the Indian party."

It can be seen that the split in India was not due to a simple align-ment into a pro-Russian and a pro-Chinese schism but rather to irrec-oncilable differences between those who wished to see a strong, inde-pendent party unified round a clear and closely argued Marxist program resting on sound revolutionary bases, and those who were content to maintain the less complicated role of political respectability within a parliamentary democracy and who hoped to "persuade" the bourgeois government to carry out the task of social revolution for them.[4]

This judgment, while rightly placing more emphasis on the ef-fect of domestic issues on Indian Communism, would seem to confirm Peking's perspective of the split. In any case, even if one agrees with Wood's evaluation of the predicament of the right-wing of the CPI, one does not understand *why* and *how* the ma-jority of the CPI became so "bourgeoized." Furthermore, Wood does not relate the crisis in Indian Communism to the dynamics of the universe of domestic politics. He does raise a very impor-tant question for students of comparative Communism: is it possi-ble for a Communist party to pursue parliamentary tactics and still maintain its revolutionary character? He does not, however, attempt to answer the question.

The 1964 split was caused not so much by Moscow's and/or Pe-king's bid to keep Indian Communism under control as by the party's own effort to establish its legitimacy within the Indian po-litical process and to affirm its independence within the interna-tional Communist movement. It was caused also by the complex interaction of the many changes that had occurred in Indian so-

[4] John B. Wood, "Observations on the Indian Communist Party Split," *Pacific Affairs*, Vol. XXXVIII (Spring 1965), No. 1.

ciety as a result of development and modernization. Keen, un-regulated, and uncontrollable competition among elite groups and gradual disintegration of traditional caste alignments had a divisive effect on almost all Indian political parties. It is in the sociology of Indian Communism rather than in the Sino-Soviet conflict that one must look for the causes of the split.

A CRISIS OF GROWTH

The crisis of Indian Communism is a crisis of growth. It is a crisis related to the "nationalization" or assimilation of Communist doctrine—Marxism-Leninism—by Indian society. "Nationali-zation" of this doctrine becomes obligatory for a Communist movement when it reaches a certain degree of maturity, when it finds itself within sight of the threshold of power and is deter-mined to make a bid to capture power. Whatever method a Com-munist party may adopt for its thrust for power, be it urban working class insurrection, protracted peasant guerrilla war, or parliamentary tactics, the party must appear to large sections of the elite as a national force and not as the instrument of an alien power. Each Communist movement or party that has succeeded in capturing power without much external assistance has had to "nationalize" Marxism.

The leaders of these sovereign revolutions have creatively ap-plied the Marxist doctrine to the concrete realities of their own societies. Thus, Lenin, Mao, Ho Chi Minh, and Fidel Castro did not copy each other's revolutions, but each wrested from Marx-ism strategies and tactics that suited the requirements of his par-ticular revolution. Each can be seen to have contributed to the general "pool" of what may be called the theory and practice of applied Communism.

Lenin was the first to make a successful Communist revolution and to usher in the world's first socialist republic. And thus Leninism came to enrich Marxism; the Communist doctrine now could claim to possess both a theoretical and an applied dimension. Mao Tse-tung, being the father of the second large revolution, has added his Thought to the expanding doctrinal and methodological "pool." Contributions have also been made by Tito, Ho Chi Minh, and Castro, all of whom led protracted armed revolutionary struggles to victorious conclusions. There has been no peaceful Communist revolution yet, but Communists dominate the ruling coalition in Chile, while in Italy, the Communist party is striving to be *elected* to lead the government, even if as the dominant partner of a coalition.

In each of these cases, the Communist party and its leaders have had to find their own strategic and tactical lines. Lenin visualized not only the diversity of Communist movements and revolutions, but also competition among the various revolutionary methodologies. "When I said to one of the best comrades among the Polish Communists, 'You will do it (the revolutionary reconstruction) in a different way,' he replied, 'No, we will do the same thing, but better than you,'" Lenin told the eighth congress of the Bolshevik party. And he added, "To such an argument I had absolutely no objection. We must give them the opportunity of fulfilling a modest wish to create a better Soviet government than ours." [5]

The "monolith" of international Communism could prevail only as long as no second revolution occurred without Soviet intervention. The Yugoslav revolution, the first largely sovereign revolution outside the USSR, found itself *competing* with the Soviet system. Next emerged the Chinese revolution, fully sovereign, and highly competitive. Each sovereign Communist revolution, then, is a constellation by itself, linked with the other constellations in collaboration and conflict, in competitive cooperation and in open rivalry.

[5] V. I. Lenin, "On the Party Program," *Selected Works*, 2 vols. (Moscow, 1947), II, 444.

Each Communist party functions in a dual environment and has a dual personality, external and internal. When a Communist party refuses to remain "forever in the primary class," to use another Leninist phrase, its internal personality must get the better of the external. In other words, it must be accepted by major sections of the elite as well as by the masses as a national political force.

It must now progressively resolve three principal problems: legitimacy, independence, and identification. Within the general framework of the Marxist doctrine, these three issues cover the entire spectrum of strategy and tactics. *Legitimacy* can be acquired by either working legally within a political system or illegally in defiance of it, depending upon objective conditions prevailing in a particular society. No Communist movement has ever made revolution without pursuing its own, *independent* strategy and tactics. *Identification* is mainly a question of tactics: a Communist party, in its bid for power, must know who are its core supporters, its allies, and its enemies.

Lenin found the supporters of the Bolshevik party in the industrial workers and its allies in the poor peasantry; one of his greatest problems was the middle-level peasants, whom he found to be vacillating and therefore worthy of particular attention. Mao drew the bulk of supporters of the Chinese revolution from the poor peasantry, and had no particular problem with the middle-level peasants, thanks to the Chinese Communist party's ability to lead the national resistance to Japanese imperialism over vast stretches of the Chinese countryside.

In fact, from 1935 onward Mao set himself to resolve the CCP's problems of legitimacy, independence, and identification. He conducted the CCP's affairs more or less independently of the Comintern. He devised for the CCP a revolutionary methodology that was distinctly different from the methodology of the Bolshevik revolution. He seized the opportunity provided by the Japanese invasion to resolve the problem of legitimacy for the Chinese

Communist Party. And, learning from the experience of the revolutionary struggle, he identified the CCP with the vast majority of the Chinese people—the rural proletariat and the urban industrial workers.[6]

The ideal situation for a Communist party in a colonial or semicolonial society is when it is able to spearhead and lead the national struggle for independence to a successful conclusion. The struggle against imperialism enables it to build a mass base among the rural proletariat which becomes the mainstay of the revolution.[7]

In the vast majority of colonial and semicolonial societies, however, the struggle for independence has been led by the national bourgeoisie, which has numerous objective and subjective links with the metropolitan power. In these societies the Communists have to work *with* and *against* the bourgeoisie simultaneously. The theoretical and tactical problems created by this objective necessity have plagued international Communism for half a century. The problem became more complicated when the Soviet Union began to use the Communist movements in the various countries, through the Comintern, at least partly to serve the interests of the Russian state. Even if this helped the cause of *international* Communism, it created additional difficulties for the indigenous Communist parties and movements in affirming their independence. The problem hit the CPI in India as soon as the country gained its independence.

THE EARLY YEARS

The Indian Communist party was created by the Comintern some time in the 1920s. It took the party more than fifteen years

[6] John E. Rue, *Mao Tse-tung in Opposition,* Hoover Trust on War, Revolution and Peace (Stanford, Stanford University Press, 1966).

[7] See Chalmers A. Johnson, *Peasant Nationalism and Communist Power* (Stanford, Stanford University Press, 1962), especially chs. 1 and 7.

to hold its first congress. For most of these years, the CPI functioned on the periphery of the Indian National Congress, along with several other leftist groups. Not that the party's first years were without any drama and excitement; the Meerut Conspiracy Case, which put the CPI on the political map of India, attracted much attention in India and abroad.

The party's impact on Indian politics and on the national freedom struggle was, however, marginal. It did useful work on the trade-union front with students and, at times, with the middle-class poor in the large cities; it also organized a few peasant protests. But it is doubtful if the CPI's main tactical line to infiltrate the Congress faction heavily and to capture the leadership of the national struggle was even taken seriously outside the relatively small coterie of intellectuals who composed its leadership. The CPI also did not appear to have had much success in radicalizing the Congress party and the Gandhian movement. Gandhi was in sole control of the Congress group and of the Indian freedom struggle; his was the most decisive voice in determining its strategy as well as tactics.

As long as India was under foreign rule, Communism's problem of legitimacy could be solved only in the crucible of the national liberation struggle. If the CPI had succeeded in strongly influencing the form and content of the Indian freedom movement, the issue of legitimacy of the Marxist dogma would not have created a major problem; it did not in China which was, in many ways, a more tradition-bound society than India. If the CPI was regarded by most Indians as basically "un-Indian," it was because of the party's failure to resolve the one problem that had dogged it since its creation: its conflict-or-cooperation relationship with the national bourgeoisie. This remained a problem for so long because the CPI could not, or perhaps would not, solve it according to its own experience and wisdom, but would look for guidance from Moscow.

Relationship with the bourgeoisie was one of the major problems of the Chinese revolution also; since the late 1930s, Mao and

the CCP resolved to solve it largely on the basis of the accumulated experience of the revolution and its strategic and tactical
objectives. In doing this, Mao had to depart substantially and vi-
tally from the formulations of the Comintern on the colonial
problem.[8] The CPI, in contrast, remained a faithful, though confused, unit of the Comintern.

Somewhat ironically, an Indian Communist, M. N. Roy, played
an important part in the formulation of the Comintern's first pronouncement on the colonial question. Lenin appeared to have a
clearer, if less radical, perception of the role Communists could
usefully perform for the liberation movements in the colonies belonging to European powers. In his first draft, Lenin stressed the
"necessity of all Communist parties to render assistance to the
bourgeois-democratic movement" in these societies. Roy, on the
other hand, wanted the Comintern to "assist exclusively the institution and development of the Communist movement in India";
he wanted the Indian Communist party, set up with Comintern
assistance, to "devote itself exclusively to the organization of the
broad popular masses for the struggle for the class interests of the
working people." [9] The pronouncement, as it finally emerged
from the second congress of the Comintern, was a compromise between Lenin and Roy. On behalf of the Comintern, Roy directed
the infant CPI during its formative years. And in doing so, Roy
"continued to oppose" the Comintern policy for India, which was
that the Communists should try to take over the nationalist movement by capturing the Congress faction from within. Roy "did
not cease trying to discredit the Congress in the eyes of the Comintern in the hope of bringing about a revision of its policy." [10]

[8] Major revisions of the Comintern thesis can be seen in Mao's several strategic
and tactical formulations including "On Coalition Government" (1937), *On New
Democracy* (1941), and *On Contradictions* (1945).

[9] *The Second Congress of the Communist International: Proceedings* (Moscow
1920), p. 478.

[10] Gene D. Overstreet and Marshall Windmiller, *Communism in India,* (Berkeley,
University of California Press, 1959), p. 28. For Roy's perspective of the Congress
party, see M. N. Roy, *The Future of Indian Politics* (London, 1926); Roy substantially changed his views later, see his *Our Differences* (Calcutta, 1938), p. 10.

M. N. Roy was the typical apocalyptic hero of Indian Communism of the 1920s. A self-taught Marxist and an indomitable revolutionary, he had no experience of working with laborers or peasants in India or abroad. A man of impressive intellect, he had taken part in the terroristic politics of Bengal before becoming a legendary fugitive from British justice. Like other terrorist leaders of Bengal, Punjab, and Maharashtra, Roy had been completely disenchanted with the Gandhian leadership of the Congress movement, which he regarded as conservative and compromising. In 1922, when the Congress faction had been remarkably radicalized by Gandhi, Roy considered it "dead as a political organization." [11] It is this perception of the Congress faction that was transmitted to Indian Communists from the Comintern in Moscow. Communist attempts to radicalize the Congress group from within made little impact in the 1920s because the CPI was psychologically unprepared to understand and appreciate the radicalism of Gandhi and the dynamics of his movement.

The CPI did not grow out of the Indian freedom movement. It was brought together by several scattered groups of self-converted Communists in the three metropolitan centers of Calcutta, Bombay, and Madras. Among them, the Bengal group alone seemed to have a certain politcal base in the Workers' and Peasants' Party —an organization set up by some mildly radical intellectuals.

A peculiarity of the formative years of the CPI was that an unusually large number of Muslims also played a leading part in its formation. Of the eight Communists tried in the Kanpur Conspiracy Case, three were Muslims. A Muslim, Maulana Hasrat Mohani, was chairman of the reception committee for the Kanpur Conference where, according to one account, the first central committee of the CPI was constituted. Of the thirty-one Communists and trade unionists arrested in 1929 in connection with the Meerut Conspiracy Case, six were Muslims.

[11] Roy, *Our Differences*, p. 44.

The first young recruits to the CPI were high caste youths of brilliant academic career—including G. Adhikari, B. T. Rana- dive, and P. C. Joshi. The first rush of new members came in the early 1930s during and after the Meerut Conspiracy Case. "In Bengal jails and camps, terrorist *détenus* started reading Marxist literature." Prisoners in the Andaman jail also did the same. Hundreds of them joined the CPI after their release.[12]

In 1934 the CPI had 150 members—an increase of 130 within a year. The party and all of its fronts were "illegal"—the CPI was, as its draft provisional statute described it, "a strictly illegal organization." During the 1930s, however, it continued to attract new recruits rather quickly—the collapse of the second Gandhian civil disobedience movement, and the worldwide depression drew the educated middle-class youth to the Communist party. The new Comintern-administered tactical line of working from within the Congress movement and building a united front from above also furnished the party with recruiting opportunity.

However, the party's social base was almost entirely middle class. Its leadership was comprised of de-classed intellectuals with university-level Indian or foreign education. Its operational base was the trade unions, the lumpen proletariat of the cities, the Congress movement, and the student community. The CPI's mind was, then, the mind of the Indian middle-class intellectual. Given the geographical and linguistic factors of the Indian polity, it was the mind of the middle-class intellectuals of the coastal provinces—Bengal, Madras, and Bombay, where Communism was building up an increasing intellectual appeal.

The former terrorists who now joined the party constituted a new radical element. However, they also brought into the CPI the old group and personal jealousies and rivalries and the strong individualism of the terrorist movement. The CPI was thus laden with some of the psychosocial problems of terrorist politics: in- tense emotional upsurge followed by sudden collapse of fervor;

[12] Muzaffar Ahmad, *Communist Party of India: Years of Formation* (Calcutta, National Book Agency, 1959), pp. 2–23, 35.

subjugation of the objective reality to the subjective goal; blind obedience to the "master"; lack of mutual tolerance and respect; and strong parochial cultural pride.

The radicalism of these middle-class revolutionaries was often one-dimensional. Many of them combined a passionate desire to see India liberated from foreign rule with social conservativeness and loyalty to traditional norms and values. An American who knew Roy in Mexico noted: "Except for desiring Indian independence, he was in no sense a radical, for he believed firmly in child marriage, the caste system, and most of the traditional evils that thus far have prevented India from achieving nationhood." [13]

The relatively small number of Indian revolutionaries, Roy among them, who functioned abroad, and some of whom tried to enlist Moscow's support for Indian freedom, were remarkable for their mutual isolation, lack of mutual respect, intense personal and group rivalries and jealousies, and self-pride. An Indian Communist who knew Roy abroad described him as "self-important and ill-tempered in discussion," and "often vehement in seeking to impose his opinion on others." A British Communist observed: "Of all Indians I have met he was the most arrogant." [14] These psychosocial traits could be found in many of the Indian revolutionaries who joined the Communist party in the 1930s.

With time, younger elements came to the party in increasing number, but they were no less intellectually and emotionally fragmented than their predecessors. In fact, they were more rooted in particularist cultures. Gradual disintegration of the traditional society made it all the more necessary for these younger revolutionaries to be incorporated into some self-transcending, authoritative entity.[15] It is hardly surprising that the younger Communists

---

[13] Carleton Beals, *Glass Houses* (Philadelphia, Lippincott, 1938), p. 44.

[14] Overstreet and Windmiller, p. 24n.

[15] As Edward Shils has said of the intellectuals of the underdeveloped societies: "Indeed, the greater his struggle for emancipation from the traditional collectivity, the greater is his need for incorporation into a new, alternative collectivity." Edward Shils, "The Intellectuals in Political Development," in John K. Kautsky, ed., *Political Change in Underdeveloped Countries* (New York, Wiley, 1967), p. 205.

found nothing wrong in the leadership's dependence on the Comintern for guidance and direction at every critical point.

The middle-class intellectuals who joined the CPI in the 1930s and 1940s were not fundamentally very different from their counterparts in the non-Communist political parties and organizations. The Communist intellectuals were de-classed only *intellectually* (if that) but not in actual working-class or peasant movements. An inquiry into the life style of thirty leading Communists in Bengal, Kerala, and Uttar Pradesh I made in 1960 showed that twenty-five of them took part in traditional Hindu festivals, twenty-one had married off their sons and daughters in the traditional religious manner, twenty-two had on more than one occasion consulted astrologers; and none thought that it would be "wrong" to perform the prescribed religious rites upon the death of their parents.

The pattern of family life of the Indian Communist was not, in most cases, different from that of the non-Communist. An all-India gathering of Communists did not differ markedly in dress, manners, language, and customs from a similar assembly of Congressmen. Until recently, the National Congress party was the platform of Indians from all parts of the country who generally came from similar social background, similar professions, and similar intellectual orientation, sharing similar political and social values and speaking a common language of politics. The same was the case with the CPI. Indian Communist leaders spoke, until the 1940s, a common ideology which was yet to be assimilated in terms of Indian reality. They engaged in endless debates but, as P. C. Joshi succinctly put it, found "no answer to the simple but vital question: what is the political situation in India?" [16]

THE ACHIEVEMENT OF LEGITIMACY

The CPI became a *legal* party in July 1942, and held its first congress in May 1943. Of the 139 delegates who attended the con-

[16] P. C. Joshi, *For a Mass Policy* (Calcutta, 1950).

gress, 86 were members of professional and intellectual groups, 22 were workers, 25 were peasants, 5 were landlords, and there was one trader.[17] Among the workers none was from the lower ranks; among the peasants none was a landless sharecropper. The first spatial expansion of the CPI took place during the war years, from 4,500 members in 1942 to 30,000 in 1945.[18] This rapid growth, the result of the central committee's decision to create a mass party, enlarged Indian Communism's middle-class, youth, and trade-union base, though not the peasant base. In 1943 the party leadership evidently felt very pleased with the expansion of membership and streamlining of organization and described the CPI as "the third largest party in our country," with an international role "next in importance to that of the Communist party of the Soviet Union and to that of the Communist party of China."[19]

World War II intensified the political crisis in India, and radicalized the masses. The enrolled membership of the Congress movement stood at 5 million in 1939 as against only 500,000 three years earlier. Of even greater significance was the emergence of the Muslim League as the mass organization of Indian Muslims. In 1940 the League for the first time articulated the demand for a separate state, Pakistan. The Congress movement refused to cooperate in the war effort, despite its sympathies for the Allies, unless Britain recognized India's claim to immediate self-government. Although Churchill would not preside over the liquidation of the empire, it became evident to perceptive people that the days of the empire were ending and that Britain would have to leave India sooner rather than later. The kind of India she would leave behind became the dominant theme of Indian politics.

[17] *People's War* (CPI weekly), June 13, 1943.
[18] N. K. Krishnan, ed., *Forgery Versus Facts* (Bombay, PPH, 1943), p. 4. These figures approximated the estimates of CPI membership in an American government intelligence report. Overstreet and Windmiller, p. 210.
[19] *People's War*, October 4, 1942.

THE CHALLENGE OF INDIA'S INDEPENDENCE

The CPI also had to face the challenge of independence. It had to think creatively about the kind of state India should be after freedom, the kind of political institutions it should create and foster. Until then, the party had apparently done little thinking on these vital issues, although much of its energies and resources had been expended on debating the hypothetical Indian revolution. During World War II, the CPI twice changed its tactical line; each time it found itself pitted against the Congress faction which, it acknowledged, would be the chief architect of the coming Indian state.

During the "imperialist war" phase (1939–1941) the CPI wanted to transform the Gandhian struggle into a general insurrection, but Gandhi refused to give battle to the British. When he gave his battle cry in 1942 with the Quit India slogan, the CPI was implementing the tactics of "people's war," which regarded Soviet (and therefore Allied) victory to be of fundamentally greater importance than India's immediate freedom or self-rule. In implementing the two opposite tactical lines, the CPI broke with the other leftist groups like the Congress Socialist party and the Forward Bloc, alienated non-Congress groups in the trade-union and peasant movements, and isolated itself from the Congress movement. Nevertheless at the end of the war its political base was stronger than before, although its strength was limited to the coastal provinces and was almost nonexistent in the Hindi-speaking north, historical Hindustan.

A careful scrutiny of the CPI's ideological formulations and tactical activity during the 1940s reveals several contradictory trends, indicating the pressures stemming from the expansion of its political base, and a desire on the part of its leadership to gain some control in matters concerning the domestic situation. With independence looming large, and the two Indian communities, Hindus and Muslims, falling tragically apart, the CPI's first concern, it seems, was the unity of India. Paradoxically, this concern was expressed in language which most Indians considered to be divisive, whereas the CPI was only exploring alternatives to the Congress concept of an Indian Union with a strong center, and the League's demand for a separate Muslim homeland.

Since 1940 the CPI had tried to "placate" the Muslim League, equating it with the Congress party as India's two mass political organizations. About this time, the CPI also began to work on its nationalities policy. Incentive came from the League's demand for the creation of Pakistan, the negotiations between the British and various Indian groups on the future political shape of India, and the several schemes or plans emanating from individuals and groups.

The CPI's nationalities program took nearly two years to be formulated. In a resolution adopted in September 1942, six weeks after the launching of Gandhi's Quit India movement, the CPI envisaged India as the home of many nationalities whose political aspirations had to be met in a scheme for independence. The resolution gave each of these "distinct nationalities" the right to a sovereign or autonomous state (the two words were used synonymously) within an Indian federation or union with the right to secede if it so desired. "Thus free India of tomorrow would be a federation or union of autonomous states of the various nationalities such as the Pathans, Western Punjabis (dominantly Muslims), Sikhs, Sindhis, Hindustanis, Rajasthanis, Gujaratis, Bengalis, Assamese, Biharies, Oriyas, Andhras, Tamils, Karnatakis, Maharashtrians, Keralas etc." [20]

The CPI recognized the "justness" of the League's Pakistan demand. The reaction in the Congress faction and among the Hindus was predictably hostile; the CPI stance only confirmed their

[20] N. K. Krishnan, *National Unity for the Defence of the Motherland* (Bombay, PPH, 1943), pp. 24–25.

evaluation of the Communists as antinationalist foreign agents. The CPI, however, was motivated by a desire to see the political unity of India maintained. While it verbalized support for the Pakistan demand, it urged Gandhi "to work out a *new* platform for the Indian national movement which satisfies the League and leads to a Congress-League United Front." [21] While it gave the autonomous states of the nationalities the right to secede, it also hastened to explain that "The grant of the right to separation should not be confused with the actual expediency of separation in this or that particular case." [22] The CPI offered the Muslims, "wherever they are in an overwhelming majority in a contiguous territory," the right to "form their autonomous states, and even to separate if they so desire" in the strong conviction, which was expressed in numerous writings and speeches of party leaders, that once the basic political aspirations of the Muslims were met and their legitimate fears of Hindu domination removed, they would not separate, and the unity of India would not be in jeopardy.

The proposal for an autonomous state for each linguistic nationality reflected, first, the sociology of the CPI and, second, the influence of the Soviet nationality model on the party leadership. As noted, the CPI's political base was in the coastal states where the party had identified itself with particularist cultural and political aspirations, the most important of which was the demand for linguistically defined provinces. The Congress faction had accepted this demand in principle, but the pressures of the national independence movement led it to emphasize the national rather than the regional aspects of the coming Indian state. The Communists were able to exploit this vacuum in Indian local politics to their advantage, and build bases among the middle classes in several parts of the country. Furthermore, the younger members

---

[21] P. C. Joshi, *They Must Meet Again* (Bombay, PPH, 1944), p. 30.

[22] G. M. Adhikari, *Pakistan and Indian National Unity* (London, Labour Monthly, 1943), p. 29. The CPI got no clear policy guideline from Moscow, nor from Soviet comments on Indian developments. These comments often contradicted one another. The British Communist party acted as the CPI's mentor. The CPI, then, was under some compulsion to contrive its own strategic and tactical concepts.

who came into the CPI in the 1930s and 1940s were rooted more to their particularist cultures than to the long-simulated all-India political culture of the Congress movement.

The challenge of on-coming independence persuaded the CPI to try to push itself into the mainstream of Indian political life, from which it had been isolated as a result of its prewar and wartime tactics. Its concept of Indian political unity within a federation of autonomous states failed to achieve this objective because it was widely misunderstood and misinterpreted as a move to balkanize India. A second decision taken by the CPI in the 1940s proved to be more helpful. The CPI accepted the legitimacy of representative government for the future Indian union or federation, and implicitly offered to work within the system of parliamentary politics. This was the first major step taken by the CPI toward *nationalization* of Communism.

THE FIRST SIGN OF POLARIZATION

In 1945 elections for the provincial assemblies were held on the basis of the Government of India Act of 1935, which provided for a very restricted electorate. The CPI decided to contest the elections. This decision is a landmark in the evolution of Indian Communism. It divided the CPI leadership into "soft-line" and "hard-line" followers. The majority of the "soft-line" followers were led by General-Secretary P. C. Joshi. Among the minority "hard-line" followers were Ranadive, Adhikari, and Ajoy Ghosh. The real issue, of course, was not the elections. The crucial question before the CPI was how to function in independent India and in its political system of parliamentary democracy without being rejected by the people as the agent of an outside power. It is the challenge of independence that divided the CPI into two polarizing factions.

As E.M.S. Namboodiripad has observed:

The internal differences of the CPI are as old as the new independent state of India; they came up again and again in different forms. The leading organs of our party. . . . tried to furnish answers to them. In the course of answering them, however, it became clear that there were different trends, different approaches within the party. This led to continuous bitter intra-party struggle, at first of an ideological and political character, but subsequently reflecting itself in the organization of our party. . . . The sixth congress held at Vijayawada in April 1961 saw this ideological organizational battle reach its zenith.[23]

Before the CPI could hold its seventh congress, it split in two.

Put in Marxist terms, the struggle centered round the question of how the CPI should use the parliamentary system and its institutions consistent with its revolutionary objectives, whether parliament should be used in the "Leninist way" or in the bourgeois way. In other words, should the CPI participate in working within the Indian political system toward gradual incremental change or should it participate so as to break the system and achieve revolutionary transformation.

Any decision involved a clear understanding and interpretation of the political situation in India as it emerged from the empire as a nation. Here the CPI leadership was faced with unusually difficult problems. In the first place, there were honest differences among the leaders in appraising the actual configuration of power alignments on the morrow of independence; some of the "hard-line" advocates apparently overrated the possibility of a revolutionary transformation of the political system. The majority evidently took a more realistic view, and came to the conclusion that constitutional Communism was perhaps the only political evolution that could be worked out, given the realities of the Indian situation.

Since neither group labored under a sense of participation and involvement in the emerging political system, the entire leadership was vulnerable to external dictation. The weakness of the "hard-line" faction was due to the absence of any revolutionary

[23] E.M.S. Namboodiripad, *Note for the Programme of the CPI* (New Delhi, Roxy Press, 1964), pp. 59–60.

base for the CPI. The weakness of the "soft-line" group stemmed from their emotional and political noninvolvement with the coming pattern of Indian politics, and their failure to apply creatively the Marxist dogma to build a revolutionary theory of constitutional Communism.

To understand this watershed period of Indian Communism and the critical dilemmas it created for the CPI, it is necessary to reflect briefly on the evolution of the *political* content of India's political culture. Each political culture is built around a dominant political idea. In the case of India, it is the idea of representative government. The idea was introduced in the nineteenth century by the first generation of English-educated Indian elite who saw in the British parliamentary system the basic framework of a political system suited to Indian aspirations and realities. The British helped in fostering the idea in the minds of the expanding Indian elite. It was indianized in the twentieth century first by Gandhi, and then by Nehru.

Gandhi broadened the base of Indian nationalism by linking the urban middle-class nationalist with the rural peasantry. Out of the Gandhian movement emerged the image of a new representative—the *Satyagrahi,* who would identify himself with the people, and give them devoted and selfless service. Gandhi, thus, brought about a marriage of modern India's two political cultures—the culture of the Western-oriented national elite and the culture of the more traditionally oriented (but modernizing) rural and small town elite.[24]

In the 1930s, the Gandhian movement reached a stalemate, and the Indian elite was in a state of intellectual stagnation and emotional frustration. Gandhism proved ineffective in meeting the challenge of reaction, secular as well as religious. The disorderly withdrawal of the second civil disobedience movement forced the

[24] See Myron Weiner, "India: Two Political Cultures," in Lucian W. Pye and Sidney Verba, *Political Culture and Political Development* (Princeton, Princeton University Press, 1969), pp. 199–244.

progressive sections of the elite, especially the younger generation, to make a frantic search for a more productive political philosophy and a more effective technique of fighting the imperialist
power.

It was at this time that the impact of Marxism began to be felt
inside the nationalist movement. Marxism, Nehru wrote in his
autobiography, lit up "many a dark corner of my mind," and
Nehru became India's greatest non-Marxist salesman of Marxism.
He brought about the second marriage of political forces in India
—a marriage of middle-class nationalism and liberal socialism. To
Gandhi's indomitable faith in the people, Nehru added a robust
faith in progress. Nehru put forth in simple, middle-class, nationalist language the kernel of Marxism without the logistic implications of a "scientific" socialist revolution. Nehru's socialism further fostered the central political idea of representative
government. The Indian image of the representative was now a
mixture of the *Satyagrahi* and the parliamentarian or the civil servant. It was a rather anomalous mixture, but it did have a great
impact on the dominant Indian political mind.

No radical political group in India, of the right or the left,
would seem to have seriously and effectively discarded or deviated
from this central political idea. The terrorists of Bengal, Punjab,
and Maharashtra did not put together any organized body of political thinking; from such political writings as are available, they
seemed to have been firm believers in a "true" Indian democracy.
Sometimes the national political image of India acquired a religious flavor as with Tilak; sometimes one could discern implicit
authoritarian strains in the political writings of nationalist
leaders—Savarkar and Subhas Chandra Bose are two names that
readily come to one's mind. But even these writings were couched
in the language of representative government. (For a further discussion of the liberal-democratic consensus core of the Indian
party system, see chapter 11.)

With its 1945 election manifesto, the CPI now embraced the

Indian political idea of representative government as well as the basic concept of the unity of India as a single political unit. The provisional governmental structure proposed by the CPI was a confederation of autonomous states—"a voluntary Union of sovereign national States"—as against the single federation plan of the Congress party and the two-federations plan of the Muslim League. The economic and social contents of the election manifesto were only mildly reformist.

Its appeal was mainly to the middle class; the CPI looked upon itself as the "unifier of the middle class with the working class in the towns and the peasantry in the villages." It envisaged industrial planning through "free and equal" cooperation of the state, management, and labor; it proposed abolition of landlordism, but with maximum holdings of 100 acres; "the party," assured the manifesto, "will not touch the small *zamindar* or the rich landlord." Adhikari came out with the reassuring statement that under the CPI program, the "middle and rich peasant would prosper more than the poor peasant." [25]

Nominating 108 election candidates for the provincial assemblies, the CPI won in only eight constituencies, representing a total popular vote of 666,723; under proportional representation the party would have won 51 seats. Six of the eight constituencies won by the CPI were labor constituencies. Even this limited success was not insignificant, considering the great handicaps the party had to fight against and the conservative character of the severely restricted electorate.[26]

As noted, the initiation of constitutional Communism met with strong opposition from the "hard-line" faction in the party. However, they did not reject representative government; what they wanted was the adoption of a line of mass struggle and of the Leninist use of parliament as a tactical instrument of mass struggle. The CPI had experimented with the tactics of mass struggle

[25] Overstreet and Windmiller, p. 230.   [26] *People's War*, October 14, 1945.

before, especially during the "imperialist war" period, but even at that time, its theoretical and tactical formulations suggested no alternative to representative government.[27] It did, of course, want to see the future Indian democracy informed with social content.

For the CPI, the challenge of Indian independence brought up a succession of tactical problems relating to Communism's legitimacy within the Indian political system. The party had failed to establish the legitimacy of revolutionary radicalism during the colonial period; its radicalism had, at no time, gone much beyond the radicalism of the Congress and other patriotic groups. In fact when independence came in 1947, the CPI could not be said to be in firm control of a large political base in India from where it could exert sustained revolutionary pressure on the political system and leaders of the ruling party. It had only pockets of influence.

The exception was Telengana, then within the princely state of Hyderabad ruled by an obscurantist despot. The peasant rebellion that formed in Telengana in 1946 was a spontaneous act of defiance by the ruthlessly oppressed peasantry, which was adopted by the *local* Communists largely on their own initiative. The Telengana peasant insurrection was essentially a *nationalist* revolt against the Nizam, who was determined to keep Hyderabad outside the on-coming independent Indian state. It was, in part, also a Hindu nationalist rebellion against a Muslim despot. It crumbled as soon as the Indian forces moved into and liberated Hyderabad. The Telengana uprising is examined in depth in chapters 10 and 11.

The overwhelming importance of domestic issues induced the CPI in the 1940s to act independently, on its own initiative, on the major issues of Indian politics. The party's history during 1939–1951 is marked by two interracting trends—independence

---

[27] See the CPI pamphlet *Proletarian Path* circulated to the delegates of the Ramgarh session of the Indian National Congress in 1939. It talked of a political general strike followed by an armed insurrection, but *not* of a proletarian dictatorship.

and submission to external direction. On each crucial occasion, the party first acted on its own, and then reversed its tactical line under external direction. The cumulative result of the experience was the emergence of two distinct trends—those who wished to assert the independence of the party, and those who preferred to follow the international line laid down by Moscow.[28]

THE ROLE OF LOYAL OPPOSITION

India's independence put the CPI face to face with the Congress party and the political system it was now to build in accordance with its own program of gradual, incremental change. Should the CPI accept the legitimacy of the emerging political system and thus establish its own legitimacy within it? Or should it declare revolutionary war on the system and its architect, the Congress party? This question was decided in 1947 in the light of the CPI's historical perspective of the Congress party, its past tactical line of united front from above, and its understanding of the character of the Indian bourgeoisie. The decision was determined also by the sociology of Indian Communism. And it was taken very largely on the party's own initiative, relying on its own intellectual and political resources, without waiting for directives from abroad.

The decision, announced in a policy statement in June 1947, made a clear distinction between the reactionary right-wing of the Congress party, which was under considerable imperialist influence but which did not control the organization, and the progressive forces in it, led by Nehru, which were in command of the Indian political situation and deserved, indeed *needed,* the support of the Communists. Only with the support of the left radical forces could the Congress leadership be expected to implement its "declared anti-imperialist program."

The CPI offered this support. "The Communist party will

[28] For documented evidence of this contradiction, see Overstreet and Windmiller, chs. 9–13, though the authors do not seem to offer this analytical interpretation.

fully cooperate with the national leadership in the proud task of building the Indian republic on democratic foundations, thus paving the way to Indian unity." The CPI was thus not only a co-sharer of the pride of independence, it also muted its earlier nationality plan, and backed the Congress government's drive to build a strong union. Only the unity of the diverse and multifarious political and social forces in India, the CPI now declared, could "decisively defeat" the "imperialist intrigues" to keep it divided and weak. In pursuance of the new tactical line of broad identification with the dominant ethos of Indian nationalism—independence and unity—the CPI worked concretely with the Indian government to control the communal riots, and even called off the powerful movement it had built up in parts of Bengal around the poor peasantry's demand for a larger share of the crops. Toward the end of 1947, the Communist party officially greeted Nehru as the one man who had "kept the traditions of the national movement alive," and expressed the hope that he would be able to set India "on the road to Socialism and prosperity." The party urged all progressive Congressmen to rally behind the prime minister.[29]

Quite remarkably, even the radicals in the CPI did not oppose this tactical line of identification with Indian nationalism and of working within the emerging political system. Ranadive, architect of the ill-fated insurrectionary line of 1948, disclosed that the radical elements in the leadership approved of the policy of loyal opposition.[30]

The loyal opposition role soon led to trouble which the CPI leadership did not have sufficient resources to resolve. In the provinces, the Congress ministries were led mostly by conservative leaders who were anxious to curb Communist influence on workers, students, and sections of the peasantry. They did not

---

[29] *People's Age,* June 29 and November 9 and 30, 1947.

[30] This disclosure came in Ranadive's review of party policy at the second congress of the CPI at Calcutta in 1948. *People's Age: Supplement,* March 21, 1948.

want to see the Communists exploit the enormous dislocations in people's lives brought about by the partition of India, the massive influx of refugees from Pakistan, and the inevitable gap between the people's aroused aspirations and the ability of the new government to satisfy them.

In Bombay, the government imposed a partial censorship on CPI journals. In Calcutta, where Congress-CPI relations had been embittered since 1938, the Communists found themselves under police surveillance. A greater threat to its trade-union base came when the Congress government set up a rival all-India trade union, the INTUC. In the countryside the Congress party began to build its political base with the powerful landlords and the wealthy and middle-level peasants. In short, the Congress organization started to use newly found political power to consolidate and broaden the political base of the newly emerging political system.

It was natural that many CPI leaders would find it difficult to offer "loyal" opposition to a government that still did not initiate economic planning or land reforms and, in foreign policy, remained almost completely tied to the British Commonwealth. To these internal factors that undermined the CPI's 1947 tactical line were added two external factors of the utmost importance—the formal outbreak of the cold war between the Soviet and the Western blocs, and the imminent revolutionary takeover in China by the Communists.

FLUCTUATIONS IN STRATEGY AND TACTICS

The four years from 1947 to 1951 were probably the most crucial period for the CPI. It was a period marked by extreme fluctuations in its strategy and tactics—from legal struggle to urban insurrection to a dogmatic imitation of Maoism and, finally, back to constitutional Communism within the framework of parliamentary democracy. For detailed accounts of Indian Communist politics of this period, the reader must turn to other studies,[31] for here we are mainly concerned with the broad evolution of the CPI as a political force prior to the split of 1964.

The cold war line was dictated to the CPI by Moscow through the British Communist party. It was adopted at the Calcutta congress of the CPI early in 1948. The Calcutta thesis saw the world divided into two antagonistic camps, in which the Indian bourgeosie, like its counterparts in other countries, could serve only as lackeys of imperialism. Gone was the distinction between progressive and reactionary sections of the Indian bourgeoisie—the CPI now declared class war on the entire national bourgeoisie, whose leader was Nehru.

The thesis urged the CPI to lead the Indian struggle for people's democracy, which was a simultaneous, single-stage struggle for democracy as well as for socialism. The struggle was to be waged through a people's democratic front built up from below. The weapons were political strikes by the urban proletariat leading to a general insurrection. However, the symbol of the struggle was to be Telengana, where the local Communists had liberated two entire districts and set up their own administration. "Telengana," declared Ranadive to the 632 delegates assembled at the Calcutta congress, "today means Communists and Communists mean Telengana."[32]

The insurrectionary line immediately exposed the intellectual and organizational weaknesses of the CPI. It failed to relate the thematic line of the party to its organizational strength and, what was worse, to the realities of the Indian political universe. It took the Indian authorities only a few weeks to round up all the important leaders of the CPI and thus paralyze its operating ma-

[31] The best accounts are to be found in Overstreet and Windmiller, and in John H. Kautsky, *Moscow and the Communist Party of India* (Cambridge, M.I.T. Press, 1956). See also Victor M. Fic, *Peaceful Transition to Communism in India* (Bombay, Nachiketa, 1969).
[32] *People's Age: Supplement,* March 21, 1948.

chinery. The party was quite unprepared for sustained underground activity.

Second, the lack of a strong rural base precluded protracted revolutionary war; it was extremely naive of Ranadive to expect the Indian state machinery to collapse as a result of industrial unrest and dislocation. The CPI soon realized that it had grossly overestimated its hold on the working class and students. Most of the attempted strikes were unsuccessful. The insurrectionary line met with strong opposition in the All-India Trade Union Congress, and so seriously threatened the Communist base there that Dange became one of its early opponents in the central committee. The All-India Kisan Sabha—the national organization of the peasantry—split. Its vice-president, N. G. Ranga, walked out, taking several provincial units with him. Significantly, in Telengana itself, the "revolutionary general staff"—leaders of the peasant uprising—was lukewarm toward the Calcutta line.

The strongest challenge to the Ranadive tactical line came from the Andhra Communists who advocated a "Maoist" line for the Indian Communist movement. The debate between the Andhra Maoists and Ranadive and his supporters has been analyzed in several studies,[33] and we need not go into this at the present moment. It should, however, be noted that the Chinese revolution had little impact on the Indian elite, including most of the Communist leaders. The Andhra group captured leadership of the CPI after the Ranadive line failed.

At a meeting of the central committee in May 1950, Ranadive was replaced as general secretary by Rajeshwar Rao, a leading Communist from Andhra Pradish, and three more of his group were elected to a new committee of nine members. Rao sought to establish links between the CPI and the CCP. The editorial board of the *Communist*, the CPI's monthly journal, sent a message to

[33] Apart from Overstreet and Windmiller and John Kautsky, a perceptive account of the debate can be found in Mohan Ram, *Indian Communism: Split Within a Split* (Delhi, Vikas, 1969).

the CCP on its twenty-ninth anniversary, declaring that the "Communist parties in the colonial world are looking upon the Communist Party of China as their model." [34] The new tactical line formulated by the CPI borrowed two points from the CCP program: a "united national front" in which the middle-level bourgeoisie and the well-to-do peasant have a place, and "armed guerrilla warfare in the countryside." The CPI asserted that India was fully ripe for such armed struggle; this alone could strengthen and expand the political base of Communism.

Under the new line, the CPI elevated the Telengana uprising to a height of symbolic grandeur (at a time when it was actually disintegrating as a result of punitive action by the Indian army), and attempted to organize, without much result, armed guerrilla peasant bands along sections of the border between West Bengal and East Pakistan.[35] The overall result of the two attempts at revolutionary mass struggle between 1948 and 1950 was a colossal depletion of CPI membership (from nearly 100,000 to 20,000), complete paralysis and stagnation in the trade unions, and the practical wiping out of peasant organizations.

The CPI stood close to "paralysis and disintegration." Its miserable state was reflected in Ajoy Ghosh's remark: "Today the reality is that nobody in the Indian party can solve this crisis. It was the international comrades who pointed out our mistakes. Since we are not agreed on the interpretation, only they can help us." [36] It was a most pathetic cry for foreign intervention by a party which only three years ago had claimed to be next in international influence only to the CPSU and the CCP!

The situation, however, was not that hopeless. For forces within the CPI that had never been persuaded of the validity of insurrectionary and armed guerrilla tactics were steadily returning to the 1947 position—the tactics of loyal opposition within

---

[34] The greeting was *not* sent by the CPI, but only by the editorial board of its theoretical journal. See *Communist*, July–August 1950.

[35] Overstreet and Windmiller, p. 300.   [36] *Ibid.*, pp. 302–3.

the Indian political system. Their leader was Joshi who, from outside the party, conducted a successful campaign against the "adventurist" lines of Ranadive and Rao, and carried the battle even to the foreign Communist parties, soliciting their support. The objective conditions in India, Joshi argued, were not ripe for armed revolution, nor could the Indian revolution blindly copy the Chinese model. Soon to Joshi's voice were added the powerful voices of Dange and Ajoy Ghosh.

This was not the first time that discipline broke down among the CPI leaders. But it was no longer a crisis of discipline. The party had tried the illegitimate lines of urban insurrection and armed peasant guerrilla warfare—"illegitimate" because such forms of struggle had not been inherited by Indian society from the colonial period. When these instruments had only brought the party to the brink of disintegration, it was left with no alternative but to return to constitutional Communism, identifying itself with the Indian political process and the Indian national ethos.

The Joshi-Dange-Ghosh protest therefore won quick support among the provincial leaders. In the spring of 1951 Ghosh succeeded Rao as general-secretary; in October, an all-India party conference approved a new program which was a first major step toward returning to legitimacy.

It was in many ways a most interesting program. The CPI discarded the tactics of violent revolution, urban or rural, and made a bid to return to the Indian mainstream. Its appeal was broadened to encompass the middle-level bourgeoisie, whom it assured that although the CPI wanted to establish socialism in India, it was not demanding a socialist transformation "at the present stage of [the country's] development." It called for a mixed economy in which private industry would receive protection, and it urged forthright redistribution of the provincial boundaries on the basis of language thereby granting self-determination to all of the nationalities.

The CPI thus did not, in its new program, recognize the Nehru government as progressive and worthy of support. It merely returned to legitimate political action within the Indian political process, but not to the 1947 tactical line of supporting the progressive bourgeoisie led by Nehru against the reactionary bourgeoisie linked with imperialism. Nevertheless, the inclusion of the middle-level bourgeoisie within the democratic forces left the door ajar for Nehru: he would evidently be supported or opposed on the merit of government policies and programs. The CPI thus did not wish to abandon entirely its public image of the last few years as opponent of the Congress regime. In taking this stance, the CPI ran into problems that assumed serious proportions several years later.

In 1950 Nehru was able to play a significant "peace" role in the Korean war; it was in Peking rather than in Moscow that his progressive role in the politics of a dangerously polarized world came first to be recognized. Toward the end of 1950 the CPI received a secret memorandum from R. Palme Dutt of the British Communist party which stressed the positive contributions already made by Nehru on behalf of peace, including his opposition to the second phase of the Korean war (the crossing of the Yalu river) and his support for Peking's claim to the Chinese seat at the United Nations.

The change coming through in Nehru's foreign policy constituted "a very important development of the present international situation." Although it was only a beginning, and Nehru's anti-imperialism was far from consistent or strong, his initiatives deserved praise and support from the Communists. They, the Communists, must welcome every step toward India's disentanglement from imperialism and organize a vigorous campaign for such disentanglement.

Palme Dutt thus placed before the CPI concrete grounds for changing the party's tactics of opposition to the national bourgeois government. Nehru was a friend of the peace camp, and even if his domestic policies had little progressive content, his foreign policy should offer strong justification for a new CPI tactic of limited and qualified support to his government.[37]

This is precisely what the CPI refused to do in its 1951 program. It placed greater importance on domestic rather than international affairs, and found it difficult to regard as progressive the foreign policy of a regime whose domestic policy was reactionary. The new program therefore emphasized that the government "essentially carries out the foreign policy of British imperialism"; moreover, it was opening India up for American imperialist penetration. While the Dutt thesis made the United States the chief enemy of all peaceloving nations including India, for the CPI, the main enemy of Indian independence was still Britain, with its strong hold on the Indian economy and influence on its foreign and domestic policy. Nehru's peace policy, the CPI declared, was "spurious." It did not serve India's basic interests.[38]

This was probably the first time when the CPI attempted to win some independence from international Communism, accepting part of the line handed down from abroad, but rejecting its most important directives. In disagreeing with Dutt's thesis, which presumably had Moscow's approval, the CPI even made a distinction between India's interests and the interests of the Soviet Union and China. However, dissent with the 1951 line within the CPI leadership was rather strong, probably because of the intense reaction of several leaders to the failure of the "hard lines" of 1948–1950. The CPI decided to contest the first general election in 1952 by and large on the basis of the 1951 program, at least officially. But it became apparent even during the election campaign that its leadership was succumbing to the *international line,* and moving rapidly toward strong support for Nehru's foreign policy.

The CPI did remarkably well in the first general election. Con-

[37] R. Palme Dutt, *Situation in India* (Bombay, Crossroads, undated.)
[38] *Programme of the CPI* (Bombay, CPI, 1951).

testing 49 parliamentary seats, it won 16 and, with 10 allies, became the largest opposition group. In four state assemblies, it
won large representation—62 in Madras, 42 in Hyderabad (where
it contested as the dominant group of the "people's democratic
front"), 32 in Travancore-Cochin (where it was the dominant
group in the "united front of leftists"), 28 in West Bengal, and
smaller numbers of seats in Bombay, Assam, Orissa, and Pepsu,
and in the electoral colleges for Tripura and Manipur. With 194
seats, the CPI was the largest party in the state assemblies after
the Congress party.

   This impressive success showed the party's strength as well
as its weakness. The CPI won only 3.3 percent of the popular
vote in the parliamentary election, and 4.4 percent of the popular vote in the state elections—both were considerably smaller
than the popular vote for the Socialist party. Its numerical strength
in the Lok Sabha and four state assemblies indicated that its political base was strong only in a few states, and very weak in Hindi-
speaking northern India. The party was strong in the industrial
constituencies and weak in the countryside. Its election strategy
showed that while it was able to form alliances with small local
groups, it could not do the same with the large national groups.
Much of its success was due to its effective championship of linguistic particularism.

APPROACHES TO THE USE OF THE
PARLIAMENTARY SYSTEM

   The election gave the CPI what it had not been able to obtain
so far: the legitimate status of an influential all-India party. The
question that now faced the party was how to make use of parliament for a social revolution. In fairness to the CPI it should be
noted that the party could hardly turn to any external source for
sound guidance. What is known in Communist literature as the
"Leninist use of parliament" clearly did not apply to India. The
Leninist parliamentary tactics were based upon the pragmatic

consideration that as long as the masses had faith in parliament, Communists must engage in parliamentary activity, not to strengthen the parliamentary way, but to destroy it—it was similar to working within the enemy camp. Lenin had used military strategy in the form of Bolshevik participation in the Duma to work toward liquidation of the assembly, just as the existence of a Bolshevik opposition within the White Russian camp helped in its defeat in the civil war.[39]

In Stalin's words, "the parliamentary struggle is only a school for, and an auxiliary in, organizing the extra-parliamentary struggle of the proletariat. . . . The fundamental problems of the working class movement are solved by force, by the direct struggle of the proletarian masses, their general strike, their insurrection." [40] In the sixth Duma, there were only six Bolshevik members; they all came from the factories, and their main duty was "to use their Duma privileges to conduct revolutionary struggle.[41]

The CPI did not appear to have made a differentiation between the parliamentary system that took shape in Russia between 1905 and 1917, and the parliamentary system the Indian ruling elite devised, based on the British model. In Russia, the belated experiment with parliamentary techniques was totally incapable of coping with the rapidly escalating revolutionary situation; they were regarded only as defense tactics by which the bourgeoisie were trying to stave off the revolution. In India, on the other hand, parliament represented the political value system of the new and vigorous bourgeoisie revolution; to the Indian ruling elite the *formal rights* of parliament were more important than the actual content of the system in terms of social and economic freedoms.

Lenin had made it abundantly clear that it was not the busi-

[39] Merle Fansoid, *How Russia Is Ruled* (New York, 1966), pp. 38–41.
[40] J. Stalin, *The Foundations of Leninism* (Moscow, 1950), p. 29.
[41] Fansoid, p. 54.

ness of Communist revolutionaries to strengthen bourgeois parliamentary systems for the reason that "the interests of the
revolution are higher than the formal rights of the constituent assembly." According to Lenin, Marxists must always make a distinction between "the form of elections, the form of democracy,"
and "the class content of the given institution."

For the toiling masses, participation in bourgeois parliaments (which
never decide important questions in bourgeois democracy; they are decided by the stock exchange and the banks) is *hindered* by a thousand
and one obstacles, and the workers know and feel, see and realize per-
fectly well that the bourgeois parliaments are institutions *alien* to
them, *instruments for the oppression* of the proletariats by the bourgeois, institutions of a hostile class, of an exploiting machinery.[42]

The Bolsheviks therefore lost no time in asking for a soviet parliament instead of a bourgeois parliament, and one of the first
things Lenin did after the October revolution was to disband the
constituent assembly. The Bolshevik experiment, then, could provide no guidelines to the CPI, which was clearly not thinking in
1951 of wrecking the parliamentary system from within, but of
working for the revolution through means existing within India's
parliamentary democracy.

Nor was the Chinese revolution of any help to the Indian Communists, even granting that they were willing to learn from it—
which they were not. Neither Lenin nor Mao rejected the theoretical possibility that in certain circumstances Communists
might choose to work within the legal framework of the given political society and through parliament or legislative assembly.
Both, however, decided that such conditions did not exist in their
countries. Mao found in the early 1940s that the CCP could not
even make a "Leninist" use of parliament, because conditions in
China were so different from conditions in tsarist Russia.

---

[42] Lenin, "Proletarian Revolution and Renegade Kautsky," *Selected Works* (2
vols.; Moscow, 1942), II, 282–92. Italics in the original.

China is not an independent sovereign state, but a semicolonial and semifeudal country; internally there is no democratic regime; but her people suffer the oppression of a feudal regime; externally there is no national independence, but her people suffer the oppression of imperialism. Because of these facts, there is no legislative assembly to make use of, no legal right to organize the workers to strike. Here the fundamental task of the Communist Party is not to go through a long period of legal struggle before launching an insurrection or civil war. Its task is not to seize first the big cities and then the countryside, but to take the road in the opposite direction.[43]

The CPI apparently decided in 1951 that, given the objective conditions in India, it had to go through a long period of legal struggle, making use of the parliamentary apparatus. Was this decision reached after serious deliberation on how the party was to use parliament to further the cause of revolution, or was the return to the parliamentary line *inevitable* after the collapse of the urban insurrection tactics of Ranadive and the armed peasant guerrilla warfare line of the Andhra Communists? Perhaps the latter rather than the former was the case. The CPI therefore failed to make any creative contribution in the 1950s and early 1960s to the general "pool" of applied Communism. Instead of devising a new tactical line to use parliament for revolution, the CPI, or at least a majority of its leaders, succumbed to the values and forms of the bourgeois parliament.

The CPI, however, began with a "Leninist" approach to parliament. This was particularly so in the constituent assembly which had a sole Communist member, Somnath Lahiri of Bengal. Lahiri sought to introduce a resolution asking the assembly to dissolve itself and convene a new legislative body that would fashion a truly independent constitution. His speeches were clearly propagandist.

However when, after the first election, the CPI found itself virtually the *leader* of the opposition in the Lok Sabha, its role un-

[43] Mao Tse-tung, *Selected Works* (Peking, 1960), II, 267.

derwent a quick change. The CPI members could no longer behave as simple revolutionaries, although in the beginning they showed a certain amount of disrespect for the governmental framework. They began to take their parliamentary business seriously, and were anxious to present themselves as better parliamentarians than their opposite numbers on the Congress benches. Some demonstrated an impressive mastery of parliamentary procedure and often quoted from British rules-of-order handbooks to make their point with the Speaker. Their tactics now could by no means be called "Leninist"; they did not aim at dissipating and overcoming the Indian bourgeois prejudices about parliament.

As Overstreet and Windmiller put it, "In the year or two preceding the second general election in 1957, the Communist party in parliament perceptibly mellowed its attitude and behavior in accordance with the new international Communist line of qualified friendship toward the Nehru government. The change was apparent in both the tone and the content of the Communist contribution to parliamentary debate." [44] The CPI did not send to the Lok Sabha and the state legislatures workers from the lower ranks. It sent its best men and women. It was these men and women, and not the agit-prop personnel, or the organizational leaders, who now came forward to build the public image of the CPI.

THE ELEVATION OF PARLIAMENTARY TACTICS
TO THE STRATEGIC LEVEL

It was not surprising therefore that the CPI should soon elevate the parliamentary line from the tactical to the strategic level. This, however, did not happen without sharp, often bitter, and continuous intraparty differences. The party leadership divided into three groups—right, left, and center. For the better part of the 1950s, the CPI was caught in a potentially creative turmoil.

[44] Overstreet and Windmiller, p. 481.

Working within the parliamentary system gained it legitimacy, of which the crowning evidence was the party's capture of power in the state of Kerala in the 1957 general election. The leadership now strove to affirm the party's independence.

However, the bid for independence brought the CPI into conflict with Moscow. The conflict stemmed from the differing perspectives of Moscow and the CPI of the class role of the Indian government led by Nehru. After the outbreak of the Korean War, Nehru's foreign policy made a favorable impression on Peking and Moscow. The CPI, on the other hand, was inclined to judge Nehru by his domestic policies, which it found to be "anti-people." As the cold war intensified, the Soviets became increasingly aware of the value of nonalignment, and they (as well as the Chinese) put Nehru in the "peace camp," and wanted the CPI to lend him increasing support. Thus, the interests of international Communism (and the power interests of the Soviet state) clashed with the interests of Communists in India, for the CPI saw nothing progressive in Nehru's economic and social programs, and was not prepared to support him because of his foreign policy alone.

This clash exposed the CPI to strong outside pressure. The party could resist the pressure only if it had a strong base in India, and if it were confident that it had found its own strategic and tactical lines that could stand by themselves. This, however, was not the case. The parliamentary tactics the CPI was following steadily "bourgeosized" the party, and led to bitter intraparty controversy. The weakness of the tactical line led the dominant leadership gradually to surrender to the tactical instructions received from Moscow. The CPI thus lost a historical opportunity to make a creative contribution to applied Communism. The failure led to a serious intraparty crisis which was partly responsible for the 1964 split.

The first serious and by all accounts bitter debate on the parliamentary method took place at the third congress of the CPI at Madurai in December 1953, in the wake of the party's impressive gains in the first general election. In Marxist terms, the central issue was the CPI's attitude toward the "national bourgeoisie"; in the esoteric Communist language of the time, this issue was debated in terms of who was the "main enemy" of the Indian people—United States imperialism or British imperialism? If it was American imperialism, then Nehru's progressive foreign policy, which had won the approbation of Peking and was winning the praise of Moscow, entitled the bourgeois government to the CPI's support; only the quality and content of support remained to be decided. If, on the other hand, the Indian people's main enemy was British imperialism, then Nehru's reactionary domestic policies must determine the CPI's relation with his regime— the CPI in that case *had* to oppose Nehru, even if at times it decided to support aspects of his foreign policy. Essentially, therefore, it was a question of priority of the Indian versus the international environment. Between the third congress at Madurai and the fifth congress at Amritsar, the CPI rapidly embraced the "international line," amounting to acceptance of the *strategy* of the parliamentary way.

At Madurai, the weight of the changing external environment was deeply felt—Nehru's foreign policy was becoming distinctly anti-imperialist, and was winning the approval of Peking and Moscow. Harry Pollitt, leader of the British Communist party, personally urged the congress to line up with the international line. However, champions of the domestic affairs cause were still in a strong position. The result was the emergence of a centrist line, of which the main authors were Ghosh, Dange, and Namboodiripad.

As Ghosh explained this position after the congress, the CPI had to choose between two alternatives: "cooperate with the government but criticize specific acts; or oppose the government but support specific acts." The CPI chose to oppose the Nehru government, but to support specific acts. The Madurai political resolution stated: "The situation does not warrant that democratic forces should give general support to governmental policies even in the international sphere. This is because the Indian government does not follow consistently a policy of peace and democracy." [45]

To a majority of CPI leadership, the contradiction between the Nehru government's policy of peace (foreign policy) and of democracy (domestic policy) dissolved in the following three years. India became a friend of China as well as of the USSR. The differences with Peking over Tibet were resolved, and India and China jointly proclaimed the Five Principles of Peaceful Coexistence. Chou En-lai came to Delhi in June 1954, and Nehru visited China the following November. And a year later, Khrushchev and Bulganin descended upon India with a massive friendship offensive.

Not only did India's foreign policy now have almost the complete approval of the two Communist powers, but the offer of Soviet participation in India's economic development convinced the CPI that Nehru's domestic policy was no longer antidemocratic. Confirming this conviction were the Congress party's adoption of a resolution in 1957 declaring the establishment of a socialistic pattern of society as the goal of its economic policy, and the endorsement of this goal by parliament.

The Soviets, on their part, left no doubt in anybody's mind about their endorsement of Nehru's *domestic* policy. On the eve of mid-term elections in Andhra Pradesh, a CPI stronghold, *Pravda* came out with an editorial lavishly praising the achievements of the Indian government both in foreign policy and in domestic reconstruction. The Congress party's thumping victory at the polls and the CPI's poor showing were partly the result of this editorial which the Congress party had distributed widely among the electorate.[46]

[45] Ajoy Ghosh, *On the Work of the Third Congress of the CPI* (1954), p. 6; and *Political Resolution* (Delhi, CPI, 1954), pp. 6–7.

[46] *Pravda*, January 26, 1955; *Current Digest of the Soviet Press* (CDSP) Vol. VII, March 9, 1955.

Under the impact of these far-reaching developments, the factions in the CPI that insisted on opposing the national bourgeoisie began to lose ground and those that stood for a policy of general support, gain. Closely following Chou En-lai's visit to Delhi in June 1954, *New Age* printed an article signed by its editor, P. Ramamurti, calling for "a national platform for peace and freedom," which implied CPI support for the Nehru government.[47] This article opened up a bitter debate in the politbureau. The central committee, meeting in September, stuck to the centrist Madurai congress line. The committee's decision, as reported by Namboodiripad, was that "there is no question of abandoning the struggle against the Congress government or revising the slogan of replacing it by a 'government of democratic unity.' The task of the democratic forces . . . is to intensify this struggle." [48]

The centrists, however, knew that their stand did not have Moscow's backing. After a trip to Moscow in December, Ghosh moved somewhat toward the "national platform" line, but still refused to endorse the government's domestic policy. "The internal policy of the Nehru government does not suit the interest of the masses, while the foreign policy does," he told a press conference.[49] When the central committee met in March 1955 to review the CPI's debacle in the Andhra Pradesh election, the differences between the cooperationists and the oppositionists became clearer and sharper. A commission set up to report on the election was unable to submit a document on which everyone agreed.

Meeting in June again, when Nehru was touring the USSR, the central committee, after a month-long debate, came out with a political resolution that was a qualified surrender on the part of the oppositionists. Nehru's foreign policy came in for eloquent praise, his domestic policy was still criticized as being hostile to the interests of the people, but members of the CPI were asked to participate in some of the development projects.[50] Yet differences

---

[47] P. Ramamurti, "Drive U.S. Out of Asia," *New Age*, July 18, 1954.
[48] *New Age*, September 19, 1954.   [49] *New Age*, December 5 and 12, 1954.
[50] *Communist Party in the Struggle for Peace, Democracy and National Advance* (Delhi, CPI, 1955).

continued to be acute, bringing party activity in several states to a standstill.

Ghosh made another journey to Moscow, and the central committee met again after his return in September. Still unable to resolve the differences, it decided to convene the CPI's fourth congress. But by the time this congress was held at Palghat in April 1956, the CPI was shaken by new developments in international Communism. At the twentieth congress of the CPSU, Khrushchev denounced Stalin, and the Russian congress adopted a new strategy for world Communism. In part, it envisaged the possibility that several of the newly liberated nations, particularly those who were neighbors of the USSR and China, could accomplish a peaceful transition to socialism. India was implicitly placed among these nations.

In the CPI, the cooperationists now quickly moved to a position of dominance. For them, the CPSU twentieth congress proposal resolved, once and for all, the contradictions between foreign and domestic issues. For the first time in the history of international Communism, peaceful transition to socialism— without the inevitability of civil war and using the parliamentary process—was elevated to the strategic level. International Communism now seemed to legitimize the program the cooperationists in the CPI had been pressing for since 1954.

The political resolution adopted at the Palghat congress was a clear victory for the parliamentary, peaceful line. Only the year before, international peace and national democracy were, for the CPI, two different areas of struggle. Now, they converged. "Life itself has shown," declared the Palghat resolution, "how the struggles for peace and defense of national freedom, for democratic rights and vital interests of the masses, are inseparable and strengthen each other."

The CPI announced its "most energetic and unstinted support" for "every step that is taken by government for strengthening national freedom and national economy against imperialist, monopolist and feudal interests." There was no longer any doubt about the role Communism was to play within the Indian political system. "In order that the Communist party may pursue such a revolutionary and flexible policy and play its rightful role as the builder and spearhead of the democratic movement, it must come forward as an *independent national force*. It must act as a Party of Opposition in relation to the present government."

In its perspective of the Congress party, the CPI now went back to its position of the 1930s and the 1940s. The Congress had within it "a vast number of democratic elements. It has an anti-imperialist and democratic tradition." Recent policies of the government had strengthened the democratic forces in the Congress party and expanded its mass following. "Our approach toward the Congress party and the method of criticising its political policies have to be such as take into account all these factors. They have to be such as do not repel honest Congressmen but draw them towards unity. They have to be such as strengthen the forces that, however haltingly, are taking a relatively progressive position." [51]

INDIAN COMMUNISM:
INDEPENDENT AND NATIONAL

The key sentence in the Palghat resolution was the one that visualized the growth of Indian Communism as "an independent national force." The exact meaning of this phrase was apparently not clear to many Indian Communists in 1956; nor did it strike even such perceptive scholars of Indian Communism as Gene Overstreet and Marshall Windmiller as particularly significant. What did Ajoy Ghosh, who drafted most of the Palghat resolution, have in mind when he used that phrase? What did *independence* imply for the CPI in 1956, and how could it develop as a *national* force?

There can be only one answer to this question: in the year of

[51] *Political Resolution* (Delhi, CPI, 1956).

the twentieth CPSU congress, at least a section of the CPI leadership visualized the growth of the Indian party as an independent, sovereign unit of international Communism. They visualized the end of the period, which had been long and costly, when the CPI allowed itself to be guided almost helplessly from Moscow. As an independent party, charting its own political path through its own accumulated experience, the CPI could hopefully develop into a strong *national* force. Independence of external control appeared to be an essential coefficient of operating within the Indian parliamentary system as the main Party of Opposition to the bourgeois government.[52]

The international situation was propitious for the CPI's independence. The CPSU had lost its control of world Communism. The manner in which Khrushchev shattered the icon of Stalin shocked many Communist party heads, some of whom, Togliatti for example, openly questioned the propriety of the CPSU action. Ghosh, who had led the Indian delegation to the CPSU congress, witnessed the reservations and misgivings entertained by several parties, notably the CCP, toward certain aspects of the new Soviet strategy. Ghosh's comment on de-Stalinization reflected the new spirit of independence the CPI now wished to grasp. "The twentieth congress . . . not only ended the deification of Stalin," said Ghosh, "but also demolished the belief in the infallibility of *any party* or any leader."[53]

The riots in Poland and East Germany and the uprising in Hungary further weakened Moscow's leadership of world Communism. The Italian Communist party made a virtual declaration of independence. In 1957 Mao openly attacked the twentieth congress line at the Moscow meeting of the major world Communist parties and by 1958 Sino-Soviet differences grew into a rift between the two nations at both government and party levels.

The CPI could have utilized the differences between Moscow

---

[52] Ghosh's main weakness as leader was that he lacked strong following in any large state unit of the CPI; he was a centrist, a mediator between warring factions.
[53] *New Age,* December 10, 1956.

and Peking to foster and consolidate the independence of India's Communism. There is evidence to suggest that this was Ghosh's intention. The Chinese Communist party had so far never tried to intervene in the affairs of the CPI, nor did it try to establish direct links of communication with it.[54] CCP leaders joined issues with the CPSU at various international Communist forums since 1949, and their tactics appeared to be to persuade the CPSU to change certain aspects of its policy rather than influence the various Communist parties against the CPSU.

The CPI was not obliged to accept the twentieth CPSU congress thesis in its entirety. Even within the framework of the concept of noncapitalist development and peaceful transition to socialism, there could be honest differences between Soviet and CPI assessments of the Indian situation. Prior to 1956, loyalty to the CPSU might have obliged the CPI to abandon its own assessment in favor of the Soviet one; in fact, this is what the party had done on a number of crucial occasions, almost always to the detriment of its own growth as a national political force. After the CPSU twentieth congress, there was no such obligation. Ghosh could therefore criticize certain aspects of the CPSU's de-Stalinization drive. He even declared that the CPI would no longer blindly follow the CPSU:

We agree that we were wrong in idealizing everything in the USSR. We should have paid more attention to the criticism of the USSR made by Socialists and non-Communist democrats. We agree that among us and in other Communist parties, the tendency developed of defending everything done by the USSR, of condemning everyone who criticized any aspect of the Soviet policy. We are deeply conscious of the damage this has done to the cause of Communist-Socialist unity and even to the cause of Socialism. We are determined to abandon this attitude.[55]

When, in the summer of 1956, the Soviet journal *New Times* printed two articles by Modeste Rubinstein declaring that India

[54] See John H. Kautsky, *Moscow and the Communist Party of India*, last chapter.
[55] *New Age*, November 25, 1956.

had already embarked upon the road of noncapitalist development, Ghosh at once joined issue with this euphoric stance, and
affirmed a vital area of disagreement between the Rubinstein
perspective and that of the CPI.

What is virtually ignored in the article is the profound truth that
"Whatever the form of transition to socialism, the decisive and indis-
pensible factor is the political leadership of the working class headed
by its vanguard. Without this, there can be no transition to socialism."
. . . The bourgeoisie, no matter how radical and progressive, cannot
build socialism which is based on new property relations. Power in the
hands of the democratic masses led by the proletariat—that is the essential condition for the building of socialism. The replacement of
bourgeois-landlord rule by the rule of the working people headed by
the working class—without this socialism is inconceivable. . . . To
conclude: There undoubtedly exists a noncapitalist path of development for the underdeveloped countries like India. But it would be an
illusion to think that the present government, headed by the bourgeoisie, can advance on that path. The Communist Party of India does not
suffer from such illusions.[56]

What the CPI did not realize in the mid- and late 1950s was
that the new leaders of the Soviet Union had embarked upon a
policy of building India as a friendly Asian power partly, at least,
as a buffer to China.[57] In other words, the CPI made no distinction between the interests of the Soviet state and the interests of
particular national Communisms and the world Communist movement.

As long as the USSR was the only socialist "fatherland," this
distinction could be ignored by all Communist parties. The survival and prosperity of the only socialist state might be construed
to coincide with the vital interests of world Communism. However, in a community of a dozen or more socialist states, and with
the recognition of each Communist party's right to travel its own
road to socialism provided that this did not violate the minimum

[56] *New Age* (monthly) October 1956.
[57] See Bhabani Sen Gupta, *The Fulcrum of Asia* (New York, Pegasus, 1970), chs.
2 and 3.

agreed-upon norms of Marxist-Leninist doctrines, there could hardly be complete convergence of the state interests of each Communist nation and the interests of each Communist party. This would apply particularly to the USSR and China, both major powers, whose *power* interests might conceivably clash (and did often clash) with the particularist interest of one or another of the numerous Communist parties.

If the CPI could maintain its independence of Moscow and build on that independence, it might have a better understanding of, and a certain sympathy for, the Chinese objections to the CPSU twentieth congress line, and the Soviet policy of a *detente* with the United States that stemmed from it. In the first place, the CPSU had fashioned its twentieth congress thesis without prior consultation with the leading Communist parties including the CCP. The CPSU, moreover, wanted the twentieth congress strategy to be accepted as the common strategy for all Communist countries and for world Communism. The national interests of the USSR and China coincided only as long as they had a common policy regarding their common enemy, the United States. Khrushchev had decided to reverse the USSR's policy toward the United States and work for a *detente* without securing the vital national interests of the Chinese People's Republic: its seat at the UN, its territorial integrity (the Formosa issue), and its national security (the U.S. military encirclement of the Chinese mainland).

What interested Mao was not peaceful coexistence with the United States, but the *liberation* of China from American imperialism. The Chinese position in the Sino-Soviet differences in the late 1950s was not such as might not have received the sympathy, if not the support, of the CPI, if only the Indian party could make an impartial, objective, and independent assessment of the disputes.

CHINA: THE "OTHER" COMMUNISM

The CPI failed to make such an assessment. It was overtaken by the nationalist upsurge in India following the outbreak of hostilities along the Sino-Indian border. Soviet support for India in its border dispute with China made the USSR India's most valuable friend, and China its treacherous enemy. If working out the strategic line of peaceful transition through the parliamentary process made the CPI a *national* force, the Sino-Indian border conflict made it a *nationalist* element. It was the nationalist stampede in the CPI in 1959–62 that finally split the party in 1964.

A remarkable fact about Indian Communism was that until the 1960s it had very few important contacts with the CCP (see chapter 10 for a detailed discussion). While the parties in other Asian countries, from Japan to Indonesia, came into various levels of communication and relationship with the CCP, the CPI kept itself more or less aloof. The Chinese party also tacitly accepted the Indian party as within the orbit of the CPSU. Throughout the 1950s the CPI made no particular attempt to study the Chinese revolution and appreciate its divergence from the Bolshevik revolution. Among the party cadres, Mao's writings were not compulsory reading. No CPI leader visited Peking; none talked with Chou En-lai or any other Chinese leader during his visits to India. The CPI welcomed the friendship that grew between the Indian and Chinese governments, and continued to look at the Soviet Union as the undisputed leader of world Communism. At one time, leaders of the CPI regarded Kardelj of Yugoslavia as the most influential Marxist outside the Soviet Union.[58] No such recognition was extended to Mao Tse-tung.

Throughout the 1950s, Chinese mass media carried few commentaries on the Indian situation except for two periods, 1950–51, and 1959, when India and China differed over Tibet. Most of the Chinese comments reflected Soviet and CPI assessments of the Indian situation. The Chinese government, as noted,

[58] This happened in 1948. According to a later intraparty report of this period by Ajoy Ghosh, the Indian radicals regarded Kardelj as the greatest Marxist thinker outside Russia; Ghosh claimed that Kardelj's writings had influenced him "most powerfully"; Ranadive hailed Kardelj as "showing us the correct Marxist revolutionary path." Overstreet and Windmiller, p. 268.

preceded Moscow in identifying Nehru and part of the Indian bourgeoisie as a progressive force in the global struggle against imperialism. In 1950–51, the Chinese made a clear distinction between these "two Indian trends," one progressive, the other reactionary, but both working together in the Indian government. This roughly echoed the CPI's own assessment of the Indian bourgeoisie. In January 1959 Ch'en Yi paid an eloquent tribute to Nehru's domestic policy, indicating thereby that the CCP had no particular objection to the strategy that was being pursued by the CPI. Three months later, the Tibetan uprising broke out. The Chinese leaders still made a distinction between Nehru, whom they regarded basically as a friend of China, and the reactionary, anti-China elements in the Indian bourgeoisie.

The first attempt to integrate Chinese Communist thinking on India was made in May 1959 when the editorial departments of *People's Daily* and *Red Flag* authored a long formulation entitled "The Revolution in Tibet and Nehru's Philosophy." Part of it reflected the CCP's differences with the CPSU assessment of the Indian bourgeoisie. The Soviet line, the article suggested, is based either on an incorrect class interpretation or on no class interpretation at all, which is worse. India's upper bourgeoisie, it said, "maintain innumerable links with foreign capital"; it has a "certain urge for outward expansion." Also, "for historical reasons, India's upper bourgeoisie has inherited and is attempting to maintain a certain legacy from the British imperialist rulers." Nehru himself is different; he has tried to keep the expansionists under control, and he sincerely desires friendship with China. However, he lacks a scientific outlook of history and has been "involuntarily" pushed by the imperialist alliance "into an important role" of cultivating world support for the Tibetan crisis.

The only occasion when the CCP publicly joined issue with a Soviet leader over the Indian situation during the 1950s was at the time of the eighth congress of the Chinese party in 1958. Mikoyan, leading the Soviet delegation, tried to equate Chinese and

Indian state capitalism, and affirmed that India was proceeding on the noncapitalist road to socialism. Liu Shao-chi, in replying to Mikoyan, made the same points that Ajoy Ghosh had made in 1956 in rebutting the arguments of Modeste Rubinstein.[59] There is, then, no evidence to suggest that the CCP had done anything during the 1950s to offend the CPI.

But China gave grave offence to the Indian nationalist elite, first, by insisting that the Sino-Indian border was undemarcated and open to dispute, next, by using force against Indian patrols and, finally, by employing military force in the border war of 1962. It so happened that the majority in the CPI leadership deeply shared the sense of injury done by the Chinese to India's national pride and what most Indians perceived to be the Chinese threat to their country's national interests. China thus created the first great crisis of conscience for Indian Communists. Unfortunately, this crisis coincided with the CPI's moment of triumph in parliamentary politics when, in the second general election in 1957, the CPI, apart from maintaining its position as the second largest party in parliament and the state assemblies, was elected to power in Kerala. Soon afterwards, the Sino-Indian border dispute came out in the open.

The dramatic CPI victory in Kerala was regarded as the first solid reward of the strategy of peaceful transition to socialism, and the party now proceeded to reconstruct its organization to better suit its role of constitutional opposition to the bourgeois government. At its extraordinary congress at Amritsar, Punjab, in March-April 1958, the CPI adopted a new constitution which "made a dramatic gesture toward 'Indianizing' the party's creed." [60] While the basis of the party's policy was still Marxism-Leninism, the creed, the preamble to the new constitution declared, must be integrated "with the realities of the Indian situa-

[59] For a fuller account of the evolution of China's assessment of the Indian situation, see Sen Gupta, chs. 3 and 4.
[60] Overstreet and Windmiller, p. 545.

tion, with the experience of India's history, with the traditions of the Indian people, with India's national peculiarities." In other words, Indian Communism must conform to what modern comparative politics calls the political culture of the country.

In a concrete effort to achieve this conformation, the preamble asserted that the CPI would strive to achieve "full democracy and socialism by peaceful means." The constitution made no mention of a proletarian dictatorship. It envisaged a people's democracy in which there would be "the widest possible extension of individual liberty, freedom of speech, press and association, including the right of political organization." [61] As Overstreet and Windmiller interpreted it, the "essence of the preamble, then, is a deep bow to the nonviolent and democratic traditions of India." [62]

Ajoy Ghosh further clarified the new creed of the CPI when he explained at a news conference that while the CPI could not guarantee that violence would never occur, it accepted the possibility of India's peaceful progress toward socialism. "And we shall try our utmost to make this possibility a reality in our country." [63]

The "peaceful transition" strategy had its opponents within the CPI leadership and its critics in the CPSU from the very beginning. Developments in India, political as well as economic, sometimes reinforced the supporters and at other times the opponents of the new strategy. In the Soviet Union, while CPSU leaders, evidently anxious to build cordial relations with the Indian government, stressed only those aspects of the Indian situation that could be said to lend support to the concepts of peaceful transition and noncapitalist growth, some members of the central committee and a strong section of the academic community took a sterner look at Indian events and grew increasingly doubtful about the applicability of the new strategy to Indian conditions.

---

[61] *Constitution of the Communist Party Adopted by the Extraordinary Congress at Amritsar, New Delhi, CPI,* 1958.
[62] Overstreet and Windmiller, p. 541.   [63] *New Age,* May 18, 1958.

The Communist government in Kerala became a test case for the new strategy. Its program was by no means revolutionary, but its style was different, and that was enough to rouse the non-Communist groups in the state to anger and outrage. The privileged property-owners received no protection from the police when peasants took "peaceful" possession of land acquired by the landlords in excess of the ceilings imposed by agrarian reform legislation. When the government came out with legislation to secularize Kerala's largely denominational education system, the Nair Service Society and the Catholic Church joined forces with the Congress party to organize a "liberation movement." In the CPI, critics of the new strategy believed that their misgivings were confirmed both by the eagerness of the chief minister, Namboodiripad, to behave like a bourgeois rather than a revolutionary, and by the sharp opposition to the Kerala ministry within and outside the state, an opposition which the central government, and Nehru himself, did little to subdue.

That within the CPSU doubts and misgivings about the Indian situation existed at a certain significant level became evident when the *World Marxist Review* printed in December 1958 an article on the Indian situation by Pavel Yudin, Soviet ambassador to China, and a member of the central committee. Yudin pointed out some of the major obstacles to India's noncapitalist growth: the country had already gone a long way toward capitalist development, and the government was incapable of preventing an increasing control of the economy by Western monopoly capital. Nehru and his party knew nothing about real socialism and had no solution for India's poverty; the middle path that Nehru was following was an exercise in abstraction.

Against this scenario, Yudin then came to the crucial point. Whether or not there would be peaceful transition would depend on the conduct of the Indian bourgeoisie. If the Communists were prevented from getting power by peaceful means, they would have no alternative but violence. Yudin then proceeded to infuse the Communist parliamentary tactics with some revolutionary content. The CPI should change its policy of total support for the Nehru government and should organize mass action to force that government to pursue progressive policies at home and abroad. Yudin drew a clear line between the progressive and reactionary elements in the Indian bourgeoisie, and asked the CPI to support the first and oppose the latter.[64]

NATIONALIST FEELINGS VERSUS COMMUNISM

The Indian authorities took advantage of the intense anti-China sentiment roused by the Tibetan rebellion and tensions along the Sino-Indian border to dismiss the Kerala ministry in August 1959. In the CPI itself, the predominant disposition was to blame Peking for the dismissal. The outbreak of border skirmishes in the fall of 1959 exposed the party leadership to a crisis of nationalist conscience. In September, the central executive committee adopted a resolution affirming the party's conviction that a socialist country could never commit aggression, and urging negotiations to settle the border dispute. The resolution raised a hue and cry in nationalist circles, who accused the CPI of treason. Some of the top Communist leaders, Namboodiripad and Dange among them, issued statements supporting the government's stand on the border issue. Ghosh, too, was steadily veering to this position.

---

[64] The publication of the Yudin article in the *World Marxist Review* and not in *Pravda* would indicate that while it reflected the perspective of a strong minority in the CPSU central committee, it did not represent the views of the leadership. This became clear at the twenty-first CPSU congress when Khrushchev lauded Indo-Soviet economic collaboration, and Mukhtidinov gave greater credit to Nehru for India's progressive home and foreign policies than to the "democratic forces." Since the late 1950s through the 1960s the Soviet academic community grew increasingly skeptical of peaceful transition in India; in the early 1960s, the CPSU conceded that India could not be expected to chart the noncapitalist road. These caveats and misgivings, however, had no impact on the Soviet government's policy to cultivate Indian friendship. In fact, Indo-Soviet state relations grew in reverse proportion to the lowering of the academic community's ideological sights about India. For a fuller documented account of Moscow's India strategy, see Sen Gupta, chs. 2 and 3.

Ghosh led the Indian delegation to the Chinese Peoples' Republic's tenth anniversary celebrations in October. Returning to Delhi, he told newsmen that he had been assured by Mao of China's peaceful intentions. Within a few days, however, a skirmish occurred between Indian and Chinese patrols in Ladakh, in which several Indians were killed and others taken prisoner. On October 24, the CPI central secretariat deplored this "tragic event." A few weeks later the central executive committee endorsed the McMahon Line as India's border in the eastern sector, maintained that the western sector was in dispute, and welcomed Chou En-lai's proposal for a meeting with Nehru.

Meanwhile, the Soviet government rallied to India's support. Ignoring Peking's objections, Moscow first came out with the now-famous Tass statement of September 9, taking a neutral stand between Chinese brothers and Indian friends. On October 31 Khrushchev, speaking at the Supreme Soviet, regretted the Ladakh incident and urged friendly negotiation to find a solution "to the mutual satisfaction of both sides." In a volunteered comment to the *New Age* correspondent, the Soviet leader suggested that China should be generous in settling the border dispute with India, as the USSR had been with Iran.[65]

It is a moot question whether the majority in the CPI leadership took an anti-China stance because of Soviet opposition to Maoism, or because of their own assessment of Chinese behavior along the border. I am inclined to take the latter view, if one must raise this question at all. In the Sino-Soviet ideological dispute, individual Indian Communist leaders obviously held partisan views, but the party as a whole would probably have had a great deal of sympathy for the CCP if Sino-Indian relations had not deteriorated so rapidly. The majority was probably persuaded that Peking had deliberately picked on India to demonstrate the fragility of the CPSU twentieth congress postulates on peaceful transition.

[65] Barnett, ed., *Communist Strategies in Asia,* p. 116.

In the circumstances, opposing China's India policy became synonymous with supporting the Soviet Union in its disputes and differences with the CCP. Both became part and parcel of Indian patriotism, a test of nationalism which the Communists were now so anxious to pass. In September 1960, the central executive committee of the CPI for the first time took the Soviet side against the Chinese. In a resolution it did not mention China by name, but supported Soviet positions on the necessity of averting war, on peaceful transition, and on creative application of Marxism. A strong minority, however, opposed the resolution.[66] The majority also got a second "intraparty" resolution passed over the objections of the minority group, condemning the CCP's handling of Sino-Indian relations over Tibet and the border issue. The resolution said that the CCP had done particular harm to the CPI especially with its mistaken assessment of the Indian bourgeoisie.[67]

This was the first time in several years that the majority in the CPI forced through major controversial political resolutions in the teeth of the opposition of a strong minority, thus breaking the golden rule of consensus and compromise that had been historically a strong factor in keeping *any* Indian party leadership together. To the injury of the passage of the intraparty secret resolution was added the salt of its leakage to the press. This was an incentive to rebellion. On October 21 the Bengal committee of the party protested and leaked the protest resolution to the press. It accused the majority of a pro-Soviet and anti-China bias, and sought to equate the CPSU and the CCP as fountainheads of revolutionary guidance. A similar resolution was passed by the Punjab party, while motions to get such resolutions adopted by the Bihar and Uttar Pradesh parties were defeated.[68]

In the federal scheme of Indian politics, no party's central leadership has ever found it easy to discipline a provincial leadership

[66] *Hindustan Standard* (Calcutta), September 8, 1960.
[67] *Link* (weekly; Delhi), September 11 and 18, 1960.
[68] *Hindustan Times*, November 14, 1960.

that is well-entrenched in its own political base. Relations between central bodies and provincial units have particularly plagued the leftist parties. The CPI has been no exception. In 1960 the CPI was not the same party that it had been a decade before. For eight years it had practiced parliamentary politics, more or less like the bourgeois parties; open, legal political activity had led to many linkages between the CPI and bourgeois institutions, groups, and personalities. Parliamentary politics also enhanced the importance of the provincial parties, especially in Kerala, Bengal and Andhra Pradesh, where the CPI's political base was the strongest.

However, the main reason why discipline in the CPI virtually broke down in 1960 was that both the majority and the dissidents were jockeying for position in the forthcoming sixth party congress. In the choice of delegates the dissidents made impressive gains in several provinces. The secretary of the Bengal committee, Promode Das Gupta, now adopted a style of rebellion that had been successfully practiced in the CPI before. He circulated a document within the party, strongly criticizing the parliamentary line, and demanding that the party follow the CCP lead.

One reason why this attempt to change the general line emanated from Bengal was that one of the provincial unit's leaders, Konar, had met with Chinese Communist leaders at the Vietnamese party congress in Hanoi in September. He had apparently heard from the Chinese not only their own version of the Sino-Soviet rift, but also their objections to the CPSU twentieth congress line.[69]

When the CPI national council met in February 1961 to prepare for the party congress, it was faced with two drafts of the main political resolution that was to come before the congress. One, prepared by Ghosh, more or less reaffirmed the prevailing party line, although it was somewhat critical of the internal poli-

[69] *Link,* February 5, October 16, 1960.

cies of the Nehru government. It found only the extreme right-wing of the Congress party and the upper bourgeoisie to be hostile to the national democratic state which the CPI now projected as its immediate goal.[70] Ghosh put forward an operational program under which the CPI would build a national democratic front from above and from below, the former being particularly necessary because the party had very little influence among the peasantry.[71] The second draft, tabled by Ranadive, took a much harsher view of Nehru, urged no alliances with local Congress committees, was more selective of the national bourgeois elements eligible for the national democratic front, and called for a line of mass struggle against the policies of the Indian government. The national council adopted Ghosh's draft, but circulated the minority draft within the party, and allowed it to be published.

The political report that finally emerged from the sixth CPI congress in April 1961 made certain concessions to the dissidents' point of view, reportedly at the prodding of Suslov, who was leading a fraternal Soviet delegation.[72] Suslov's speech set the tone for the congress; it was the tone of the CPSU twentieth and twenty-first congresses. The struggle the CPI was to wage was to be against "imperialism and the remnants of feudalism," and not against the ruling bourgeoisie; the technique was to bring about a "single national democratic front of all patriotic forces interested in India's advancement along the path of social and economic progress,"—not socialism.

The elections to the top party bodies created a situation of potential deadlock between the two groups. The majority of the parliamentary-line advocates in the national council was greatly re-

[70] The concept of the "national democratic state" was incorporated in the 1960 Moscow statement of world Communist parties. It was evidently coined by the CPSU to replace the Maoist concept of a "new democratic state." The crucial difference between the two seems to be that while in the "new democratic state," the Communists must be in firm control of the political coalition of democratic forces, in the "national democratic state," Communist partnership, not control, is essential. See also footnote 10 in chapter 6.

[71] *New Age*, March 5, 1961.

[72] *New Age*, May 7, 1961. For a detailed report on the congress, see Savak Katrak, "India's Communist Party Split," *China Quarterly* (July–September 1961).

duced, which was a victory for the dissidents. However, the majority utilized their reduced number in the council to cut back the dissidents' representation in the central executive committee and the central secretariat. Thus, the majority got stricter control of the general direction of the party and the day-to-day management of its affairs.[73]

The border situation worsened in the summer and autumn of 1961. In November, Nehru reported to parliament on a series of Chinese provocations and violations. There was an immediate nationalist uproar in India in which Ajoy Ghosh now joined with a statement on his own initiative, expressing surprise and regret at the official disclosures. In December, *People's Daily,* of Peking, came out with a bitter denunciation of Nehru's "anti-China campaign," and for the first time attacked Ghosh publicly for having "trailed behind Nehru and hurriedly issued a statement in condemnation of China . . . without bothering to find out the truth or look into the rights and wrongs of the case." [74] The Bengal committee of the CPI came out with a resolution declaring that Ghosh's statement represented the sentiments of only a section of the party; articles published in the Bengali organ of the CPI castigated Nehru's home and foreign policies, and some of these were translated and printed in the Chinese press.[75]

By the end of 1961 the CPI was in a state of internal upheaval. At this juncture Ghosh died. The central executive appointed Dange to the newly created post of chairman, and Namboodiripad as general-secretary.

THE STAMPEDE TO NATIONALISM

The border war broke out on a large scale on October 20, 1962, with a massive Chinese attack. Seven days later, Peking media came out with a bitter ideological attack on Nehru, the Indian

[73] In both bodies there were a few centrists who were trying hard to reconcile the two groups. The most prominent among them were Namboodiripad, Jyoti Basu, and Bhupesh Gupta.
[74] *People's Daily,* December 7, 1961.
[75] Barnett, ed., *Communist Strategies in Asia,* pp. 133, 147.

bourgeoisie, the CPSU twentieth and twenty-first congress line, and the CPI, which was now described as the "so-called Marxist-Leninist party" that "trailed behind" the Indian bourgeoisie.[76]

The CPI had already made a total commitment to the nationalist cause. The national council, meeting in the last week of October, adopted a resolution condemning Chinese "aggression." It asked the Indian people to unite behind the government "in defense of the motherland." It even approved Indian acquisition of defensive arms "from any country on a commercial basis." [77] Dange personally assured Nehru of the CPI's complete support in the war. In an article in the party journal, Dange called India's war against China "a just war" which the Communists were duty bound to support.

The three dissident members of the central secretariat resigned in protest, while Namboodiripad remained isolated and powerless as a centrist. At this time the police rounded up a large number of dissident leaders, allegedly with useful information supplied by the dominant group.[78] Some of the dissidents were threatened by angry Indians with dire consequences if they persisted on their antinational attitude.

Taking advantage of the disappearance of dissident leaders, who had gone into hiding, the Dange group captured the party machinery and newspapers in Bengal and Punjab. The dissident leaders hit back by organizing undercover centers to mobilize their followers against the Dange group. In December Dange traveled to Moscow to discuss CPI affairs with the CPSU. In February, the national council endorsed the actions of the party chairman and his group and denounced the CCP's ideological position in the Sino-Soviet conflict.

Namboodiripad now resigned as general-secretary as well as edi-

---

[76] "More on Nehru's Philosophy in the Light of the Sino-Indian Boundary Question," *Peking Review*, November 2, 1962.

[77] Barnett, ed., *Communist Strategies in Asia*, pp. 148–52.

[78] Wood, "Observations on the Indian Communist Party Split."

tor of *New Age*. The following month, the Chinese denounced the CPI leadership in the most violent terms. Dange was called a Titoist revisionist who had betrayed and split the Indian party by succumbing to the bourgeoisie and its leader, Nehru.[79]

For the next twelve months, the CPI remained one party in name only, for the "parallel centers" set up by the dissidents functioned virtually as a separate party. The main interest during this period lies with the centrists, who bent their efforts to avoid a formal split. The theoretical formulation of the centrists came from Namboodiripad. In two carefully thought-out papers, he expressed strategic and tactical concepts that differed from those of either group. It was the middle-class intellectual base of Indian Communism, said Namboodiripad, that exposed it so mercilessly, tragically, and repeatedly to the dangers of revisionism and dogmatism.[80]

The centrist mediation efforts broke down after a number of deadlocked meetings. The central control commission of the CPI, asked to investigate the "parallel centers," reported toward the end of 1963 that "some members of the CEC of likemindedness on political and ideological issues" had been functioning in Delhi since November 1962 more or less as a rival party. They regarded the national council as "thoroughly revisionist and so bitterly anti-China that it would not take any initiative that does not have the approval of the government of India."

According to the report, Gopalan and Ramdas were building the all-India parallel center while Surjeet, Sundarayya, and Ramamurti were busy organizing state units. The parallel centers were already running four weeklies, in Tamil, Telugu, Malayalam, and Bengali. The control commission's report was so disquietingly accurate and the open functioning of the parallel party in Delhi created such an embarrassing situation for the Dange group that

[79] *People's Daily*, March 9, 1963.
[80] *Revisionism and Dogmatism,* and *Note for the Programme of the CPI* (Delhi, 1963).

the CEC had to call a meeting of the national council for April 10, 1964, in order to discredit the "splitters."

About a month before the date set for the meeting, the Bombay weekly *Current* published letters Dange allegedly had written to the British authorities when he was in prison in 1924 offering his services as a political agent if they would release him. The letters had been lying in the National Archives in New Delhi for many years, and their publication in March 1964 was apparently a calculated move by the dissidents not only to destroy the political image of Dange, but also to question the revolutionary fiber of many of his colleagues. The authenticity of the letters was indignantly denied by Dange and his friends, but they could not bring out reliable evidence to prove that the letters were forgeries. The "Dange letters" placed the kiss of death on all efforts to paper over the differences and avoid a split.[81]

The parallel group met in Delhi at the beginning of April and offered a peace plan. They demanded that Dange step down from chairmanship of the CEC's preparatory meeting on April 9 so that there could be a full discussion of all ideological issues and of a draft party program for the national council meeting. When Dange refused to vacate the chair, the dissidents walked out of the CEC meeting. They walked out of the national council also when the majority turned down their demand for a full ideological debate. During this walkout, their number rose from 16 to 32 in October 1963. The dissidents now moved to form a new Indian Communist party. They were able to assemble 146 delegates to the All-India Indian Communist Convention which met at Tenali, in Madras, in July.

The split in the CPI was, then, the result of the combined impact of nationalization and nationalism on Indian Communism. It was the result also of the CPI's failure to control the impact of international events on the domestic situation. Acceptance of the

---

[81] For an insight of lack of mutual trust and respect in the CPI politics in the 1920s and 1930s, see Muzaffar Ahmad, *The Dange Letters* (Calcutta, 1964).

peaceful parliamentary way helped in the nationalization of the CPI; it also exposed the Communists to the influence of bourgeois sentiments and values. In 1961–62, the Indian Communists would not tolerate the stigma of being called traitors to the cause of national independence, although during the "people's war" tactical period, they had not minded being called traitors.

The crisis that faced the CPI and tore it asunder in 1964 was, thus, primarily a crisis of independence. Ironically, it made the parent CPI helplessly dependent on Moscow. However, this dependence was self-willed. It was *earned* by the Dange group if only for disregarding the warnings given by Moscow against a total surrender to nationalism.

The warning came at least twice during the Sino-Indian conflict. First it came in the *Pravda* editorial of October 25, 1962, in which the Soviets, for a brief while, appeared to support the Chinese position on the border conflict. The Soviets called upon the Indian Communists to make "more active efforts" for a peaceful settlement and not to yield to "nationalistic influences and move over to chauvinistic poisitions" which were "useless in questions of struggle for peace." Again, when Dange met with Khrushchev in Moscow in December 1963, the Soviet leader reportedly remonstrated against the national council resolution as being unnecessarily outspoken in condemning Chinese aggression, and criticized the CPI for not qualifying its support of Nehru.[82] The CPI was more nationalistic than the Soviets wanted it to be. As John Wood has put it:

The Chinese aggression turned the CPI's gradual slide to the Right into a stampede; the 30 CPI members in the Lok Sabha were instructed to rally behind the ruling Congress Party and adopted political attitudes that could only be described in Marxist terms as 'bourgeois nationalist.' Thus at this historic juncture the CPI found itself, perhaps for the first time in history, an ally of a strong Indian nationalist upsurge. Its isolation was thus temporarily ended, but only at the cost of

[82] Barnett, ed., *Communist Strategies in Asia,* p. 139.

abandoning any separate or revolutionary programme, with the result that political initiative was left in the hands of the national bourgeoisie.[83]

Those who broke away from the CPI to form a new Communist party apparently refused to surrender the independence and sovereignty Indian Communism had been able to secure for itself after 1956. The "Marxists" were not pro-Chinese, as soon became clear; they wanted to take up an independent position in the Sino-Soviet disputes and conflicts, judging each issue on its merit. On the Sino-Indian border problem, they did not absolve China of all blame, nor did they wish to swallow only the official Indian side. It would be frustrating to call all of them "leftists."

In the final alignment of the leaders between the two parties, ideological radicalism did not appear to be the dividing line. In fact, it is not easy to find in many CPI leaders consistent and persistent trends of "rightist" or "leftist" reflexes. Thus, Rajeshwar Rao, the Andhra group's "Maoist" leader in the early 1950s, became a leading theoretician of the Dange group, while the anti-Maoist Ranadive became a prominent leader of the Marxist group. P. Ramamurti, who had raised the slogan of a "national platform for peace and freedom" in the mid-1950s, joined the dissidents, while Bhupesh Gupta, a vocal critic of Dange during the party crisis, remained with the chairman. Namboodiripad joined the Marxists almost at the last moment, and not without reservations on several portions of the political documents adopted at Tenali. Muzaffar Ahmad took a clearly anti-China stand on the border question, but finally joined the new Communist party.

If there are any perceptible dividing lines between the "Communists" and the "Communist-Marxists," these have to be looked for in the past history of individual leaders, their age and caste. Most of the parliamentarians remained with the parent party, while most of the activists joined the Marxists. More trade union-

---

[83] Wood, "Observations on the Indian Communist Party Split," p. 51.

ists than peasant-front workers remained with the CPI. The CPI continued to enjoy the loyalty of a majority of the leaders who were over fifty-five, who were known as "intellectuals," and who belonged to the upper castes. The CPI's political base was in the Hindi-speaking north and in Maharashtra, while the CPI(M) was much stronger in Bengal, Madras, Kerala, and Andhra Pradesh. The youth front in these states went over to the CPI(M), whereas those in the Hindi-speaking areas remained mostly with the CPI.

The official report of the Tenali convention declared: "Our party as an independent sovereign unit in the world Communist movement shall arrive at its own independent decisions after a full democratic discussion in the entire party. No question of either pro-Peking or pro-Moscow shall arise whatever our enemies shout to slander the cause of Communism. We should not resort upon criticism and attack either on the CPSU or the CPC until our party concludes its inner-party discussions and arrives at its own conclusions." [84]

With the split, the parent CPI remained a willing camp follower of Moscow. The new party, the CPI(M), proclaimed itself an independent, sovereign body, partisan to neither Moscow nor Peking. Five years later the third party, the CPI(ML), once again voluntarily attached itself to Peking.

[84] H. S. Surjeet, *Tenali Convention of the CPI,* mimeographed.

2

TWO CPIs: CONFLICT — COOPERATION — CONFLICT

The history of Indian Communism between 1964 and 1966 is one of intense rivalry between the two groups into which the CPI split in its quest for legitimacy and independence. The rivalry, however, was at times punctuated by parallel action against the ruling Congress party and the dominant economic and social forces. While each party's leadership directed its attack at the leadership of the other party, each visualized eventual reunification of the Communist movement along its own strategic and tactical lines. Each party aimed at penetrating the political and social base of the other. However, there was a reluctance to carry the split immediately to the principal front organizations, the All-India Trade Union Congress, and the All-India Kisan Sabha. In the former, the Dange group was dominant; the latter had all but ceased to function except in name.

Paradoxically, the most intense phase of the rivalry between the two CPIs—during the fourth general election in February 1967—was followed by a dramatic closing of the ranks in the formation of the united front governments in Kerala and West Bengal. This "unity," however, led to a wider and often deeper conflict both from within the government and without. Communism became involved in the bewildering dynamics of Indian party politics.

This conflict–cooperation–conflict syndrome of relations between two factions is to be seen in the dual background of the dominance of internal realities and the relative inability of Moscow or Peking to control the Indian Communist movement. It became clear that Communism in India would from now on be shaped primarily by Indian realities rather than by the power and prestige of external fountainheads. The collapse of the "monolithic" phase of international Communism—of Moscow's control of the world Communist movement—thrust independence on each national Communist party. Thus, even the truncated CPI, at its first congress (after the split) in Bombay in 1964, was obliged to make a formal declaration of independence.

The conditions in which national Communist parties have to function demand full freedom for each national party to work out its own policies in relation to its specific problems, within the framework of an agreed international line and nonintervention by any party in the internal affairs of other parties. The unity of the international Communist movement can now be based only on the full recognition of this reality, not only in theory, but in practice.[1]

This affirmation was, however, accompanied by a complete endorsement of the Soviet (and total rejection of the Chinese) position in the Moscow-Peking ideological conflict. One reason for this affirmation of autonomy was probably the CPI's fear that Moscow might intervene to restore the unity of the Indian Communist movement. For, the Soviets were concerned at the disruption of the democratic forces at a time when "India has become the scene of bitter struggle between capitalism and Socialism, la-

---

[1] *Proceedings of the Seventh Congress of the Communist Party of India: Documents* (Delhi, CPI, 1965), I, 91.

bour and capital." [2] Soviet media had praised Dange for his effort to prevent the split, and had carefully refrained from blaming the "splitters." [3] In September 1965, Sundarayya, general secretary of the Marxist party, went to Moscow for medical treatment and was visited in hospital by Suslov. In 1967 Soviet media acknowledged the existence of two Communist parties in India. The CPI(M) was called the "parallel Communist Party."

TWO DIFFERENT LINES [4]

The Marxist party, in a major theoretical document adopted at its Calcutta congress in November 1964, attributed the split to the struggle that had been "going on for the last ten years against the repeated attempts to take the Communist Party and the working class movement on to the path of class collaboration." There had been two contradictory lines within Indian Communism, it said: the line of class struggle and the line of class collaboration. The "persistent" differences between the two lines had certainly been accentuated by the ideological differences within the world Communist movement.

But it must be realized that the differences inside the party had been accumulating long before the ideological differences in the world Communist movement came into the open and these relate to the assessment of the political-economic situation in India, of the role of the bourgeoisie in our domestic revolution, of the shifts inside the bour-

[2] *New Times*, June 10, 1964. Commenting on Nehru's domestic policy after his death, this journal said: "Nehru did not accept scientific Socialism as the people's path from poverty to prosperity. The method Nehru . . . had chosen in an attempt to abolish inequality without revolution . . . was bound to fail."

[3] See *Pravda*, June 22, 1964.

[4] This comparative analysis in this section is based on the documents adopted at the Bombay and Calcutta congresses of the two CPIs. As far as possible, the actual wording of policy formulations has been maintained. For the CPI, see *Proceedings of the Seventh Congress* . . . Vols. I and II. For the CPI(M), see *Programme of the Communist Party of India; Resolution of the CPI; Fight Against Revisionism; Statement of Policy* (Calcutta, 1965). See also, *New Age*, January 5 and 12, 1965; *People's Democracy*, November 8, 15, and 22, 1964.

geoisie, of the class character of the government of India, of the attitude the working class and its party should adopt towards the bourgeoisie, its party and government, and of the role of the working class in our domestic revolution.

Thus, the Marxists attributed the split primarily not to the external environment, but to the cumulative differences between the class protesters and class collaborationists about the strategy and tactics of Indian Communism.

Now that the two different lines faced one another in open conflict, it should be useful to sum them up briefly on the basis of the documents adopted at the congresses of the two CPIs in 1964. In attempting this summing up, it should be noted that the Marxist formulations were sketchy until 1967, mainly for two reasons. In the first place, the majority of the Marxist leaders were in prison when the CPI(M) congress met in Calcutta, and they were not released until a year and a half later. Second, while the parent party could now claim to represent a very largely united point of view, the dissidents who formed the rival party were far from unanimous on most of the burning domestic and foreign issues.

Three points agreed upon that bound them together were: a resolution to chart a "truly revolutionary course" and not "trail behind" the bourgeoisie; a commitment to affirm the autonomy of Indian Communism in practice; and the rejection of Dange's leadership of the Communist movement. On either of the first two points, serious differences existed among the various state groups, and among what might be called moderates and radicals of the new party.

As a result of these differences, and also because of the forced absence of a majority of the leaders from the Calcutta congress, the Marxist party adopted a number of resolutions that were rather empty of theoretical underpinning. It deferred its decisions on the differences within the international Communist movement and asked its members not to comment on these until the party's stance had been announced. On the domestic situation, the congress, somewhat curiously, reaffirmed a political resolution the united CPI had adopted in 1951, although its radical overtones came to be substantially softened in subsequent formulations. The only major document the congress adopted was one that gave its own history of the split. Compared to the Marxists, the CPI was well prepared with its theoretical assertions and its action program.

The CPI saw the state of India as the "organ of the class rule of the national bourgeoisie as a whole," while the CPI(M) saw the state as controlled by the upper bourgeoisie in alliance with the major landowners. Both saw India overtaken by the crisis of capitalist development. This crisis was reflected in the rising cost of living, food scarcity, hoarding and profiteering, corruption among politicians and civil servants, and the increasing misery of the masses.

The CPI, however, took a mellower view of the capitalist crisis than its rival party. According to the CPI, capitalist growth in India had strengthened the economic base of nationalism; in other words, India had by and large proceeded on the line of *independent* capitalist growth. For the CPI(M), capitalist development had led to the strengthening of the monopolists, to an increasing penetration of foreign, especially American, capital, and to an increasing dependence on foreign imperialist economic aid. For the CPI, the "ushering in of the bourgeois democratic state was a historic advance over the imperialist-bureaucratic rule over our country." For the CPI(M), the strategy of capitalist development by the Indian monopolists, aided by foreign imperialist capital, constituted a threat to the country's national independence.

The CPI(M) saw the major landowners as the joint classowners of the Indian state. The CPI took no such view of the role of the landlord class. "The national bourgeoisie compromises with the landlords, admits them in the ministries and governmental compositions, especially at the state levels, which allows them to hamper the adoption and implementation of laws and measures of land reforms and further enables them to secure concessions at the cost of the peasantry."

The CPI(M) held that the national bourgeoisie was compromising with imperialism both in domestic and foreign policy spheres. The CPI took a more differentiated view of the national bourgeoisie. The upper bourgeoisie was getting more and more differentiated from the rest, and only the monopolist groups and feudal circles represented the main antidemocratic forces of reaction.

For the CPI, India's first task was to complete the national democratic revolution. It had to go through the stage of completing the anti-imperialist, antifeudal, democratic revolution before embarking on the socialist road. Completion of the national democratic revolution was beyond the means of the present government. What was needed was a national democratic front, "bringing together all the patriotic forces of the country, namely, the working class, the entire peasantry including the rich peasants and agricultural laborers, the intelligentsia, and the non-monopolist bourgeoisie." The worker-peasant alliance would be the basis and the pivot of the front. The national democratic state in the hands of the national democratic front would be a transitional stage in which power would be jointly exercised by all those classes which were interested in eradicating imperialist interests, routing the semifeudal elements and breaking the power of monopolies. "In this class alliance, the exclusive leadership of the working class is not yet established, though the exclusive leadership of the bourgeoisie no longer exists." However, the working class would "increasingly come to occupy the leading position in the alliance."

For the CPI(M), the present stage of the Indian revolution was the agrarian stage, "which is directed not only against the landlords and imperialists but also against the Indian bourgeoisie." The objective was to "replace the present antidemocratic and antipopular government by a new government of 'people's democracy.' " The "people's democratic government" would be a "coalition of all democratic, antifeudal, and anticapitalist forces in the country." Such a government must be

capable of effectively guaranteeing the rights of the people, of giving land to the peasant gratis, of protecting our national industries against competition of foreign goods and of ensuring the industrialization of the country, of securing a higher standard of living to the working class, of ridding the people of unemployment and thus placing the country on the wide road of progress, cultural development, and independence.

The struggle for "people's democracy" had to be waged through a "people's democratic front, which is essentially a front of the democratic classes and political parties and organizations" that reflect these classes. The front was to be built out of mass struggles of the trade unions, peasants' organizations and the people.

"In the course of the struggles and campaigns people's political consciousness should be heightened, the futility of the capitalist path of development should be exposed, and the alternative path of people's democratic development should be clearly placed before the people so that more and more they come to accept the program of People's Democracy."

Thus, the CPI recognized the national bourgeois state of India to be a solid achievement toward independence, and sought to convert it into a "national democratic state" through a "national democratic front" from above. The CPI(M), on the other hand, considered the upper bourgeois-landlord–controlled state to be "anti-people," and sought its replacement with a people's democracy. This was to be wrought through a "people's democratic front" built from below on the basis of mass struggles against the present ruling forces. Neither party promised socialism in the immediate future. Both assured sections of the bourgeoisie and landlords a secure position in the new society they contemplated. The CPI excluded only the well-to-do bourgeoisie—the monopolists—from its "national democratic front." The CPI(M) excluded both the upper bourgeoisie and the major landholders, from the "people's democratic front."

PEACEFUL OR NONPEACEFUL TACTICS

The CPI believed that the "national democratic state" could be achieved through the parliamentary process. "India's parliament has provided a forum for the people to intervene in the affairs of the state in a measure and to voice the cause of peace, national freedom, and democracy, to counter imperialist conspiracies, and to demand social transformations in favor of the people such as land reforms, working-class rights, curb on monopolies, etc." A struggle was growing among the various sections of the national bourgeoisie "to get hold of the parliamentary machine in order to wield power over the budget and other economic measures, laws, and policies, and to shape them in their own particular group interests."

The "monopolist groups and feudal circles" were trying to shift parliament and government policies to the right. "Hence the democratic and socialist forces back the strengthening of the state sector (in the economy) and its democratic control and parliamentary democracy." For these forces, extraparliamentary mass struggles were an "effective vehicle of influencing and changing the course of parliamentary policies in favor of the masses and against the monopolists, which in effect means the defense of democracy and Parliament itself."

The limitations of parliamentary democracy arose from the class role of the bourgeoisie. "It is the right reactionary forces which undermine the parliamentary system, both from within and without, by making it an instrument of their narrow class interests and to repress the toiling masses. The Communist party defends the parliamentary and democratic institutions and strives to preserve and develop them further, to make democracy full and real for all." The CPI, thus, elevated the parliamentary way to a strategic level.

The CPI(M), on the other hand, preferred to make only tactical use of parliament. It was skeptical of fundamental structural changes in Indian society resulting from the parliamentary process. This skepticism, it claimed, came from the Indian experience itself.

There are a large number of people who think that this government can be replaced by a People's Democratic Government by utilizing the parliament ushered in by the new Constitution. . . . Even a liberal would now feel ashamed to maintain, let alone the Communist party and other democrats and revolutionaries, that this government and the classes that keep it in power will ever allow us to carry out a fundamental democratic transformation in the country by parliamentary methods alone. Hence, the road that will lead us to freedom and peace, land and bread . . . has to be found elsewhere.

Each country had to seek its own path to revolution. The correct Indian path could not be Russian or Chinese. The Indian path had to be based on a firm alliance, in theory and practice, between the working class and the peasantry. As a tactical line, however, "we must fight the parliamentary elections and elections in every sphere where the broad strata of the people can be mobilized and their interests defended."

For fighting parliamentary and state assembly elections, the CPI(M) would endeavor to forge an electoral alliance on the basis of a common program with socialist and leftist democratic parties, groups, and progressive individuals. "It must adopt flexible tactics, without compromising its political principles, so as to enhance the party's representation in the state legislatures and parliament." The CPI(M) visualized the possibility of forming non-Congress coalition governments at the state level.

While it will be a dangerous illusion to imagine that a state government formed by the Communist party together with its allies can transform the economic and political set-up in the state, nonetheless the formation of such a government will be of great importance in today's conditions. It can play a positive role. . . . Apart from enabling the solution of a limited number of local problems which such a government can without doubt do, its existence and functioning will bring greater morale to the democratic masses everywhere and thus strengthen the democratic movement. It can become a weapon in the hands of the masses in the struggle against the "anti-people" policies of the central government. It will at the same time further intensify the struggle between the forces of progress and reaction inside the ruling party itself.

The CPI did not mention the issue of violence in the resolutions and documents adopted at its Bombay congress. Its explicit adherence to the parliamentary method presumably excluded the deliberate use of violence as a tactical weapon. It, however, stressed the need of large-scale mass action. The party's attitude toward violence was explained after the congress by G. Adhikari in an article in *World Marxist Review*. Adhikari shifted the tactical line of the CPI considerably to the left of the line suggested by the Bombay congress documents.

The CPI, Adhikari said, did not set forth the objective of the "immediate" overthrow of the existing government; however, it had to "develop struggle against the government" to prevent a reversal of progressive policies and to "isolate and eliminate the reactionary forces." This struggle was to be waged on the basis of an alternative, noncapitalist way of Indian development put across to the people by making the maximum use of the bourgeois freedoms available to the CPI and also by waging mass mobilization struggles. The CPI was still wedded to the "peaceful way," but with a qualitative change, the emphasis now shifting to mass struggle and to "parliamentary democracy won by our national liberation struggle." The CPI hoped that confronted with the dire consequences of capitalist policies, the masses, activized by struggle, would progressively elect for the alternative program of national democracy. If this did not happen, and if capitalism grew stronger and the progressive policies of the national bourgeois government continued to be eroded, the Communists, Adhikari declared, would have to change their strategy and tactics.

Everything would depend on whether the force of peaceful mass struggle, isolating the ruling class, compels them to surrender or whether they hit back with their armed might at one stage or another. The proletariat and its party must never lose sight of this possibility, and it should be prepared for it. Given such a basic preparation, a switch-over to non-peaceful methods, when required, should not be difficult.[5]

The CPI(M) did not take an essentially different position with regard to peaceful and nonpeaceful methods.

The Communist Party of India strives to achieve the establishment of People's Democracy and socialist transformation through peaceful means. By developing a powerful mass revolutionary movement, by combining parliamentary and extraparliamentary forms of struggle, the working class and its allies will try their utmost to overcome the resistance of the forces of reaction and to bring about the transformation through peaceful means. However, it needs to be borne in mind that the ruling classes never relinquish their power voluntarily. They seek to defy the will of the people and seek to reverse it by lawlessness and violence. It is, therefore, necessary for the revolutionary forces to be vigilant and so orientate their work that they can face up to all circumstances, to all twists and turns in the political life of the country.

If this affirmation of the Calcutta congress is read together with a somewhat mystical stance on violence that had been adopted by the united CPI in 1951 (which the Marxists now invoked), the CPI(M) would seem to have been, in 1964, at least less sanguine than its rival party about the possibility of a peaceful transformation of the Indian capitalist-semifeudal society. The 1951 stance, as expressed in a document cited by the Calcutta congress, was described as "Leninist." The document asked the Communists to cultivate a "Leninist understanding" of the Indian situation,

---

[5] G. Adhikari, "The Problem of the Non-Capitalist Path of Development of India and the State of National Democracy," *World Marxist Review*, November 1964, pp. 34–40. Adhikari's article is significant also for its comparison of the CPI strategy with that of the CPI(M). Printed several months after Nehru's death, it reflected a harder stance of the Indian political and economic situation. Adhikari, however, did not seem to have convincing arguments to support his belief that the Indian capitalists, after years of capitalist growth of the economy, might still voluntarily surrender their power.

which would persuade them that the "main question" before the revolution was *not* whether it would be violent or peaceful or whether or not there should be armed struggle.

It is the reactionary ruling classes who resort to force and violence against the people and who create the issue of whether our creed is violence of nonviolence. Such an issue is an issue of Gandhian ideology which, in practice, misleads the masses and is an issue of which we must steer clear. Marxism and history have once and for all decided the question for the party and for the people of every country in the world long ago. All action of the masses in defense of their interests to achieve their liberation is sacrosant. History sanctions all that the people decide to do to clear the debris of decadence and reaction that blocks their path to progress and freedom[6]

In early January 1965, the Indian government brought serious charges of violence and antinationalism against the CPI(M). Home Minister Gulzarilal Nanda first voiced these charges in a radio broadcast on January 1, and followed this up by placing a 45-page White Paper before parliament in February.[7] Nanda's charges were designed partly to justify the arrest of some 800 active workers and leaders of the Marxist party, and partly to alienate the electorate in Kerala where a mid-term election was scheduled for March. In his broadcast, Nanda accused the CPI(M) of "preparing the rank and file for armed struggle and guerrilla warfare," of serving as "Peking's instrument," and of attempting to work out "an internal violent revolution to synchronize with a fresh Chinese attack."

The White Paper alleged, with a measure of truth, that the Marxists, at their conference at Tenali, had adopted a draft manifesto criticizing peaceful methods of seeking power and calling on members to lead the workers in "revolutionary struggle." It

[6] *Political Resolution, 1951* (Calcutta, CPI [M], reprinted 1965), p. 22.
[7] For the text of the broadcast, see *The Statesman*, Delhi, January 2, 1965. The White Paper was entitled *Anti-National Activities of Pro-Peking Communists and Their Preparation for Subversion and Violence* (Delhi, Ministry of Home Affairs, 1965).

claimed, with little reliable evidence, that the subsequent Calcutta congress had planned to organize party supporters for rebellion and guerrilla warfare. In support of this contention, the White Paper cited excerpts from the Marxist party's press writings and from published reports of speeches of some of its leaders. The Tamil journal of the party, for example, had written: "After twelve years we hear the voice of revolution throughout India. This government cannot be removed by parliamentary methods. . . . There is no doubt that our revolutionary campaign will sweep away all their tactics. . . . Let us follow the teachings of Mao Tse-tung." One of the arguments advanced by Nanda to prove his charge of the CPI(M)'s alleged loyalty to China was that "the program accepted by the Calcutta congress was Peking's prescription of People's Democracy as distinguished from Parliamentary Democracy which we have in this country."

From prison, five Marxist leaders sent letters to Prime Minister Lal Bahadur Shastri and to Nanda himself protesting these charges and asking the government to prove them in a court of law. They also asked an eminent lawyer-member of parliament, N. C. Chatterji, to file a defamation suit against the home minister.[8] The letter to Shastri took some pains to explain the historical evolution of the strategy and tactics of the united CPI and the genesis of the split. The burden of the letter was that there was no fundamental difference between the CPI(M) and the CPI position on the question of peaceful and nonpeaceful methods.

ATTITUDES TOWARD THE CONGRESS PARTY
AND THE NATIONAL BOURGOISIE

The two parties in their 1964 formulations differed substantially in their assessment of the ruling Congress party and the other parties of the national bourgeoisie. The CPI took a much kindlier view of the Congress party than did the CPI(M). The role played by the Congress party under Nehru's leadership, said

[8] *Reply from Prison*, Calcutta, CPI(M), 1965. The five leaders in jail were P. Sundarayya, M. Basavapunniah, A. K. Gopalan, P. Ramamurti, and H. S. Surjeet.

the CPI, had consolidated, and given a mass base to, India's independence; the mass base "extends to all classes including large sections of the working class, peasantry, artisans, intellectuals, and others." The influence of the Congress party, though much less than what it was in the days of the freedom struggle, is "still a very important factor in the political life of the country." The division between "the masses that follow the Congress party" and the "masses that follow the democratic opposition" is the "most important division in our democratic forces today." There are contradictions within the Congress party between the "anti-people" forces that dominate the government and its mass base. The CPI looked forward to programmatic cooperation with the leaders of the Congress mass base.

The CPI(M) no longer regarded the Congress party as a progressive force. "For, despite the relatively progressive policy declarations of the Congress party, and despite the subjective good intentions of some of its leaders, the fact remains that the Congress party as a whole is dominated by reactionary elements the bulk of whom are in it." However, the Marxists agreed with the CPI assessment of the mass base of the ruling party. The "bulk of the masses who are to be won over to democratic policies and into the democratic front are more or less equally divided into those who follow the Congress party and those who rallied round the non-Communist opposition parties. . . . Sections of Congressmen are interested in a leftward shift in government policies."

The CPI(M) ruled out a "general united front" with the Congress party while the CPI regarded this as a possibility. The two parties had almost identical attitudes toward the Swatantra and Jan Sangh parties and to the smaller parties of the left. Cooperation with the rightist parties was ruled out, while the socialist parties and groups were considered fit for the respective national or people's democratic fronts even though their leaders sometimes pursued reactionary and opportunistic policies.

There was, however, no agreement in the two parties' assessment of India's foreign and defense policies. The CPI affirmed that the foreign policy of the Indian government was "in the main, a policy of peace, nonalignment, and anticolonialism. It conforms to the interests of the national bourgeoisie, meets the needs of India's economic development, and reflects the sentiments of the mass of people. . . . It is sometimes vitiated by lapses and compromises, but as a whole the main character of the policy has been generally preserved." For most of the lapses and compromises, the CPI blamed Peking.

The Marxists, on the other hand, believed that the domestic policies of the government were pro-monopolist and pro-imperialist and were influencing its foreign and defense policies also. They saw the government as steadily surrendering the rights and prerogatives of an independent India to the advancing interests of the imperialists, particularly U.S. imperialism. To them the government had gone back substantially on its anti-imperialism, and was paying only lip service to nonalignment.

PARTY SOCIAL BASES
AND PARTY ORGANIZATION

A mood of self-criticism and sadness at the disruption of the Communist movement was noticeable at the 1964 congresses of both the CPI and its Marxist rival. "Our party is passing through a critical period in its history just like the one the international Communist movement is also passing through," confessed the CPI in its Organizational Report. "Our party is split, throwing party members, sympathizers, and the masses behind it into confusion. The party has received the biggest shock in its life." The CPI(M), like all breakaway groups, took a more optimistic view, but candidly admitted organizational and ideological weaknesses in Indian Communism.[9]

[9] *Proceedings of the Seventh Congress*, p. 97. *Fight Against Revisionism;* and *Programme of the CPI.*

The CPI claimed, however, that the rival party could count on just about a third of the membership of the united organization. Except in West Bengal and Karnatak state councils where the Marxists were in a small majority, and in Tripura where the position was "undecided," the National Council "commands overwhelming support." There was, at the same time, "a neutral trend" among many party members and cadres "who have not joined either party." The CPI(M), countering this claim, asserted that it commanded the loyalty of 60 to 80 percent of the party membership in "the major states like Kerala, Tamilnad, Andhra Pradesh, West Bengal, and Punjab," and that at the Calcutta congress, the 447 elected delegates represented 100,000 of the 150,000 party members.[10]

It soon became evident that the Marxists were in a much stronger position in the coastal states and in Punjab where the Communist movement had been able to build a sizable political base. The CPI's strength was scattered thinly over a much wider area than was the rival party's, but whatever political base it had was in the Hindi-speaking areas where the Congress party and the Jan Sangh were strongly entrenched.

Only the CPI(M) gave an indication of the social background of its Calcutta congress delegates. Of the 482 delegates who returned a form sent out by the credentials committee soliciting information about the social background, occupation, and educational status of party members, 204 belonged to the middle class, 106 were middle-level peasants, 62 came from the working class, 44 were poor peasants, 30 were rich peasants, 21 were landlords, and 16 were agricultural workers. Occupationally speaking, there were 315 full-time party workers, 39 peasants, 12 businessmen, 14 lawyers, 8 teachers, 6 journalists, 7 office employees, 5 workers, and 4 each students and doctors. Regarding education, there were 100 college graduates, 130 matriculates, 37 intermediates (with

[10] *Proceedings of the Seventh Congress*, p. 108. *Fight Against Revisionism*, p. 57.

two years of college after matriculation), 130 who had passed middle school, and 63 who had passed primary school; only 2 were illiterate. As to political activity, 81 had served or were serving in a representative capacity ranging from that of member of parliament to that of village *panchayat;* 147 were working in the trade unions, 137 in the party, 144 in peasant organizations, 12 among students and youth, 6 among women, 3 among teachers, and 2 in cultural fronts; 31 were listed as agricultural worker delegates. The bulk of the delegates—391—were under the age of fifty, while 71 were between fifty and sixty and only 16 over sixty. Of the delegates, 192 had joined the party since 1948; 290 had joined between 1938 and 1947.[11]

While the CPI released no such information of the social base of its membership, it tacitly admitted that it was predominantly middle class. Parliamentary politics, it confessed, had developed the "tendency of bourgois habits" in the party. Members were influenced by "love for the easy-going life, selfishness, hankering after places in bourgeois parliamentary institutions, scant respect for collective decisions, individual functioning, indulging in revolutionary phrasemongering, and doing nothing. . . . In some cases, corruption also crept in." [12]

Both parties acknowledged their weakness among the peasantry, particularly the poor peasant and the landless agricultural worker. The CPI(M) admitted:

But we must note that our trade union front is weak, vast masses of workers remain unorganized, a large number of organized workers remain completely under reformist influence. Our trade-union work is

---

[11] *Resolutions,* pp. 38–40.

[12] *Proceedings of the Seventh Congress,* p. 112. The CPI(M) too attributed to parliamentary politics the bourgeois degeneration of Communists. "Without that revolutionary fervor born out of the revolutionary Marxist theory and practice, with activities in the parliamentary, legislative, cooperative, and such spheres being on the ascendant, with the colossal growth of bourgeois corruption in social and political life all around, Communist norms of life were getting shattered and bourgeois habits and mode of life—softness and easy-going life—began to grip party comrades, particularly at the top levels." *Fight Against Revisionism,* p. 95.

permeated with economism. So far as the peasant front is concerned, our weakness is more pronounced. For the last several years, the mass organizations of peasants and agricultural workers were getting more and more weakened. In many places, their existence became only formal. This utter neglect of *kisan* front shows that we were victims of revisionism in our understanding of the role of the peasantry in building the democratic front.[13]

The CPI claimed a certain measure of strength on the trade-union front. "It is no exaggeration to say that except on the trade union front, there is no clear-cut mass line on any other mass front. This is one of the main reasons why the trade union front is alive and functioning whereas other fronts are almost sleeping." The CPI appeared to take comfort from the fact that the united party's mass influence had always far exceeded its membership. "The mass influence of the party is far more than what is reflected in its membership. This gap between the mass influence and organization of the party has to be bridged if it has to discharge its political responsibilities." [14] Implicit in this was the CPI's desire, translated into a decision at the eighth congress in 1968, to convert itself into a mass-based party. The CPI(M), on the other hand, decided to keep its membership restricted only to carefully trained and indoctrinated cadres.

Interestingly, the two parties adopted new constitutions that were almost identical not only in the framework of party organization and functioning, but even in language. Each constitution listed the "rights of party members" and enumerated "the guiding principles of democratic centralism," presumably to guard against the "undemocratic" practices of the leadership of the united CPI, which were alleged to be one of the reasons for the split. Each party was to hold a congress once every three years, and extraordinary congresses whenever necessary. Each would have a national council of not more than 101 members, of whom at least one-fifth

[13] *Fight Against Revisionism,* p. 87.
[14] *Proceedings of the Seventh Congress,* pp. 92, 119.

would be newcomers. Each national council's work would be conducted by a central executive committee. The CPI constitution
provided for a chairman. Thus in all essentials the two parties
continued with the constitutional framework of the old CPI devised at the Amritsar congress.

The CPI, as the parent party, continued to be officially affiliated with the international Communist movement. Its congresses
were attended by delegates from foreign Communist parties—the
Bombay congress was attended by Boris Ponomarev as head of the
CPSU delegation. Invitations to send delegates to foreign Communist party sessions came to the CPI.

The CPI(M), in contrast, remained officially isolated from the
world Communist movement. In 1965 it applied to the CPSU for
recognition as a Communist party, but Moscow did not oblige although, as already noted, Sundarayya was treated in a Soviet hospital in that year and was visited by Suslov. The Marxist party
did not seek the CCP's recognition. At the Tenali convention,
pictures of Mao were displayed side by side with pictures of
Marx, Lenin, and Stalin, but pictures of Mao were conspicuously
absent at the Calcutta congress. Unofficially, however, the
CPI(M) received party documents from a number of countries including the USSR, Poland, Italy, North Vietnam, and Peking.[15]

THE IMPACT OF DOMESTIC CONDITIONS

During 1965–66, the impact of conditions within India made it
necessary for both Communist parties to change their tactics with
regard to the ruling faction and also with regard to each other.
The changes were made mainly in three directions: the CPI was
forced to shift its tactical position somewhat to the left, the
CPI(M) somewhat to the right; and despite the growing intensity

[15] Interviews with CPI(M) leaders.

of mutual conflict, the Communists were forced to seek areas of joint action.

As noted, the Marxists came under severe government attack which was justified on the ground that their "pro-Peking policy" had made them unpatriotic and antinational. With most of their militant leaders in jail, the Marxists were hard put to organize their new party in the various states. Among the leaders who were not arrested were Namboodiripad and Jyoti Basu, both known to be centrists rather than radicals in terms of the intraparty conflict in the united CPI. The activists still at large, many of whom went into hiding, devoted their energies to building the new party in those states where it had a strong political base, notably Kerala, Bengal, Andhra Pradesh, and Punjab. The result was that the Marxists lost to the CPI whatever little following they had in the Hindi-speaking north.

The CPI, however, soon was due for its first post-split shock. In the Kerala elections in March 1965, the Marxists, with most of their candidates in prison, won 40 seats in the state assembly, as against a mere 3 by the CPI, out of the 84 seats contested. Both groups together won only 27 percent of the vote, but the Congress party, which won over 45 percent, was also divided, and no party therefore had an overall majority. President's rule was therefore reimposed on the state. While the CPI could derive some comfort from the fact that the CPI(M) did not come to power in Kerala, its rout in this state was a traumatic shock. G. Adhikari admitted that the bulk of the cadres and the mass base in Kerala had gone over to the CPI(M).[16]

The national council, in taking stock of the debacle in Kerala, came to the conclusion that only a harder line of opposition to the government would enable the party to win back some support in the Communist strongholds. In a resolution adopted in April, the council noted "certain very serious shifts" toward the right in

[16] *New Age,* April 6, 1965.

the government and some "reactionary" policies having been "intensified." The national council therefore demanded "concrete mass actions" and mass political activity in order to "compel the government . . . to change its course." It called on "all leftist parties, progressive forces, and personalities, including democratic Congressmen," to rally round the CPI and defend living standards, help the peasantry, attack "pro-monopoly economic policies," take action against government "vacillations and weaknesses," and release all political prisoners. The council also proposed a "united campaign on the language issue" to replace English by the regional language in each state and declared that it was ready to "offer cooperation" on these issues without demanding support for others.[17]

In 1965 India faced perhaps the worst economic crisis since independence. It became increasingly clear that the Third Five Year Plan was a failure. Prices soared—the wholesale price index number (March 1953 = 100) rose to 184 by the end of May 1966. The all-India working-class consumer price index (1949 = 100) which rose by 23 points between 1951 and 1961, increased by 39 points during the Third Plan period (1962–1967), from 127 to 166. The cost of living thus rose three and a half times faster during the Third Plan period than during the first two. The number of unemployed at the beginning of the Third Plan was 8 million; at its close, the number of registered unemployed reached 12 million.

Except for the bumper harvest of 88 million tons in 1964–65, thanks to a very favorable monsoon, annual food production throughout the Third Plan period averaged 79 million metric tons. The drought of 1965 brought it down to 76 million metric tons. Imports of food grains which stood at 3.5 million metric tons in 1961–62, shot up to 6.4 million metric tons in 1964, 7.4 million metric tons in 1965, and more than 10 million

---

[17] CPI, *National Council Resolutions* (New Delhi, 1965).

metric tons in 1966. Industrial production also faced a crisis, particularly after the India-Pakistan war of September 1965, leading to many closures and layoffs and considerable retrenchment.

In the spring of 1965, India and Pakistan had clashed in the Rann of Cutch, on the west coast. In August, Pakistan sent in several thousand armed infiltrators to spearhead a widespread rebellion in Kashmir, and this led to intensive military action by the Indian army for an entire month. The second Kashmir conflict between India and Pakistan since independence led to the first full-scale war between the two neighbors. China aligned itself with Pakistan, supporting the Kashmiri people's "right to national self-determination" and, during the most crucial phase, threatened military intervention along the India-Sikkim-Tibet border. The Soviet government, alarmed by Chinese influence over Pakistan, changed its strategy for the subcontinent. Instead of supporting the Indian position on Kashmir, Moscow now tried to be a friend of *both* India and Pakistan. The India-Pakistan war thus changed Pakistan's foreign policy in a fundamental manner. While it still maintained a formal alliance relationship with the United States, Pakistan moved out of the U.S. political-military orbit, and began to seek friendly relations with China as well as the USSR. Peking now treated Pakistan as a more progressive force than India in its global struggle against U.S. imperialism.

Indian politics also changed perceptibly in style as well as in the dimensions of factional conflict and rivalry. After Nehru's death in June 1964, Lal Bahadur Shastri was *made* prime minister by the Congress Party "High Command," who now tried to control the prime minister. As the authority of the central government weakened, the state chief ministers became stronger. In the linguistic controversy, the southern states now made their voice felt as never before; in India's continental politics, the rise of the south became a significant new development. Shastri died before he could consolidate the powers of the prime minister vis-a-vis the "High Command," and was succeeded by Indira Gandhi, another "High Command" choice. The opposition parties seized every weakness of the ruling party to advance their own interests. The decline of the economy enabled the conservative elements to bring pressure on the government to reverse or slow down some of its "socialistic" measures. Within the ruling party itself, a greater anxiety to preserve the status quo rather than accelerate the direction of social change began to surface.

It was within this baroque environment that the divided Indian Communist movement had to operate. Domestic events made it feasible for the two CPIs to work together, but interparty rivalry precluded unity.

The first serious attempt to forge united action was made in April 1965. Both parties had given the call for a mass protest against the high price of food grains, and against hoarding and profiteering. On April 19, Namboodiripad and Jyoti Basu, the two centrist leaders of the CPI(M), met with Bhupesh Gupta and Bhowani Sen, of the CPI, to discuss unity in action. It is significant that three of the four participants came from Bengal— divisions and rivalries in Bengal were apparently somewhat less acute than elsewhere in the country. A program of common action was agreed upon but, as the CPI leaders made clear in a statement on April 25, the reuniting of the two parties was *not* discussed.[18]

CRISES WITHIN BOTH CPIs

Early in 1965, the CPI was faced with an internal crisis. Bhupesh Gupta rose in rebellion against Dange's leadership with a memorandum that questioned the correctness of the tactical line of the Bombay congress, and accused the party chairman of departing

[18] *The Statesman*, New Delhi, April 26, 1965.

from even that line. Gupta threatened to resign from the central executive committee and the central secretariat unless his accusations were answered. The case came up before the central executive committee in July, but was shelved so that it could be taken up by the national council. The primary aim of the Gupta thesis was to seek a way of saving the Communist movement in India, which was being steadily undermined by the ideological conflict between the two groups. One of Gupta's main demands was that the CPI work out a program of common action with the CPI(M) and conduct negotiations for reunification.

When the controversy came before the national council in August, CPI General Secretary Rajeshwar Rao started to refute some of Gupta's charges. Council members broke out in a storm of personal attacks on one another. Gupta was clearly not alone in denouncing the leadership. He was, however, thrown on the defensive when Dange offered to resign which was quickly followed by a similar offer from Rao himself. The threat of resignation from three top leaders led immediately to a compromise. Gupta was persuaded that his advocacy of unity at any price implied the CPI's virtual capitulation to its rival's viewpoint. In any case, the majority of the national council members would not accept such capitulation. Gupta finally withdrew his memorandum. The issue was shelved, not resolved.

One result of this episode was a certain loss in power and prestige for Dange. The national council had already appointed a committee to look into his handling of party funds. Apparently the council disapproved of the way in which these funds were sometimes kept in accounts under Dange's own name and those of his relatives. The council now authorized Rao to keep an eye on the chairman's handling of party funds.

After the national council meeting, a CPI spokesman claimed that the party had emerged "more united and stronger." It seemed to be a questionable claim. The council had met to discuss reform of party policy and organization in the light of its experience following the Bombay congress. Apparently these questions were not discussed. The meeting was dominated by Gupta's thesis and its emphasis on unity between the two Communist factions. Gupta's defeat seemed to underline the strong opposition within the CPI for unity except on its own terms. It widened, rather than narrowed, the gap between the two Communist factions.

Nor were the Marxists without their own internal troubles. As already noted, one of the first tasks before the CPI(M) was to secure the release of its leaders and activists from prison. The letter sent from prison to Prime Minister Shastri by Sundarayya, Gopalan, and three others was intended to refute the officially made charges that the Marxists were unpatriotic agents of the CCP.

Ironically, the issue of patriotism confronted the CPI(M) when the Chinese government announced its unreserved support of Pakistan in the India-Pakistan war of September and, in the small hours of September 18, handed an "ultimatum" to the Indian charge d'affaires in Peking. The "ultimatum" asked the Indian authorities to demolish certain military structures the Indian army was alleged to have built in 1962 on Chinese territory along the Sikkim-Tibet border. If these structures were not dismantled within seventy-two hours, India, the Chinese note warned, would face "grave consequences."

In New Delhi the Chinese threat was interpreted as a maneuver to intervene militarily at the most crucial phase of the war with Pakistan. The CPI condemned the Chinese move, and pledged its support to the government in any measures it might take to secure the defense of India. Indians waited impatiently and not without anger to see what the CPI(M) would do. The Indian nationalist mood was expressed in Shastri's declaration in parliament, "China is the greatest menace to the freedom of India and of Asia."

Namboodiripad who, in Sundarayya's absence, was the CPI(M)'s general-secretary, issued a statement in September arguing that the government's plea for national unity in the face of the war with Pakistan could not be achieved unless it included every political party. The Marxist party, Namboodiripad said, stood for the defense of India against any foreign attack, whether it came from Pakistan, China, or any other country.[19] While this statement did not satisfy Indian nationalist sentiment, it apparently raised within the Marxist party's leadership the same crisis of nationalist conscience that had been one of the major factors leading to the split. At its Calcutta congress, the CPI(M) had taken considerable pains to show how chauvinistic the Dange group had been in lining up with bourgeois nationalism against the "Chinese aggression." Was Namboodiripad trying to take the CPI(M) along the Dange line?

The party organ, *People's Democracy,* printed a lengthy article signed by Sundarayya, Gopalan, and their three other prison colleagues explaining the party's attitude toward the war. While they accused Pakistan of aggression against India, they declared that they would "not characterize Chinese action as aggression." *People's Democracy,* however, affirmed in an editorial that the CPI(M) combined "patriotism with proletarian internationalism, and we are ultimately responsible to the people of India. Never have we been the agents of any foreign Power." A week later, *People's Democracy* welcomed Soviet initiative to settle the India-Pakistan war, even though this was strongly resented by the Chinese. Commenting on Kosygin's letter to Shastri on the India-Pakistan conflict, the journal said that it "underlined the anxiety of countries friendly to India for an immediate cease-fire and negotiations for a peaceful settlement."[20]

The India-Pakistan war brought together, in a complex pattern of conflict and collaboration, the four nations that among themselves comprise most of the sprawling Asian land mass—the USSR, Pakistan, India, and China. A significant aspect of this de-

[19] *People's Democracy,* September 12, 1965.
[20] *Ibid.,* September 19 and 26, 1965. See also *ibid.,* August 14, 1965.

velopment was that the Western powers, including the United States, had only a residual role to play. The Communists were confronted once again with the problem of reconciling patriotism with international proletarianism. This was not just a case of Chinese "aggression" toward India. India's traditional enemy was Pakistan, which was being befriended by China. The Chinese however, perceived Pakistan as more anti-imperialist than India, a view that both the CPI and the CPI(M) rejected. However, the Communists had a more difficult problem when the Soviet Union, with its Tashkent diplomacy, tried to bring Pakistan within its own friendship orbit. The CPI, of course, would predictably go along with Moscow's policy. Interestingly, the CPI(M) also warmly supported the Soviet drive to win Pakistan's friendship. Thus it was during and after the India-Pakistan war that the CPI(M) openly rejected Chinese policy for South Asia, and supported the Soviet stratagem.

OUTSIDE PRESSURES FOR UNITY

The knowledge that it had considerable influence on the leadership of the CPI(M) perhaps encouraged Moscow to publicly put pressure on the CPI in mid-1965 to forge at least a program of unity in action with the rival party. This pressure became visible when *Pravda,* welcoming the "new upsurge" in the Indian working-class movement, also warned that its strength was being dissipated by the divisions among the Communists. *Pravda* also pointed out the advantages enjoyed by the Indian National Trade Union Congress, the working-class front of the ruling party; neither INTUC nor the other socialist-controlled trade unions wanted to be associated with the Communists. This attitude made unity in the Communist ranks even more important.

The timing of the *Pravda* article was significant. The Dange group, which controlled AITUC, was facing an increasingly militant challenge from the Marxists. If AITUC also split in two, not only would its influence among the workers suffer, it would also further polarize the division among the Communists. The Communist unions, after a long period of inactivity, were now trying to rouse their members by summoning an all-India conference in August 1965. This was to be led by the Rashtriya Sangram Samity (National Militant Association), which had been set up in 1964 to act as a unifying committee for the unions' campaign. Dange was its president. *Pravda*'s comment was evidently meant to persuade the CPI that it must do all it could not only to maintain AITUC as a common platform of the two Communist parties, but also to strengthen Communist unity through more militant working-class action.

Pravda's next comment on the Indian situation came in November after seven leftist groups, including the two Communist parties, had assembled in New Delhi to thrash out an agreement, hoping to create a united leftist front to contest the fourth general election. Suslov had already talked with Sundarayya in a Moscow hospital. As a gesture of goodwill to the CPI(M), and also to show that it did not regard the CPI as the only legitimate Communist group in India, *Pravda* in reporting the New Delhi meeting, described the CPI(M) as the "parallel Communist Party." [21]

No report has been published on the Sundarayya-Suslov conversations in Moscow. According to a pro-CPI weekly in Delhi, Sundarayya's letters from Moscow to his colleagues in India indicated a positive shift from his earlier extremist position and placed him in "heated controversy" with the CPI(M).[22] Returning to India after five months in Moscow, Sundarayya plunged into a series of discussions with his colleagues.

Meanwhile, Moscow kept up the pressure for unity. On February 12, 1966, *Pravda* reported, with evident approval, Rajeshwar Rao's effort for a united front with the CPI(M) and other

[21] *Pravda*, July 16 and November 12, 1965.   [22] *Link,* Delhi, February 13, 1966.

leftist groups to oppose the central government. Rao was reported to have stated; "The concerted action of both parties is essential. . . . Our movement can be united if we focus our attention on questions that disturb the people and fight for them jointly. In the past six years we have conducted endless discussions, and our work among the masses has fallen off. . . . To be sure, much bitterness has accumulated in the relations of the two parties. In the course of struggle it will grow less."

On April 20, a group of CPI leaders arrived in Moscow "for an exchange of views on the problems of the international Communist movement and other questions." [23] They were all members of the central secretariat, with the exception of the secretaries of the state committees of Kerala, Bengal, and Punjab. A joint statement issued on May 1 by this group and the CPSU said that the Soviet party had urged the CPI to "struggle for unity of the ranks of the country's Communist and democratic movements." [24]

The CPSU's pressure on the CPI, however, had little impact on Indian Communist politics. The growing militancy of the CPI in 1966 was the result of its own response to the deepening economic and political crisis rather than to advice from Moscow. For instance, a document circulated at a CPI national council meeting in Hyderabad in June 1966, reportedly emphasizing the importance of conspiratorial and clandestine activity, had little apparent effect on the work-style of the party.[25]

An acute food shortage and steadily rising prices created a situation in India which the Communists could not fail to exploit to their advantage. With the fourth election in the offing, all opposition parties sought to wean the electorate away from the ruling Congress party. The Communists were particularly active in Kerala and Bengal. In Bengal, the Communists were helped by the first major crisis in the Congress party since independence. As a result of factional fights between the dominant group of Atulya

---

[23] *The Statesman,* April 3, 1966.   [24] *Pravda,* May 2, 1966.
[25] *Asian Analyst,* October 1966, p. 20.

Ghosh, a member of the "Syndicate," and the Midnapur group of Ajoy K. Mukherji, president of the Bengal congress, the latter left the party in September with his followers, and set up the Bangla Congress (Bengal Congress). Food riots spread from Calcutta to the district towns and villages. The Congress government found itself increasingly isolated from the people. Ministers could not address meetings or move about freely without police escort.[26] In Kerala, the absence of popular government gave the Communists a greater opportunity to mobilize people belonging to several parties to protest cuts in the rice ration.

In this situation of political crisis, the CPI could enhance its electoral prospects only by adopting a militant stance. It therefore abandoned its policy of "critical support" for Congress governments in the states as well as at the national level. Its particular targets of attack were three cabinet ministers—Ashoke Mehta, C. Subramaniam, and Sachin Chaudhuri—who were believed to have been responsible for the devaluation of the Indian rupee in June 1966 under pressure from the United States and the World Bank. The CPI organized an impressive "people's march" on parliament on September 1 demanding the resignation of the three ministers. Toward the end of September, the attack was extended to include Mrs. Gandhi. In a signed article in *New Age*, Bhupesh Gupta, its editor, demanded her resignation.[27]

INSIDE PRESSURE AGAINST UNITY

The increasing militancy of the CPI was matched by an equally increasing militancy of the CPI(M). By the spring of 1966 most of

[26] *Amrita Bazar Patrika*, September 22, 1966.

[27] *New Age*, September 25, 1966. *Pravda*'s praise for Mrs. Gandhi's government on August 15, India's independence day, put the CPI in an embarrassing position, particularly because the rival party wondered which really was Moscow's line—praise for the Indian government or criticism of its policies. *New Age* in its September 18, 1966, issue denied that it shared *Pravda*'s attitude toward Mrs. Gandhi, even declaring that *Pravda* was wrong.

the imprisoned CPI(M) leaders and activists were released, and they brought to the party a more militant stance than its moderate leaders might have taken on their own. The leftist unity talks proceeded gingerly. In July the two CPIs entered an election pact with seven other left-wing parties and agreed not to pit CPI and CPI(M) candidates against each other in the fourth election, but almost immediately after the meeting, arguments broke out about the allocation of constituencies.

As negotiations proceeded tortuously, three trends became evident in Indian Communism. The first was that the militants on either side were opposed to making concessions to the other side and were confident of triumphing over their rivals. With these militants were joined those of the leaders who, more for personal rather than ideological reasons, found working with their rivals extremely distasteful. Under the combined pressure of the militants and these pathologically antiunity forces, the moderates in both parties who wanted at least electoral unity lost ground.

The second trend that came to the surface was the supremacy of the regional over the national leadership in determining crucial questions relating to electoral unity. Indeed, the central leadership of either Communist party could hardly impose its decision on the powerful state parties. Thus, in the allocation of constituencies, it was the state parties of Bengal that had the determining voice; so it was in the case of Kerala and Andhra Pradesh.

The third major factor was that the Communists found it easier to align with local caste or religious groups than with national secular parties. Thus, the CPI(M) was able to enter into electoral agreements relatively smoothly with the DMK party of Tamil Nadu (Madras) and the Akali party of Punjab. In contrast, it found electoral aspirations of leftist parties like the PSP and the SSP difficult to accommodate.

Behind the surface efforts to organize a leftist united front there was keen rivalry between the two CPIs to capture each other's political bases. Where there was little room for doubt about the strength of either party's political base, an electoral adjustment became possible. In Kerala, for example, the 1965 election had conclusively shown that the CPI(M) base was much stronger than that of the CPI. It was therefore relatively easy for Namboodiripad to work out a constituency adjustment with the CPI and five other non-Congress parties including the Kerala Muslim League. In Bengal, however, the situation was extremely fluid. The two parties had had no occasion to test their respective strength, and the emergence of Bangla Congress as a potential rallying point of the Congress left complicated the situation still further. As many as twelve "leftist" groups, including the Bangla Congress, had to be united into a leftist front; each of these groups claimed a strong political base in one or the other of the districts of West Bengal.

While the two CPIs were still working together in AITUC and AIKS (All-India Kisan Sabha), the Bengal branches of both fronts were controlled by the Marxists, and this added an edge to the rivalry. The militants in the CPI(M) would rather lose the election than surrender their bases to the CPI. In fact, the moderate leaders of the CPI(M), in their quest for electoral unity, had to constantly defend themselves from the militants' charge that they were as anxious to engage in parliamentary politics as the revisionists of the CPI.

After July 1966, the central leadership of the two parties apparently gave up the idea of unity, and relinquished the problem to the state parties. In Bengal, the initiative was now taken by Bangla Congress. The negotiations, however, broke down on the irreconcilable constituency demands of the two CPIs. Eventually, two "united left fronts" were assembled, one under the leadership of Bangla Congress, the other of the CPI(M). In the first, which was called the United Left Front, were the CPI(M), the Forward Bloc (Marxist), the Revolutionary Socialist Party, the Revolutionary Communist Party of India, the Workers' Party of India, the

Socialist Unity Center, and the Samyukta Socialist Party. In the second, called the People's United Left Front, were Bangla Congress, the CPI, Praja Socialist Party, the Bolshevik Party, the Gorkha League Forward Bloc, and the Lok Sevak Sangh (People's Service Society). In Andhra Pradesh, no electoral adjustments were possible, and the two CPIs fought one another in multicandidate contests.

THE STRUGGLE WITHIN THE AITUC

In 1951, the united CPI had come to the conclusion that "peasant struggles along the Chinese path alone cannot lead to victory in India." One reason was that "we have a large working class and that it has a role to play, which can be decisive in our form of struggle. The grand alliance of the working class and the peasantry, acting in unison, the combination of workers' and peasants' struggles, under the leadership of the Communist Party, and utilizing all lessons of history for the conduct of the struggles is to be the path for us." [28] At its Calcutta congress, the CPI(M) invoked this "grand alliance" as its tactical line.

In putting this tactical line into action, the CPI(M), however, was confronted with the stark fact that while it had practically no peasant base to speak of, its trade-union base also was weak and very limited. It was therefore natural for the party to try to build up its own working-class and peasant bases. Since AIKS was practically moribund, an acute struggle developed in 1965 between the two CPIs within AITUC. At their 1964 congresses, both parties had declared that they would do everything they could to maintain the unity of the workers' and Kisan fronts. From the accusations either party made against the other in 1965 for trying to disrupt AITUC, it became clear that, for the CPI, unity meant continuation of its control of the trade-union front, while for the

[28] *Statement of Policy* (Calcutta, 1965), p. 6.

CPI(M) it meant increasing its representation on the top decision-making bodies.[29]

The conflict within AITUC dominated the organization's twenty-seventh meeting in Bombay in May 1966, its first general meeting since the CPI split. The Marxists tried to mobilize their full strength at the meeting,[30] whose importance was enhanced by the presence of fraternal delegates from the USSR, Yugoslavia, France, and several other countries, and of Renato Bitossi, president of the World Federation of Trade Unions. As soon as the meeting opened, the CPI(M) delegates, led by P. Ramamurti, demanded the resignation of Dange as general-secretary of AITUC. The demand was rejected, and eventually the factions agreed to retain S. S. Mirajkar, of the CPI(M), as president of AITUC, while the CPI group appointed the secretaries.

Dange's report and Ramamurti's speech both led to heated controversies. Ramamurti asked the delegates to reject Dange's report because of its attack on China and its "soft line" toward the Indian government. In his own speech, which was violently antigovernment, he demanded a reversal of AITUC's stand concerning India's internal affairs. The general-secretary's report was, however, passed by 1,827 votes to 617. Mirajkar and Dange were reelected, as had been agreed upon beforehand. The CPI(M) failed in its bid to replace Dange with Ramamurti, and in the process, Ramamurti lost his vice-presidency. The CPI(M) won only one vice-presidency out of seven and one secretaryship out of five. The session closed with a resolution to build up a united trade-union movement in India.[31]

The struggle between the two CPIs within the trade-union and

[29] See *Proceedings of the Seventh Congress,* pp. 98–110; *Fight Against Revisionism,* pp. 26–35.

[30] *People's Democracy,* May 8, 1966, urged all unions to send to the session "the maximum number of delegates."

[31] *New Age,* May 6, 13, 20 and 27, 1966; *People's Democracy,* May 8, 15, 22 and 29, 1966; *Times of India,* May 17, 18, 19, 20, 21, 22 and 23, 1966.

peasant fronts followed a similar pattern until both the AIKS and the AITUC were split, the former toward the end of 1967, and the latter in May 1970. In the Kisan Sabha, the CPI sought to dislodge the CPI(M) from its control of the top-level decision-making bodies, while in AITUC it was the CPI(M) that tried to dislodge the CPI from its control of the central institutions. In both cases, the conflict took an acute form in the states, especially in those where the fronts were either strong or were being made so.

3

THE CHALLENGE
OF INDIAN POLITICS

Ever since India achieved political independence in the late 1940s, the Communist movement in the country has been increasingly under pressure from the domestic situation within India. Its crucial problem has been how to gain control of national or local affairs and escape direction from Communist fountainheads outside India. In simpler terms, Indian Communism has been under pressure to be increasingly Indian. After the split in the CPI in 1964, the challenge of India—its social and political culture and systems—has been, and continues to be, the principal preoccupation of the two Communist parties. We must therefore look at the strategic-tactical progress and activity of the two parties in the larger context of Indian society and politics.

To attempt a profile of Indian society and politics within the limits of a few hundred words is an extremely sobering task. India is vast and diverse—more diverse than vast. It is one of the most complex societies in the world. Joan Robinson is said to have once remarked that whatever one may say about India is true; its opposite is also true. Nevertheless, India has been functioning as a viable political society for twenty-five years. Indian society has changed, and is changing—hastening slowly toward modernization. The Indian political system has endured, and has tried to adjust to the changes that have occurred in the social ecology. We shall try to explore in this and the final chapters only those features of the Indian cosmos that are most relevant to the problems and promises of the Communist movement.

India is one of the most populous and poorest countries in the world. According to a noted Indian economist, India is "probably the poorest among the community of nations." [1] If mass poverty and misery by themselves fathered revolution, the pages of Indian history would have shown the imprint of many revolutions. The fact, however, remains that there has been no political and social revolution in India in historical time. There have been local rebellions by sections of the peasantry, but these have been isolated deviations from the general pattern of docility and submission to fate that have characterized the collective conduct of the Indian poor.

The country by and large lacks a revolutionary tradition—which distinguishes it from China. Independence came in 1947, not as a result of political revolution, but of a political arrangement between the British, the Congress faction, and the Muslim League. India has not had an industrial revolution. "There has been no bourgeois revolution, no conservative revolution, no peasant revolution." [2] The advent of the modern world has not led to political and economic upheavals. In Marxist terms, objective conditions for revolutionary change have existed in India

---

[1] The 1971 census puts the total population tentatively at 547 million, indicating a slight decline in the rate of growth during the last ten years. Only 29.35 percent are literate, one of the poorest literacy growth rates in the world. V. M. Dandekar and Nilakantha Rath, "Poverty in India: Policies and Programmes," *Economic and Political Weekly*, January 9, 1971, p. 143.

[2] Barrington Moore Jr., *Social Origins of Democracy and Dictatorship* (Boston, Beacon Press, 1967), p. 314.

for a long time. The subjective conditions, however, have been conspicuously lacking.

The immense heterogeneity of Indian society creates cultural and psychological problems inhibiting motivations for radical change in the social structure. People in the various layers of society live very different kinds of lives and consequently have very different outlooks toward their social universe. Individuals and groups harbor within themselves sharply conflicting evaluations. The ideals of modernization are pitted against these conflicting evaluations with the result that even among "radical" individuals, value conflicts lead to frustrating mental compromises.[3] The Indian elite have to some extent assimilated Western political concepts of representative democracy. However, the concept of democratic radicalism is still alien to them.

The democratic radicalism of Europe has its roots in the eighteenth-century belief in the rationality, innate goodness, and perfectability of man, and in the natural order as an "attainable, indeed inevitable and all-solving end." [4] It is difficult to find such belief in India's traditional political culture. "Political Messianism"—which legitimizes political ideas as derivatives of an all-embracing and coherent philosophy, and enables the field of political activity to embrace all human action—is still alien to Indian society. Myrdal found in India's social and political culture much that is change-resistant; he came to the conclusion, therefore, that in India, change had to be *induced* by modernization agencies.[5] Parliamentary democracy can permit only slow and gradual change; one reason why the Indian elite have found parliamentary democracy such an acceptable political system is

[3] D. R. Rangnekar, *Poverty and Capital Development in India* (London, Oxford University Press, 1958), pp. 80–82.

[4] J. L. Talmon, *Origins of Totalitarian Democracy* (London, 1952), pp. 1–3, 249, 253.

[5] Gunnar Myrdal, *Asian Drama* (New York, Pantheon 1968), Vol. I, chs. 1–3. Myrdal's analysis of Indian valuations and their interaction to modernization and development deserves carefully study and calls for further investigation and research on several related premises.

that it agrees with their preference for gradualism in social change.

In India, democratic planning has proceeded for some twenty years without much social discipline, and without any compulsion; indeed this has been projected as a basic point of difference from the practice in Communist countries. Democratic planning, however, has not brought about any fundamental change in the social structure; its cumulative social consequence has turned out to be increasing disparity of incomes between social groups and greater stratification. According to both Moore and Myrdal, success in planning for development is possible only when obligations are placed on people from *all* strata of society, and when compulsion plays a strategic role in the rigorous enforcement of those obligations.[6] Broadly speaking, the fundamental contradiction in India today is the contradiction of the political system of parliamentary democracy and the inequalities and stratification resulting from democratic planning.

THREE POLITICAL UNIVERSES

The Indian political system is made up of three universes: the village, the state, and the nation. Each has its own distinctive structures, rules, and style of political behavior, each its own social and cultural environment. At the same time, each is related to the other, interacting on the other. The three universes are being woven together by the process of modernization. The will to modernize is churned out of a highly traditional and change-resisting society by the conflicts of electoral politics which are integrative as well as divisive.

The impact of these conflicts is the greatest on the universe of state politics, where the three universes meet and mingle.[7] The national political universe is a superstructure of modern political

[6] Myrdal, I, 66–67; Moore, pp. 408–10.
[7] Duncan B. Forrester, "Electoral Politics and Social Change," *Economic and Political Weekly*, Special Number, July 1968, pp. 1075–94.

style and rhetoric. It gets increasingly "provincialized" as it draws on the state universe for strength and sustenance. The state universe carries to the village the language and will of modernization. The state, then, is the center of gravity in the entire political system. State politics impinge on the village at countless points. So do national politics on the state. At one end of the political spectrum is the member of parliament who speaks mostly the language of the politics of modernization with an increasingly provincial accent. At the other end is the *panch* of the village *panchayat,* or elected council, who speaks the language of the politics of tradition with some imported words of modernization. The MLA—member of the state legislative assembly—is the gap-filler, a bridge between the two extremes, the nation and the village.[8]

The cultural, linguistic, and social diversities of the states tend to make them distinct political units. Redistribution of boundaries on linguistic lines has made them *natural* units also. In the first years of the Indian Union, there was a certain resemblance between the national universe of politics and those states which were bi- or multilingual. This resemblance exists no more. Each state is a natural cultural-political unit dominated by a linguistic nationality with its own political culture and style of politics. This naturalness has been further sharpened by the increasing use of the vernacular as the medium of internalization and communication. The emerging elite groups can assimilate modern political concepts only in their own vernaculars, which makes communication among the various linguistic elite an increasingly difficult problem.

FEDERAL PULLS GET STRONGER

Partition of British India into India and Pakistan smothered true federalism in the Indian state, and enabled the Congress party leaders to write what is essentially a centralized constitu-

[8] W. H. Morris-Jones, *Government and Politics of India* (London, Oxford University Press, 1962), p. 56.

tion. The provinces (later, states) were given only limited autonomy, while the central government reserved for itself enormous power to keep the states under control.

Nevertheless, over the years, the natural federalism of Indian politics has tended to assert itself. The system has been moving toward an accretion of strength by state political figures. Even when the Congress party was a truly centralizing force, members of its "High Command" were subjected to strong local pulls, while state officials were identified with local interests. Much of the Congress intraparty disputes had their roots in genuinely conflicting provincial interests. Since the death of Nehru in 1964, the federal system has been triumphing in India at the cost of the unitary system. The provincial "bosses" chose Shastri as Nehru's successor. The chief ministers were now in power in Delhi. The federal process was carried a step further when the provincial "bosses" chose Indira Gandhi to succeed Shastri. Neither the Congress "High Command," nor the central parliamentary caucus, nor the Union Cabinet, nor the super-cabinet Planning Commission, was any longer able to dictate to the powerful "bosses" in the states. The great weakness of this federalism, however, was that it was within the Congress party and not of all-Indian political forces.[9]

The first real challenge to the unitary system came after the fourth general election in February 1967, when the Congress party lost its majority in as many as eight of the states (in a few, as a result of defections). In these eight states, parties and groups other than the Congress party formed coalition governments, and two of these coalitions, in Kerala and West Bengal, were dominated by the CPI(M). The CPI joined these two coalitions and three others—those of Bihar, Uttar Pradesh, and Punjab. In the central government, the majority of the Congress party was reduced to a bare 55.

[9] Wayne Wilcox, *Political Modernization in South Asia* (Santa Monica, Calif., Rand Corporation, 1968), memeographed.

The Congress party began to disintegrate at the state level in late 1966. Breakaway groups like the Bangla Congress of West Bengal made the formation of non-Congress coalitions possible in most of the states where the party lost its majority in the fourth general election. In two states, however, local caste-oriented parties were propelled to power—DMK in Madras and Akali Dal in Punjab, the former winning an absolute majority in the state legislature, the latter in coalition with other non-Congress groups, including the CPI.

With this remarkable change in Indian politics began a period of increasing strain on the political system. Shifting loyalties of a handful of legislators led to several changes of government in Bihar, Uttar Pradesh, Haryana, and Punjab. The Communist-led united front government in West Bengal was dismissed by Delhi after being in office for ten months, and the state was brought under President's rule. Mid-term elections had to be held in Bihar, Uttar Pradesh, Punjab, and West Bengal in February 1969; in each of the four, the Congress party suffered worse reverses, and in West Bengal, the CPI(M) emerged much stronger than in 1967.

At the national level, the government of Mrs. Gandhi was reduced to a minority after the Congress party split into two rival organizations in November 1969. Its survival depended on the support of left-wing groups like the CPI and DMK. Faced with the problem of survival, Mrs. Gandhi shifted her own faction, the ruling Congress, to the left by nationalizing fourteen large Indian banks and by bringing in legislation depriving the former rulers of the ex-princely states of their privy purses—allowances that had been granted by the government while integrating these states into the Indian Union. Taking tactical advantage of the popularity of these actions, the prime minister dissolved the Lok Sabha and held a mid-term parliamentary election in March 1971; mid-term elections were also held simultaneously for the state assemblies of Madras, Orissa, and West Bengal. (In West

Bengal, the second united front government had collapsed in 1970 as a result of intense rivalries between the constituents, primarily between the CPI(M), Bangla Congress, and the CPI; the state had been under President's rule for a second time since 1967.)

Mrs. Gandhi's Congress party won more than a two-thirds majority in the Lok Sabha, and in West Bengal emerged as the second largest party after the CPI(M). The immediate result of the impressive victory of the ruling Congress party was that in several states—Uttar Pradesh, Mysore, Gujarat, and Andhra Pradesh—Congress legislators who had either joined the rival Congress faction or had defected from Mrs. Gandhi's faction, hurried back to the ruling Congress party and, on the surface, the Congress party looked almost the same as it had before the split.

The 1971 parliamentary election was remarkable not because it revealed a massive popular support for Indira Gandhi and her party, (it got only 3 percent more votes than the undivided Congress party got in 1967), but because the voters shifted their support in large number from the opposition factions. Only 54.81 percent of the electorate voted. Mrs. Gandhi's Congress party won 43.64 percent of the votes cast; in other words, it was supported by only 23.91 percent of the electorate. All of the non-Congress parties except the Communists lost in electoral support. However, the ruling Congress faction's landslide victory in terms of parliamentary seats (350 out of 515) was due to the simple majority system of election sanctioned by the constitution. Under the system of proportional representation, the ruling Congress faction would have won 226 seats, just 6 more than it had in the dissolved Lok Sabha, and well short of an absolute majority.[10]

Two parliamentary elections in four years, three assembly elections for West Bengal in four years, and two elections in four

[10] M. R. Masani, "Poll Results in Perspective," *The Statesman,* April 14, 1971.

years for eight state legislatures, quick succession of coalitions at
the state level, long spells of central rule over a number of states
—all of this happening between 1967 and 1971—would indicate
that the Indian political system has entered a critical period of
stress and strain. The splitting of political parties into rival factions led to an unprecedented competition among elite individuals and groups for political power and also to an unprecedented
political mobilization of the masses. With the 1967 election, India
faced a crisis of consensus, and entered a more controversial and
fluid stage in respect to both leadership cohesion and policy ori-
entations.[11]

PARLIAMENTARY POLITICS
AND SOCIAL CHANGE

The parameters of electoral politics may not be adequate to measure the changes that have occured during the last twenty-four
years in the innermost core of Indian society. Despite a decade
and a half of planned economic development, the number of poor
people in India has steadily increased, and inequalities of income
and consumption between the well-off and the badly-off have
steadily widened. A recent study of poverty in India comes to the
conclusion:

During the past decade, the per capita private consumer expenditure increased by less than half a percent per annum. Moreover, the small
gains have not been equitably distributed among all sections of the population. The condition of the bottom 20 percent urban poor has defi-
nitely deteriorated, and for another 20 percent of the urban population,
it has remained more or less stagnant. Thus, while the character of

[11] Rajani Kothari, "The Political Change of 1967," *Economic and Political
Weekly*, Annual Number, January 1971.

rural poverty has remained the same as before, the character of urban poverty has deepened further. This is the consequence of the continuous migration of the rural poor into the urban areas in search of a livelihood, their failure to find adequate means to support themselves there, and the resulting growth of roadside slum life in the cities. All the latent dissatisfaction about the slow progress of the economy and the silent frustration about its failure to give the poor a fair deal, let alone special attention, appear to be gathering in this form. Its shape today is probably no more than hideous; allowed to grow unheeded and unrelieved, it will inevitably turn ugly.[12]

The gathering dissatisfactions and frustrations of the Indian poor do not seem to be reflected in electoral politics. The Congress party's support among the electorate declined sharply in 1967, but the decline was by no means catastrophic for the party. The poor and the underprivileged appeared to have voted in great strength for the Congress party in 1967, and again in the 1971 parliamentary election except in West Bengal, Kerala, and Madras. It was mostly among the white-collar workers and the better-off sections of the electorate that the party lost support in 1967. The bulk of the rural and illiterate voters stood by the Congress party. However, it failed to attract the young, post-independence generation of voters both in the urban and rural areas.[13]

A remarkable feature of India's electoral politics is that most political parties draw their support from the same social base, which accounts for major upheavals in election results if even a relatively small portion of the electorate shifts its loyalty from one party to another. In 1967 the Congress party lost only 3 percent of its 1962 voters, but the electoral consequence was unnerving to the party. In 1971 the ruling Congress faction gained back the 3 percent that the undivided Congress had lost in 1967, and the re-

[12] V. M. Dandekar, "Poverty in India—I," *Economic and Political Weekly*, January 2, 1971, p. 40. Dandekar's study was sponsored by the Ford Foundation.

[13] Kothari: "Younger age, higher education and urban exposure . . . contributed to the alienation from the Congress party in 1967." His findings are based on a series of studies in the 1967 vote conducted by the Center for the Study of Developing Societies, Delhi, of which Dr. Kothari is director.

sult was a thumping majority in the Lok Sabha. A second note-worthy feature of voting behavior in India is that only two par-ties, the Congress and the Communists (the two CPIs together) have a large number of regular supporters, while the support bases of the other parties are highly uncertain. More than 50 per-cent of those who identify with the Congress party are "regulars," that is, they have voted continuously for it. Communist "regulars" account for 39 percent of those who voted for either CPI in 1967.[14]

DIFFERENCES IN PARTY BASES [15]

If there are any significant differences among the social bases of Indian political parties, it is between those of the Congress party and the two Communist parties. While the Congress party draws a great deal of its support from voters aged thirty-five or older, about a quarter of the supporters of the Communist parties are under twenty-five. "It seems that the politically aware youth, who have entered the electorate for the first time but most likely have not yet entered the adult period of earning a livelihood, tend to be attracted by the appeal of the Communist parties on the one hand and the regional parties on the other." While the Congress party draws its support proportionately more or less equally from all the educational strata, the Communist parties draw sizable support from the more educated strata.

The Congress and Communist parties have their supporters proportionately distributed both in the urban and the rural sec-tors. Occupationally, however, the Communists received greater support in 1967 from white-collar workers than the Congress party did. "The Communist parties' real strength lies among the working class. Thus in the urban areas a polarization of party

---

[14] *Ibid*.

[15] Material on differences among social bases is drawn from D. L. Seth, "Profiles of Party Support in 1967," *Economic and Political Weekly*, Annual Number, Janu-ary, 1971.

support is evident between the Communist parties on the one hand and the Jan Sangh party on the other."

Castewise, the higher castes tend to vote more for the Congress party than for the Communists, who draw greater support from the lower castes. Harijans and tribals, on the other hand, tend to vote heavily for regional parties and the Socialist groups, although their voting for the Congress party is larger than their voting for the Communists. The Communists have a good portion of their supporters among the lowest income groups, but they are also supported by a sizable portion of voters in the highest income groups. The wealthy and well-to-do landholders vote more for the Congress than any other party, while the Communists have a strong support base among the landless and those having less than five acres of land.

The Congress party, then, has a "relatively more heterogenous and differentiated social, economic, and demographic support base, compared to all of the other parties." Second to the Congress party are the Communists, although their total support base is much smaller. But, contrary to the earlier position, by 1967 the Communists' support base was fairly evenly spread among both rural and urban areas.

PARTY BASES IN FOUR STATES [16]

Within this all-India framework of the impact of electoral politics on social groups and classes, we have to look more closely at each state, for India, we have noted, is diverse, and each state is a social universe unto itself. A recent study of the 1969 mid-term election in Punjab, Uttar Pradesh, Bihar, and West Bengal gives some insight into the social base of the party system in each of these north Indian states. Among themselves, these states are

---

[16] Material on party bases in four states is drawn from Ramashray Ray, "Patterns of Political Instability: A Study of the 1969 Mid-Term Elections," *Economic and Political Weekly,* Annual Number, January 1971.

fairly representative of the Indian social terrain. West Bengal has had the largest rate of urbanization in India (24.5 percent), while Bihar is one of the least urbanized (only 8.4 percent). Punjab is fairly urbanized (20.1 percent), while Uttar Pradesh (with 12.9 percent) belongs to a middle-level category. In literacy, West Bengal and Punjab, with 29 and 24 percent respectively, are far ahead of Uttar Pradesh and Bihar (about 18 percent each).

On the composite index of development, West Bengal ranks the highest, followed by Punjab, Uttar Pradesh, and Bihar, in that order. In Bengal, the core of economic activity consists of a predominantly secondary, that is, manufacturing sector; the growing pace of industrialization also acts as a catalyst for agricultural development as the creation of the necessary inputs becomes possible (the state has had a succession of bumper crops). Punjab follows more or less the same pattern. Per capita income is the highest in West Bengal, and the lowest in Bihar, but West Bengal spends much less than Punjab on developmental activity.

Each of the four states spends a major portion of development funds on education: Bengal, 36.6 percent; Punjab, 38.1 percent; Uttar Pradesh, 35.6 percent; and Bihar, 29.4 percent. Education and public health accounts for 54.5 percent of West Bengal's development expenditure. Despite the high per capita income, West Bengal's developmental expenditure is much lower than Punjab's, probably because the modern sector of its economy is dominated by non-Bengalis, and a large part of their earnings is exported outside the state. Unemployment is the highest in West Bengal— one out of every 52 employable persons being without work. In Punjab, it is one in every 264, in Uttar Pradesh, one in 625, and in Bihar, one in 682. "Punjab and West Bengal represent two extreme poles of economic development. While West Bengal is industrially well developed and enjoys the largest per capita income, most of its earnings are either exported or consumed in providing and maintaining civic amenities in urban areas. As a consequence, it is left with inadequate resources for carrying out developmental programs. In contrast, Punjab earns well and spends well on developmental activities."

Further, West Bengal represents a bifurcated culture of frustrated middle-class existence and parasitic absentee landlordism with a stranglehold on the rural farm economy. Growing economic distress, lagging developmental efforts and the 'pull' of urban life operating on the upward mobile and aspiring young educated generation—all these factors add to political disaffection. In Punjab, the dynamic, self-reliant yeomanry, the infrastructure of small-scale industries and a fast developing economy succeed in muting dissatisfaction. However, the salience of religion and the anxiety to preserve Punjab's separate identity incline people in the upper social strata to articulate communal feelings in politics.

In Uttar Pradesh and Bihar, the dominance of agriculture and the slow pace of industrialization and urbanization preserve the relevance of traditional social order and act as a barrier to secularizing tendencies. Caste mobility is therefore much greater in Punjab and West Bengal than in Bihar and Uttar Pradesh. In these two states deep and widespread poverty, made less bearable by promises expounded by political leaders that are rarely translated into reality, appear to have resulted over the years in the decline of the Congress party. In the absence of a viable alternative, politics takes the shape of competition among fragmented parties and groups articulating local, regional, and personal loyalties.

Except in West Bengal, the Congress party continues to be the most conspicuous in the party system. The Congress party support base, however, is nibbled away by competing parties and groups, most of whom have not been able to develop their own distinct support bases. In Punjab, the Congress party has to compete with the CPI and the particularist Akali Dal. However, ideological loyalties of the voter are far from sharply drawn, and this is reflected in voter movement among the three contending parties. Punjab's electoral politics since 1967 has created a situation in which neither the Congress party nor the Akali Dal is able to rule by itself. Nor can they rule in coalition for very long. The Congress party, however, is still the party of the rural poor and the underprivileged communities, while the Akali Dal draws most of its support from the higher social strata of the Sikhs.

In Uttar Pradesh, electoral contests take place along a triangular path—a centrist tendency represented by the Congress party and the breakaway groups assembled together in the BKD party, a moderate left-of-center tendency represented by the two socialist parties, SSP and PSP, and a rightist tendency represented by the Jan Sangh and Swatantra parties. The fourth tendency—radical left—plays only a marginal role; the two CPIs together got only 4 percent of the total votes cast in 1969. The Congress party still enjoys considerable support among the lower social strata: "the lower the socio-economic status, the smaller the support for both right and Socialist parties."

In Bihar, the arena is crowded with a host of parties forming a cluster of five political tendencies: the bifurcated Congress party, the Communists, the Socialists, the rightists, and the local and regional parties. There is considerable movement to and from the Congress party, but, despite the proliferation of parties, and a greater magnitude of cross-party movement, voter loyalties are quite strong, and there is little movement of voters from right to left or vice versa. "However, of late a radicalization of voting choice is evident from the movement of votes from the Socialist parties to the Communists without any trace of an opposite movement."

Party orientation is highest in West Bengal. The centrist tendency is represented by the Congress party, which is still the party of the young voters and whose support base consists of the higher strata of society. Proliferation of left groups prevents left

unity. The Communist support base has expanded in recent
years, and no movement of votes from the Communists to other
parties was noticed in the election of 1969.

COMMUNISM, PARLIAMENTARY POLITICS,
AND REVOLUTION

Since 1952, Communism has been operating in India within
the system of parliamentary democracy, and although a certain
cynicism has grown in the CPI(M) about whether the parliamentary path can lead to revolution, no single alternative tactical line
has so far crystallized. Parliamentary politics can be said to have
influenced the two CPIs more than the CPIs have influenced parliamentary politics. For instance, both CPIs have had to enter
into electoral alliances with "reactionary" parties and groups—
the CPI(M) with the Muslim League and the Kerala Congress in
Kerala, the CPI with such rightist groups as the Jan Sangh and
the BKD in Uttar Pradesh and Bihar (in coalition governments)
and Akali Dal in Punjab.

The Indian Communist movement has been long exposed to
the influence of the castes, particularly in those states where caste
loyalties are strong. Donald S. Zagoria says that the Indian Communists "have succeeded only by playing on caste, religious, and
regional loyalties." [17] While this is an overstatement, a deep bow
to caste and regional pulls of Indian society by the CPI was unavoidable when it decided to enter parliamentary politics. As
Namboodiripad himself has observed: "Almost every political
leader invariably takes into account the caste composition of the
electorate in a constituency when it selects its candidate." [18] The
CPI(M) reminded its delegates at the Calcutta congress that in
the struggle for power in India, individuals and groups used the
hold of castes and other pre-capitalist social organizations and became the champion of this or that caste; "the phenomenon that,

[17] Donald S. Zagoria, "Communism in Asia," *Commentary*, February 1965.
[18] Quoted, *ibid*.

while religious practices based on caste are dying out, politics based on caste has been in the ascendancy has to be taken into account." [19]

When the leftist faction of the CPI broke away in 1964 and formed the CPI(M), it had no tactical alternative to the parliamentary line. Some of the leaders were conscious of the bourgeoization of the CPI because of adhering too closely to the parliamentary line but, as we have noted in chapter 2, the Marxists were highly ambivalent in their Calcutta congress resolutions on the question of adopting sharper forms of class struggle, particularly on the question of violence. The Marxists' electoral victory in Kerala in 1965 strengthened the parliamentarians.

However, continuation of President's rule in Kerala, the long imprisonment of several hundred CPI(M) leaders, and the government offensive against the party in 1965–66, precluded any overt enthusiasm on the legitimacy of the Indian political system. Among the rank and file of the CPI(M), however, rejection of the parliamentary line gained some popularity.

Throughout 1966 both the CPIs played a leading role in organizing widespread mass protest in West Bengal and elsewhere against mounting food prices, for better wages, and for statutory rationing in large sections of the country affected by an acute shortage of food grains. In Bengal, these struggles embraced sizable portions of the rural population for the first time. The mass protests and their limited successes bred a certain amount of militancy in the cadres of the Marxist party. In the latter half of 1966, some opposition seemed to exist in the CPI(M) leadership to continued employment of parliamentary tactics. Opposition was much stronger among cadres.

However, the party decided to contest the 1967 election. Neither the Marxists nor the CPI expected the Congress party to lose control of the government of eight states. It was not so much the

[19] CPI(M), *Fight Against Revisionism* (Calcutta, 1965), p. 74.

electoral successes of the CPIs as the defeat of the Congress party that opened up an unprecedented opportunity of sharing power in several states. The pre-election rivalries of the two factions notwithstanding, both took part in united front governments in Kerala and West Bengal, while the CPI also joined the coalition governments of Bihar, Uttar Pradesh, and Punjab.

Within a few months, however, the CPI(M) leaders were obliged to defend their continued adherence to parliamentary tactics in the face of a challenge emanating from a group of "ultra-left revolutionaries" who had the support of the Chinese Communist party. The CPI(M) politbureau dismissed these "left adventurists." Partly because the Marxists' adherence to parliamentary tactics had drawn the wrath of the CCP, and also because the "ultra-left" line had apparently some appeal to the party cadres, the leadership was obliged to defend the parliamentary line in the columns of the party weekly.

In a series of articles, Ranadive and Basavapunniah confessed the numerical and organizational weakness of the CPI(M) and conceded the superior strength of the bourgeoisie. The party had to use parliamentary tactics to increase its influence over the masses.

Ranadive argued that the Indian national bourgeoisie element was much stronger than the forces ready to line up with the proletariat; wide sections of the masses were still under the influence of parties "not hostile to the state." A revolutionary party like the CPI(M) has to make a realistic assessment of the strength of its opponents and of its own strength and cannot indulge in "summary revolution." It is because of the weakness of the Communist movement in India that "partial" and "auxiliary" struggles still have revolutionary possibility; they offer "immediate recruiting ground for drawing the masses into the revolutionary struggle." The CPI(M) had not become a parliamentary party ("Who has ever talked of power through elections?"), but it had adopted the correct strategy of contesting the election and joining the left coalitions in West Bengal and Kerala. The objective of this strategy is "isolation of the main party of the bourgeoisie, advancement of the ideology of the party, and releasing the people and the working class from the grip of bourgeois ideology and increasing people's confidence in themselves as against the bourgeois-landlord government led by the big bourgeoisie." The very fact that the "ruling Congress gentry" saw the main danger to its hegemony arising from leftist coalition governments is evidence of their revolutionary potential. The leftist coalitions must function parallel to "constant pressure of the mass movement from below"; the "strategic position of the ministries" can be used to "deliver a blow at the vested interests." Ranadive claimed that in West Bengal "the struggle around the ministry has become the symbol of the class struggle among the contesting forces." [20]

The situation in India was not yet ripe for armed peasant struggle. No genuine peasant movement was possible "without overcoming the present weakness of the peasant movement." In a more candid confession, Basavapunniah wrote:

We are not oblivious of the fact that ours is a society with a predominantly petty-bourgeois class composition, that it is still politically backward with an extremely low level of class consciousness, that the proletarian and semiproletarian element is weak in the composition of the party, that Marxist-Leninist education is far from satisfactory, and that it will have to travel yet a long and difficult path before it becomes a mass revolutionary proletarian party capable of fulfilling its historic role.[21]

The CPI(M) in 1967, then, was nowhere near the revolutionary seizure of power; it decided to follow the parliamentary path in view of its organizational weakness vis-a-vis the national bourgeoisie. However, the Marxists intended to follow a militant parliamentary line, in which governmental power at the state level

[20] Ranadive's articles appeared in *People's Democracy* between July and November 1967. For reference to the points made here, see the issues dated July 16, pp. 5–9, and August 13, pp. 3, 12.

[21] *People's Democracy*, July 23, 1967, p. 3.

would be used to expand the party base and radicalize the masses, and extraparliamentary struggle from below would supplement the work of the leftist coalition ministries. In theory as well as in practice, this was a departure from the parliamentary tactics of the CPI, as we shall see later. The Marxist party did try to evolve in 1969 a radical and militant parliamentary line which, however, led to the collapse of the leftist coalitions in Kerala and West Bengal and to the CPI(M)'s isolation from most of the other leftist groups, including the CPI.

REGIONAL AND NATIONAL POWER

The parliamentary lines followed by the two parties between 1967 and 1971 brought significant rewards for Communism in India. The Communists were leading the state governments in Kerala and Bengal; they could influence from within the governmental policies and decisions in three other north Indian states. After the Congress party split in November 1969, when Mrs. Gandhi's government at the national level was reduced to a minority, the Communists were in a position to influence the policies and decisions of even there. Yet, there was much in this Communist success that was deceptive; moreover, success brought in its train organizational and operational problems that seriously taxed the leadership of both parties.

As a social force with grass-roots support, Communism in India is more of a regional than a national factor. The Marxists are strong in West Bengal, Tripura, and Kerala; the CPI has a certain social base in Bihar, and some following in Kerala, West Bengal, and Punjab; in the two south Indian states of Madras and Andhra Pradesh, both parties' social base is tenuous.

In the 1967 Lok Sabha elections, the CPI contested in fifteen states and Union territories, and the CPI(M) in twelve. The CPI's 23 seats came from Bihar (5), Kerala (3), Uttar Pradesh (5), West Bengal (5), Maharashtra (2), Assam (1), Andhra Pradesh (1), and Manipur (1). The CPI(M) won a total of 19 seats: 9 from Kerala, 5 from West Bengal, 4 from Madras, and 1 from Uttar Pradesh. Thus, in sixteen states and Union territories, the Marxists failed to secure any seat, and in nine of them they did not try. The CPI did not contest in two states, and did not secure any seat in twelve.

In the 1971 mid-term Lok Sabha election, the CPI(M) won 25 seats, but all but 3 of these were from West Bengal and Tripura; it won only 2 seats in Kerala (where it also supported a winning independent candidate, V.K. Krishna Menon), and 1 in Andhra Pradesh. The CPI got 23 seats: 5 in Bihar, 3 each in Kerala and West Bengal, 4 in Madras, 1 in Andhra Pradesh, 2 in Punjab, 4 in Uttar Pradesh, and 1 in Orissa.

In 1967 the Marxists had won 4 seats in Madras as a result of their electoral alliance with DMK; in 1971, DMK's electoral allies were the CPI and the ruling Congress party, which accounted for the Marxists' zero showing, and the CPI's four victories. In Bihar, Uttar Pradesh, and Punjab also, the CPI in 1971 had electoral adjustments and understanding with the ruling Congress faction; the Marxists fought alone, although the CPI accused them of entering into unwritten electoral pacts with the "Syndicate" Congress.

In the total number of Lok Sabha votes as well as in the percentage of all valid votes cast, the Marxists, despite their strictly regional showing, had in 1971 a slight edge over the CPI (Table 3.1); their total votes in certain states were significantly less than

TABLE 3.1. LOK SABHA VOTING FOR CPI AND CPI(M)

	Total Valid Votes		Percentage of Valid Votes	
	1967	1971	1967	1971
CPI	7,564,180	7,059,327	5.19	4.89
CPI(M)	6,140,738	7,184,560	4.21	4.97

Source: *Times of India,* March 31, 1971.

TABLE 3.2. COMPARATIVE VOTER SUPPORT FOR CPI AND CPI(M) IN STATES WHERE THE CPI(M) WON NO SEATS IN LOK SABHA

	CPI		CPI(M)	
	Valid votes polled	Seats won	Valid votes polled	Seats won
Bihar	1,467,146	5	113,373	0
Madras	866,399	4	260,833	0
Orissa	194,273	1	81,843	0
Punjab	253,800	2	89,543	0
Uttar Pradesh	842,818	4	39,821	0

Source: *Times of India,* March 31, 1971.

the CPI's (Table 3.2). Among the states in which neither Communist party won any seat, the CPI received 170,977 votes in Assam and the CPI(M) 42,772, while the Marxists got 45,188 votes in Mysore against the CPI's 6,914.

In the 1967 state elections, the Communists parties combined were second only to the Jan Sangh among the non-Congress parties, winning a total of 247 seats (out of a total of 3,347). The comparative strength of the two CPIs is shown in Table 3.3.

TABLE 3.3. CPI AND CPI(M) IN STATE ASSEMBLIES IN 1967

	CPI	CPI(M)
Andhra Pradesh	10	9
Assam	7	0
Bihar	24	4
Kerala	19	52
Madhya Pradesh	1	0
Madras	2	11
Maharashtra	10	1
Mysore	2	0
Orissa	7	1
Punjab	5	3
Rajasthan	1	0
Uttar Pradesh	14	1
West Bengal	16	43

Source: *Seminar,* June 1967.

In the mid-term elections in Bengal, Uttar Pradesh, Bihar, and Punjab in 1969, in the Kerala mid-term election in 1970, and in the West Bengal second mid-term election in 1971, what emerged with considerable clarity was that the CPI(M) support base existed primarily in West Bengal, Tripura, and Kerala. Thus, the main difference between the two parties' support base strongly influenced their strategic-tactical lines.

The CPI, lacking a support base in depth anywhere, but possessing various degrees of electoral support over a wide portion of India, adopted the tactical line of a united front from above, and regarded the ruling Congress faction, after the Congress split, to be a progressive force eligible for the national democratic front. The Marxists, on the other hand, were more concerned with protecting and enlarging their regional base in Bengal and Kerala; their tactical line aimed at a united front from below, and they regarded Mrs. Gandhi's Congress faction as the party of the bourgeoisie and landlord classes. The CPI tactics were aimed at sharing power with the democratic parties at the national level as well as in the states. The Marxist tactics were to build up regional areas of deeply entrenched Communist strength, to bring together leftist fronts under Communist hegemony, and to confront the central government. Put another way, the CPI appeared to believe that it could influence India's national politics as a significant partner of the national democratic front. The Marxists were skeptical of getting power at the national level, and were aiming at building strong regional bases first, and from those bases, to attack the national government.[22]

THE CPI AND NATIONAL POWER

The split in the Congress party in 1969 reinforced the CPI's hope of establishing a Communist presence at the level of na-

[22] The reader may be tempted to see in this an echo of the Soviet and Chinese revolutionary tactics. The CPI may seem to concentrate on the cities, while the CPI(M) can be said to have devised an Indian version of the Maoist tactical line of first capturing the countryside and then advancing toward the cities. The analogy, however, must not be drawn too far.

tional power. Mohit Sen, a CPI theoretician and member of the politbureau, saw in the fracture of the Congress party a "profound crisis that has now gripped the entire post-independence structure of India, both economic and political."

What took place in the twenty-two years, according to Sen, was the formation of what might be called a dual economy—both aspects of it capitalistic but differing in their significance and potential. On the one side grew the Indian private sector, with the aid of foreign capital, leading to a great strengthening of the oligopolistic groups. On the other side there was the "undoubted growth of the independent base of the economy, the development of economic relations with the socialist states, [and the] the striking growth of the state capitalist sector (where the oligopolists and their foreign allies do not have exclusive control)."

In the rural areas one had the intermeshing of the persistence and strengthening of landlordism with the emergence of a peasant bourgeoisie. This dual economy continued with a "happy competitive coexistence" for a considerable time. The coexistence came to an end with the onset of the recession in 1966 and especially after devaluation (of the rupee). Meanwhile, the capitalist path of development, while it generated new productive forces, "also produced the conditions for rebellion and revolutionary consciousness." There was a general desire that the entire post-independence structure should be recast. Some of this consciousness was diverted into revivalist and separatist channels, but the "mainstream of it followed Leftwards—into the traditional political formations of the Left as well as into the Congress."

Within the Congress party itself, Sen perceived the emergence of two "basic strategies" to deal with the crisis. One strategy, finally adopted by the "Syndicate," was "completing the economic coup of devaluation by the political coup of an authoritarian Rightist takeover, the setting up of a neo-colonialist, neo-fascist state power." The other strategy was to move the center of the Congress party to the left, "to attempt a new national consensus

on the basis of some radical changes in structure." The forces of
the center refused to surrender to the right. The forces of the left
took "convergent action" against the right as well as deciding to
support the center. A rift developed in the center-right coalition
that had been ruling the country during the 1960s. "It is this balance of political power forces that led to the [Congress] split."

The "Syndicate" faction now wanted to forge a coalition with
the explicitly right-wing parties like Swatantra and Jan Sangh.
"In the Congress led by Indira Gandhi are to be found the bulk
of the center (which remains the strongest element), all the left
forces in the ruling party (more consolidated and active than perhaps at any time in the history of the Congress), and a strong section of the right." The rightist elements in this Congress faction
would like to "sabotage" the organization from within and at the
same time work with the "Syndicate" faction and its rightist allies.
"The strategy of the center is, in the main, to cut the right down
to size, make the minimum necessary concessions to the people,
conciliate the left and utilize its support, but also to do its utmost
to avoid an alliance with it as well as prevent its gaining further
strength. The center wants the left only to the extent that it is
necessary to overwhelm the right and assert centrism."

In such a situation, Sen prescribed a triple strategy for the left,
including the Communists. First, the left should build up its own
independent strength and "establish maximum possible unity of
all its forces including those in the Indira Gandhi Congress." It
must abandon all "schematism"—that is, it must not insist on left
unity separately from unity with the progressive forces in the Indira Gandhi Congress party. Second, it must come out "as the
foremost and most effective opponents of the right coalition."
Third, it must follow a tactical line of "unity as well as struggle"
with the center in the Gandhi Congress party for the implementation of a minimum program of national rejuvenation.[23]

[23] Mohit Sen, "Congress Split and the Left," *Economic and Political Weekly*, December 13, 1969.

The CPI's vision of Communist partnership of national political power was articulated somewhat less sophisticatedly by Dange himself at the international Communist conference in Moscow in June 1969. After the mid-term elections in four Indian states, Dange said, "Everybody now realizes that the last days of Congress monopoly of power at the Center have arrived." The alternative of the coming power structure at the national level was either a leftist and democratic front "forged in time to take over power," or a reactionary combination of right-wing parties and groups.

The Indian monopolists and their foreign allies are trying to set up a new right-wing reactionary coalition party to take over the state power on their behalf. In such a situation, our party attaches the greatest importance to the urgent task of forging a left and democratic united front on the basis of a minimum program to serve as a viable alternative to Congress rule at the Center. . . . Our party is fully taking into consideration the concrete conditions of state power in India and the manner in which the fight for power at the Center has to be conducted.[24]

The CPI, then, is aiming at partnership of a center-left coalition at the national level. This strategy is based on two major premises. First, the Congress party led by Mrs. Gandhi is a progressive force and is interested, or will be made so by the compulsion of forces, in effecting structural changes in Indian society. The second premise is that it is possible to forge a united front of the leftist parties and groups on the basis of actual struggles against the policies of reaction and an agreed minimum program of national reconstruction.

THE CPI(M) AND NATIONAL POWER

The CPI(M), on the other hand, has been lukewarm about the Communists being a junior partner of a coalition government at

[24] For the text of Dange's speech at the Moscow meeting, see *New Age: Supplement*, June 22, 1969.

the national level. Moreover, the CPI(M) has had little reason to expect friendly treatment from those of the united Congress who broke away to form the new Congress of government leaders. Gulzarilal Nanda as home minister had arrested nearly a thousand CPI(M) leaders and activists and made it very difficult for the party to establish itself after the CPI split. The Marxist leaders could not easily forget the charges of treason and pro-China activities hurled against them by Nanda; these charges were often repeated explicitly or implicitly by Congress leaders, including Mrs. Gandhi, during the mid-term election campaign in 1968–69. While touring Kerala to campaign for the Congress party, Mrs. Gandhi attacked the CPI(M) much more than the other partners of the united left front.

Earlier, at the Hyderabad session of the All-India Congress Committee in January 1968, the decision taken by the Working Committee that the Congress party try to replace the left coalitions in the states by coalitions under its own leadership was taken by the Marxists as objective evidence of the class character of the Congress party.[25] Romesh Thapar, the Delhi columnist of *Political and Economic Weekly,* described the Congress party's decision as "a declaration of war against the non-Congress coalitions, especially those led by the Communists." The Marxists saw the operation of this resolution in the central government's dismissal of Bengal's united front government in the autumn of 1968.

More fundamentally, the CPI(M) differs from the CPI in its evaluation of the progressiveness of the Congress "center." While the CPI believes that no radical change is possible "without replacement of the Congress government at the Center," the CPI(M) is more eager to strengthen its political base in Bengal, Kerala, Andhra Pradesh, and Punjab.

An interesting debate took place between the two parties on replacing the central government soon after the fourth election.

[25] *People's Democracy,* January 9, 1969, and February 22, 1968.

The CPI(M) position was that the CPI was "naive" in its perspective of the national bourgeoisie. It expected the Congress government to fall through defections. This was considered sheer parliamentary maneuvering that had nothing to do with the masses—the CPI was trying to defeat the Congress government in parliament, not through mass struggles. "We too stand for a non-Congress alternative but we do not base it on defections nor divorce it from the mass struggle."

The revisionists, the CPI(M) argument continued, not only talked about coalition government at the national level, but also spread "illusions" about a peaceful transfer of power from the upper bourgeoisie-landlord state to a state of the people. Why should the revisionists protest, then, if they were called parliamentarians? They had even amended Bernstein by claiming that a bourgeois parliament could be the organ of the people! The coming struggle in India was not only against the Congress government but also against the bourgeoisie-landlord clique. It was necessary to isolate all parties toeing the line of the upper bourgeoisie/landlords.

The "no-untouchability doctrine" of the CPI was only a gimmick to cover parliamentary coalition while pretending to fight reaction outside and inside parliament, said the CPI(M). The revisionists refused to understand the crisis of capitalist development. They raised the possibility of a non-Congress democratic coalition at the national level—in which presumably the Swatantra and the Jan Sangh parties too would take part. For, had not the revisionists joined coalitions with the Jan Sangh in Uttar Pradesh and Punjab? The revisionists thought of the Congress party as a peaceful, nonaligned, anticolonial force, whereas in actuality the Congress government was supporting American imperialism and permitting American interference in India's economy at an increasing pace. The CPI still underestimated "the American threat." [26]

[26] For the CPI(M) formulations, see *People's Democracy*, April 2, April 30, and June 11, 1967. For CPI reply to the CPI(M), see *New Age*, May 7, 1967. The main

This Marxist stance has continued through 1970, without any significant variation. If anything, it has somewhat hardened, in response to the collapse of the Namboodiripad ministry in Kerala and to the united front regime in Bengal, as well as to the CPI's readiness to form coalitions at the state level without the CPI(M). Namboodiripad and Jyoti Basu, who as leader of the Marxist team in the Bengal coalition was instrumental in constructing the party's parliamentary strategy in that state, tried from the beginning to build up a climate of confrontation and struggle between the Congress regime in New Delhi and the two CPI(M)-led regimes at the state level. Both men maintained a studied difference in their style of direct and indirect negotiations with the national government from that of the leaders of other non-Congress state governments. Namboodiripad alone came up with an alternative draft of the fourth five-year plan and an alternative economic policy for the country. At meetings of the National Development Council, a body of senior national ministers and state chief ministers, Namboodiripad and Basu (who was deputy chief minister of the second Bengal united front government) sometimes tried to offer alternatives to the policies and plans of the central government. In parliament, the CPI(M) members proved to be much stronger critics of the government than were their CPI colleagues.

For the CPI(M), problems of center-state relations were not just problems inherent in India's federal-unitary constitution. It was a problem that "reflects the struggle of two contending class policies—the policies of the bourgeoisie-led state and the policies which the democratic movement stands for in the interests of the common people and for which the non-Congress democratic governments fight. It is an intense class struggle and its intensity is again and again seen when the Congress resorts to the most undemocratic methods to throw out these governments." [27]

CPI counterargument was that the Marxists were too dogmatic to see that class forces in India were changing. This was evident in the defeat of the Congress party and the victory of the Communists and other leftist and democratic forces.

[27] "Center-State Relations," *People's Democracy,* March 23, 1969.

It was a struggle of class policies because the "ruling Congress party has been pursuing policies which are in favor of Big Business, the big landlord, and the foreign monopolists. The democratic movement in the country has all along opposed these class policies of the big bourgeoisie and the ruling party and put forward its own class policies in favor of the toiling people and the real advance of the nation. With the formation of non-Congress democratic governments, this confrontation between the two class policies has been projected into relations between the Center and the states." [28]

As if to polarize their differences with the CPI over the issue of national power, two CPI(M) leaders, Namboodiripad and A. K. Gopalan, chose the second week of July 1968, when the Congress party was going through an acute crisis at its AICC session in Bangalore, to issue a statement explaining the party's parliamentary tactics. The CPI(M), they declared, has no illusion that the masses can capture power through the existing constitution and through the parliamentary method. The party's objective is to capture power for the masses by making the fullest use of the constitutional machinery and thereby "to break the constitution from within." Real democracy cannot be ushered in "without a thorough change of the constitution." Namboodiripad and Gopalan defended Ranadive's earlier statement in London that the task of the leftist governments in Kerala and Bengal was to "unleash the discontent" of the people rather than to "give relief."

The CPI(M), of course, could not dismiss as a "non-event" the crisis that overtook the Congress party in July and led to its split in November. Sundarayya welcomed Mrs. Gandhi's executive order nationalizing fourteen leading Indian banks, but hastened to add that this action, in itself, did not mean that the Congress government had become a progressive force. P. Ramamurti expressed delight at Morarji Desai's resignation from the central

[28] *Ibid*. The CPI(M) in 1969 further developed the theoretical basis of the center-state "class struggle." See chapter 5.

government, for wasn't Desai "one of the staunchest champions of Indian monopoly and foreign collaboration?" When, toward the end of July, Mrs. Gandhi tacitly sponsored V. V. Giri for the presidency in opposition to the official Congress candidate, N. Sajiva Reddy, and the ruling party stood on the brink of a split, Ramamurti played an active role in mobilizing support for Giri's election. However, the CPI(M) perspective of the crisis in the Congress party was very different from the CPI's. The Marxists saw the conflict between Mrs. Gandhi and the "Syndicate" fundamentally as a factional conflict. Insofar as it represented a split in the Congress leadership, the democratic forces must exploit it to their favor. But it would be a mistake to believe that Mrs. Gandhi had made a real break with the basic Congress policies or had given the Congress party a leftward swing.[29]

In the months that followed, the CPI(M) welcomed the split of the Congress party and opposed the right-wing parties' move to pass a motion of "no-confidence" in the government of Mrs. Gandhi. The CPI(M)'s central committee, at a five-day meeting in Calcutta, devoted considerable time to outlining a tactical line of "politicking" in Delhi in the context of "the serious inner-party crisis that has erupted in the ruling Congress party." This tactical line, as explained by Sundarayya at a press conference, was that, in the context of the "immediate political situation," the prime minister's faction needed the support of the democratic forces against the "greater enemy," the "Syndicate." Whenever conflicts arose in the ruling party, Sundarayya said, "it will be our task to isolate the greater enemy." Whatever limited support might be given to Mrs. Gandhi, it is not because "she has changed and turned a democrat overnight." CPI(M) members of parliament gave Mrs. Gandhi "limited support" for several months, but voted against her in a "no-confidence motion" (which the prime minister survived by a comfortable margin). By that time Mrs. Gandhi

[29] *The Statesman* Weekly, July 12 and 26, 1969.

had given her blessing to the CPI-led, Congress-supported government in Kerala which isolated the CPI(M) from practically the
entire political spectrum in that state.

THE TWO PARTIES FALL FARTHER APART

The tactical lines of the two CPIs were put into operation during
the 1971 mid-term parliamentary election and the simultaneous
elections to the state assemblies of West Bengal, Madras, and
Orissa. Mrs. Gandhi took the country by surprise when she dissolved the Lok Sabha in January and set a mid-term election for
March 10.

The CPI, encouraged by the Kerala model—where a CPI-led
ministry had been functioning since February 1970 with the support of Mrs. Gandhi's Congress party—and by the ruling party's
minority in the dissolved Lok Sabha, made an active bid for a formal national electoral alliance with Mrs. Gandhi and other centrist or leftist parties. The ruling Congress faction, however, rejected a formal alliance, but worked out local alliances with
several groups, including the CPI. Thus, in Punjab, Uttar Pradesh, and Bihar as well as in Kerala and West Bengal, the ruling
Congress group and the CPI made local electoral pacts.

The curious thing about these pacts was that they did not eliminate all contests between the ruling Congress faction and the
CPI, but only kept these contests at the minimum. The CPI
blamed the rightist faction in the ruling party, and its president,
Jagjivan Ram, for denying it its legitimate share of parliamentary
seats in Punjab, Uttar Pradesh, and Bihar. In Kerala an amicable
adjustment was arrived at rather easily. In Madras, the ruling
Congress party, in an electoral pact with the DMK, agreed not to
enter the contest for the legislative assembly; the CPI thus came
to a profitable adjustment with the DMK for assembly seats. The
Lok Sabha seats were divided between the DMK, the ruling Con-

gress party, and the CPI. In West Bengal, the state unit of the CPI refused to obey the central committee's instruction to strike an electoral understanding with the Mrs. Gandhi's Congress faction. Instead, the CPI worked out a united front with seven other leftist parties. The CPI(M) brought about a six-party leftist front in which it was much more than an equal of the other groups. However, although the electoral contest in Bengal was quadrangular—the two Congress factions and the two left fronts—in a large number of constituencies, the CPI worked with the Gandhi Congress faction against the Marxist party. The bitter fruits of interparty rivalry during and after the 1969 united front experiment pushed the two Communist groups farther apart than ever before.

The electoral results came as a sharp disappointment to the CPI. The ruling Congress party won a two-thirds majority in the Lok Sabha, and had therefore no need of CPI support. In fact, instead of a national democratic government being set up in Delhi, the party led by Mrs. Gandhi was safely in power for five years, and it now began to draw back to its fold most of those members who had left it in 1969. The CPI leadership, however, hailed the election result as a victory for its tactical line, as the poll had witnessed the rout of the rightist forces like the Jan Sangh, the Swatantra, and the "Syndicate" Congress faction.[30] In fact, the leadership mildly criticized the West Bengal committee for going against the central directive. If the state committee had lined up with the Gandhi Congress faction, it might have wrested more seats from the CPI(M). Thus, humiliating the Marxist party was, in 1971, more important to the CPI than defeating the Congress party in Bengal.

The politbureau of the CPI(M) declared that the victory of Mrs. Gandhi's Congress faction "cannot be considered a victory of the people, of the democratic and toiling masses." While it wel-

[30] *Patriot,* March 19, 1971.

comed the debacle of the rightist parties, its main attack was the
"most treacherous role" of the CPI and some other leftist groups
"in undermining the growing alternative of a united front" of
leftist and democratic forces. "What is needed once more is the
restoration of a united front of the democratic parties and forces
which will be considered by the people as an alternative to Congress rule." The CPI(M) appealed to the CPI to revive the democratic united front. The CPI, however, declared that it could
have no dealings with the Marxists unless they publicly gave up
their tactics of "murder and violence." [31] In West Bengal, the
CPI(M) emerged from the election as the largest single party in
the state assembly, but Mrs. Gandhi's Congress faction, with fewer
seats than the Marxists, was able to form a government with the
participation of CPI and several other groups.

In the spring of 1971, then, the CPI(M) held no governmental
power in any state in India, while the CPI was leading the coalition in Kerala and was a major constituent of the coalition in
West Bengal.

An immediate impact on the Marxist party was a certain polarization between the parliamentary and extraparliamentary groups
in the leadership. Those who were skeptical of the revolutionary
relevance of parliamentary tactics gained status, and those who
still wanted to tread the parliamentary path were thrown somewhat on the defensive. A noted Indian political commentator
reported that, within the Communist movement, there were
two contrary pulls, one toward increasing militancy, the other
toward parliamentarianism. These pulls worked as a linkage
among the three Communist factions, the CPI, the CPI(M), and
the CPI(ML) or the so-called Maoists. "The pull exerted on the
CPI's ranks by the CPI(M)'s militancy and its uncompromising
opposition to the new Congress is paralleled by the Maoist pull
vis-a-vis the CPI(M)."

[31] *Times of India,* March 19, 24, and 26, 1971.

All over India, reported this commentator, the Marxist party had been losing cadres to the Maoists since 1968: "The process may now accelerate because the promise of power in West Bengal has proved illusory." Within the CPI(M) leadership, Ranadive was said to be leading the group that was against further pursuit of the parliamentary and ministerial line. "The CPM leadership never found it easy to justify its participation in the parliamentary process to its ranks."

In 1967 the leadership plunged into elections on the plea that the breaking up of the Congress party's monopoly of power was a necessary first step toward revolution. The mid-term elections of 1969 and 1970 and the formation of a non-Marxist coalition in Kerala once again polarized the parliamentarians and the militants. In 1971 the leadership's parliamentary tactics drove the Marxists into a grand isolation from most, if not all, of the left and democratic parties: "The outcome has underscored the harsh truth that the CPI(M) cannot win power via the ballot box."

Pressure to abandon the parliamentary path was now expected to increase: "The groundwork for the move may have been laid already." In fighting the Maoists' attempt to liquidate CPI(M) cadres, the party had built up, during the past three years, an underground party apparatus. "In the special situation of West Bengal, emphasis was placed on the collection of weapons and the training of men to handle them. The immediate objective was to deal with the 'Naxalites', but the distant aim was to equip the party for a future showdown with the law-and-order machine." [32]

[32] Dilip Mukherji, "The Communist Dilemma," *Times of India*, March 19, 1971. Mukherji reported that during the election in Madras, the state committee of the CPI(M), without the politbureau's approval, worked out an electoral adjustment with the "Syndicate" Congress led by K. Kamaraj.

4

REGIONAL BASE
OF COMMUNISM:
WEST BENGAL

Perhaps the most significant difference between Communism and other major political forces in India is that despite the claim of the CPI to be a "national" party, Communism is in practical reality still only a strong regional element. Communism thrives in two extreme corners of India—in the southwestern coastal state of Kerala and the eastern state of West Bengal. Its once-strong base in Andhra Pradesh disintegrated largely because of intraparty and, then, interparty conflicts, and also because the urban-oriented undivided CPI rapidly lost ground as soon as the Congress party was able to identify itself with the linguistic subnationalism of the Telugu-speaking elite.

The CPI's strong base in Andhra Pradesh had been built in the late 1940s and early 1950s, first, around the linguistic-nationalist demand for a separate Telugu-speaking state and, second, around the land-hungry, oppressed peasantry of Telengana. The peasant base collapsed when the CPI abandoned the Telengana struggle in 1951, and during the 1950s and 1960s, the Congress party succeeded in building a strong peasant base with the help of the landowning castes in the coastal districts. The CPI also steadily lost its middle-class support after the creation of Andhra Pradesh on a linguistic basis; the middle-class elite now found the Congress party abler to reward its loyalties. The absence of an industrial proletariat reduced Andhra Communism to factional rivalries among a relatively small number of middle-class, high-caste intellectuals.

In the formerly bilingual state of Bombay, the CPI had a certain support among the Marathi-speaking middle classes as long as the demand for a separate Marathi-speaking state remained unfulfilled. After the inauguration of Maharashtra in 1956, the CPI rapidly lost its middle-class base, and its influence was confined to a section of unionized industrial workers in Bombay.[1]

In Madras, the rise of Tamil subnationalism led to the triumph of the DMK and the decline of the Congress party in 1967; the trend has continued. Here, Communism can operate only in alliance with Tamil nationalism—witness the small but not insignificant gains of the CPI(M) in the 1967 election and the comparable gains of the CPI in the 1971 election, in either case the result of an electoral pact with the DMK. Similarly in Punjab, Communism is pitted against the much stronger force of Sikh subnationalism, and its political arm, the Akali party.

Communism in India, then, has to confront not merely the "nationalism" of the national elite, but also the ascendant subnationalism of the various nationalities. The slow pace of industrialization and urbanization and lack of structural changes in agrarian relations have tended to strengthen and consolidate the

---

[1] Causes for the sharp erosion of Communist influence in Andhra Pradesh and problems faced by the Communists in adopting linguistic-cultural subnationalist elites are further discussed in chapter 11.

particularist nationalisms of the linguistic elite and to keep the rural poor in a state of docility and quiescence.

Viewed from this angle, Hindi-speaking northern India would seem to suffer from a disadvantage in comparison with non-Hindi states like Madras, Andhra Pradesh, Maharashtra, and Punjab. Linguistic Hindi nationalism is more or less synonymous with Indian nationalism; it offers no particularist cultural and political barrier to Communism. If Communism has made a poor showing in the Hindi-speaking states so far, it is mostly because of the extreme backwardness of these societies and the still powerful grip of traditional social institutions on the peasantry.

If Communism has made any significant progress outside Kerala and Bengal in recent years, it is in Bihar where, in the 1967 election for the legislative assembly, the two Communist groups together polled about 10 percent of all valid votes. Bihar's countryside is exposed to the same political winds that blow over West Bengal. A conscious sense of deprivation may lure the rural poor and urban middle classes in Bihar and Uttar Pradesh to Communism more easily than the same social groups in those states where there exist strong sentiments of subnationalism.

The regional character of Communism creates organizational as well as psycho-cultural problems for the two Communist parties, more so for the Marxists who, as noted, have their strong bases far away from the seat of national power. How this reality influences the tactical perspectives of the CPI(M) we have already discussed in the foregoing pages. Also of profound significance for the organizational and operational character of the CPI(M) are its social composition and the regional character of its support base.

The party's central committee in 1968 attributed most of Communism's shortcomings and failures in India to its preponderant middle-class composition. Among the "chronic" shortcomings listed were unstable and fluctuating membership, passivity of the bulk of the members, precarious dependence on a "handful of organizers," and, above all, "a strong element of instability in upholding and executing the political line." [2] The central committee was also conscious of the concrete problems of building a nation-wide Communist movement in multinational and multicultural India. It is easy to build a well-centralized Communist party in a single-nation state; but India is not only multinational, it is different from all the other multinational states in the world. The Communist party, like all other political parties, "is state- and state-language-based in its day-to-day work and agitprop." It is "curious to note" that while the central committee of the CPI(M) was "compelled to be content with running an English weekly as its organ, in a language not known to 99 percent of the people in any state, seven state committees run their language weeklies and three among them run their daily organs." The language barrier "prevents the central leadership from coming into direct and close contact with the cadres and their day-to-day work in different states."

All these factors stood against the building of a united, centralized Communist party in India. Parochialization was already evident in the Marxist party: "what predominates today in most of our state committee leaders is one's state consciousness rather than all-India Communist Party consciousness." The tendency was apparently toward the growth of local chieftainships rather than disciplined cadres of a national political movement. Self-criticism was either completely absent or grossly inadequate; "localism" was rampant. "A sort of 'state exclusiveness' and the absence of an all-India consciousness is gaining currency in the party leadership, let alone among the bulk of our party members." [3]

The remedies prescribed by the central committee could be implemented only over the long run. Meanwhile, a decision it made concerning the state committee representation in the chief organs of the party as well as its plenums and congresses reflected the regionalization of Indian Communism. The Communist movement

---

[2] *Our Tasks on Party Organization*, (Calcutta, CPI(M), 1968), pp. 17–20.
[3] *Ibid.*, pp. 60–65.

had unevenly spread in the different states, being weakest in the Hindi-speaking belt. In the old, united CPI, states with "loose but large membership" were "over-represented" in the highest echelons, and a weighted representation was given to the smaller states over the larger states. This brought to the head of the party its "most backward sections . . . with no deep mass struggle experience," breeding revisionism and leading to the party split.

The CPI(M) therefore had to provide for a weighted representation in the delegations to be elected to party conferences and congresses "on the basis of the strategic importance of the party movement in certain areas and on the basis of mass struggles launched." [4] Since these characteristics were to be found only in the coastal states and in Punjab, these were the areas that would inevitably predominate the party conferences and congresses and find larger representation in its central organs. In more specific terms, the leadership of the CPI(M) had to remain very largely a collectivity of Bengali, Malayalee, Telugu, Tamil, and Punjabi Communists.

Apart from the label of regionalism this would apparently put on Indian Communism, which could be changed only with the spread of militant movements in the Hindi-speaking belt, the communication problem of Indian Communism must also be taken into account. While there exists a large area of communication between the three south Indian linguistic groups—most Malayalees and Telugus also speak Tamil—there is practically no communication between the Bengali and the south Indians or the Punjabi and the south Indians except through English, although a Punjabi and a Bengali could at least try to reach one another through their own varieties of Hindi.

A potentially significant aspect of this restricted south-north milieu of Indian Communism, which may assume far-reaching importance in the coming years, is the strategic advantage it places

[4] *Ibid.*, pp. 62–65.

at the disposal of the Communists in Bengal. It is Bengal (and to a much lesser extent, Punjab) that represents northern India effectively in the more radical of the two Communist parties. Students of the history of Indian politics cannot but be impressed by the similarity of this phenomenon with the early, pre-Gandhian, stage of the Indian nationalist movement.[5]

THE IMPORTANCE OF WEST BENGAL

The achievement of a strong base in West Bengal has invested the Communist movement in India with an importance it could hardly claim as long as its base was confined to Kerala and to parts of Andhra Pradesh. Bengal has been historically the fountainhead of Indian radicalism; even in the nationalist movement, it traditionally occupied a leftist position. The radical nationalist movement in the eastern wing of Pakistan is essentially a Bengali movement; at the time of writing,[6] leaders of this movement have declared an open rebellion against the military regime, and proclaimed the independent republic of Bangla Desh. Whatever the outcome of this movement, there is a possibility that the armed resistance now being offered against Pakistani rule will be progressively taken over by the radical elements in East Bengal. Such a turn in the politics of East Bengal, if it comes about, may well establish in the northeastern flank of the subcontinent a stronghold of leftist radicalism. In any case, the outbreak of an armed nationalist rebellion in East Bengal and the possibility of protracted guerrilla warfare there add a new dimension to the Communist movement in West Bengal.

West Bengal occupies a vantage point in the economic, cul-

[5] The similarity may be more superficial than real. The fact remains, however, that between 1885 and 1914, the Congress leadership was predominantly south Indian and Bengali. The third strong element was Maharashtrian. It was Gandhi who integrated the Congress party with the Hindi-speaking north.

[6] May–June, 1971. See also chapter 11.

tural, and political life of India. Its strategic importance is unsurpassed by any other part of the country. Around the city of Calcutta lies the nerve center of the engineering, jute, and tea industries, currently India's chief leading exports. Central revenues from excise, customs and income tax earn the nation about Rs 600 crore (over $1 billion) per year. The port of Calcutta handles nearly 50 percent of India's foreign trade. It is the outlet for all of the export commodities of the Ganges valley, including the iron ore of Orissa and the manganese of Bihar and Madhya Pradesh. In spite of the phenomenal growth of industry in Bombay, Bangalore, Ahmedabad, Poona, and the Ludhiana-Amritsar region of Punjab, West Bengal still has the largest concentration of industry and is the strongest center of Indian capitalism. Since most of this capital has come from outside of Bengal, Calcutta is the most cosmopolitan city in India. West Bengal is strongly integrated with northern and western India economically, culturally, and politically.

Partition largely shattered the economy. Resources needed to restore that economy could not be found within the state, nor were they forthcoming from the central government. Partly responsible for this neglect of West Bengal's pressing needs was the Bengali's apparent lack of interest in economics: "The Bengali, it must be accepted to begin with, is a political and not an economic animal. . . . Throughout history, the Bengali has been a rebel with little thought of profit to himself." [7]

Government expenditure on West Bengal is just about one-third of what it is for Maharashtra; the Indian armed forces do little recruiting in Bengal, where there are very few Plan pro-

[7] A C B, "Not Forever Amber in W. Bengal," *Economic and Political Weekly,* April 18, 1970. The writer says: "So parochial a people are Bengalis that it is perhaps necessary to remind non-Bengalis that Bengal is not Kerala; India can survive Kerala but not Calcutta. Were the industrial, mineral, and agricultural production of West Bengal (which commands Assam) and the Calcutta port denied to India, without coal, jute, tea, iron and steel, and machine tools, the industries of the rest of India would collapse, military defense would be impossible, exports vanish, and very quickly political freedom would be destroyed."

grams. The Calcutta port works at half of its capacity, handling only 6.9 million metric tons of traffic against a possible 12.5 million metric tons. This reflects the neglect of the Hooghly river, where the drafts have fallen so low since independence that only ships under 6,000 metric tons can now be handled. The industries of the Calcutta area draw the surplus humanity from the countryside in Orissa, Bihar, and Uttar Pradesh; to this endless stream of the lumpen proletariat has been added some 4 million refugees from East Pakistan—a steady trickle of 200,000 refugees every year is expected to continue indefinitely.

The result is appalling in every direction. Over a third of the city constitutes the worst slums in the world. The jobless and the underemployed can be counted in many thousands. Fifty percent of the population live in one room per family, and their children grow up making the streets their homes. Schools and colleges are the most overcrowded in India. The transport system is completely chaotic and grossly inadequate—commuters not only crowd the aisles and platforms of suburban trains, buses, and trams, but even cling to the windows outside and quite a few are thrown off and get killed or maimed. The wages of factory labor in Calcutta is about the lowest in India, for industries can always hire expatriates from the neighboring states where the wages of agricultural labor is considerably lower than in Bengal.[8]

SOCIAL STRUCTURE

The social structure of Bengal is different from that of the rest of India in several important ways. Five hundred years ago, when caste restrictions were becoming more and more rigid in the rest of the country, Chaitanya Deva of Bengal led a rebel religious movement preaching the equality of man and the supremacy of

[8] Wages of agricultural labor in West Bengal, at Rs 490 ($64.00) per head per year, is the highest in India. *Economic Times*, March 6, 1970. The number of refugees from East Pakistan does not include the 3.5 million Muslims and Hindus who migrated to West Bengal from "Bangla Desh" since March 25, 1971.

the human being in all creation. The Bengali Brahmin has always been a meat-eater, so much so that the old scriptures described Bengal, Orissa, and Assam as the habitat of "fallen Hindus." The writ of the powerful Mughal emperors of Delhi reached Bengal only through semiautonomous provincial governors. In the intrigues that led to the downfall of Siraj-ud-Doulah, Bengali merchants and moneylenders conspired with the British to overthrow Muslim rule.

Then followed a period of political quiescence, an intellectual and cultural revolution which, in time, gave birth to the Indian nationalist movement. As a strong reaction to the new generation's attraction for Christianity, the liberal eclectic humanism of Ramakrishna was born. It further weakened the shackles of the castes. The Bengali started the nationalist movement, but later broke away from it to indulge in group terrorism; he led spectacular revolts against Gandhi within and outside the Congress. But he was almost completely blind to the economic stagnation of Bengal.

To a large extent this was the result of the permanent settlement introduced by the British at an early stage of their rule. The landed aristocracy was assured of a minimum income, and felt no incentive either to increase agricultural production or to invest in industry. On the contrary, it developed its own culture of elegant dissipation.

The cultural and intellectual revolution of the nineteenth century was, in part, the new urban middle class's rebellion against the decadence of the landed gentry. For well over a century, it is the middle class that has dominated the life style of Bengal, while in Bombay, industrialists and businessmen won for themselves leadership of economic, social, and political development. The Bengali middle class was the first to obtain English education in great numbers, was the largest group to join the nationalist movement and was the first to get disenchanted with it. It swelled the ranks of clerks, teachers, lawyers, doctors; created the best of Indian literature, drama, poetry and the fine arts—while, in the meantime, Bengal's economy, where it was not controlled by the British, slipped into the greedy grasp of up-country businessmen and capitalists.

Unlike Bombay, where industrialists took care to develop a planned city, the non-Bengali capitalists of Calcutta were interested only in taking as much as they could out of it. After independence, the Bengali middle class, its parochial pride wounded, found that it was being rapidly overtaken by the rising middle classes of the rest of the country. This sharpened the Bengali's sense of relative deprivation, and made his mood rebellious.[9]

THE MISERY OF CALCUTTA

The city of Calcutta in many ways symbolizes the plight of the Bengali middle class, which is being steadily reduced to the world's largest and most volatile lumpen proletariat. Overconcentration of industry, trade, commerce, culture, and administration in Calcutta has blighted Bengal's economy for over a century; no effort has been made to create a balance by diverting some of these to a second city. According to the 1961 census, 53.72 percent of West Bengal's population live in the Presidency Division, of which Calcutta is the center. Also in this division are located 55

[9] The noted novelist Bankim Chandra Chatterji, who is regarded as "the father of the Indian fiction," depicted the typical Bengali middle-class intellectual in *Rajani*. "He did not disclose his business, nor could I ask him outright. So we discussed social reform and politics. I found him an accomplished conversationalist. His mind was cultivated, his education complete, and his thought far-reaching. There being a pause in the conversation, he began to turn over *The Shakespeare Gallery* on my table. . . . Amarnath did not come to business even after the plates of *The Shakespeare Gallery* had been gone over, and began to discuss the pictures. . . . From Shakespeare's heroines he came to Shakuntala, Sita, Kadamvari . . . and he analyzed their characters. The discussion of ancient literature led in its turn to ancient historiography, out of which there emerged some incomparable exposition of the classical historians—Tacitus, Plutarch, Thucydides, and others. From the philosophy of history of these writers, Amarnath came down to Comte and his *lois des trois etats* which he endorsed. Comte brought in his interpreter Mill and then Huxley. . . . Amarnath poured the most entrancing scholarship into my ears, and I became too engrossed to remember our business." Translated from Bengali by Nirad C. Choudhuri in his *Autobiography of an Unknown Indian* (New York, Macmillan, 1951), pp. 59–61.

percent of the state's hotels, motels, inns, and rest houses; 56 percent of its shops; 57.74 percent of its business and commercial establishments; 66.65 percent of its industry; 70.21 percent of its restaurants and eating places; 50 percent of its cinema houses and other entertainment centers; and 57 percent of its medical institutions, hospitals, and health centers. This extraordinary concentration of wealth, enterprise, and humanity in a relatively small area has created a dangerous political imbalance: any party that can control four of the seventeen districts of West Bengal—24-Parganas, Midnapur, Hooghly, and Murshidabad—as well as the Calcutta-Howrah industrial complex, can control the entire state.

Within this "immature metropolis," there is a rural universe—the *bustee*—in which live one-third of the population. Here are the slums of Calcutta. It is a "rural spot in an urban milieu," except that it is extremely overcrowded. "In addition to underindustrialization, unemployment, and lack of integration with the city as a whole, the arrival of immigrants from East Pakistan and the retreating of minority groups from isolated areas or from majority groups result in a higher concentration of population. After each social or communal conflict, moreover, the slums reach a new peak of overcrowding. There are cases of more than one couple residing in the same room with arrangements being made every night for visual privacy."

The *bustee* has remained multi-ethnic—Hindus and Muslims, Bengalis and non-Bengalis, live together in remarkable amity. Although the poor predominate, the typical *bustee* dweller is literate, young (under thirty), semiskilled or unskilled, and defiantly protective of his slum home. The main social groups are unskilled workers and manual laborers who constitute about 90 percent of the slum population, small traders and small businessmen and skilled workers employed as low-grade personnel of government or commercial organizations, and hut-owners and relatively stable businessmen. There are a small number of educated people also. They live as compact residential groups, closely bound together by kinship, devising solutions to their own problems, always fighting eviction from the only shelter they have in a cruel and hostile city.

"In their attempt to solve the problems of a rural people in an urban setting, the clusters of kin groups have evolved a coherent way of life in the slums and have progressively engulfed and assimilated many of those who had been outside their normal social range." [10] They help one another in times of need, collectively protect their common interests, settle petty disputes through their own *panchayats* (elected councils), and bargain with political parties and leaders with their votes. The incidence of crime in the *bustee* is remarkably low, and strict segregation of women prevents large-scale sexual immorality. "The feeling of insecurity itself, generated by socio-psychological factors, makes *bustee* dwellers adhere more rigidly to traditional norms of behavior and guard themselves even more zealously against degeneration and disorganization. . . . The painful awareness of how they are looked down upon by those outside the slums is also a factor in the preservation of organized life in the slums." [11]

The *bustee* is the traditional entry area for thousands of landless peasants who have been squeezed out of their rural abodes, and for the refugees from East Pakistan. The remarkable thing is that there is very little upward movement from the *bustee* to a normal residential area. For this rural humanity the *bustee* therefore is the last haven in its struggle for existence. It is also an ugly haven, with no water supply, no electricity, no modern latrines, and no removal of garbage for days and weeks. The law was until recently a disincentive to even ordinary repairs and improvements in the huts. The dwellers get accustomed to the unspeak-

[10] Very few studies have been made of the nature of the Calcutta slums. An interesting study, from which the writer has borrowed, is M. K. A. Siddiqui, "Life in the Slums of Calcutta," *Economic and Political Weekly*, December 13, 1969, pp. 1917–1921. Siddiqui found in one slum a senior lecturer in a degree college and a journalist working in a leading Bengali daily.

[11] *Ibid.* There are, however, many slums where women work as household help during the day and as prostitutes at night.

able squalor and do nothing to solve collectively the problems of unsanitation and uncleanliness.

LAND TENURE: TOO SMALL AND TOO FRAGMENTED

West Bengal is the second most thickly populated state in India, with an average of 1,032 people per square mile. The

TABLE 4.1. LANDHOLDINGS IN WEST BENGAL AND ALL-INDIA

Size of holdings	West Bengal No. of landholders	Percent	All-India (Percent)	West Bengal No. of acres	All-India (Percent)
Under 5 acres	2,368,000	74	62.98	5,114,000	18.88
5 to 10 acres	601,000	18.88	18.2	4,128,000	19.7
10 to 15 acres	170,000	5.31	8	2,001,000	13.8
15 to 30 acres	53,000	1.65	7.18	1,033,000	22.15
Over 30 acres	3,000	.09	3.39	133,000	25.17

Source: drawn from National Sample Survey, 16th Round Draft Report No. 122, New Delhi, 1958.

heaviest concentration is to be found in the five southeastern districts: Calcutta, 24-Parganas, Howrah, Hooghly, and Burdwan, which together support 47 percent of Bengal's population on 30 percent of the total area. Calcutta, with a density of 73,642 persons per square mile, is one of the most overcrowded cities in the world. The northern districts of West Dinajpur, Malda, Murshidabad, and Nadia have an average density of 931, and the eastern districts of Birbhum, Bankura, Midnapore, and Purulia, 731. It is only in the northern districts of Darjeeling, Jalpaiguri, and Cooch-Bihar that the density is as low as 606 per square mile. The state's average rural density is 787. In the plains, a density of 1,000 (including 200 agricultural workers) is the norm.

Of West Bengal's 11.58 million working population, 38.8 percent are "cultivators," owning plots of land of from less than 2.5 acres to over 15 acres. A large portion of the working population,

15.3 percent, are agricultural laborers, either without any land or with plots too small to count as "land." Thus, as an occupation, agriculture, supports 54 percent of the total population. The number of large-plot holders is very low, and the number of holders of small plots too high.

TABLE 4.2. LANDHOLDINGS IN WEST BENGAL AND LAND AVAILABLE FOR DISTRIBUTION

Size of holding	No. of land-holders	Total acres in possession	Acres allowed to be retained	Acres available for distribution
Over 33⅓ acres	20,000	1,000,000	700,000 (ceiling: 33⅓)	300,000
Over 25 acres	40,000	1,600,000	1,000,000 (ceiling: 25)	600,000
Over 20 acres	60,000	2,300,000	1,350,000 (ceiling: 20)	950,000
Over 15 acres	120,000	3,200,000	900,000 (ceiling: 15)	2,300,000

Source: Bhowani Sen, *Evolution of Agrarian Relations in India* (New Delhi, PPH, 1962), p. 201.

Too many small holdings and large numbers of landless agricultural workers are not the only features of the land-tenure system of West Bengal. By introducing the permanent settlement in Bengal, Bihar, Assam, and Orissa, the British created what Marx called "a caricature of large-scale English landed estates." The experiment was doomed to failure because it did not spring spontaneously out of historical development but was an alien system grafted on to Indian society only to provide the East India Company with a steady income from land revenue every year. The English manoral system was the product of social conditions completely different from that of India. The *zamindars* created by the permanent settlement in Eastern India were merely rent-grabbers; their creation deprived the rack-rented peasants of their traditional rights without conferring on them any new rights under the law, and brought about rapid disintegration of the peasantry.

Apart from the fact that there were many categories of *zamindars,* most of them absentee landlords, a whole hierarchy of rent collectors came into existence as a class of ruthless exploiters of the tenants. These intermediaries between the landlord and the peasant multiplied in course of time; in most parts of eastern India there were from 10 to 20 *categories* of them, and in some parts there were as many as 52.[12] In the absence of any institutional service to the peasants, these rent-collectors and many of the *zamindars* themselves also became moneylenders who charged exhorbitant rates of "interest" on loans to illiterate and helpless peasants. The law of inheritance, litigation, and other factors led to frequent fragmentation of *zamindaries,* thus multiplying the number of absentee landlords whose dissipated living in town depended entirely on what they could squeeze out of the peasants.

The tenants in Bengal came to be classified into three categories: *raiyats,* under-*raiyats,* and *bargadars* (sharecroppers). The first two were divided into occupancy tenants and non-occupancy tenants. Only a portion of the *raiyats* and under-*raiyats* enjoyed some protection from eviction under the law; the vast number of non-occupancy *raiyats* and sharecroppers had no protection at all. Even in the early 1950s, 20 percent of land under cultivation in West Bengal was tilled by sharecroppers, of whom there were 600,000 families comprising a population of 3 million.[13]

The prevailing system of cultivation is age-old and continues unchanged in spite of the "reforms" of the Congress party in 20 years of

[12] Abdullah Rasul, *Krishak Sabhar Itihas* (History of the Peasant Association) in Bengali (Calcutta, 1970), p. 98.
[13] Bhowani Sen, *Evolution of Agrarian Relations in India* (New Delhi, PPH, 1962), pp. 116–17.

independence. The petty landlord or *jotedar* generally cultivates his land by leasing it out to *bargadars* or *adhiars,* on a crop-sharing basis. If the *jotedar* provides seeds, bullocks and plough and manure, the crop is shared on a 50-50 basis between him and the *bargadar.* If he provides nothing except the land, he gets 40 percent of the crop and 60 percent is retained by the *bargadar.* The system suffers from many disadvantages. There is no certainty that the *jotedar* will retain the same *bargadar* for the next season, and this lack of security does not encourage the *bargadar* to look beyond immediate returns. Further, instances are not uncommon where the *jotedar* loans paddy to the *bargadar* during the pre-harvesting season and collects the loan plus "interest" in kind from the next harvest. On the other hand, the *bargadar* has every opportunity to conceal a part of the crop and often successfully avoids giving the full share to the *jotedar.* . . . The system breeds distrust, puts a premium on dishonesty, and has built-in brakes on progress on the farm front.[14]

The *jotedar* combines three functions: he is absentee landlord, money-lender and the village political leader. He has numerous links with the town and the city; normally, he exports his income from land to the town or the city where he maintains numerous connections with the political bosses and with urban finance. The *jotedar* could be a catalyst of change in rural Bengal, but unlike the self-confident Punjabi yeoman, he is mainly the exploiter of the small peasant and the *bargadar.*

The disintegration of the peasantry, which began all over India during the early stages of British rule, has been most acute in West Bengal, Bihar, and parts of Uttar Pradesh. Only in Bengal, however, has the progressively dispossessed peasantry offered organized resistance for its rights. In fact, the history of the Indian peasant movement till the 1940s is by and large the history of peasant struggles in Bengal and certain areas in the Deccan, notably Telengana. "Since 1939, the *bargadars* have been waging big agrarian struggles in West Bengal; the movement reached its highest peak in 1946, again to be resumed in 1948." According to

[14] C. R. Irani, *Communism in Bengal*, pp. 17–18.

a CPI(M) historian of the peasant movement, however, the peasant struggle in Bengal, as in the rest of the country, had begun to lose its "class consciousness" since the early 1940s.[15]

THE SOCIAL BASE OF COMMUNISM

In this urban-rural milieu of West Bengal, it is not surprising that Communism should appeal to the people; what is surprising is that it has taken a very long time for Communism to build a social base of any depth and size. Several explanations can be suggested for the Bengalis' resistance to Communism until recent years. If egalitarian ideas took roots in Bengal earlier than in other parts of India, it was not the radical egalitarianism of class conflict, but the synthesizing humanism of Buddhism, of the Bhakti cult of Chaitanya Deva, and the love cult of Ramakrishna. Thus M. N. Roy failed to convert C. R. Das to Marxism; to Roy's disappointment Das, in his presidential address at the 1923 session of the Indian National Congress, rejected the concept of class conflict as "un-Indian."[16] Bengal's disenchantment with Gandhism did not mean that the Bengalis turned to Marxism-Leninism; rather it was largely urban terrorism that got a greater and readier response because it was closer to the cult of Kali. Later, the charisma of Subhas Bose made him the symbol of Bengal's rejection of Gandhi.

Until the mid-1930s, Communism in Bengal was confined to a relatively small group of alienated angry young intellectuals, many of them educated abroad, and a section of Calcutta's unionized workers. The first major conversion to Marxism occurred among the Bengali *détenus* in prison in the late 1930s. During the 1940s, the movement began to spread among students. In 1948, at the time of the CPI's Calcutta congress, the social base of

[15] Sen, p. 204; Rasul, p. 149.
[16] Mitra's *Annual Indian Registrar* (Calcutta, 1923), I, 957–67.

Communism was still the middle-class intelligentsia in the cities and towns, and the industrial belt in the Calcutta metropolitan area. The peasant movement had gathered some momentum in the 1930s, but this was lost in the 1940s largely because of the CPI's isolation from the mainstream of the nationalist movement.

During the 1950s, parliamentary politics posed problems for the CPI in Bengal which were different from those faced in Kerala, Madras, and Andhra Pradesh because Communism lacked a viable social base. In those three southern provinces, Namboodiripad, Ramamurti, and Sundarayya had captured for Communism almost the entire social base and party organization of the Congress Socialist party; this was a classical takeover of a nationalist movement by a Communist group. Nothing comparable happened in West Bengal. In fact, the CSP never did flourish in Bengal, while the only non-Congress party with a middle-class social base, the Forward Bloc, was in conflict with the CPI from its very creation.

In the south, Communism was able also to find a caste base, which it could not in Bengal because of the relative fluidity of the caste structure of Bengali society. In Kerala, Namboodiripad was able to establish himself at the forefront of a caste renaissance. In Andhra Pradesh, many of the first generation of Communist leaders belonged to the Kamma caste of rich landlords, which gave Communism a social base outside the cities. In West Bengal, on the other hand, the state committee of the CPI in 1954 was almost equally composed of persons from the three upper castes—Brahman, Baidya, and Kayastha—with a sprinkling of Muslims. A majority of the members, in fact, 65 percent, were "intellectuals."

However, the fact that the committee had neither a working class nor a rural proletariat representative confirmed Communism's almost exclusively middle-class social base. It is with this social base that the CPI in Bengal entered parliamentary politics. Since elections in India are won or lost in the villages, the CPI could at best hope to capture a number of urban seats. It won 28 seats in 1952, 46 in 1957, and 50 in 1962, a good portion of them in the Calcutta metropolitan area, in the adjacent industrial belt, and in rural constituencies in 24-Parganas which are in close proximity to Calcutta. In a majority of the West Bengal districts, the CPI won no seats, nor could it win any in the constituencies reserved for the Scheduled castes and tribes. In other words, the CPI's social base did not extend much beyond the Calcutta industrial belt, the urban middle classes, and the refugees from East Pakistan who swelled the numbers of Calcutta's lumpen proletariat.

Even in the Calcutta area, the undivided CPI could not penetrate the "rural universe" of the slums, especially those inhabitants who were rural expatriates from Orissa, Bihar, and Uttar Pradesh. This was not so much because the non-Bengalis tended to vote in accordance with the political traditions of the regions they migrated from as it was because the CPI could not reach them or break the barriers of middle-class inhibitions, language, and culture. Where these barriers were broken or lowered, as in some of the industrial constituencies, the non-Bengali workers voted in some strength for the CPI. Taking the non-Bengali workers as a whole, however, the Communists in Bengal could not get the support of even 10 percent of the voters in 1957.[17]

In the 1960s, the social milieu in Bengal changed markedly in favor of the Communists, who emerged as the only viable opposition to the Congress party. The rapid escalation of defense expenditure hit the economy. Prices began to rise. Inflation went on spiraling upward. Nehru's grip on the party's leadership loosened. In 1962 B. C. Roy, the Congress stalwart who had been West Bengal's chief minister for twelve years, died. Immediately, Congress leader Atulya Ghosh came into the limelight and brought the

---

[17] Donald S. Zagoria: "The Social Bases of Indian Communism," in Richard Lowenthal, ed., *Issues in the Future of Asia* (New York, Praegar, 1969), p. 116.

organization under his firm control. Factionalism came into operation.

The worsening economic condition and the weakening of the Congress organization behind the false facade of a strong leadership created the objective situation for the spread of Communist influence. The subjective condition was provided by the increased militancy of the Bengal CPI and its opposition to the nonradical parliamentarianism of the central party leadership. From the early 1960s the Bengal Communists began to organize mass protests, mostly in the Calcutta area, but also in the districts. Repression by the government enhanced their public image.

The CPI split did not affect the Bengal unit more than marginally; a majority of its leadership and two-thirds of its members broke away to join the CPI(M). After the split, the CPI(M) threw itself into a series of mass actions—over food shortages and distribution, high prices, a move to raise tuition fees in colleges, and similar politically loaded economic issues of immediate concern to the public. The split in the CPI activated both Communist groups. For the first time in nearly fifteen years, Communists in Bengal, as in the rest of the country, made a serious bid to increase party membership.

1967: VOTING PATTERNS AND WHAT THEY REVEALED

In India, it is somewhat risky to measure the social base of a political party by the percentage of the valid votes it may win in an election. However, as we have noted in chapter 3, party identifiers and regulars are to be found more among supporters of the Congress and the Communist parties than of the others. We may therefore take the voting figures in 1967 as a reflection of the changes that came over the social base of Communism in Bengal between 1962 and the fourth election. The Congress party, we have noted, was opposed by two "united" fronts, and the CPI(M) and CPI fought each other in thirty-nine constituencies. Our first concern, however, is with the Communist performance as a whole and, in this regard, certain pictures emerge (Tables 4.3–4.6)

From these tables several generalizations can be made about the Communist social base in West Bengal at the beginning of 1967. It is necessary to bear in mind that there was no public expectation at the time of the election that the Congress party would lose, and nobody seemed to know with any amount of certainty how the Communists would fare. What the poll showed was that Communism had built considerable support bases in rural Bengal, a "presence" in at least twelve of the seventeen districts, and a base in depth in three districts adjacent to Calcutta

TABLE 4.3. SUPPORT FOR COMMUNISTS IN CITY
AND NON-CITY CONSTITUENCIES

		Seats won			Percentage of votes	
	Seats contested	City	Non-city	Total	City	Non-city
Congress	280	20	107	127	41.1	44.1
CPI(M)	135	10	33	43	18	29.3
CPI	62	5	11	16	6.5	7
Jan Sangh	28	–	–	1	1	0.1
RSP	–	3	1	4	–	–

Source: *Fourth General Election: An Analysis* (New Delhi, Ministry of Information and Broadcasting, 1967).

TABLE 4.4. INTENSITY OF PARTY SUPPORT IN CITY
AND NON-CITY CONSTITUENCIES

	Over 40%		30% to 40%		20% to 30%		10% to 20%	
	City	Non-city	City	Non-city	City	Non-city	City	Non-city
Congress	37	223	–	19	–	–	–	–
CPI(M)	25	49	–	47	–	–	2	12
CPI	3	–	4	16	–	37	–	–

Source: Same as Table 4.3. The Congress party polled 57.5 percent of the votes in one constituency, the CPI got 5.7 percent in two constituencies.

TABLE 4.5. VOTES POLLED BY CONGRESS PARTY PERFORMANCE
IN WEST BENGAL DISTRICTS AS PERCENTAGE OF
TOTAL VALID VOTES

District	1952	1957	1962	1967
Bankura	40.8	49.9 (+9.1)	49.5 (−0.4)	44.4 (−4.7)
Birbhum	30.8	37.2 (+6.4)	40.1 (+2.9)	40.7 (+.06)
Burdwan	41.6	46.4 (+4.8)	49.6 (+3.2)	45.8 (−3.8)
Calcutta	40.1	42.5 (+2.4)	47.3 (+4.8)	44.5 (−2.8)
Cooch-Bihar	60.7	53.6 (−7.1)	41.1 (−12.5)	43.4 (+2.3)
Darjeeling	29.3	26.4 (−2.9)	31.1 (+4.7)	39.2 (+8.1)
Jalpaiguri	56.4	49.2 (−7.2)	44.9 (−4.3)	41.6 (−3.3)
Hooghly	46.7	56.0 (+9.3)	50.8 (−5.2)	43.7 (−7.1)
Howrah	37.8	46.9 (+3.1)	50.7 (+9.8)	40.3(−10.4)
Malda	48.4	45.4 (−3.0)	43.8 (−1.6)	44.9 (+1.1)
Murshidabad	43.2	49.0 (+5.8)	39.3 (−9.7)	46.1 (+6.8)
Midnapore	31.6	48.6(+17.0)	52.9 (+4.3)	40.1(−12.8)
Nadia	50.6	54.5 (+3.9)	44.0(−10.5)	38.4 (−5.6)
Purulia	–	37.3	40.1 (+3.2)	35.5 (−4.9)
24-Parganas	33.1	42.2 (+9.1)	48.5 (+6.3)	36.9(−11.6)
West Dinajpur	57.6	44 (−13.6)	42.1 (−1.9)	43.4 (+2.3)
Total	38.9	46.1 (+7.2)	47.3 (+4.8)	44.5 (−2.8)

Source: Dr. Ashoke Mitra in *The Statesman*, March 23, 1967.

TABLE 4.6. AVERAGE VOTES POLLED BY PARTY CANDIDATES
IN ASSEMBLY AND LOK SABHA ELECTIONS

	Average votes	
Party	Assembly	Lok Sabha
Congress	18,602	125,178
CPI(M)	17,302	125,782
CPI	13,385	106,882
Bangla Congress	16,844	168,417[a]

Source: Same as Table 4.5.

[a] Bangla Congress concentrated its parliamentary electoral effort in only one district, Midnapore; this high average figure is therefore somewhat misleading.

as well as in some of the frontier districts with tea plantations. In a constituency like Alipur, for instance, the CPI(M) won 5 out of the 7 "base" seats (seats in the assembly), while the Lok Sabha seat went to the CPI.

The Communists made as much use as they could of state power to expand and consolidate their party position in the cities, towns, and villages of West Bengal. The Marxists, of course, gained more than the CPI. A tribute to party achievements in Bengal was paid by the CPI(M) central committee at its meeting at Calicut, Kerala, in October–November 1967. The committee also took up some of the problems an expanded social base had begun to create for Communism.

"Our problems are problems of growth," observed the central committee in a lengthy resolution on the tasks of party organization. These problems arose from the central task of consolidating "our mass influence into proper party organizational form." The document pointed out the instability of CPI membership since the 1950s. During the Amritsar congress in 1958, the united CPI had a membership of 220,000; by the time of the next congress at Vijaywada in 1961, there was a drop of 40,000. In 1964, before the split, CPI membership was 145, 000, of which 25,000 were said to be new recruits. Thus between 1958 and 1964, party membership had dropped by nearly 50 percent. This problem also dogged the CPI(M) after the split. "At our Seventh Party Congress in November 1964, the total membership that had rallied behind our party stood at 104,000, with another 15,000 as candidate members. But now, after another three years, as latest reports reveal, it does not exceed 75,000." The unstable and fluctuating character of the primary party membership prevailed in every state *"except West Bengal."* [18]

"It is mainly in Bengal we see the working class going on general strike in sympathy with the demands of other sections and on general democratic and political demands along with its class de-

[18] *Our Tasks on Party Organization*, pp. 5, 14–15. Italics added.

mands." However, also in Bengal, the party membership of 16,000 did not "correctly reflect" the depth or the level of mass movements. The "intensity of mass struggles is the greatest and the most widespread" in Bengal, followed by Kerala, with Andhra Pradesh a somewhat lagging third. But even in Bengal, "in the Calcutta industrial belt, we are very strong but in the rural belts, especially as we go farther and farther from Calcutta, it becomes weaker and weaker. We are far stronger among middle-class employees than in jute or in some other important industries." [19]

Thus, even toward the end of 1967, after the Communists had used state government power for party expansion and consolidation, the social base of Communism in Bengal, as in the rest of India, was predominantly middle class. The CPI(M) central committee laid the greatest emphasis on changing this middle-class characteristic of party organization which also reflected on its functional style.

A fairly large proportion of our members are recruited from the peasantry and the different strata of urban and rural middle classes, instead of the urban and rural proletariat. This, of course, is intimately connected with the nature and pattern of our mass work which is not yet decisively oriented to the basic classes. Even from the trade-union run for decades under the leadership of our party, no concerted efforts were made to recruit the largest number of trade-union militants into the party and thus build the party among the working class. As long as this pattern and class composition of the party continues, the element of unstability will persist with all its attendant evils. While not minimizing the need of our party's intensive work among the students, youth, and urban middle classes, our party will have to mainly base its recruitment on the urban proletariat and rural poor." [20]

1968: THE CHANGING CHARACTER
OF PARTY MEMBERSHIP

At the West Bengal state conference of the CPI(M) in December 1968, it was disclosed that the party's membership in

[19] *Ibid.*, p. 50.
[20] *Ibid.*, p. 49.

the state still stood at 16,066, of which "only some 400 had been expelled" for ultra-left "adventurism." The general-secretary of the West Bengal party, Promode Das Gupta, claimed that the party had been able to consolidate its social base in all of the seventeen districts, though "many weaknesses" of organization, leadership, and ideological indoctrination still remained to be solved. However, West Bengal happened to be "one of the strongest units of our party in India," and at least in five districts, organizational weaknesses had largely been overcome. The central committee's order to strengthen the *kisan* front had taken most of the state leadership's attention. Although much had been accomplished during the preceding year, the task of building up the *kisan* movement "on an extensive contiguous area," remained "yet to be achieved." [21]

The state conference was attended by 430 of 432 elected delegates from all districts, with weighted representation for the five districts where the party was the strongest. These districts are 24-Parganas, Howrah, Hooghly, Burdwan, and Calcutta. Ten party members came from the Naxalbari area, showing that the CPI(M) had been able to gain some ground there since the expulsion of the entire local leadership for ultra-left adventurism in the fall of 1967. The party's growing influence in the state was demonstrated by the huge rally at the open session. "The *maidan* (ground) could hardly accommodate one lakh (100,000). But there came many more. From distant Murshidabad came peasants in a chartered bus; from Bishnupur, in Bankura, came sympathizers in trucks. And besides *lakhs* of people who came by train to Dum Dum, there were numerous processions from all parts of Calcutta, Howrah, Hooghly—and, of course, from 24-Parganas." [22]

[21] "The practice of recruiting trade union, *kisan*, student, or middle-class militants directly as candidate members has to be given up. Such militants thrown up in the process of mass struggles should be grouped into compact auxiliary units and kept under the guidance of the concerned higher unit. Candidate membership should be given only for those amongst them who prove their worth and whose ideological political consciousness meets the requisite party standards after a fairly good period of work and observation in their auxiliary groups." *Ibid.*, p. 22.

[22] *People's Democracy*, December 15, 1968.

It was probably too early to expect the changing character of party membership to be reflected in the state committee elected at the conference. The large majority of the thirty-three members were still high-caste, middle-class intellectuals, although many of them had been hardened in mass struggles. Six were Brahmin, twelve Kayasth, and eight Baidya, while only one probably belonged to a low caste. Two were Muslim and one non-Bengali.[23] The 110 delegates elected for the eighth congress of the CPI(M), however, included a significant minority of lower-caste peasants and trade-union workers.

That the CPI (M)'s principal achievement during 1967–68 was an expansion of its influence among the rural poor became evident at the nineteenth conference of the West Bengal Kisan Sabha held in June 1968 at Rajpur in the 24-Parganas district. Harekrishna Konar, president of the state AIKS, reported "significant advances" in the peasant movement which had now spread to "new areas in each district." Though the movement "was still weighed down by the pull of the old reformist understanding," intensified protest against evictions and for land "made the Kisan Sabha, though not always consciously, go to the lower strata of the peasantry, that is, the poor peasants, sharecroppers, and agricultural laborers." The movement "steeled itself to some extent, has overcome some of its weaknesses, has made itself conscious about the weaknesses to be overcome, and has created some awareness among its cadres about the need for consciously building up a militant movement based on poor peasants and agricultural laborers."

There were 676 delegates who came from all districts, in addition to 106 observers and 83 fraternal delegates. Of the 676 delegates, 71 were agricultural workers, 228 sharecroppers and poor peasants, 20 nonagricultural rural workers, 115 middle-level peasants, 204 middle-level peasants, and 7 others. Among the delegates were 103 full-time cadres. The primary membership of the

---

[23] For the list of members of the state committee, see *ibid.*

state Kisan Sabha reached 400,000 at the beginning of 1969.[24] Describing the mood of the conference, a correspondent of *People's Democracy* wrote:

A general heightening of class consciousness was evident not only in the discussions but in the character of the delegates also. Unlike any conference before, there were 319 agricultural workers, sharecroppers, poor peasants and nonagricultural rural workers among the total 676 elected delegates. Even that does not give an idea of how the events of the last eight months have initiated the peasantry of West Bengal into the class struggle. Every peasant that I talked to in one way or another talked about the agricultural revolution, "our" class and "their" class, "permanent revolution," etc. When I told this to a veteran kisan leader, he said he had been conducting the affairs of the Kisan Sabha of the state from 1943 and participation of the most oppressed sections in such large numbers and their heightened consciousness was something he was witnessing for the first time.[25]

Another way in which the CPI(M) sought to build up its organizational base in Bengal was the formation of "auxiliary groups." These were the activists of the party who were now being transformed into cadres. In July 1968 nearly a thousand auxiliary groups were formed in the different districts, with five to ten members in each group. Each local committee, at the district and lower levels, was instructed to organize at least one auxiliary group under its guidance. The objective evidently was to build up several thousand fully trained cadres at the local level— something that had not existed in Bengal before.[26]

The protest movement in West Bengal in 1968 was indicative of the expanded social base of Communism. Some 15,000 people braved arrest in Calcutta and the districts; for the first time, sections of the peasantry joined industrial workers, blue-collar employees, and the general mass of middle-class people in the largest and longest protest movements organized in the state. The mass

---

[24] *People's Democracy*, June 16, 1968.   [25] *People's Democracy*, June 9, 1968.
[26] Communique issued by the Bengal committee. *People's Democracy*, July 21, 1968.

struggles further improved the CPI(M) influence on the newly politicized elements. In the selection of candidates for the midterm election in February 1969, the party was able to draw on some of its newly expanded bases. Among the candidates there was now a significant number of Communists belonging to the lower castes, the peasantry, and the industrial proletariat.[27]

The election results indicated an impressive expansion of the support base of the two Communist factions, especially that of the

TABLE 4.7. TOTAL VOTES, PERCENT OF POPULAR VOTE, AND NUMBER OF SEATS WON BY MAJOR PARTIES, 1967 AND 1969

	1967			1969		
	Total votes	Percent	No. of seats	Total votes	Percent	No. of seats
Congress	5,207,930	41.13	127	5,538,622	41.32	55
CPI(M)	2,293,026	18.11	43	2,676,981	19.97	80
CPI	827,196	6.53	16	938,472	7.0	21
Bangla Congress	1,286,028	10.6	34	1,094,654	8.17	30

Source: West Bengal Information Bureau, New Delhi.

CPI(M). However, the leftist gains were to a large extent due to the contests between the Congress party and a single united front of the leftist groups as well as Bangla Congress. The leftist gains were more in terms of assembly seats than popular vote. The Congress vote was still more than double of that of the CPI(M)— it declined only by 0.71 percent from that of 1967.

Of greater interest is the Communists' performance in some districts where they were evidently successful in building up strong support bases. It will be seen in the Table 4.8 that the CPI(M) support was quite strong in 1969 in Burdwan, Howrah, 24-Par-

---

[27] For reports of the protest movement, see *Economic and Political Weekly*, Annual Number, January 1968. The movement was organized by several parties, but the Communists were clearly leading it in Calcutta and most of the districts. In any case they seemed to have gained more than the other groups from the protest movement.

TABLE 4.8. NUMBER AND PERCENTAGE OF VALID VOTES OF
MAJOR PARTIES IN WEST BENGAL DISTRICTS, 1969

Districts	Valid votes	Congress	CPI(M)	CPI
Bankura	591,153	228,086(38.58)	104,161(17.62)	29,711(5.03)
Birbhum	435,300	163,456(37.55)	57,695(13.25)	no contest
Burdwan	1,113,013	458,251(41.17)	478,437(42.99)	26,357(2.37)
Calcutta	1,090,231	476,831(43.75)	253,921(23.29)	111,068(10.19)
Cooch-Bihar	390,179	206,680(52.97)	42,819(10.97)	no contest
Darjeeling	164,677	71,556(43.45)	11,228(6.82)	no contest
Hooghly	933,534	399,922(42.48)	226,790(28.58)	58,948(6.31)
Howrah	872,291	355,609(40.77)	280,394(32.14)	no contest
Jalpaiguri	428,497	215,585(50.31)	26,199(6.11)	40,110(9.34)
Malda	448,086	355,609(47.17)	22,489(5.02)	63,263(14.12)
Midnapore	1,789,325	767,357(42.96)	85,624(4.79)	312,382(17.49)
Murshidabad	820,325	273,480(33.34)	20,988(2.56)	23,014(2.81)
Nadia	683,432	295,096(43.18)	112,948(16.53)	26,157(3.83)
Purulia	384,268	138,836(36.13)	no contest	19,611(5.10)
24-Parganas	2,824,747	1,102,455(39.03)	849,450(30.07)	186,257(6.59)
W. Dinajpur	438,270	173,948(39.69)	63,874(14.57)	41,703(9.52)

Source: Same as Table 4.7.

ganas, Hooghly, and Calcutta, but nowhere except in Burdwan
was it stronger than that of the Congress party.

In no district did the Congress party poll less than 30 percent
of the valid votes; in two districts, Cooch-Bihar and Jalpaiguri, it
got more than half of all valid votes cast, and in eight districts,
more than 40 percent. The CPI(M) got more than 40 percent
only in one district, above 30 percent in two, and above 20 percent in two more. It polled more than 10 percent in five. The
CPI secured more than 10 percent in two districts, but in none
was its share more than 20 percent. In the Calcutta area, the Congress vote was more than the total vote of the two Communist factions put together.

1971: A DEEP AND BROAD MARXIST BASE

It was not before the mid-term election of March 1971 that the
gains made by the CPI(M) in terms of a popular support base

could be measured with some certainty. The election came after some fifteen months of President's rule. While this provided the Marxists with an opportunity to mobilize public opinion in favor of restoration of parliamentary rule, the instability and interparty conflicts of the two united front regimes between 1967–69 made sizable portions of the urban population cynical about popular rule and generally disposed to a stint of central government administration if that would bring stable government and orderly civic life.

Law and order began to erode after 1969, and interparty rivalries began to erupt in murder and physical injury. While all of the political parties indulged in violence, murder and physical assault on a large scale were more or less confined to the "Naxalites" and the Marxists. In 1969–70 the dominant "Naxalite" group in West Bengal adopted what in practical reality amounted to urban guerrilla terrorism, and its victims were the so-called class enemies of the people and the Marxists. (The "Naxalite" movement is discussed in chapter 9.)

It was also the period of the CPI(M)'s isolation from other main non-Congress factions. Thus, when Mrs. Gandhi dissolved the Lok Sabha in January 1971 and called for a new election, the question concerning Bengal was whether the central government could hold a parliamentary election in the state, yet postpone a local election on the ground of lawlessness. The Marxists alone came out strongly in favor of a state assembly election; the other parties were at first opposed and then lukewarm toward the idea.

However, when the elections were fixed for March 10, a weird process of bargaining started among the political groups; the final outcome was a pattern of five-way contests. The Congress party was split into three factions: Mrs. Gandhi's or the new Congress party, the "Syndicate" Congress party, and the Bangla Congress party. The left was split into two "united fronts," one led by the CPI which embraced the major leftist factions, and the other by the CPI(M). A new phenomenon was the revival of the Muslim League in West Bengal—it joined the "united front" of the CPI.

As the election tempo speeded up and violence and murder became a daily norm, the non-CPI(M) groups arrived at electoral "understandings" in many constituencies. Of these, Baranagar, an industrial suburb of Calcutta, assumed symbolic importance. Here the Marxist candidate was Jyoti Basu, deputy chief minister in the two united front governments of 1967 and 1969, against whom stood Ajoy K. Mukherji, chief minister of the same two governments and Bangla Congress leader. Both the new Congress party and the CPI withdrew their candidates and rallied to the support of Mukherji, thus making Baranagar a symbolic trial of strength between the Marxists and the non-Marxist forces in Bengal.[28]

However, electoral pacts broadly reduced the contests in the entire state to a trial of strength between the Marxists and others. The non-Marxist parties, with the support of the state government, succeeded in persuading large portions of the urban electorate that the CPI(M) was directly and indirectly responsible for the violence and lawlessness that had gripped West Bengal since 1969. The CPI(M), of course, tried its best to refute this allegation, repeatedly pointing out that its own cadres had been the worst-hit victims of violence and murder—206 Marxist cadres were said to have been killed in 1970 by "Naxalites," the police, and others. When polling took place, army units and some 50,000 armed police were guarding "disturbed" areas—which meant districts where the CPI(M) was believed to be strong.[29]

In terms of interparty bitterness, it was the grimmest election fought anywhere in India since independence. The city of Cal-

[28] Basu won the contest with a majority of over 5,000 votes. Mukherji, however, was returned from another constituency in Midnapore district.

[29] *People's Democracy,* March 7, 1971; *The Hindustan Times,* March 9, 1971. The CPI(ML) boycotted the election. In pockets in Calcutta could be seen posters and slogans of the party proclaiming loyalty to Chairman Mao and asking the people not to be deceived by parliamentary politics. The unusually low-level voting in Calcutta, 40 percent, could be partly attributed to CPI(ML) propaganda, but was largely due to the climate of violence and murder and the presence of the army which seemed to have frightened the poor more than the middle classes.

cutta was figuratively covered with posters, many of which spat hatred and venom; what was more remarkable was that slogans were scribbled on the mud walls of huts, schools, and shops in villages remote from cities and towns.

When I toured the districts of Burdwan, Nadia, and 24-Parganas three weeks before the election, I was impressed by two developments hitherto nonexistent in the Indian countryside. In the first place, a "class line" had been drawn in the villages between the "haves" and the "have-nots;" the latter, embracing the poor peasant, the landless agricultural worker, and many nonagricultural workers in the small towns (like cycle-rickshaw drivers) and villages (petty shopkeepers and daily wage-earners) appeared to be solidly behind the CPI(M). Second, the Marxists appeared to have built a disciplined and working organization in most of the villages around the Kisan Sabha units. Their election meetings were numerous, and were attended by peasants from every village in the area, indicating a mass base that had penetrated deeply into the countryside. All of these meetings were addressed by peasant cadres who were evidently in charge of the election campaign, and there was a tendency to allow decisions and programs to emanate from the "class conscious" peasants rather than to impose them from above.

Two other aspects of West Bengal politics which appeared to be significant were the psychological bewilderment of the middle classes in Calcutta and other major urban centers (most of the people I met confessed to a loss of faith in "all political parties," in other words, the political system) and second, the near-absence of non-Marxist mobilization among the rural poor in the districts visited. The Marxists seemed to have a clear field in the largest single constituency of the Indian electorate—the rural proletariat.[30]

[30] In the industrial belt of West Bengal, several trade unions were found competing with one another, and the Marxists were clearly not in complete command of the workers' allegiance. However, cadres of the non-Marxist parties, including the CPI, admitted that in the villages "the CPI(M) is very strong."

The election results generally confirmed these impressions. The CPI(M) could not produce an absolute majority in the West Bengal assembly as its leaders had boasted that they would, but it emerged as the dominant political group both in terms of electoral support and seats in the legislature. For the first time in West Bengal, the Congress party popular vote was lower than the popular vote of the Communists, even of the CPI(M).

In the assembly election, the CPI(M) polled 31.98 percent of the valid votes cast, as against 18.20 in 1967 and 19.97 in 1969. The ruling Congress party's share of the vote was 28.20 percent, and that of the "Syndicate" Congress party 5.50 percent. Bangla Congress polled a mere 5.18 percent, and the CPI, 8.13 percent. In terms of seats, the Marxists and their allies got 123 seats, 17 short of an absolute majority in a House of 280. Next came the ruling Congress party, with 103 seats. The CPI won 13. Leftist groups like the Forward Bloc and the PSP were practically eliminated.[31]

In the Lok Sabha election, the CPI(M) won 20 of the total number of 40 West Bengal seats. The Marxists got 37 percent of the total vote (as against 20 percent in 1969), while the combined share of the two Congress factions and Bangla Congress was 39 percent (Mrs. Gandhi's party got barely 28 percent). For the Lok Sabha seats, the CPI(M) average vote was 118,000 as against 115,-000 of the ruling Congress party. For the assembly seats, it was 18,000 as against 15,000. But for a remarkable setback in Calcutta, where the Marxists could win only 5 of the 23 seats, the CPI(M) would have won an absolute majority in the legislature. "Of the total decline of 400,000 votes cast between the two elections, more than 200,000 are accounted by the decrease in voting in Calcutta itself; almost entirely this decline in vote has been to the cost of the CPM."

Electoral data underline several other important aspects of the

[31] "The West Bengal Vote," *Times of India,* March 25, 1971. Also, "Performance of CPM in West Bengal," *Times of India,* March 19, 1971.

Marxist vote. The CPI(M) support base now extended across seven districts: Calcutta, 24-Parganas, Hooghly, Howrah, Burdwan, Birbhum, and Bankura, containing the bulk of West Bengal's population, industry, and mineral resources. The base is probably stronger among the rural poor than among the urban industrial workers. In the industrial areas, it includes sizable portions of Hindi-speaking workers from the north Indian hinterland.

Several observations can be drawn from Table 4.9. The ruling Congress faction's most impressive performance was in Calcutta and 24-Parganas, indicating that the urban middle class was

TABLE 4.9. SEATS WON BY MAJOR PARTIES, 1971 COMPARED TO 1969

District (total seats)	CPI(M)		CPI		Ruling congress [a]		Bangla congress	
	1971	1969	1971	1969	1971	1969	1971	1969
Bankura (13)	8	4	–	1	3	–	–	6
Birbhum (12)	7	3	1	–	–	–	–	1
Burdwan (25)	21	17	–	1	1	2	–	2
Calcutta (23)	5	8	1	4	16	5	–	–
Cooch-Bihar (8)	–	–	–	–	7	6	–	–
Darjeeling (5)	1	–	–	–	2	1	–	–
Hooghly (18)[b]	10	9	1	1	4	2	–	–
Howrah (16)	12	8	–	–	3	1	–	1
Jalpaiguri (11)	1	–	–	1	9	7	–	–
Malda (10)	2	–	1	3	5	4	–	–
Midnapore (35)	6	2	8	10	12	7	4	11
Murshidabad (18)	3	–	–	1	8	5	–	2
Nadia (14)	9	2	–	1	1	5	–	3
Purulia (11)	1	–	–	1	9	3	–	1
24-Parganas (50)	24	24	1	7	14	4	1	5
W. Dinajpur (11)	–	2	–	–	11	3	–	1

Source: *Desh* (Nation), Calcutta (Bengali weekly), March 16, 1971.

[a] In the case of ruling Congress, the 1969 figure shows seats won by the undivided Congress party.

[b] In this district the "Syndicate" Congress won 1 seat.

strongly drawn in 1971 by the charisma of Mrs. Gandhi's "social-ism" and repelled by violence and anarchy, for which it held the CPI(M) at least partly responsible, and generally disillusioned by the performance of the united front governments. The Congress party's traditional stronghold continues in the districts of north-ern West Bengal, which are predominantly rural and relatively backward, and where the CPI(M) was not able to build a strong peasant protest movement in 1968–70.

In the more developed, industrialized, urbanized, and popu-lated districts of West Bengal, however, the Marxists have suc-ceeded in extending and deepening their urban-rural base. These districts border on Bihar and Orissa. They provide the CPI(M) with a large continuous urban-rural base with a strong potential impact on the urban-rural economy of adjacent Bihar. This base is to be seen in the context of the general disarray of the bour-geois and non-CPI(M) leftist factions in West Bengal, its deepen-ing political instability, and serious economic and social crisis. It has also to be seen in the context of West Bengal's strategic im-portance for the rest of India, its traditional contribution to In-dian radicalism and secularism, as well as the developing situation across the border in Pakistan.

The CPI National Council, meeting in Delhi toward the end of April 1971, came to the following assessment of the Marxist party's performance in the March election:

The CPM as the result of its wrong and thoroughly disruptive line has lost heavily in every state except West Bengal and Tripura. In Kerala it has been reduced from 9 seats to a bare 2 seats. In Tamilnadu (Madras), it has lost all its 4 seats, its stalwarts losing their deposits. In the whole Hindi belt, it has been wiped out to zero. Indeed, out of the 25 seats it has secured, 20 seats have come from West Bengal and 2 seats from the adjoining Tripura state. The election has thus revealed the fact that the position of the CPM as an all-India political party has been seriously eroded. The CPM is trying to use its success scored in West Bengal to cover up its wrong and disruptive all-India general line which has brought it disaster as an all-India political force to every state except West Bengal and Tripura. But in West Bengal it-self, the victory scored by it in terms of seats has been out of all pro-portion to its actual relative strength compared with other parties. Due to the fact that there were multicornered contests in most of the constituencies, the CPM as the party with a significant mass strength and organization throughout the state was able to benefit most from the situation. Second, its policy of terrorism, supported by the major section in the police bureaucracy, appears to have paid it dividends in its major strongholds only because it could not be effectively coun-tered as the anti-CPM forces were not sufficiently united and orga-nized, with the result that in many of their strongholds the CPM armed terrorism held full sway.[32]

Implied in this assessment was a rebuke to the West Bengal committee of the CPI for violating the party's all-India line to enter into an electoral alliance with Mrs. Gandhi's Congress party and other anti-CPI(M) elements. Apparently, the West Bengal party was sharply divided on this issue even after the election was over. The *Times of India* reported on March 18 that "a section of CPI cadres is openly critical of the state leadership's refusal to toe the party's, all-India line and its insistence on a policy of equi-distance from the CPM and the new Congress." However, after the CPI joined in a Congress-dominated coalition ministry led by Ajoy K. Mukherji, Bangla Congress leader, about a third of the members of the state committee was said to be critical of this ac-tion.[33] At the time of this writing (May 1971), the fate of this ministry, the fourth coalition in West Bengal in four years, is ex-tremely uncertain.

[32] *New Age,* May 2, 1971.   [33] *Times of India,* April 18, 1971.

5

REGIONAL BASE
OF COMMUNISM:
KERALA

If unique were not a word too often profaned, one would be tempted to use it to describe Kerala's position in the Indian socio-economic universe. In the nineteenth century, Kerala impressed Europeans with its tropical indolence. In the latter half of the twentieth century, it represents tropical ferment. Still lovely to behold, especially when the eye of the beholder has grown accustomed to the brown, scrubby expanse of India's central plain, the whole length of Kerala's 100 miles is green up to the edge of the white beaches, on which the Arabian Sea makes its small assaults and retreats. A New York *Times* correspondent once wrote: "If India's planners are ever so grotesquely successful in their efforts to haul this country into the American Age as to create a Miami Beach, it will have to be located in Kerala."

The almost unbroken shade of a thick canopy of palm trees tends to hide from the visitor's eye a topography of vast social imbalance and deepening destabilization. Here 20 million people are huddled together in 15,000 square miles of land—the population density is the greatest in India, the land most fragmented, with the average holding being about 1.5 acres. Nearly half of the population are agricultural workers and/or sharecroppers with wages that are the lowest in India. And yet Kerala boasts the highest literacy rate in the country and is the only area in India that lies outside the world's sprawling low-pressure zone in literacy. The desire to educate the young beyond the grade-school level is conspicuous even among the lowest castes. No other Indian state has therefore so many educated unemployed in perpetual quest of the few jobs available.

Nor in any other part of India has the caste system been traditionally stronger or old customs more tyrannical. Until recently, the untouchables in Kerala had to keep a prescribed minimum physical distance away from not only the upper-caste Brahmins and the Nairs, but even the lower-caste Kammalas and Ezhavas. Vertical divisions of caste, community, religion, and economic pursuits have been traditionally more rigid in Kerala than anywhere else in India; even today Hindu society is divided into four slowly melting caste groups: Brahmins, Nairs, Ezhavas, and Scheduled castes (untouchables). Keralan polity is the sum total of interactions among these Hindu caste groups and the two other major communities—Christians (who are themselves splintered into Catholics, Syrian Christians and Marthomites) and Muslims.

A strong tendency of sanskritization—by which people belonging to the lower strata in Hindu society "adopt" members of the higher strata as reference groups and try to move upward—makes the caste a dynamic rather than a static social institution and tends to destabilize the caste base of political parties.[1] A stronger force that cuts through caste barriers and softens up the tradi-

[1] K. C. Alexander, "Changing Status of the Pulaya Harijans in Kerala," *Economic and Political Weekly: Special Number,* July 1968, pp. 1071–74.

tional alignments of social forces is secularization, to which Communism's contribution has not been insignificant.

In the whole of India, Christians, as an organized social force, play a significant political role only in Kerala, although secular influences seem to be changing the political behavior of the community, albeit rather slowly. More distinctive is the political role of the Muslims. They occupy a social position to be found nowhere else in the subcontinent. In spite of their particularist political role, Muslims, who constitute 16 percent of Kerala's population, share whatever unitary culture the region may claim. Their women do not wear the veil. In dress, language, psychological outlook, and social behavior, Muslims here are more Keralan than Indian, and have very little in common, except Islam, with the Muslims of the north and the west.

The cultural integration of Muslims in Keralan society is reflected in Malayalee literature written by Hindu and Christian writers. When feudalism was at its height, the poor, simple, and illiterate Muslim was the villain of many Malayalam dramas and poems. "In the changing social situation, the dynamic and hardworking Muslim has emerged as the hero in novels, plays, and cinemas. It is the caste Hindu who is portrayed as the respresentative of the decadent class." In no other Indian literature, including Bengali, is the Muslim emotionally integrated with the rest of society.[2]

Kerala's participation in India's struggle for freedom has been conspicuous, but its contribution to the nationalist leadership has been strangely slight. No Keralan has sat among the topmost hierarchy of the Congress party leaders. None of the Congress party's ministers from Kerala had a status comparable to that of C. Rajagopalachari of Madras, T. Prakasam of Andhra Pradesh, Govind Ballav Pant of Uttar Pradesh, B. G. Kher or Morarji Desai of Bombay, or B. C. Roy of Bengal. For historical and social reasons,

---

[2] "Report on Kerala," *Economic and Political Weekly,* October 18, 1969.

the Congress base in Kerala has remained one of its weakest and most fragmented in the country. In contrast, Kerala's contribution to the Indian pool of creative writers, educators, jurists, administrators, and technologists has been, and continues to be, remarkably high. The relative weakness of the intellectual base of the nationalist movement in Kerala would seem to have rendered the soil fertile for radical thoughts and movements. It seems somewhat remarkable that the two Keralans, K. M. Pannikar and V. K. Krishna Menon, who were able to exert an influence on India's post-independence foreign and domestic policies, were both men of leftist persuasion.

1957: COMMUNISTS CAPTURE A BASE

India's smallest state leapt into world headlines when its electorate elected a Communist government in 1957 with a clear, though small, majority of seats in the legislative assembly. In the thirteen years that have since passed, Communists have built a strong base in Kerala. They have ruled Kerala, either singly or in coalition with other parties and groups, for a little over five of the thirteen years, which is also roughly the same amount of time the state government has been in the hands of the Congress party or the PSP supported by Congress.

The Communist social base in Kerala is conspicuous because it was acquired in the late 1930s through methods different from those used in northern India. The CPI was born in Kerala only in 1939. The man most responsible for that birth was Elumkulam Manakal Sankaran Namboodiripad, then a thirty-year-old socialist, who belonged to the highest Brahmin caste in India, and to a prosperous landlord family. He and his friends controlled the Kerala unit of the CSP, a leftist group that formerly functioned from within the Indian National Congress. In the late 1930s, E.M.S., as Namboodiripad is popularly called, joined the CPI and practically brought the entire CSP organization in the area into the sphere of the Communist party.[3] This, however, also happened in Andhra Pradesh and Madras, where Sundarayya and P. Ramamurti effected similar coups d'état.

What gave the Communists in Kerala a stronger and stabler social base was that E.M.S. was also able to establish himself at the forefront of a caste renaissance in his home province. The beginning of the twentieth century had seen the establishment of caste groups that were pledged to rid their respective castes of some of the more undesirable customs and to work for the moral and educational upliftment of entire castes. From the early years of the CPI's founding, its policy in Kerala under E.M.S.'s leadership was to infiltrate caste organizations and gain control, thereby making important contacts, providing screens for otherwise illegal activity, and enabling individual Communists to become community leaders. Thus K. P. Gopalan became one of the early leaders of the Ezhava caste which constitutes one-fourth of Kerala's population and is to this day the mainstay of Communist strength in the state.

E.M.S. himself became president of the Namboodiri Yogekshema Maha Sangh—the progressive caste organization in his own community. He carried on valuable work among the major caste and communal organizations through the 1940s and 1950s. In 1945 he organized a conference of nine such organizations and presented them with a program designed to build bridges between the various castes and communities.[4] In this way, as one

[3] E.M.S. Namboodiripad, Communist partiyepatti pradhana chodyangal (Landmarks in the Life of the Communist Party), (Ernakulam, Prabhathan), p. 15. For an account in English of the beginnings of the Communist movement in Kerala, see Namboodiripad, "Founding of the Party in Kerala," New Age, April 1958. How E.M.S., and other South Indian leaders of the CSP clandestinely embraced Communism and then took over the entire party organizations on behalf of CPI is described by E.M.S. in his New Age article; by Jaiprakash Narain in Toward Struggle (Bombay, 1946), p. 170; and by Gene D. Overstreet and, Marshall Windmiller Communism in India (Berkeley, University of California Press, 1959), pp. 160–66.

[4] For a brief political biography of Namboodiripad (and also of Dange and Jyoti Basu), see Sen Gupta, "Diverse Leaders of Communism in India," in Roger Swearingem, ed., Leaders of the Communist World (New York, Macmillan, 1971).

Keralan social scientist has pointed out, E.M.S. was able to avoid a direct clash between the rising CPI and theistic Hinduism.[5]

No Indian Communist intellectual and leader has a greater "localist" image than does E.M.S. Namboodiripad. Born in the most exalted caste of the Malayalee Brahmin, he had a standard Namboodiri upbringing, with traditional instruction in Sanskrit for ten years. Dropping out of college, he joined the Gandhian civil disobedience movement in 1931, and soon became a prominent Congress leader in Malabar. His intellectual and emotional progression has been consistently toward a leftward direction: from the Congress party to the CSP to the CPI to the CPI(M).

E.M.S. is one of the few Indian Communist leaders who have tried to apply Marxism creatively to an interpretation of Indian social realities. A Marxian analysis of Keralan society persuades him that Kerala is riper than most other parts of India for radical social change. To Namboodiripad, the principal distinctive feature of Kerala is the fact that "field cultivation here does not, in a normal year, require artificial irrigation canals and other forms of public works." According to Marx, the foundation of oriental despotism and the Indian village communities was based on agriculture's dependence on artificial irrigation. This precluded the development of feudal private property. E.M.S. believes that this Marxian feature has been historically absent in Kerala. However, centralized government could not develop because "it had no role in production."

Medieval Kerala, according to E.M.S., "actually developed a pattern of society which partakes of the character of both Asiatic society as described by Marx as well as of feudal society on the model of medieval Europe." Kerala developed its own national language—Malayalam—fairly early in history. It also developed certain peculiarities which distinguished it from the rest of India. "If ancient and medieval Indian society as a whole failed to de-

[5] R. K. Nair, in an unpublished paper read at the Rajasthan University Political Science Conference in 1965.

velop a strong class of merchant capitalists, Kerala developed it
even less than India." Thus Kerala offered an open field for Jew-
ish, Christian, and Arab merchants.

The establishment of British rule "stabilized the political divisions of Kerala as they existed at the end of the eighteenth century." Thus the natural process of formation of nationalities was
"artificially checked by violent interference of a foreign imperialist power." Since then, however, the history of the forming of nations took a new course—the development of a colonial economy
under imperialist domination, the growth of capitalist relations
subordinate to it, and the perpetuation of feudal landlordism.

The process gave birth to the class of national bourgeoisie. The
national bourgeoisie, however, were unable to lead the national
movement because of their alliance with imperialism, despite
their conflict with it. Thus in Kerala, according to Namboodiripad, the historic role of leading the national movement "has
fallen on the working class allied with the peasantry." [6]

THE WEAKNESS OF KERALA'S BOURGEOISIE

Whether or not one agrees with this class interpretation of
Kerala's national bourgeoisie, one has to admit that the ability of
the bourgeoisie in Kerala to control political power and direct social change has been far more limited than that of its counterparts
in the rest of India. One reason is the geopolitical composition of
Kerala. The state came into being on November 1, 1956, as part
of the reorganization of provincial boundaries. It consists of the
former princely state of Travancore-Cochin (less the five southern
subdivisions which were given to Madras, now known as Tamil
Nadu), plus the Malabar district and the Kasargode subdivision
of Madras.

The political center of the state is Travancore, where the Congress movement was weak. An enlightened native princely house

[6] E.M.S. Namboodiripad, *The National Question in Kerala* (New Delhi, PPH,
1958).

had been able to enlist the active collaboration of a major portion of the elite in ruling Travancore. Its celebrated Dewan (prime minister), C. P. Ramaswamy Ayyar, was known for his ruthlessness as well as his passion for modernization. In the absence of a strong Congress movement, the struggle of the poor against social and economic repression was taken over and led by the Communists, who bore the brunt of the regime's repressive methods. Thus, in September 1946, the army of Travancore crushed an "armed rebellion" of Communist-led workers and peasants in two villages, Vayalar and Punnapra, in Alleppey district; to this day Vayalar-Punnapra remains a symbol of heroism in the history of the Communist party in Kerala.

Similarly in the 1940s, in the economically depressed Malabar region of Madras state, the CPI was able to organize a strong movement of plantation labor and landless agricultural workers. Between 1948 and 1952 the Congress government in Madras with considerable ruthlessness suppressed Communist agitation for "democratic rights" at Surnad, Edappally, and in north Malabar.

When the state of Kerala was created, it was already a weak base of the Congress party and a relatively strong base of the Communists. This was illustrated by the fact that in the first election in 1957, the Communists, with five independents supported by them, won an absolute majority in the legislature.[7]

This upsetting event led to much study of whys and wherefores by politicians, journalists, social leaders, and scholars. They all seemed to agree on three main points: chronic factionalism in Keralan society, which plagued the bourgeoisie more than the Communists; organizational superiority of the Communists and the "dedication" of their cadres to the ideals of Marxism-Leninism; and the ease and sophistication with which the Communist leaders were able to utilize to their advantage the divisions within

---

[7] Ramakrishnan Nair, *How Communists Came to Power in Kerala*, (Trivandrum, Kerala Academy of Political Science, 1965), chs. 1–3. See also *The Red Interlude in Kerala* (Trivandrum, Kerala Pradesh Congress Committee, 1959).

the ranks of the bourgeoisie. Analysts found that politics in Kerala was caste-bound, but the alignments of castes and political parties were far from rigid and stable. The social base of the Congress party in Kerala was comprised of Brahmins, Nairs, and Christians, yet the issues dividing these groups were so numerous and sometimes so dynamic that the Congress party leadership could hardly reconcile their rivalries and maintain a cohesive political organization.

To illustrate: in no state in India is education controlled by private institutions on the scale that it is in Kerala; here, the Catholic Church and the Nair Service Society control 70 percent of the schools. When P. Govinda Menon was minister of education in the second Congress ministry in Travancore-Cochin in 1951, he brought forward an education scheme which aimed at curtailing the powers of the managers of private schools and improving the working conditions of teachers. He became highly unpopular with the leaders of the Nair caste as well as those of the Catholic Church, so much so that his leadership of the Congress party was regarded as one of the main reasons why the party lost the support of the Nairs in the 1957 election. Similarly, the report of the Christian Missionary Activities Committee appointed by the government of India had adverse repercussions on

TABLE 5.1. DISTRIBUTION OF VOTES IN THE 1957
KERALA ELECTION

Castes or communities	Congress party	CPI
Christians	1,250,000	170,000
Ezhavas	200,000	1,200,000
Muslims	350,000	150,000
Nairs	200,000	200,000
Scheduled castes	120,000	250,000

Source: Jitendra Singh, "Communism in Kerala," in B. E. Pentony, *Red World in Tumult* (San Francisco, Chandler, 1962), pp. 244–50. The figures are approximate.

the attitude of the Christians toward the Congress party in Kerala.[8]

These figures demonstrate that while Communism in Kerala penetrated each of the major castes and communities in 1957, its main constituency was the untouchables and the lower castes that constitute the rural and urban proletariat of the state. Thus, the castes did not prove to be an insurmountable barrier to Communist influence in Kerala. The CPI sought to *secularize* the castes and, at the same time, became exposed to caste influences.

HOW SUCCESS WAS ACHIEVED

Parliamentary tactics have helped in socializing Communism in Kerala. The Communists were able to put themselves on the political map of Kerala not by waging class struggle, but by agreeing to work within the Indian political system—that is, by accepting the parliamentary process of political and social change.

The CPI had been active in Travancore-Cochin and Malabar since 1937, waging several struggles on behalf of landless peasants, agricultural laborers, and plantation and industrial workers. In the 1948 Travancore-Cochin election, however, not a single Communist was elected, while many candidates lost their security deposits, having failed to poll the minimum of 5 percent of the votes cast. Three years earlier, not a single Communist candidate had been returned to the Madras assembly from Malabar; among those defeated were Namboodiripad and A. K. Gopalan. The Communists won only 25 seats in the Travancore-Cochin assembly in 1952, in spite of the fact that they had spearheaded "the struggle to defend the people's democratic rights," while other non-Congress groups and independents won 30 seats.

The CPI's spectacular success in Kerala in 1957 could not have been won only because of its organizational superiority and factionalism among the bourgoisie, although these were undoubt-

[8] Nair, *How Communists Came to Power,* ch. 2.

edly helpful factors. The main reason lay elsewhere. As a Keralan political scientist has put it:

Certain developments during 1953–56 which indicated that the Communist Party of India had started believing in peaceful and constitutional means to achieve socialism, that the party's attitude to the Nehru government was profoundly changed for the better, that the party was prepared to function as a parliamentary opposition, that the ideological difference between the Indian National Congress and the Communist party as regards the goal had been considerably narrowed down with the former's adoption of the goal of socialistic pattern of society, were responsible to a large extent for making a large number of nonpolitical and non-Communist people of Kerala, including several communalists and capitalists who were disgusted with the Congress regime, vote in the 1957 elections for the Communist party, the best organized, the most united, and the most active party and the principal rival to the Congress party in the state.[9]

Acceptance of the parliamentary process, of the strategy of peaceful transition, and subscription to the broad national consensus of the 1950s with regard to the goals of economic planning, then, earned the Communists in Kerala the *legitimacy* which they had failed to secure through the class struggles of the 1940s and early 1950s. Legitimacy had to be conferred by the non-Communist political elite, which in 1957 apparently looked upon the CPI in Kerala as the most effective "loyal opposition" to the Congress party. This is reflected in the evaluation of the Kerala CPI by a leading Malayalam daily, a supporter of the Congress party:

Deep-rooted in the soil of Kerala and tended by the constant care and attention of its activists is the Communist party of Kerala. In every remote village there are Communist activists who are closest to the most downtrodden of the people and who have identified themselves with these sections. It might be that this activist may not be well known. It might be that he goes about like a vagabond. But in his village, he keeps daily contact with all individuals. And he takes the message of the party to every heart. He has an objective which keeps

[9] Nair, *How Communism Came to Power*, p. 48.

him inspired. And to achieve that objective he devotes his self-sacrificing endeavors.

The better tomorrow may perhaps be a mirage, but to him it is the complete truth. And the means to achieve his aims he finds in the Communist party. The party is his body and soul.[10]

To one of the most influential bourgeois newspapers in Kerala, the CPI, or rather the "Communist party of Kerala," was in 1957 not the "fifth column" of an alien power, nor the propagator of an alien ideology, nor a revolutionary force determined to destroy the existing pattern of society, but a force that was "deep-rooted in the soil" of the state, inspired by an idealism, and armed with dedicated workers which the Congress party, in contrast, lacked. This was an exalted bourgois image of the CPI as a loyal opposition within the Indian political system, an opposition that could be looked upon to provide an alternate government without seriously upsetting the politics of gradual change.

CHANGES IN POLITICAL ALIGNMENTS

This bourgeois image of Communism in Kerala changed as soon as the first CPI government embarked upon a program of mild structural change in the educational system and a somewhat deeper structural change in agrarian relations. The Commmunist attempt to bring about a "revolution through legislation" united the bourgeoisie against the CPI in 1958–59 in the "liberation struggle." This unprecedented unity of the bourgeoisie succeeded in its immediate objective—the Communist government was dismissed by the central government. However, when the next poll was taken in Kerala, the CPI was found to have built up an extensive social base in the countryside among the rural poor.[11]

[10] *The Mathrubhoomi* (The Motherland), March 21, 1957, quoted in English translation in H. D. Malvya, *Kerala: A Report to the Nation* (New Delhi, 1957), p. 18.

[11] The Communists increased their voting strength by about 1 million over the 2.06 million they had polled three years before. 84.4 percent of the electorate voted.

The anti-Communist unity of the bourgeoisie collapsed soon after the CPI's impressive electoral victory in 1960. The following years witnessed a simultaneous process of fission and fusion of traditional and secular elements in Keralan politics, a solid social base of Communism being one of the major contributing factors.

The politics of Kerala still centered round the four major groups—Nairs, Ezhavas, Christians, and Muslims. But the ability of group leaders to manipulate block votes steadily declined. Also, the communal blocks became increasingly fragmented, partly because of the waning influence of the old established leaders and the emergence of new competitors, partly also because of the impact of secular forces. This is evident in the zigzag shifts of political alignments as seen in Table 5.2.

This kaleidoscope of Kerala's shifting political alignments in the last decade suggests a number of hypotheses. People's voting decisions have become more politicalized and secularized than ever before, and caste and communal loyalties have been softened by an increasing awareness of secular interests.[12] Second, proliferation of bourgeois groups has made politics more competitive. The proliferation has been caused by, and has caused, a further decline in the ability of traditional caste and communal operators to manipulate block votes. Third, as Communism has become socialized, it has also entered a *cul de sac* in Kerala politics.

Basically, all this seems to be the result of a crisis in the operational effectiveness of parliamentary tactics. If the Communists use state power in Kerala as an instrument of confrontation with the national bourgeoisie and against the political system, seeking to wreck it from within—as the Marxists tried to do during 1967–69—they run into organized resistance from all or most of the non-Communist forces, which they are not powerful enough to break without abandoning the parliamentary process, if then. Unsuccessful confrontation with the united force of all or most of

[12] Horst Hartman, "Changing Political Behavior in Kerala," *Economic and Political Review: Annual Number,* January 1968, p. 167.

TABLE 5.2. SHIFTS IN POLITICAL ALIGNMENTS IN KERALA SINCE 1959

Year	Electoral Alliances	Government Coalition	Reasons for Fall
1960	Congress, PSP, ML	Congress-PSP (supported by ML)	Dissension between PSP and Congress, also among factions within Congress; Chief Minister P. T. Pillai, PSP, removed in 1962 from Kerala; Congress govt. formed by R. Sankar
1962		Congress, with Ezhava Chief Minister Sankar	Nairs and Christians rebel against Ezhava rule; new actors defy old communal leaders; finally Nairs, Christians, and Muslims vote down the Sankar ministry in Sept. 1964; President's rule imposed
1965	Political pattern more fragmented; Congress dissidents form KC, with Catholic Church and Nair Service Society support; CPI split into two; CPI(M) has electoral arrangements with SSP, ML; Congress, anxious to retain Ezhava support, shuns any understanding with KC, campaigns alone, like CPI; altogether 556 candidates for 133 seats	No party able to form government; President's rule extended	
1967	CPI(M)-led united front of seven parties including ML; Congress campaigns alone; so does KC	United front of seven groups including two CPIs, and ML	Differences within the front, mainly between two Communist groups over CPI(M)'s alleged bid for hegemony
1969		"Minifront" of five groups, including CPI and ML, supported by Congress	Resignation by chief minister with recommendation for mid-term poll
1970	CPI, new Congress, ML, and other groups versus CPI(M) and SSP; old Congress campaigns alone	Coalition of CPI, ML, and other groups supported by new Congress	

their opponents undermines the tactic of the united front and, what is worse, tends to erode the Communists' social base, especially among the urban population. If the Communists, on the other hand, decide to use state power for incremental welfare of the poor and the semipoor within the existing political system they, in effect, perpetuate the system and identify themselves, at best, with the progressive elements of the bourgoisie.

THE COMMUNIST BASE IN 1967

In Kerala each major caste or community has a distinct economic base. Hindus constitute 61 percent of the population, and are divided into four main *caste groups:* the Nairs, who are 25 percent of the Hindu population, form, together with Brahmins, the predominant landowning class; Ezhavas—44.4 percent of the Hindus—are mainly urban workers and landless peasants; the Scheduled castes make up 20.4 percent of the Hindus and are the most depressed and worst exploited of the rural poor. Christians constitute 23 percent of Kerala's population. They are mostly landlords, traders, and administrators; many Roman Catholics are, however, among the rural poor. Muslims—16 percent of the population—are to be found in trade and business, but a majority of them are poor peasants.

The Communist strategy for the past two decades has been to build a statewide secular constituency of the poor which, in terms of social stratification in Kerala, would mean the poor peasant whose small holding does not exceed one acre, the agricultural laborer, the plantation worker, the industrial worker, and the lower middle class. Kerala has an extraordinarily high concentration of agricultural laborers who are also sharecroppers and / or owners of small holdings. Such "propertied" or sharecropping laborers are more independent than the completely propertyless laborer and, therefore, are more susceptible to radicalization. These radical peasant elements and plantation labor constitute the militant Communist base in Kerala.

Communist activism has aimed at weaning the poor and land-less peasantry from the caste and communal elites, the vast majority of whom are anti-Communist. This has brought the Communists into sharp and widespread conflicts with "sanskritization"—the competitive element that makes the castes dynamic rather than static. It has been suggested, for instance, that between the Communists and Exhavas there has been "no fundamental meeting of minds, but a rather fortunate confluence of program and action." [13] Or, as Zagoria puts it: "The relationship between the Communists and the Ezhavas . . . is a marriage of convenience, not a permanent alliance. The Ezhavas look to the Communists to elevate their community socially and economically, and the Communists look to the Ezhavas for political support." What Zagoria means by "Ezhavas" here, of course, is the caste leaders and the emerging urban elite among the Ezhava community. The Communists, in aligning themselves with the Ezhava caste in its conflict with Nairs, Brahmins, and Christians, have also been trying to build their *secular* or *class* base among the agricultural laborers, who constitute the bulk of Ezhavas.

However, the rapid spread of education and the absence of rigid and strong barriers between country and town in Kerala tend to sanskritize portions of the rural Ezhava community that may seek traditional paths to status and influence. This has been happening in Kerala during the past decade to an extent that endows it with some political significance. Those of the rural poor who, with education, migrate to the small towns and swell the number of white-collar employees have tended to vote against the Communists. The most remarkable evidence of this changing voting pattern in Kerala came in 1968 when the united front fared badly in a number of municipal elections.[14]

[13] Michael St. John, "The Communist Party and Communal Politics in Kerala," cited in Zagoria, p. 108.

[14] For an interesting study of the changing electoral behavior of urban middle classes in Kerala, see K. G. Krishnamurthi and G. Lakshmana Rao, *Political Preferences in Kerala* (Delhi, Radhakrishna Prakashan, 1968).

One of the objectives of the Communists' united front tactics is to weaken and break up the traditional base of bourgeois politics. In practice, this means primarily keeping the Congress party out of power, since that party is the rallying point of the bourgeoisie. The Communists have learned by experience that even if the Congress party in Kerala has long ceased to be able to control state power on its own, it is still the largest political force in the state (as in the country), and is capable of offering various rewards to political groups. The Communists have therefore tried to outbid the Congress party in attracting non-Congress political groups.

Their success can be measured by changes in the Muslim League during the last decade. In Kerala, no political group is more anti-Communist than the leadership of the League. Concentration of the Muslim population in Malabar lends strategic importance to the League as a balance-keeper in Kerala politics. The League played a major role in the "liberation struggle" against CPI rule in 1958–59; its alliance with the Congress party and the PSP brought about the electoral rout of the Communists in 1960. The Congress party, however, refused to share power with the League because the latter is a communal organization.

In 1966, the CPI(M) succeeded in bringing the League into the united front against the Congress party. After the electoral victory in 1967, the League was given a major share of state power—a League member held the important portfolio of minister of education. The CPI went even a step further in 1970. As a reward for the League's remaining in the united front without the Marxists, the coveted portfolio of minister of internal administration was given to a League member. Both Communist groups worked together to create a new Muslim-majority district in Malabar, and named it Malapuram.

In spite of this "placating" of the League leadership, however, there was a constant struggle between the League and the Communists. The Communist, especially Marxist, endeavor was to weaken the Muslim communal leaders' traditional hold on the masses and to secularize the latter's voting decisions. According to one observer of the contemporary Kerala scene:

The Muslim League leadership, as a group, has not played any part in bringing about the new social and economic situation (in Kerala). In fact, some of the League leaders are among the most backward-looking people in Kerala. But no other political group has benefited as much as the League from the new developments. Now there are new stirrings in the Muslim community and if a struggle for power between the Muslim League and left Communists takes place, the League's hold over the Muslim masses will be seriously challenged.

Until recently the Muslim League was in a position to tilt the balance between Congress and Communists. Now the League can survive as a political party in Kerala only with the support of the privileged sections of Hindu and Christian communities which are represented by Congress, Jan Sangh, and Kerala Congress. Obviously this sort of an alliance will not be popular with the poor Muslim masses.[15]

The Muslim League faced a struggle for power with the Marxists in the mid-term election of September 1970. It did fairly well because the League was in an electoral alliance with the CPI and the new Congress party. The League, then, has already been reduced to a situation where it must choose between one or the other of the Communist factions in order to survive as a political force in Kerala. The Kerala Congress party, the political tool of the Christians, has also been reduced to a similar situation, for in the mid-term election it joined hands with the CPI(M) against the two Congress factions, and with the CPI in the 1971 mid-term parliamentary election.

The Communists' united front tactics, then, earned them a stable position on Kerala's political map. As Namboodiripad pointed out:

Anti-Communism—both in its original form of hostility to Communism in general as well as in the subsequent form of hostility to the

[15] "Kerala: Moving Toward a Poll," *Economic and Political Weekly,* October 18, 1970, p. 1659.

CPI(M) in particular—has been steadily weakening. Large masses of people who, in the 1950s and in the early 1960s, could be mobilized on an anti-Communist platform began to see that anti-Communism was merely a cover for the defense of vested interests, for attacks on the common people. . . . The mass of Christians as well as Muslims found from their own experience that the only way in which they can safeguard their interests was to help bring into existence a non-Congress government.[16]

THE PRICE OF A UNITED FRONT

Credit for this achievement of importance goes mainly to Namboodiripad, undisputed architect of the united front of 1967. He brought it about with engineering skill and political flexibility but not without paying a price which was to hurt the Marxists three years later. Formation of the united front was announced six months before election day. The common-policy declaration of the seven groups carefully avoided controversial issues. It was also made clear that the united front applied only to Kerala and not to national politics.

The CPI(M) made a number of concessions to make the policy declaration acceptable to the Muslim League. The crucial problem of distribution of seats to the constituents was resolved four months before the election. Namboodiripad had the advantage of the undisputably strong position of his party in Kerala. By finally agreeing to contest only 59 seats (they had originally asked for 65), the Marxists demonstrated that it was not their intention to capture office on their own. If they were strict with any group, it was the CPI. The CPI(M) refused to permit the rival party to contest even a single parliamentary seat in Malabar, where the electoral adjustment was confined to the CPI(M) and the Muslim League, with a few seats contested by the SSP, with Marxist and/or League support.[17]

[16] E.M.S. Namboodiripad, "Kerala and Bengal: Vanguard of Emerging Alternative," *New Age: Kerala Supplement,* March 16, 1969.

[17] Collaboration with the Communists created a crisis in the League. A conservative group broke away to form the Samastha Kerala Muslim League. However, it failed to get a single seat in the assembly.

The election results came as a stunning blow to the Congress party. In a House of 133 seats, it could get only 9. The Kerala Congress got 5, and a small local communal group, 2. All the other 117 went to the united front. In the parliamentary elections, the united front captured 18 out of a total of 19 seats in the Lok Sabha—the Marxists 9, the CPI 3, the SSP 3, the League 2, the RSP 1; the Congress party got only 1 seat.

TABLE 5.3. SEATS WON BY MAJOR PARTIES
IN 1965 AND 1967 ELECTIONS

	CPI(M)		Congress		CPI		League		SSP	
Districts	*1965*	*1967*	*1965*	*1967*	*1965*	*1967*	*1965*	*1967*	*1965*	*1967*
Cannanore	7	7	1	–	–	–	–	1	3	3
Kozhikode	6	6	–	–	–	–	6	8	5	5
Palghat	11	10	1	–	–	–	–	2	2	2
Trichur	2	5	7	3	1	3	–	1	1	1
Ernakulam	3	9	5	2	–	2	–	1	–	–
Kottayam	4	4	1	1	1	4	–	–	–	1
Alleppey	4	7	4	1	–	1	–	–	–	3
Quilon	–	2	7	–	1	8	–	–	1	1
Trivandrum	3	4	10	2	–	2	–	1	1	4
All Districts	40	54	36	9	3	20	6	14	13	20

Source: Adapted from Hartman, p. 175. The Marxists helped the Muslim League and the SSP to increase their seats in the assembly.

The voting pattern revealed the organizational strength of the CPI(M) in Kerala. It alone of all political groups, including the Congress party, won seats in eight of the nine districts both in the 1965 and the 1967 elections. The Congress party won seats in eight districts in 1965 and in five in 1967. The CPI had a winning presence in three districts in 1965, and in five in 1967. The League had won only 6 seats in 1965, all of them in one district; it won 14 in 1967 in six districts. The SSP had won seats in six districts in 1965; in 1967 it won seats in eight.

The voting pattern in 1967 did not reflect a fundamental and stable realignment of social forces in Kerala. It, however, indicated a major shift of electoral support away from the Congress party as the ruling one. In contrast with the rout of the Congress party as a parliamentary force, the percentage of popular vote for the party *increased* to 35.43 percent from 33.53 percent in 1965. Caste and community considerations still apparently influenced people's voting behavior more than secular factors. Nevertheless, "the election results also showed that none of the communal leaders . . . who tried to swing their respective communities from the Kerala Congress party to the Congress party was able to command the same support as in the past. . . . This warrants the hypothesis that a larger section of the people than ever before were influenced by secular considerations in their voting decision.[18]

THE 1970 MID-TERM ELECTION

In the course of a bitter encounter between the two Communist factions in the Kerala assembly toward the end of 1969, T. V. Thomas of the CPI threw a dramatic challenge to the Marxists. "We shall meet at Kurukshetra," he declared,[19] drawing a parallel between the fratricidal battle of the Kerala Communists and that of the royal princes of ancient India, depicted in the epic *Mahabharata*. The "Kurukshetra" to which Thomas referred was, of course, the mid-term election held on September 18, 1970. The Indian press hailed the results as a great victory for Mrs. Gandhi's Congress faction and the CPI, and as a debacle for the Marxists. What the election actually demonstrated, however, was that electoral politics had rendered political alignments in Kerala extremely unstable, and that the Communist movement, despite impressive gains, had arrived at a stalemate which could hardly be resolved without further radical change in social relationships.

The necessity to go once again to the electorate put the various political groups in Kerala into utter confusion. All kinds of elec-

---

[18] Hartman, pp. 117–78.   [19] *Link*, New Delhi, September 13, 1970.

toral alliances and/or arrangements were tried. Finally, three broad alliances emerged. The first was the alliance between the CPI, Muslim League, the PSP, and the RSP, which had a "firm electoral pact" with the ruling Congress party. The second alliance brought together the CPI(M), the SSP, and three other smaller groups, each a partner in the first united front ministry. The third combination was comprised of the rightist groups—the

TABLE 5.4. THE 1970 MID-TERM ELECTION: PERCENTAGE OF POPULAR VOTES WON BY THE MAJOR PARTIES IN 1970 AND 1967

Parties	1970	1967
Congress (Ruling)	18.70	35.43
Congress ("Syndicate")	3.15	–
CPI(M)	22.55	23.51
CPI	9.22	8.57
Muslim League	8.70	6.76
SSP	4.00	8.40
Kerala Congress	6.00	7.56
Independents *	24.30	8.47

* Includes several small groups allied with CPI(M).
Source: *National Herald* (New Delhi, September 20, 1970).

"Syndicate" Congress party, the Kerala Congress party, the Jan Sangh, and the Swatantra.[20] The real battle, of course, was between the CPI-Congress parties and the Marxists. The former contested all the 133 seats, the latter alliance 94, while the third alliance set up candidates for 80 seats. Altogether 506 candidates fought for 133 seats. The Marxists supported 25 independents.

The ruling Congress party came out of the poll as the single largest party in the Kerala assembly, a tremendous comeback after its rout in 1967. It won 32 seats. The CPI-led alliance secured 36. With one independent, the CPI-Congress combination com-

[20] *Ibid.*

manded an absolute majority. The Marxists got only 27 seats, their allies 16. On the face of it, the election was a serious setback for the CPI(M).

This, however, was only one side of the picture. The Marxists got 700,000 more popular votes in 1970 than in 1967, and the CPI-Congress alliance 300,000 fewer votes in 1970 than in 1967. For the first time in Kerala, the Communists' popular vote surpassed that of Congress party—the CPI(M) alone polled more popular votes than the two Congress factions put together.

The combined Communist popular vote totaled 31.77 percent of the votes cast. The CPI as well as the Muslim League increased their popular votes from 1967; in the case of the former, this is indicative of the impression the CPI-led ministry had made on the urban voter in 1969–1970. The CPI(M) got 1 percent less of the popular vote in 1970 than in 1967, which shows that voting in the mid-term election having been very heavy, the Marxists were at least able to hold on to their political bases. The total rout of the Jan Sangh (0.60 percent) and the Swatantra (0.13 percent) showed that rightist parties had little or no appeal to the Kerala electorate.

TABLE 5.5. CONGRESS PARTY AND CPI(M) POPULAR VOTE: 1970 AND 1967

Party	1970 (total vote: 7.4 million)	1967 (total vote: 6.5 million)
Congress (Ruling and Syndicate combined)	1.6 million	2.2 million
CPI(M)	1.7 million	1.5 million

Source: Same as Table 5.4.

Of some significance was the Marxist inroad into the Muslim electorate. The League, as Table 5.4 shows, increased its popular vote, but got three seats fewer in the assembly than in 1967. It

TABLE 5.6. THE PATTERN OF MUSLIM VOTING
IN THE 1970 MID-TERM ELECTION

Constituency	Party	Votes	Total votes polled
Perinthalmanna	ML	28,436	53,552
	CPI(M)[a]	23,865	
Malapuram	ML	39,682	62,895
	CPI(M)	22,379	
Kuthipuram	ML	30,081	55,048
	Ind[b]	23,870	
Mattancherry	Ind[c]	38,580	56,706
	ML	17,460	
Beypore	CPI(M)	30,260	68,479
	ML	27,945	
Guruaayur	Ind[d]	26,039	46,290
	ML	20,987	

Source: Same as Table 5.4.

[a] The Marxist radical, Imbichi Bawa, lost this contest to the League.

[b] A Muslim candidate supported by the Marxists.

[c] The League lost this seat to a Christian supported by the Marxist alliance.

[d] Supported by CPI(M), thus another Muslim League loss to the Marxist alliance.

won all the seats from Malapuram, the new Muslim majority district created in 1969. The League, then, was still able to "deliver" the block votes of Muslims, but the Marxists who contested the League in many constituencies were able to penetrate deep into the Muslim masses. If Marxist votes came mainly from the poor peasants and/or agricultural laborers—as they presumably did—secular considerations have apparently made deep inroads into traditional Islamic society.[21]

[21] "So, though the Muslim League maintains its influence on the mass of Muslim voters broadly in the whole of Kerala, in Malapuram district, where the Muslim masses are in a majority, there is a big drop in the percentage of vote of the League-Right Communist-Congress combination. This indicates that our party has made a considerable dent in this area even among Muslim masses. . . .

"But remembering the class character of the Muslim League leadership, which consists of landlords, merchants, and capitalists, we should have made determined

The Marxists were less successful in softening up the communal base of the Kerala Congress party, the political organization of the Christians, which increased its strength in the assembly from 5 seats in 1967 to 13 seats in 1970, and thus emerged as a major force in political bargaining. Of the 13 seats, 8 were won in the Christian-majority Kottayam district. In nearly every contest, the Kerala Congress party held its own against both the CPI(M) and ruling Congress party candidates. However, the Marxists built up a sizable presence in some of the traditional Christian constituencies.

TABLE 5.7. THE PATTERN OF CHRISTIAN VOTING
IN THE 1970 MID-TERM ELECTION

Constituency	Party	Total votes polled
Kanjirally	KC	22,307
	CPI(M)[a]	20,700
Thodupuzha	KC	19,750
	Congress	12,233
	Ind[b]	18,115
Kallooppara	KC	17,864
	CPI(M)	15,431
	Cong	14,995

Source: *National Herald,* September 19, 1970.

[a] The Marxists lost this seat to the Kerala Congress party. The anti-KC votes were split by three independents, one of whom, supported by the Congress party, got 8,985 votes.

[b] Supported by CPI(M).

The Marxists made an impressive showing in the Ernakulam industrial belt where their base had been poor in 1967. In a three-way contest among the ruling Congress party, CPI(M), and the "Syndicate" Congress, the first won by less than 5,000

and serious efforts to approach the Muslim masses on their economic problems, roused their democratic consciousness, and brought them into common mass movements and organizations. But there is a big failure in this regard." *Review of Kerala Election* (Calcutta, CPI(M), December 1970), pp. 15–18.

votes.[22] The Marxists were in firm control of their stronghold in Palghat district, where they and their allies won all of the 10 seats. They also drew some comfort from the defeat of the extremist leader, K. P. R. Gopalan, who had been leading a "Naxalite" group in Kerala since 1967. The CPI(M), however, had to swallow the defeat of two of its ministers in the first united front government, Imbichi Bawa and M. K. Krishnan.

The mid-term election, then, explicitly demonstrated that the Marxists had built a strong political and social base in rural Kerala, and succeeded to a fair extent in secularizing the traditional pattern of electoral behavior. To a significant degree they had also polarized Keralan politics between country and town. While the electorate in the urban areas was evidently swayed by the "socialist-democratic" image of the ruling Congress faction of Mrs. Gandhi and impressed by the CPI's leadership of the "minifront" ministry, the rural electorate stood more or less firm by the Marxist party.[23]

The voting in the mid-term election made it clear that although the Marxists by themselves were still not in a position to rule Kerala, neither could any other party or group of parties. In fact, the CPI-Congress victory seemed to create as many problems as it might have solved. The ruling Congress party refused to join a coalition with the CPI alliance as this would have been a vindication of the CPI strategical objective of a national democratic front. The CPI's electoral alliance with the Muslim League, which was blessed by Mrs. Gandhi's Congress faction, led to the

[22] *National Herald,* September 19, 1970. The "Syndicate" Congress party contested 39 seats, and lost in each one of them. In a number of constituencies, the CPI(M) and "Syndicate" Congress parties campaigned for the same candidates, though there was no formal electoral understanding between the two.

[23] *National Herald,* which supports Indira Gandhi, wrote editorially, "The massive support that the Kerala electorate has given to the Congress party is proof of their approval of the party's program, particularly the socialist measures which the Indira Gandhi government have boldly taken after the split in the Indian National Congress. . . . The prime minister's stress on democracy and socialism during her recent tour of the state evidently appealed to the people." September 19, 1970.

revival of the League as a political force in northern India, and the Congress party itself came to an electoral pact with the League in West Bengal in 1971, sharing power with it in the anti-CPI(M) coalition ministry set up in Calcutta after the poll.

THE CPI(M) AFTER 1970

The Marxists' political base in Kerala in 1970 was a mixture of strength and weakness. In December 1968, membership of the CPI(M) in Kerala stood at 20,912, the highest in any Indian state, and an increase of nearly 3,000 since 1964. The party's state conference held in November 1968 at Palghat was attended by "over 190 delegates" and "over 6,000 sympathizers organized in groups." Agricultural laborers formed the main part of the 30,000 who staged a militant demonstration before a mass rally that concluded the conference; the rally itself was attended by about 100,000 people. The party had a 40,000-strong volunteer force, organized since 1965 under the leadership of A. K. Gopalan. The volunteers combined party work with rural construction work such as road-building and helping the peasant in the field. The training program included drilling and marching.[24]

The party, however, suffered from several serious weaknesses. Some of its leaders were far from being in good health: Namboodiripad had been hospitalized in East Germany in recent years; Gopalan and Mrs. Gowri were both heart cases. The party's strongest base was among agricultural laborers in Palghat district, but organization was "very poor," and most of the rural cadres were said to have a petit-bourgeois outlook. The trade-union base was "very strong" only in Cannanore and Kozhikode, where the party could by itself bring about "a complete standstill in all industries." It was, however, weak in the industrially advanced

[24] *People's Democracy*, December 8 and March 3, 1968. The volunteer force is popularly called "Gopala Sena" (Gopala Force).

district of Ernakulam; elsewhere the party had lost several bases to the CPI and/or the "extremists." Not all trade-union activists were reliable followers of the party line. There was a "tendency among some comrades to lapse into economism and hurl a tirade against our ministry and thus play the Congress game. There was also a tendency to fall victim to revisionist provocation and form new unions without preparing mass support." [25]

A strong dissident group functioned within the party, putting pressure on the leadership for more radical policies. Radicalization seemed to be more prevalent among the young party members and those recruited from among the poorer peasants. A. K. Gopalan, Ezhava leader of the peasant front of the CPI(M), was considered more radical than the trade-union leaders and intellectuals. Imbichi Bawa, a Muslim Communist leader, was said to be even more radical than Gopalan.

Some of the radicals opposed the parliamentary line, and wanted the party to promote revolutionary mass struggle, with the peasants as its primary base. They opposed the party's attitude toward the USSR, and shared Chinese evaluation of the CPSU leadership. The radicals seemed to be particularly strong in Trivandrum district. At the district plenum in 1968, they challenged the party program and other central committee documents and passed a resolution demanding their revision. "In Trivandrum, only the opponents of the CC documents were elected as delegates to the state plenum. . . . To some extent the same thing happened in Quilon. In Cannanore the delegates holding different views were elected to the state plenum." [26]

At the state plenum, however, a resolution to postpone discussion of central committee resolutions was defeated by 227 votes to 67. The dissidents mustered 86 votes to back an amendment which would support the Chinese concept of U.S.-Soviet collusion

---

[25] *Political-Organizational Report of the Eighth Congress of the CPI(M)* (Calcutta, CPI(M), 1969), pp. 299, 261–62.

[26] *Ibid.*, p. 228.

for world hegemony. This was about one-third of the total dele-
gate strength at the plenum.

Apart from this radical wing within the CPI(M), there was the
group of extremists, the "Naxalites," who also exhorted the Marxist leadership to adopt more radical tactics. Although only 5 percent of CPI(M) members were said to have defected to the
"ultra-leftist group," the extremists had a forceful and widely
respected leader in K. P. R. Gopalan, one of the veterans of the
Communist movement. The Marxists had lost a number of trade-
union and peasant bases to the "extremists," who had joined with
anti-Communist elements to discredit the CPI(M) and its ministers in the united front government.[27]

STALEMATE IN 1971

The formation of the anti-Marxist, CPI-led government in
Kerala in the autumn of 1970 put the CPI(M) on the defensive.
The party launched a number of protests, including a strike by
government employees. However, the CPI(M) leadership was apparently caught between two pressures, one coming from the CPI
and its leftist allies, the other from the radical elements within
the Marxist group as well as the "Naxalites." The first pulled the
leadership toward the right, the second toward the left. The main
problem was how to expand the support base of the party in the
rural as well as urban areas.

In the urban areas, the "socialist" image of Indira Gandhi drew
the uncommitted middle classes, especially the youth, toward the
new Congress faction, and the militant parliamentarianism of
the CPI(M) looked somewhat barren in view of the failure of the
Marxist-led united front to solve Kerala's chronic problem of educated unemployment. Namboodiripad's tactics of confrontation
with the central government evidently alienated those sections of
the urban population whose job prospects lay mostly outside the

[27] *Ibid.*, p. 289.

state. In the rural areas, the Marxist party was unable to devise tactics of militant peasant struggles without risking violence and thus succumbing to the "Naxalite" line.

It was from its "grand isolation" that the CPI(M) contested the mid-term parliamentary election in March 1971. The CPI worked out an electoral pact with Mrs. Gandhi's Congress party and the partners of the coalition regime, including the Muslim League. The CPI(M) got the support of only a few tiny local groups— only with the Kerala Congress party could it work out a few seat adjustments. The Marxists had their own candidates in 11 of the 19 parliamentary constituencies.

Where it had its own candidates, the party polled 42.41 percent of the total valid vote, as against 51.32 percent secured by the new-Congress-CPI-Muslim League united front combination. In the eight other constituencies, the independents supported by the CPI(M) got 36.24 percent of the vote as against 55.60 percent secured by the combination. For the whole of Kerala, 40 percent of the electorate voted for the CPI(M) and its allies, and 53 percent for the larger combination. In terms of seats, however, the CPI(M) got only 2, as against 9 in 1967, and only one of the independents it supported, V. K. Krishna Menon, was successful. While the Marxists' support-base remained strong, their ability to get parliamentary seats was severely reduced. Moreover, it was once again confirmed that the CPI(M) needed strong allies to win elections in Kerala, while its tactics of militant parliamentarianism alienated most of its prospective allies.[28]

The CPI congratulated itself on the success of the anti-CPI(M) combination in Kerala; it was evidently pleased that the parliamentary poll could be interpreted as an expression of the electorate's confidence in the coalition it had led since 1970. However,

[28] *People's Democracy*, March 28, 1971. The CPI(M) total vote came to 1,611,442 (25.1 percent) as against Mrs. Gandhi's Congress party vote of 1,289,601 (20.1 percent), and CPI's 593,761 (9.2 percent). The CPI(M) vote alone was higher than the combined vote of the two Congress factions. *Times of India*, March 31, 1971.

as already noted, the CPI's tactical line of a national democratic front suffered a setback. Its postelection tactical line consisted of general rather than selective support to Mrs. Gandhi, close liaison with the Congress left, and bitter opposition to the CPI(M).

6

COMMUNISTS IN POWER: WEST BENGAL

In 1957 the united CPI won the Keralan assembly election and formed what was described as the first *elected* Communist government anywhere in the world. The Communists governed for a little over two years until they were overthrown by the "liberation movement." Ten years later, Communists once again found themselves in power in Kerala and West Bengal. The intervening decade, however, had witnessed vast changes in the political and economic milieu in India.

Perhaps the most significant of these was a crisis in the Congress "system" at the state level. The dynamics of the Congress leadership's socioeconomic programs appeared to have been largely exhausted in 1967. Even the relatively slow pace of modernization in India created social cleavages that became politically relevant. The Communist movement had split. Rivalry between the two Communist factions persuaded each faction to seek mass support.

In 1967 neither faction could control the state government in

Kerala and West Bengal. In Kerala, as we have noted, the recognized superiority of the CPI(M) enabled it to forge a coalition of non-Congress groups to contest the election and itself to come out as the leader of the united front government. Its leadership, however, rested on the survival of the coalition and involved compromises even on fundamental issues. In West Bengal, the two Communist parties fought each other at the polls; it was only the defeat of the Congress party and the prospect of forming a non-Congress government that brought them and other non-Congress groups together in a united front after the election. The CPI(M), though the leading partner of the front, had to accept the leadership of the Bangla Congress party in the government. Here again, it had to pay a price for its first taste of power.

It became evident in 1967, although it had not been unknown to perceptive observers of the Indian scene, that the Indian political system was much more vulnerable at the state level than at the national level; if the system decayed and disintegrated, the process would begin at the state level—where it might already have started. The strategic-tactical lines of the two Communist factions during this period were put together in the context of the crisis brewing at the base-level of the political system; the CPI(M) tactics were explicitly designed to accelerate the crisis.

The crucial question for the Marxists was how to work the parliamentary line without becoming a victim of bourgois parliamentarianism and how to work within the system for a revolutionary transformation of the system. The CPI(M) tried during this period to formulate a tactical line of militant parliamentarianism. At the state level, this tactical line meant the building up of *controlled* militant action by the masses in order to push forward limited structural reforms and to politically mobilize large sections of the urban and rural proletariat. At the national level, it implied using the Communist-led united front regimes to wage a "class struggle" with the central government.

This militant parliamentary line did not emanate spontaneously from the leadership; it was the result of pressures from the radical elements within the party and from the "Naxalite" extremists. Partly it also emanated from the deep conflicts between the CPI(M), the CPI, and the bourgeois parties led by the Congress party. The new line, to which Namboodiripad and H. K. Konar seemed to have made significant theoretical contributions, however, isolated the Marxists from almost the entire spectrum of the liberal left, including the CPI. It also exerted a continuing pressure on these leftist groups, particularly the CPI. The pressure on the CPI was greater in West Bengal than in Kerala because of Bengal's acute economic problems and the traditional radicalism of its politics.

Even more significant was the Communists' decision during this period to bring the rural poor within their orbit. For the first time in India, the two Communist parties addressed themselves seriously to the rural proletariat. Here again, the Naxalbari peasant uprising and the birth of the "Naxalite" movement worked as a catalyst; the CPI(M) condemned the "ultra-left" adventurists, but not without realizing that the future of Indian Communism lay with the party's ability to build a radical peasant movement. The precipitate adoption of the "Naxalite" rebellion by Chinese mass media forced the Marxist leadership formally to declare their ideological independence of Peking and reject the CCP's interpretation of Indian realities. The Marxist party was now thrown on its own resources in working out a new tactical line which would be a marriage of militant parliamentarianism and controlled peasant protest.

This tactical line was devised in 1968, during the months between the dismissal of the first united front government in West Bengal and the installation of the second after the mid-term poll of February 1969. Toward the formulation of the tactics of peasant struggle, the West Bengal unit of the CPI(M) appeared to have made a major contribution. Harekrishna Konar's tactical thinking that in the existing socioeconomic milieu in India, the rural proletariat claimed priority over the urban proletariat, and its acceptance at the eighth party congress marked a turning point in the Indian Communist movement.

In 1969 the CPI(M) in West Bengal showed how to build a militant peasant base by utilizing governmental power. The Marxist tactics persuaded the CPI also to cultivate the rural poor; its "land grab movement" in 1970 at least helped in focusing national attention on the growing polarization in the countryside. Land reforms returned to the Congress party's agenda after more than a decade, and the inability or unwillingness of the chief ministers to translate the new rhetoric into reality once again underlined the strength of the liaison that had grown in the country since the mid-1950s between the ruling party and the landed gentry.[1]

PROBLEMS INHERENT IN A UNITED FRONT

The third important lesson of the period of CPI(M) leadership of the governments of West Bengal and Kerala related to the concept and tactics of a united front. Students of international Communism are aware of the many animated debates and bitter controversies that have attended the united front or coalition tactics of the various major Communist parties. The question: who are our allies and who are our enemies? has been answered suc-

---

[1] The political influence of the "kulaks" is indicated by the fact that agricultural income is not taxed in India, not even after the "Green Revolution." The central government pleads inability to tax agricultural income because it is a state subject; the state governments show no inclination to impose direct taxation on farm income. On the contrary, the state subsidizes farm output by buying grains from the farmers at "procurement prices" which are often higher than the market price. Since 1967, the state governments have been in an expansive mood to abolish the age-old land revenue from their fiscal system. Ostensibly this is supposed to give relief to the small holder. In actual practice, abolition of revenue on land even up to 7–10 acres benefit the "kulak" rather than the small holder. This is because of the extremely unequal pattern of landholdings in India. See *The Economic Times*, May 14, 1971.

cessfully only by those Communist parties that have made successful revolutions.

By its very definition, Communism is an aggressive doctrine: its
foundation is on class war leading to the dictatorship or hegemony of the proletariat. If it collaborates with other classes or
sections of classes, it is always with the final objective of over-
throwing the bourgeoisie and establishing the class rule of the
proletariat. The nature of collaboration and united action is determined by the prevailing class alignments in a given society,
and the strength and capability of the party of the proletariat.

This is what Lenin meant when he wrote that for "revolutionary Social Democrats, insurrection is not an absolute slogan, but a
concrete one." [2] As a revolutionary situation builds up in a society, it is, as Lenin postulated, the task of the Communist party
"to split up the bourgeoisie as much as possible, to derive from
the bourgeoisie's temporary appeals to the people the greatest
possible advantage for the revolution, and meanwhile to prepare
the forces of the revolutionary people." In such a situation, Lenin
added, "It is to our advantage that the bourgeoisie should appeal
to the people, for by doing so it provides material that will help
to rouse and enlighten politically those huge backward masses of
people to reach whom through Social Democratic agitation would
be sheer utopianism for the time being." [3] The purpose is not to
collaborate with the bourgeoisie to run the capitalist system better, but to enhance the prospects of revolution.

It goes without saying that to further agitation and struggle in this
connection, temporary agreements with various groups of revolutionary bourgeois democrats . . . are especially expedient. But here we
must, on the one hand, steadfastly preserve the class individuality of
the party of the proletariat, and must not for a single moment abandon our Social Democratic criticism of our bourgeois allies; on the
other hand, we should be failing in our duty as the party of the ad-

[2] Lenin, "Playing at Parliamentarianism," *Collected Works* (Moscow, 1962), IX,
273.
[3] Lenin, "Boycott of Bulygin Duma, and Insurrection," *ibid.*, pp. 180, 182.

vanced class if in our agitation we failed to produce an advanced revolutionary slogan at the present stage of the democratic revolution.

A revolution in itself is nothing, Lenin warned the Russian Communists in 1905, if it does not bear the imprint of a socialist revolution.

Undoubtedly the (bourgeois democratic) revolution will teach us and will teach the masses of the people. But the question that now confronts a militant political party is, shall we be able to teach the revolution anything? Shall we be able to make use of our Social-Democratic doctrine, of our bond with the only thoroughly revolutionary class, the proletariat, to put a proletarian imprint on the revolution, to carry the revolution to a real and decisive victory, not in word but in deed, and to paralyze the instability, half-heartedness and treachery of the democratic bourgeousie?

Lenin thought that it was permissible for the Communist party to take part in a revolutionary provisional government, not to make it work, but to wreck it from within and without. In a revolutionary period, a democratic-Communist coalition was only another form of class war; the bourgeoisie would try to take away the gains of the revolution from the proletariat "in the desperate struggle between them for power." The Communists could not join the coalition as a "tail-end" of the bourgeoisie; their participation could be only for two purposes: "a relentless struggle against counterrevolutionary attempts, and the defense of the independent interests of the working class. Even if the Communists were able to act from above, it must "in any case exert pressure" from below.[4]

In China, the question of allies and enemies has preoccupied Mao Tse-tung since 1926, when he wrote his tract analyzing the classes in Chinese society. It was not before 1935, however, that Mao actually got an historic opportunity to mobilize broad sections of the Chinese people in the national liberation struggle

[4] Lenin, "Two Tactics of Social-Democracy in the Democratic Revolution," *ibid.*, pp. 17–32.

against Japanese imperialism. He now enlarged the concept of a
people's republic to be created by a broad national revolutionary
united front. All the social classes, even including those that did
not wish to fight American or British imperialism, were eligible
at the front only if they were ready to join the struggle against
Japan. This people's republic would "encourage the development
of industrial and commercial enterprises of the national bourgeoisie rather than confiscate them." Four years later, Mao further
sharpened his concept of the Chinese revolution. Now he called it
a bourgeois-democratic revolution, "the joint revolutionary-
dictatorship of several revolutionary classes over the imperialists
and reactionary traitors," the "joint dictatorship of several parties
belonging to the Anti-Japanese National United Front." [5]

In 1949 Mao founded the People's Republic, which he conceptualized as the "people's democratic dictatorship" based on "an alliance of the working class, the peasantry, and the urban petty
bourgeosie," but "mainly on the alliance of the workers and the
peasants." [6] In the progression of an increasingly class-oriented
conceptualization of the Chinese revolution, at no stage did Mao
deviate from the firm postulate that in each passing coalition, the
Communists must securely retain leadership of the united front.

In 1928, Mao expressed the view that a bourgeois-democratic
revolution could be completed in China "only under the leadership of the proletariat." Here he was clearly echoing Lenin's postulate that it was the task of the Communists to place the proletarian imprint on the bourgeois-democratic revolution. While
formulating the concept of a people's republic in 1935, Mao made
it clear that its mainstay would be the Communist party and the
Red Army; indeed, the success of the revolution would depend
on the hegemony of the Communist party. "The essential part of

[5] Mao Tse-tung: "Analysis of All Classes in Chinese Society," in Stuart Schram,
The Political Thought of Mao Tse-tung (New York, Praegar, 1966), pp. 143–47; *On
the Tactics of Fighting Japanese Imperialism* (Peking, 1953); *The Chinese Revolution and the Chinese Communist Party* (Peking, 1949).
[6] Mao Tse-tung, *On People's Democratic Dictatorship* (Peking, 1949).

our program must be the protection of the interests of the basic section of the masses—the workers and peasants." [7] In 1939 Mao again laid down that the success of the two-fold revolution—the bourgeois and the proletarian—"rests on the shoulders of the party of the Chinese proletariat." The united front or coalition tactics of Lenin and Mao, then, were only an expedient instrument in establishing Communist leadership or hegemony of the revolutionary struggle and, finally, a dictatorship of the proletariat. [8]

The Marxist technique of coalition is different from the coalitions often formed in capitalist societies not because there is conflict among the partners—conflicts exist in all coalitions which are, in essence, more or less temporary combinations of competing groups—but because the Communists must, in the first place, dominate the coalitions and, second, steadily weaken and finally eliminate the non-Communist elements. The Marxist technique emanates from the concept of antagonistic relations between the bourgeoisie and the proletariat, one of which must dominate the other. According to the Marxists, coalitions exist in capitalist societies because the constituents belong to the same class, the bourgeoisie, and conflicts among them are not antagonistic. When Communists join coalitions with the bourgeoisie as "tail-enders," they are inevitably ousted by the bourgeoisie.

In Kerala and West Bengal in 1967, the Communists could have ruled singly, or almost singly, had they not split into two rival groups. In the existing circumstances, the CPI(M), as the single largest group, was in need of allies among the bourgeoisie;

[7] Mao Tse-tung, "The Hegemony of the Proletariat in the Bourgeois-Democratic Revolution," in Schram, ed., pp. 147–49; *On the Tactics of Fighting Japanese Imperialism* and *The Chinese Revolution and the Chinese Communist Party*.
[8] In Yugoslavia, Tito invited all the followers of former democratic and liberal political parties to join the Popular Front to fight the Germans and the Chetniks, but in order to maintain an unchallenged Communist leadership of the Front and to prevent factionalism, the Communists would accept followers of these parties only as individuals, not as groups. Jossip Broz Tito, *Narodna Fronta i Borba za Mir* (Pittsburg and Philadelphia, 1947), p. 13.

the hostility of the CPI did not permit the Marxists to assume formal leadership of the coalition in West Bengal. The CPI elected to pursue its own variation of the tactical line incorporated in the concept of the National Democratic State in the Moscow Declaration of 1960.[9] It joined the coalitions in Punjab, Uttar Pradesh, and Bihar more or less as "tail-enders." And in Kerala and West Bengal, its main concern was to prevent Marxist hegemony of the coalitions. The united front politics in these two states thus became highly dynamic between 1967 and 1969.

There were, in the first place, the fundamental and antagonistic conflicts between the Marxists and the bourgeoisie-democratic groups. Second, there was the increasingly bitter rivalry between

---

[9] The 1960 Moscow Statement was a crude amalgam of Soviet and Chinese positions on major controversial issues in international Communism. The "national democratic state" was defined as one that had won complete economic independence from the imperialist world and assumed close economic ties with the Socialist bloc; had adopted an anti-imperialist foreign policy; had built a predominant state sector in its economy; and had achieved a list of democratic reforms and democratic freedoms, the major two of them being land reforms and freedom of activity for the Communists. The tactical line to achieve this strategic objective is laid down:

"Today in a number of capitalist countries, the working class, headed by its vanguard, has the opportunity, given a united working class and popular front or other workable forms of agreement and political cooperation between the different parties and public organizations, to unite a majority of the people, win state power without civil war, and ensure the transfer of the basic means of production to the hands of the people. Relying on the majority of the people and resolutely rebuffing the opportunist elements incapable of relinquishing the policy of compromise with the capitalists and landlords, the working class can defeat the reactionary, antipopular forces, secure a firm majority in parliament, transform parliament from an instrument serving the class interests of the bourgeoisie into an instrument serving the working people, launch an extraparliamentary mass struggle, smash the resistance of the reactionary forces, and create the necessary conditions for peaceful realization of the socialist revolution. All this will be possible only by broad and ceaseless development of the class struggle of the workers, peasant masses, and the urban middle strata against big monopoly capital, against reaction, for profound social reforms, for peace and socialism.

"In the event of the exploiting class resorting to violence against the people, the possibility of nonpeaceful transition to socialism should be borne in mind. Leninism teaches, and experience confirms, that the ruling classes never relinquish power voluntarily. In this case the degree of bitterness and the forms of the class struggle will depend not so much on the proletariat as on the resistance put up by the reactionary circles to the will of the overwhelming majority of the people on these circles using force at one or other stage of the struggle for socialism."

the two Communist factions. As against this, the united front governments compelled the varies groups to work together on the basis of mutually agreed upon programs. The constituents found it easier to draft such programs than to implement them.

The Marxists proved to be cleverer than the other groups in employing governmental power to extend their mass base. Soon they threatened to take over the limited political bases of the other leftist groups. These groups found themselves fighting for survival. Bitter rivalries ensued, often leading to violence and murder, and the "Naxalites" made a further major contribution to political violence and murder after 1968. Under the cumulative impact of all of these conflicts, and also because of the central government's hostility toward the CPI(M), the Marxist-dominated coalitions in Kerala and West Bengal collapsed in 1969–70.

THE FIRST UNITED FRONT
IN BENGAL

The first united front government was set up in West Bengal on March 2, 1967 after weeks of hard bargaining. During these negotiations, two former Congress leaders played the inevitable role of mediator in any Indian impasse; both of them later played a major role in the front's disintegration. One was P. C. Ghosh, a septuagenerian disciple of Gandhi, who had been ousted as West Bengal's first Congress party chief minister in 1950, and who had since nursed many personal grievances against the Congress leadership. The other was Humayun Kabir, former education and petroleum minister in the national government, who saw himself in the role of a protector of Muslim interests.

The united front government was led by the Bangla Congress leader, Ajoy K. Mukherji, who took over general administration, including the police. In the nineteen-man cabinet, the Bangla Congress party and CPI(M) were each allowed three ministers,

CPI and Forward Bloc two each, and eight smaller groups one each. The nineteenth minister was Ghosh, an "independent." The Marxist leader Jyoti Basu became deputy chief minister in charge of finance. Among the major portfolios, the two other Marxist ministers got land and land revenue, and relief and rehabilitation; a CPI minister got irrigation and waterways; Ghosh got food and agriculture. The ministerial groups set up a united front committee of party leaders and members of the cabinet to oversee the work of the government, resolve differences among the constituents, and generally function as a watchdog of the interests of the various groups.

An eighteen-point common program became the platform of the coalition. The government's initial actions included predictable political gestures such as the release of a large number of political prisoners, withdrawal of charges against many more accused of various crimes during the food agitation of 1966, the decision not to renew the West Bengal Security Act which the Congress governments had systematically used against their political opponents, and the dismantling of an inquiry commission set up in 1966 to probe into the causes and effects as well as justification of police firings during the food protests. Jyoti Basu, in one of his first actions, ordered the British-owned Calcutta Tramways Company to defer a rise in fares that had been sanctioned by the Congress regime.

During the first fifty days of its existence, the united front government took several measures that gave some indication of the thrust of its socioeconomic policies. It instructed the Calcutta Corporation to reduce the tax on slums and increase the tax on buildings with an annual valuation of Rs 15,000 ($2,000). No tax or cess was to be realized in the drought-affected area where 60 percent of the crops had failed. Elections were ordered for twenty-five municipalities on the basis of adult franchise; these elections had been pending for some time, and some of the municipalities had ceased to function. It was announced that landless peasants and sharecroppers would be given free of cost up to one-fourth of an acre of homestead land from lands vested in government. Higher minimum wages were ordered in thirteen different industries without, according to their owners, considering the industries' capacity to pay. Over 100,000 government employees were given tenure; more than 600 state transport workers who had been dismissed on charges of sabotage were given back their jobs; higher cost-of-living allowance, involving an annual expenditure of Rs 15 crore ($2 million), was granted to government employees and school teachers. The Communist-led state government employees' union was recognized, and it was announced that political affiliations would no longer be a bar to employment.[10]

The united front's eighteen-point common program included a policy directive on industrial relations which was now translated into a government decision with far-reaching consequences. Bengal was in the grip of acute and widespread industrial unrest. The chief minister issued orders in April asking police officers not to intervene in labor disputes without prior consultation with the minister for labor, Subodh Banerji. This order was modified in June and replaced by another. It said:

The government would like to impress upon all officers, especially those connected with maintenance of law and order, that the police must not intervene in legitimate labor movements and that, in case of any such complaint regarding unlawful activities . . . . the police must first investigate carefully whether the complaint has any basis in fact before proceeding to take any action under the law.[11]

At the party level, the CPI(M) lost no time in putting into effect the tactics of mass mobilization with a view to exerting pressure on the united front government to keep it moving in the proper direction. On March 27, the party's state committee directed its cadres all over Bengal to "mobilize public support to

[10] C. R. Irani, *Communism in Bengal*, pp. 9–12.   [11] Quoted, *ibid.*, p. 66.

defend the united front ministry against attacks from the Congress reactionary forces and from an imperialist conspiracy" to overthrow it. The party also decided to organize mass movements and to rouse popular enthusiasm "to keep the ministry on the right track to serve the causes of the people." Trade unions and *kisan* organizations were asked to hold conventions *within a fortnight* "to formulate demands to be placed before the ministry." [12]

The first major trouble for the united front regime came on March 27 from a most unexpected quarter. Violent riots broke out in the northern parts of Calcutta between Sikhs and Bengalis, the first such incident in Bengal. Quick remedial measures taken by the government, which included the stationing of army units in the troubled area, brought the situation under control. Even then, six men were killed and one hundred injured, thirty-five of them seriously. The work style of the Communist ministers made an impression on the public: Jyoti Basu and CPI leader Bishwanath Mukherji personally escorted a Sikh procession to a *gurudwara* and arranged for the installation of the Granth Sahib there. In April, Chief Minister Mukherji attempted to reorganize the top level of the civil service by transferring ten senior officials to other posts; some of the transferred officials were able to get the support of their ministers to resist this order, which had eventually to be "modified." [13]

Serious problems concerning food and labor began to surface in urban as well as rural Bengal. On May 13, in a confrontation between railway police and an angry crowd of 10,000 at Ranaghat station near Calcutta, three persons were killed when police fired. A few days later, Mukherji disclosed that the government had been receiving "disturbing reports from different parts of West Bengal . . . that individuals, individually and collectively, occupied or have been trying to occupy houses and lands belonging either to the government or to private individuals. In such cases,

[12] *The Statesman,* March 23, 1967.   [13] *Ibid.,* March 30, April 29, and May 5, 1967.

there are reports even of use of *lathis* (sticks), bows, arrows, spears, etc. In some other cases, certain landholders have been seeking unlawfully to evict old sharecroppers in order to bring such lands under their direct control." [14]

On May 10, there had been a major clash in the Defense Ministry's gun and shell factory at Cossipore in which "at least six people were injured, three seriously." The central government ordered the army to guard the factory, while Basu worked out a settlement between labor and management. About this time, the central government announced the appointment of Dharam Vira, a retired civil servant known for his "toughness," as governor of West Bengal, without apparently consulting the united front ministry. Toward the end of May, Hindu-Muslim riots broke out in parts of Calcutta.

In an evaluation of the ministry's work in the first hundred days, *The Statesman* in Calcutta said that "despite the zeal shown and the hard work put in by individual ministers," it had "not yet been able to create the impression of having initiated the kind of major change that the people had expected. This seems, at least in part, due to the lack of effective functional cohesion among the constituent units of the coalition." Differences persisted particularly on the government's food, land, and labor policies. [15] In June, the tension building up on the labor front and in some of the rural areas began to tell upon the cohesiveness of the united front and tended to create a crisis between the West Bengal government and New Delhi.

THE PROBLEM OF FOOD

In dealing with the three problems which perpetually affect the life of the poor—food, land, and labor—the united front found itself far from united. The food problem has to be seen against the background of the severe drought of 1965–66, and the near-famine conditions in most of Bihar and in large areas of several

[14] *Ibid.*, May 30, 1967.   [15] *Ibid.*, May 11 and 23, 1967.

other states. An acute shortage of grain, particularly rice, had in 1966 compelled the government to introduce statutory rationing in the greater Calcutta area. To meet the requirements of statutory rationing, the state government must have a certain assurance of the minimum supplies needed. Most of this had to be procured by the state government itself from the producers, who were required to sell their officially fixed surplus grain to the Food Corporation of India at prices regulated by the government.

In 1967, West Bengal needed a minimum quantity of 600,000 tons of grain to feed its population, half of it for the rationed areas. By the time the united front government came to power, the best months for procurement had already passed; during those months, the Congress government then in office had procured just about 50,000 tons mainly through a 50 percent levy on the rice mills. The united front government had only two alternatives—either to press the procurement drive with the utmost vigor, or to persuade the central government to give West Bengal a generous portion of the surplus from those few states which grew more than they consumed.

In 1966 the central government had given West Bengal more food grains than it had promised, but in 1967 it had also to look after the needs of famine-stricken Bihar and other scarcity areas, and was unlikely to oblige West Bengal especially when procurement had been "shamefully neglected in all the states during the pre-election period." In West Bengal "a good deal of the harvest is still in the villages, mostly with the better-off farmers who account for most of the marketable surplus." [16] The question for the united front government was whether measures should and could be taken to persuade or coerce the 200,000 families owning ten acres or more to sell to the official agency at least a third of what was needed to fulfill the minimum needs of the rationed areas.

The cabinet was divided on this question. Lack of agreement

[16] "Grasping the Nettle," editorial, *ibid.*, March 17, 1967.

delayed the announcement of a food policy by a month and, when it came, the policy lacked precision. The district officers, for example, had no clear idea from where the procurement target of 200,000 tons was to come. Food committees of officials, members of the legislature, and party representatives were set up in each district, but the differences within the cabinet were soon transmitted to these committees, paralyzing their work.

A climate favorable for "persuasion" seemed to exist in the villages; wherever ministers carried their appeals "people came forward with promises to deliver substantial quantities of rice stocks." The district authorities found "everywhere a surge of popular feeling for the united front government." [17] But who were these people? They were mostly the rural poor who had neither land nor grain to sell, or those who had already sold their surplus and resented that others should manage to avoid selling theirs. Forces "opposed or indifferent to the new government," wrote a correspondent of *The Statesman* (a Swatantra party-oriented newspaper) were the "ricemillers and *jotedars* (landlords) and sections of the Congress party organization which resent the ascendancy of the United Front." The Congress party, the administration, and the "ricemiller-*jotedar* combine" being the only three agencies with a "widespread functional network in the rural areas," the united front government met with strong resistance to its procurement drive.

It apparently did not get the full cooperation of the district administration. For one thing, the "administration is not used to methods of persuasion," and for another, "a section of it may be involved in the interaction of rural power groups" and could not act as "an effective initiator of a popular movement of persuasion for the success of the food policy." Nor did the civil service in Calcutta entirely cooperate with the new regime. This became

[17] *Ibid.*, May 5, 1967.

known when it was revealed in early May that a cabinet decision to compel the chief growers to sell paddy to the official agency had not been "adequately emphasized" by "some officials" who had "communicated this order to the district authorities." [18]

The main obstacle was Food Minister Ghosh who, as a Gandhian, was opposed to restriction and control on the movement of food grains as well as to any kind of coercion of the well-to-do growers. The procurement drive was therefore a failure, and in June the weekly rice ration had to be cut. The central government failed to meet its monthly commitments to the state. The food situation became "desperate" in the middle of June, and *The Statesman* put the blame on the right culprit: "It is the West Bengal government itself which is primarily responsible for the present crisis." In the cabinet the Communists were sharply critical of the policy of the food minister, who threatened to resign in July but was persuaded by Mukherji not to.[19]

In the absence of an effective food policy of its own, the government could only look to the central government; its tactics from now on were to blame New Delhi for "starving" the people of West Bengal as a punishment for their rejection of Congress rule. The cabinet, at its meeting of July 1, apparently decided to build up a confrontation with the central government over the food question, which suited the Communists very well. New Delhi admitted its failure to send the committed monthly quota to Bengal; in fact, it was obliged to cut the supply of rice to all the states by nearly 20 percent.[20]

The Bengal cabinet decided to carry the battle to New Delhi. It warned the central government early in August that a "grave threat to law and order" existed in the countryside of Bengal, and the situation "might go beyond the state government's control" if

---

[18] *Ibid.*, April 27 and July 27, 1967.   [19] *Amrita Bazar Patrika,* July 5, 1967.
[20] *Hindustan Standard,* July 2 and 5, 1967.

the central government did not increase Bengal's monthly quota by 10,000 tons of wheat.[21] Mukherji, Ghosh, and Basu journeyed to New Delhi to talk to the prime minister and other ministers. They came back with an "assurance of goodwill" but no grain.

The cabinet then made a startling decision. At least eight ministers would stage a *dharna* (sit-in) outside the prime minister's house in New Delhi if the state government's demand for 10,000 tons of extra wheat per month was not met. Six ministers arrived in the capital on August 22 to start the *dharna,* but the crisis was resolved at "a gruelling round of talks" between them, the prime minister, and the central food minister, and Bengal was promised 105,000 tons of wheat, barley, and milo in August. On August 23, the united front government organized a one-day general strike in West Bengal to "strengthen the campaign against hoarders and black marketers, to expose the conspiracies of the Congress and the reactionaries, and to protest against the central government's policy of denying West Bengal's legitimate demand for food." [22]

Apparently the serious differences over food policy deeply undermined the cohesion of the united front in the summer of 1967 because the coalition no longer worked as a team. The state Congress party was stirring back to life. Within the coalition there were elements ready to respond to these stirrings. However, of much greater divisive consequence was the two fundamentally different concepts of how the united front was to function. Mukherji, Ghosh, and several others believed that the partners should set aside their respective ideologies and maintain "pro-

---

[21] *Ibid.,* August 10, 1967. Violence did occur in rural Bengal over the food shortage. In Nabadwip, Nadia district, a violent crowd attacked a police station, raided petrol pumps, uprooted rails and cut telephone wires and food demonstrators were dispersed by the police who fired, killing two and injuring eight. *The Statesman,* August 13, 1967.

[22] *The Statesman,* August 11, 12, 15, 22 and 23, 1967. *Hindusthan Standard,* August 23, 24, 25, 1967. The "sit-in" threat by Bengal ministers was not entirely novel. In 1958 the Communist ministers of Kerala organized a "sit-in" before the prime minister's residence in New Delhi. Such protest teachniques in India claim legitimacy from the Gandhian concept of *Satyagraha.*

grammatic unity." [23] The Communists and their allies took an entirely different view; in any case, they would not separate the program from the ideology that shaped it.

The first open fissures in the united front occurred in June when five Bangla Congress members defected to the Congress party. "In an unprecedented demonstration of mass anger," reported *The Statesman,* "a large number of people *gheraoed* [encircled] the West Bengal Assembly for over six hours [on June 26], demanding the resignation of the five [defectors]." About a month later, the united front failed to get one of its two nominees elected to the upper house of the state legislature; his Congress rival won, evidently with the support of several united front voters. [24]

Of much greater import for the future of the coalition was the growing coolness between Mukherji and Basu. In July, when Mukherji was in Delhi talking with the president, the prime minister, and the home minister, Basu brought about a masterly *coup de grâce* by announcing the government's decision to take over the Calcutta tramways. The matter had been brought to a head by the British company's directors in London, who suddenly informed the government that the company was unable to meet its payroll unless it could increase the fares. Basu, as deputy chief minister and minister for transport, hit back with a decision that was at once popular and energetic. The cabinet gave its endorsement and the central government lost no time in approving the united front government's bill bringing the tramways under public control, but Mukherji could not help expressing his resentment that Basu should have taken such a major decision without consulting him. [25]

---

[23] This was the argument put forward by Ghosh. See *The Statesman* editorial "In Cold Storage," June 5, 1967.

[24] *Ibid.,* June 27 and July 23, 1967.

[25] *Ibid.,* July 5, 6, 8, 10, 11, 15, 17, 18 and 20, 1967.

Mukherji now waited for an opportunity to show Basu that he, not Basu, was chief minister. Basu, as finance minister, set up a pay commission in late July to recommend revisions in the pay-scales of government employees, and appointed members to the commission apparently without the concurrence of the chief minister. Mukherji stopped publication of the list in the official gazette. In August, differences in the united front cabinet appeared to be "heading toward a rift." [26]

LAND AND THE LANDLESS

The coalition's land policy took time to evolve. The common program promised nothing beyond gradual, incremental benefit for the rural poor. Konar, who was CPI(M) minister for land and land revenue, did not begin with any explicit commitment of government support for "legitimate" peasant militancy. His main problem in the spring of 1967 was how to control the militancy of peasants in areas where the food protests of the year before had activized and politically mobilized sizable numbers of the rural poor.

One such area was Naxalbari, in northern Bengal, where peasants rebelled against landlords, under the leadership of an extremist wing of the CPI(M). This uprising showed how sensitive and explosive the land problem was in West Bengal, but Konar presumably was not prepared to launch a militant movement without adequate preparation at both governmental and organizational levels. The prompt support of the Naxalbari uprising by the CCP created a critical problem for the CPI(M) for which it was evidently not at all prepared. But for Peking backing, the Naxalbari rebellion might have provided Konar with the kind of mass support he was obviously looking for before he could initiate a militant land policy. The emergence of the "Naxalbari path," blessed by the Chinese as the only true path to the Indian revolution, created for the CPI(M) an ideological-organizational

[26] *Ibid.*, August 6, 1967.

problem which it had to settle before Konar could embark upon a militant land policy.

Konar's main problem in the spring and summer of 1967 was to get an accurate estimate of the land that had been misappropriated by the landlords over and above of the 25-acre ceiling imposed by the land "reform" measures in the 1950s. That this misappropriation had been done on a large scale was well known. The ceiling was imposed not on a family, but on an individual registered as a single unit. Many landlords had taken advantage of this provision to keep all the land they had before the "reforms"; they had only to split the land among individual members of a joint family, and often "register" land in the names of individuals who did not exist. However, each document filed with revenue officials had the appearance of legality, and it was no mean job to find out which land was fraudulently held. The search for *benami* land (land registered under false names) therefore was time-consuming.

Nor was it much easier to recover all the *khas* land (land belonging to the government). Until the beginning of 1959, the Congress government had "obtained" 125,000 acres of *khas* land as a result of agrarian "reforms." This land was allowed to remain with the landlords. Three or four years later, it was discovered that most of the 600,000 acres that might have been obtained by the imposition of the 25-acre limit had "disappeared." [27] Among those responsible for the disappearance were tea plantation owners in north Bengal, and some of the leading landlord families, including ministers during Congress rule. Konar's investigations revealed startling instances of land cheating, one of which was reported in *The Statesman.*

There are cases where landlords have realized several *lakhs* of rupees as compensation from the government without losing an inch of land from the hundreds of acres they boast of.

[27] Bhowani Sen, *Evolution of Agrarian Relations in India* (New Delhi, PPH, 1962), p. 202.

A typical case, recently unearthed, relates to a *zamindar,* formerly a minister who, jointly with his brother, owned over 1,000 acres before the [Land Reform] Act came into force in April 1955. Apparently he had come to know well in advance that the legislation would be introduced; the joint property was then first transferred under the *ryotari* [direct tenancy] arrangements among five sons of one of the brothers who, in turn, distributed part of their land among their wives and children and sub-*ryots.* Among the *benamdars* [tenants with false names] were also servants of the family and others.

Since such distribution of land covered less than half of the total holding, 534 acres of the farming land were declared fisheries, although the land was being used for farming.

As the Act came into force, both the sub-*ryots* and *ryots* (who were mostly members of the family) started paying rent directly to the government. As the original owners of the land—the two brothers and the *ryots* (i.e., five sons) were entitled to compensation from the government. They received Rs 700,000 [about $100,000] as compensation while retaining within the family's possession whatever land they owned originally.[28]

By the end of July, Konar appeared to have drawn up the broad framework of a land policy that included controlled peasant militant action. "The primary task" he wrote in a brief article in a left-wing weekly, was "abolition of large-scale holdings and distribution of land to the landless. The next step would be for the government to explain to the peasants the disadvantages of small holdings. The peasants will then voluntarily take to collective farming. Private ownership of land will thus be done away with." [29] In accomplishing the "primary task," Konar was meeting with obstacles. "The machinery of the Government cannot carry out land reforms even though there are honest officers in the administration. The efforts of the administration have to be strengthened and supplemented by the conscious and organized participation of the peasants and the people at large."

[28] *The Statesman,* April 5, 1968. The West Bengal government paid Rs 1.40 crore (almost $7 million) to compensate the landlords. Sen, p. 238.
[29] H. Konar, "Our Land Problem," *Mainstream,* July 29, 1967, p. 25.

In the spring and summer of 1967, the CPI(M) leadership was evidently more concerned about food procurement in West Bengal and Kerala than about a radical agrarian policy. In May, Sundarayya asked the three Marxist ministers in the Bengal government to press the party viewpoint on food procurement with greater vigor. If necessary they should openly criticize parties and ministers who might adopt a pro-rich-peasant attitude.[30] The politbureau, meeting in May, issued a note on the food situation in Bengal and Kerala, accusing the central government of "political discrimination" against the two states. The note, however, had nothing to say about agrarian reforms.[31]

The first clear indication that the party was evolving an agrarian policy came in August, when the Bengal state committee of the party met for four days apparently to prepare for the session of the central committee held later in the month. The committee blamed the chief minister and the food minister for their "failure" to carry out the "main directive" of the common program on the food problem. The committee demanded radical land reforms and decided to support the struggle of the *kisans* for distribution of land to the landless and for stopping the eviction of sharecroppers.[32] This tactical line was approved at the Madurai session of the CPI(M) central committee, which gave a radical direction to the party's activity in Bengal as well as in Kerala. Both Namboodiripad and Basu came in for criticism. While they had taken the "correct stand" on all major issues, "they should have taken a firmer stand to overcome the resistance of others" on the basic question of grain procurement.

LABOR CONFRONTATIONS: THE
TECHNIQUE OF GHERAO

The brief regime of the first united front in Bengal will probably be remembered for two symbolic phrases with which it en-

[30] *The Statesman,* May 21, 1967.   [31] *Hindustan Standard,* May 21, 1967.
[32] *The Statesman,* August 5, 1967.

riched India's indigenous political vocabulary. The first is "Naxalbari," which has come to connote anything resembling violent
populist anarchism. The second is *gherao,* which symbolized
working-class militancy. If urban working-class unrest was conspicuous in Bengal in 1967, there was very good reason for it.

The slump in the economy after 1965 had hit the engineering
and allied industries in the Calcutta metropolitan area more than
any other major organized industry in India. Retrenchments were
postponed by the general body of employers in 1966 largely because they did not wish to make things difficult for the Congress
regime in an election year. As soon as the election results were
out, lay-offs began on a large scale. The laboring force was already
feeling the pinch of inflation and rising prices, and the lay-offs increased its resentment and anger. But this was only one of the several reasons for the working-class upsurge.

The workers' deep resentment against the pattern of industrial
relations had been growing for two decades. The industrial relations machinery in India operates at two levels. At the enterprise
level, there exist such arrangements as works committees, griev-
ance committees, joint consultative machinery, and collective bargaining. At the government level, there is the fourfold machinery
of conciliation, court of inquiry, arbitration, and adjudication.
There are also nonstatutory forums like the Indian Labor Conference, the Standing Labor Committee, and so on.[33] The government machinery has failed, if not on any other count, on the
grounds of the delay it entails.

This is a real dilemma of Rule of Law in a democratic set-up. Full opportunities have to be given to the parties in a dispute to prove their
case up to the level of the Supreme Court. In normal circumstances,
the time lag between raising a dispute and the pronouncement of the
highest court of the land is at least four years, which means more

---

[33] G. K. Sharma, *Labour Movement in India* (Delhi, University Publishers, 1963),
ch. 10; S. A. Dange, *Crisis and Workers* (Bombay, AITUC, 1959); V. B. Karnik,
Strikes in India (Bombay, Manaktala, 1967).

hardship to the employees than to the employers. Not only are the two parties denied vindication of their cause for a long time, but there is frustration at not getting the opportunity to resolve the issues at the first opportunity." [34]

Legalism in industrial relations has bred a sense of instability, "a burning desire to defeat the system by a shortcut method of 'quick justice.' "

Another factor that has contributed to the explosive situation is the intense rivalry among the four major trade-union federations. The installation of the united front government gave an unprecedented fillip to the movement for registration of trade unions. Between March and September 1967, 591 trade unions were registered, 170 of these belonging to the CPI(M) and 140 to the CPI. Given the long-standing unresolved grievances of the workers, it was inevitable that the political parties would take advantage of the changed political situation to resort to militancy in order to compete for the loyalty of a restive and distressed working class.

The technique that the workers employed to get quick justice was called *gherao,* which is comparable to the techniques used by students in some American universities to take over buildings or surround presidents and other administrative officers for the redress of their grievances. A special bench of the Calcutta high court defined *gherao* as "the physical blockage of a target, either by encirclement or forcible occupation. The target may be a place or a person or persons, usually the managerial or supervisory staff of an industrial establishment. The blockade may be complete or partial." [35]

The "creative genius" behind *gherao* was Labor Minister Banerji, leader of the Socialist Unity Center, who claimed to be

[34] Nitish R. De and Suresh Srivastava, "Gheraos in West Bengal—II," *Economic and Political Weekly,* November 29, 1967, p. 2062. This study, in four parts, is the best made so far of the *gherao* movement in Bengal. For less reliable and more value-oriented approaches, see Govinda Lall Banerji, *Gherao* (Calcutta, Mukhopadhaya, 1969); Irani, pp. 57–86.
[35] Cited in De and Srivastava.

more revolutionary than the CPI(M). The Marxists did not originate the movement, nor did they disown it; what they did was to
use the advantages of industrial dislocation to enlarge their hold
on unionized workers. The SUC's trade-union base was relatively
weak, but even such unions as were under its control took no part
in *gherao*. It was a somewhat Gandhian-anarchist movement.
"There was apparently no prior planning by the federated trade
unions to resort to *gherao* in industries. There was no evidence
that the more militant trade union associations like AITUC and
UTUC (United Trade Union Congress) made any concerted attempt at intimidation of managements by the *gherao* movement."

It was somewhat peculiar that Banerji's *gherao* tactics met with
Chief Minister Mukherji's sympathetic approval at least in the initial stages, while Konar's bid to use the poor peasants for generat-
ing a climate for land reforms did not. Between March and August 1967, there were 1,018 cases of *gherao* in 503 establishments.
Of the incidents that occurred, 85 percent were in the districts of
Calcutta, 24-Parganas, Howrah, and Burdwan, Calcutta leading
with 363 cases. The typical *gherao* was the "physical blockade" of
managerial or supervisory staff of industrial establishments, but
there were atypical cases too in which students, neighborhood res-
idents, tenants, hawkers, and office employees used the technique
to seek redress of long-felt grievances.[36]

In a way, the *gherao* movement came to symbolize social conflict in urban India. As a mode of confrontation between authority and the governed and as a tool of intervention to resolve social
conflict, it had some potential because of its claim of legitimacy in
the Gandhian *satyagraha* (nonviolent resistance and protest).
However, this potential remained severely limited because *gherao*
did not spread beyond West Bengal and, to some extent, Kerala;
a few attempted *gheraos* in Maharashtra were quickly broken up
by the police.

[36] *Ibid.*, p. 2022.

The Congress regime in Delhi was adamantly opposed. The *gherao* found no favor with those non-Congress ministries in office in a number of states. At a session of the Indian Labor Conference in New Delhi in May, labor ministers from all non-Congress states, excepting Kerala, opposed *gherao,* which found supporters only among the Communists. Banerji made a stout defense of his labor policy, and stressed that *gherao* was not a cause of industrial conflict but an "inevitable" result of the Congress party's labor policy. He was in a hopeless minority. The Conference adopted a resolution disapproving "coercive and intimidatory tactics," including *gherao,* in resolving industrial disputes, whereupon Dange staged an angry walk-out.[37]

Home Minister Chavan carried the war into the enemy's camp when, presiding over the Eastern Zonal Council meeting in Calcutta on May 19, he expressed New Delhi's deep concern over industrial unrest in West Bengal and warned against any "further erosion of the rule of law." *Gherao,* said Chavan, was "no longer an isolated spontaneous demonstration of a brief duration. It has created fear and a sense of insecurity." Chavan was thus able to confuse the Bengal government's perspective of *gherao;* it was more than an industrial conflict; it was a threat to the rule of law, to social order, and to cohesion. The Communists alone protested Chavan's remarks and his "intervention" in Bengal's internal affairs. In the Lok Sabha, Gopalan described *gherao* as "a new version of peaceful picketing" and as a "form of militant struggle" in the same breath, but he knew he was speaking to an unresponsive house.[38]

When the issue came up at the All-India Congress Committee

---

[37] *The Statesman,* May 11, 1967. Banerji described the resolution as "meaningless." He disclosed that some of the state governments had taken a dismal view of the enhancement of the cost-of-living allowance of Bengal government employees. *Ibid.,* May 12, 1967.

[38] *Ibid.,* May 20, 30, and June 28, 1967. The Union Home Ministry passed orders making *gherao* by Union government employees illegal. In the upper house, Bhupesh Gupta defended *gherao,* backed by several other Communists.

session in New Delhi in June, Darbara Singh, of Punjab, introduced a new element into the controversy. *Gherao* did not stem from the present economic difficulties, but from the strategic location of Bengal, he declared. The same people who had been ready to "welcome" the Chinese invaders in 1962 were "raising their heads" again, while the West Bengal government seemed to be oblivious of the danger. Congressmen from Bengal saw in *gherao* a political movement designed to undermine the economy of the state.[39]

Industry in Bengal took full advantage of this denunciation of *gherao,* and refused to make concessions to the workers unless forced to do so. At several joint conferences of representatives of industry and labor, convened by the united front government, the former rejected the latter's demand for a year's, or a half-year's, moratorium on lay-offs. Within the united front government itself differences arose soon after Chavan's visit to Calcutta. Mukherji himself appeared to have lost some of his initial enthusiasm for the movement after he had had a long talk with the central government's home minister. Instruction given in March to the police authorities about nonintervention were modified, and the police were told to act in certain cases of proven coercion and distress to managerial and supervisory personnel. By the time the high court declared *gherao* illegal, the united front government was more relieved than frustrated.[40]

The *gherao* movement, however, left an impact on unionized working-class politics in West Bengal. The movement provided a

---

[39] *Ibid.,* June 26, 1967.

[40] *Ibid.,* June 4, May 5, 1967. The chief justice who delivered the judgment declared that while a *gherao* was not an offense as such, if it was accompanied by restraint or confinement, assault, criminal trespass, mischief to person or property, unlawful assembly, or other criminal offenses, used as coercive measures, it was "unconstitutional and violative of the laws of the land."

The state government revoked the orders restricting police intervention in "legitimate trade union activity." It set up machinery for periodical review of all labor disputes and to work out a mutually acceptable basis for settlement of the issues in dispute.

"blood and sweat" program of apprenticeship to the grass-root level trade-union leaders.

On the one hand, the "local" leaders who are part and parcel (physically and psychologically) of the employees of an enterprise have moved, through this movement, from a state of "adolescence" to a state of "adulthood" in their relationship with the "national" leaders (professional politicians who have taken the reins of a number of trade unions in a region). The bureaucratic control of the "nationals" have, in fact, been challenged by the "locals." By confronting the managerial elite, the locals have in effect confronted their elders and mentors, the "nationals." The movement is, in some sense, an assault on the trade-union oligarchy.[41]

Gheraos brought about constant flux in intertrade-union relations. In 1967, enterprise-level *gheraos* were sought to integrate workers emotionally and physically so as to orient them toward leftist ideology. During this period the two Communist parties often worked together, and there was evidence that they succeeded in achieving their objective to an extent.

In 1969, however, this unity gave way to intense organizational rivalry. The aim this time was to create a different kind of orientation. The Marxists were in a dominant position in the 1969 united front government, and the CPI was afraid of losing its industrial base in the metropolitan area. The two parties, as well as other leftist groups, now sought to use *gheraos* to establish their respective superiority and hegemony among the politically organized and militant workers. Apparently the Marxists believed that they had gained at the cost of the CPI and other leftist groups. That is the main reason why they broke away from AITUC to set up their separate Calcutta-based Central Trade Union Congress in 1970.[42]

[41] Nitish R. De, "Gherao as a Technique for Social Intervention," *Economic and Political Weekly: Annual Number,* January 1970, pp. 201–8.

[42] The *gherao* movement stirred the central labor ministry to a fresh examination of the existing practices of registration of trade unions and reference of disputes to arbitration and adjudication and for implementation of judicial awards. *The Statesman,* June 4, 1967. The Bengal government brought forward several

THE CONGRESS PARTY TOPPLES
THE UNITED FRONT

The food, land, and labor policies of the united front government did, then, generate considerable tension in the social and economic life of West Bengal, within the coalition itself, and between the coalition and the central government. The cumulative impact of these tensions loosened the determination of the constituents to keep the coalition intact. However, neither the Congress party nor the central government had the patience to wait for the coalition to disintegrate by itself.

Congress party maneuvers to bring down non-Congress governments in the states began in June, but without immediate success. Attempts to induce members of the ruling groups in Punjab, Uttar Pradesh, and Haryana to "cross the floor" led to equally unprincipled but more successful moves on the part of these groups to buy additional support for the coalitions with the offer of ministerial jobs.[43]

In West Bengal, the Congress party was of "two minds." One group, encouraged by five defections from the united front, wanted to challenge the coalition's majority in the assembly, while the other preferred to wait until the front's image was sufficiently tarnished. The former group, which related to the Congress high command as well as to Governor Dharam Vira, believed that consolidation of the united front government would

pieces of legislation to improve upon the central legislations for compensation of disabled workers and workers' overtime wages. These legislations were passed by the state legislature and sent to the central government for the President's consent. Consent, however, was withheld and the legislations were sent back to the government for revision.

The Marxist reaction to the high court order came from Konar. "I make no comment on the judgment. As I read it in a newspaper this morning I was reminded of Lenin's theoretical proposition that 'in a class society, justice also is class justice.' " Mr. Konar said he hoped that "people would realize the truth of the statement through experience." *Ibid.*, October 1, 1967.

[43] "Topplers Toppled," editorial, *The Statesman*, June 22, 1967. For a study of the malaise of defection of footloose legislators, see Subhas C. Kashyap, *The Politics of Defection: A Study of State Politics in India* (Delhi, National Publishers, 1969).

mean "virtually the extension of the sphere of influence of the Marxist Communist Party"; this argument appeared to find confirmation in the sweeping Marxist victories in the municipal elections held in Bengal in early summer.[44]

At this juncture, the initiative to scuttle the coalition shifted to the Congress high command in New Delhi and to the governor's mansion in Calcutta. Four men apparently played crucial roles in ousting the united front regime: Gulzarilal Nanda, who followed the Congress high command; Governor Dharam Vira, who was presumably working with the approval, if not under the instruction, of the Union Home Ministry; Humayun Kabir, who was now determined to replace the united front with a coalition minus the Marxists; and P. C. Ghosh, whose Gandhian abhorrence for coercion was now matched by a desire to see himself installed as Bengal's chief minister.

From Delhi, Nanda came to Calcutta in September with a plan to replace the provincial Congress committee by an "ad hoc" committee. The real objective of his plan was to bring Ajoy K. Mukherji back to the Congress fold. Governor Dharam Vira arranged a meeting between himself, Mukherji, Kabir, and Bengal's defeated Congress chief minister, Prafulla Sen. At this meeting Mukherji was offered chief ministership of a Congress-led coalition that would exclude the Marxists, if not the CPI also.

The united front government seemed to be finished on October 2; Mukherji was holding himself incommunicado, while an announcement was made on his behalf that the ministry would continue to function "at least tomorrow," and Kabir told reporters that "it is certain that Mr. Mukherji will resign." On October 3, "desperate political activity" went on in two different directions until late in the night. One was to save the ministry led by

---

[44] *The Statesman,* June 2, 1967. In the elections, the Congress party lost control of most of the municipalities, including those in Howrah and Asansol. "Leftist parties have done uniformly better in the municipal elections than in the general election just over three months ago." Editorial, *ibid.,* June 1, 1967.

Ajoy Mukherji, even without the participation of Communists and other allied parties, and the other was to form an alternative government to be headed by P. C. Ghosh. The Congress party was apparently willing to join either coalition. The Communists, anxious to keep the Congress party out of power, offered to quit the united front coalition but to lend it support if Mukherji would form a ministry without the Congress party. Meanwhile a sizable rebellion broke out within Bangla Congress; some twenty legislators decided to "disown" Mukherji for conducting "secret negotiations" with the Congress party "for the last two months" to topple the united front government.[45]

On October 4, Mukherji staged an about-face and announced his decision *not* to resign. In a remarkably frank confession at a cabinet meeting, he admitted that he had held secret negotiations with the Congress party on the possibility of forming an alternative government with Congress support. What he did not disclose was what made him change his mind.

The reason for his temporary vacillation was that "he had intelligence reports to show that the left Communists [Marxists] were up to a dangerous game in West Bengal; he had been informed that they were smuggling arms into West Bengal. It would be against his creed and faith to continue to be with them in the same cabinet." Next day Mukherji issued a statement announcing that the united front government would continue; apparently he had been able to wring certain concessions from the Marxist ministers, who offered him their unconditional cooperation.[46] The only minister who did not attend the cabinet meeting where differences were "resolved" was P. C. Ghosh.

Tensions in the coalition continued. Jehangir Kabir threatened to resign. The CPI(M) demanded a mid-term election. A Bangla

[45] *Ibid.*, October 3 and 4, 1967. *Hindusthan Standard* October 2, 3, 4, 1967; *Times of India*, October 3, 1967.

[46] *The Statesman*, October 5 and 6, 1967. The chief minister did not make it clear whether the intelligence reports had come from the state police or from the central home ministry.

Congress member resigned only to return to the party in three days. About a week later, seventeen legislators defected from the united front to form a coalition with the Congress party; their leader was Ghosh.

Governor Dharam Vira asked the chief minister to convene a session of the assembly by November 21 to test the majority of the united front party, but Mukherji wanted more time. The governor dismissed the united front ministry on November 21 on the ground that it had lost the support of a majority of the legislators. The governor's action was protested the next day by one of the largest public demonstrations ever held in Calcutta. It was broken up by the police with considerable brutality. At a large rally in the *maidan,* several united front leaders, government officials only two days before, were severely beaten by the police.[47]

Ghosh now formed a new government first with the support, then the participation, of the Congress party. However, when the assembly met on November 29, the speaker refused to recognize the legality of the new government and prorogued the house. While this created a first-class constitutional crisis from which the pundits of the central government's law ministry now tried to find a way out, a group of Congress party legislators revolted, depriving the new coalition of a majority in the legislature. Thus within some three weeks West Bengal had the taste of four governments—the united front, the minority Ghosh government, the Ghosh-Congress coalition, and Governor's rule. In the com-

[47] The following report was published in *Yugantar,* a Bengali daily owned by a former Congress minister of Bengal: "The mounted police rush towards the jeep (which brought the united front leaders to the venue of the meeting announced prior to the dismissal of the ministry) and drive the crowd from its vicinity. Simultaneously, *lathi* police (police armed with sticks) fall upon the leaders and the others in the jeep. The jeep is smashed. . . . Under the *lathi* blows, the former law minister starts bleeding profusely from the head. Arun Babu (leader of the Gandhian Lok Sevak Sangh) receives a severe blow on the arm. Biswanath Babu (former Irrigation minister and younger brother of Ajoy Mukherji) . . . and other leaders are also injured. Their companions get no respite when they fall to the ground under the police blows. They are subjected to assaults without respite. However, within 10 to 15 minutes the assaulting police forces leave the place." Quoted in *Economic and Political Weekly,* December 2, 1967, p. 2082.

plete impasse thus created, Dharam Vira had no other alternative but to dissolve the legislature and impose President's rule on West Bengal.[48]

The bizarre events of October–November seemed to signify a deep crisis in the non- and anti-Communist forces in Bengal. Almost all of the non-Communist parties and groups were torn by internal dissensions. The Bangla Congress party proved to be as fragile as the Congress party itself; hardly any "leader" remained who did not try to give Bengal an anti- or non-Communist government. The civil service also appeared to be divided—some senior officers reportedly helped the governor to topple the united front regime. The central government's antipathy toward the united front government in Bengal was clearly revealed. What was worse was the apparent lack of unity in the central Congress leadership as well as in the central cabinet.[49]

The day the united front government was dismissed, the army was alerted for action in the event of a major threat to the peace. Spokesmen of organized industry came out openly in support of a

[48] Romesh Thapar blamed the united front rather than the central government for the dismissal of the Mukherji cabinet. The main fault of the central government, he said, was that it did not exercise "greater patience." The Marxists' tactics were "to compel the Center to throw out the government." *Economic and Political Weekly,* November 18, 1967.

[49] "This reporter's firm belief is that the role of some officials has been very murky ever since the united front government entered the Writers' Building. They had an ally in Governor Dharam Vira, a former ICS official of moderate competence who always knew which side his bread was buttered on. The whole gang, Chief Secretary M. M. Basu, the inspector-general of police, Upananda Mukherji, and some other officials mildly punished by the united front government had excellent allies in L. P. Singh, union home secretary, and S. P. Verma, director of the intelligence bureau. Whether General Maneckshaw, the regional army chief, was equally involved is not very clear. What, therefore, looks like a Congress political coup may well have been engineered by the faceless bureaucracy." Flibbertigibbet's "Calcutta Diary," *Economic and Political Weekly,* December 2, 1967.

Flibbertigibbet who happens to be a leading journalist-intellectual of Bengal, and works as a writer on *The Statesman,* articulated the Bengali's wounded chauvinism when he wrote: "The unimportance of West Bengal has been emphasized often enough. The ruins around New Delhi are surely points to another possibility."

S. K. Patil openly opposed the Nanda plan for the Bengal Congress. Romesh Thapar, in his column in *Economic and Political Weekly* (Nov. 18), gave the impression that Indira Gandhi was less in favor of dismissing the united front government than were some of her cabinet colleagues.

non-Communist coalition. The British spokesman of the Indian Engineering Association, a joint body of British and Indian interests representing about 200 engineering establishments in West Bengal, hinted at direct participation in state politics "to help the parties in the government which wanted to restore law and order." It was reported that the sixteen legislators who defected from the Congress party and thus brought down the Ghosh ministry did so as soon as the government decided to impose a levy on the food stocks of the richer peasants.[50]

MARXIST REACTION

The Marxists saw the crisis as an "open and growing confrontation" between the capitalistic and socialistic forces in India which, unless checked by a complete reversal of policies being pursued by the Congress party, "might conceivably lead to a civil war." In putting forward this perspective, a Marxist economist of Bengal, Ashok Rudra, saw no future for the Congress party in the state at all, just as it had also none in Kerala. "If the peoples of these two states more and more overwhelmingly cling to the socialist programs of the Communist parties, the question naturally arises: how long would peoples of these states continue to tolerate a state of affairs which prevents them from carrying out their socialistic programs in their own states? How long would they tolerate a Centre that would more and more autocratically impose upon them a capitalistic order?"

Rudra evidently did not regard India as a single political entity, but as a federation of several states whose autonomy the central government could not keep forever under control. The idea of a civil war, he hastened to add, appeared to be "remote and unreal" at this point, especially in view of the huge concentration of

[50] *Economic and Political Weekly,* December 7, 1967.

economic and military power in the central government. Yet, given the continental scale of Indian politics, "how long can this authoritarian rule by one part over another continue?"

Rudra offered a somewhat ingenious class interpretation of the crisis in the Congress party. "If it is accepted as a plausible hypothesis that the Congress party represents the class interests of the two ruling classes of this country, the class of industrial monopoly capitalists and the class of rich peasants, then an analysis of the economic crisis that has engulfed the country during the last five years could show that the alliance between the two classes has been under very great strain." The failure of the rich peasantry, despite all the benefits it had received from governmental projects and financial aid, to increase agricultural output had made the industrial capitalist class "doubt the capacity of the rich peasantry to make agriculture grow at a rate at which it has to grow if industry is to grow at a rate at which industrial capitalists can make it grow."

Underproduction in agriculture had caused a slump in industrial production and profit. "Industrial capitalists have been talking about intervening directly in agriculture; they are looking hopefully to the as yet incipient class of modern capitalist gentlemen farmers. There is no interlocking of economic interests between the monopoly capitalists in industry and the rich peasantry in the countryside; the alliance is a purely political one. The importance of the rich peasantry lies in the dominant position it enjoys in the rural sector. It is its members who procure the rural Congress votes. The question that is facing the monopoly capitalists is: is it possible to break the alliance with the rich peasantry, to divert state patronage from them to the new class of gentlemen capitalist farmers without losing political hold over the country?"

The monopoly capitalists, Rudra continued, faced another crisis: "they have been under relentless pressure from their other class ally, American monopoly capital." The strategy of Indian monopoly capital during the post-independence period was to develop with the help of both American and Soviet capital, "but as a capitalist force in its own right." However, the aid-giving Western countries had been increasingly attacking the independence of Indian monopoly capitalists. "The game is up—the game of Indian monopoly capital to grow without doing anything to generate surpluses within the country, hiding its real class interests behind a facade of socialism meant for the Russians and a facade of the parliamentary democratic alternative to the Chinese revolution meant for the Americans. . . . The monopoly capitalists of India, subject to simultaneous attack from two sides by their most important class allies, are in utter disarray." [51]

THE NEW MARXIST PARLIAMENTARY LINE

The year 1968 witnessed a statewide mass movement against President's rule in West Bengal and for a mid-term election. Drawing upon the experience of this struggle and also in the light of the events of the preceding year, the CPI(M) evolved in 1968 a tactical line that was more militant than the one pursued so far. The central committee of the party, at its Madurai session, was confronted with three major developments in India and outside.

The first was the peasant rebellion at Naxalbari, and its quick "adoption" by the Chinese Communist Party as a Maoist-type revolutionary beginning in India. In rejecting peasant insurgency as unsuitable under Indian conditions, the party moved toward peasant militancy as the principal instrument by which it could identify itself firmly with the rural and urban poor.

The second development was the Congress party's decision to disrupt non-Congress governments in the states and, wherever possible, to form coalitions either under Congress leadership or with Congress participation. The Marxists' response to this Congress political offensive was a more militant parliamentary policy, combining parliamentary and extraparliamentary struggles to win tactical victories.

[51] Ashok Rudra, "End of the Honeymoon," *ibid.*, December 9, 1967.

The third factor was the extreme fluidity in bourgeois politics, making all coalitions highly instable. At Madurai, the Marxists resolved to adopt a militant line within the coalitions, even risking their disruption. In other words, the CPI(M) decided that it would not be in the interest of the party to make concessions to the various leftist groups at the cost of its basic policies and principles.

The theoretical framework of the new parliamentary tactic was formulated by Namboodiripad in a series of articles in the Malayalee journal of the party, *Deshabhimani,* in the summer of 1968. These articles, however, also threw interesting light on inner-party conflicts in the CPI(M). The Kerala chief minister admitted candidly that differences within the top leadership over major issues were not uncommon, but he claimed that these were almost always resolved through "criticism and self-criticism." Attempts by the party's opponents to divide the leadership between moderates and extremists were therefore nothing but "meaningless propaganda." The all-India leadership of the party "functions with much stronger unity than any other party in India." However, Namboodiripad confessed that there existed within the party a dissident group whose strength he placed at 20 percent of the membership.[52] The dissidents apparently favored a more militant line than the leadership was prepared to sanction.

It seems that the militant parliamentary tactic that Namboodiripad articulated was a compromise between the leadership and the more radical dissidents. The line represented a more "dynamic" and "revolutionary" approach to united fronts as well as to relations with the central government. "It is as important to form the non-Congress united front," affirmed Namboodiripad, "as it is to clearly state the independent stand of the party on basic issues on which there are differences with the constituent units including the Rightists (that is, the CPI)."

[52] What Namboodiripad wrote was: "Thus the CPI(M) has a political line which has been adopted with the support of 80 percent of the party membership."

The Marxists apparently were now trying to apply to India some of the coalition tactics used by Mao Tse-tung in the 1940s, for Namboodiripad referred approvingly to the CCP stand: "A coalition government if possible; civil war, if necessary." For the Marxists, participation in a coalition meant combining "administration and agitation." Agitation was important in terms of both state politics and state-central government relations. Experience had shown that "ideological conflicts will take place inside the [United] Front. It is also clear that they cannot be confined to the four corners of the united front."

The Marxist tactics would be, first and foremost, to maintain the united front; a "wrong tendency had begun to raise its head inside the Party, the tendency to disrupt the united front itself and sacrificing the election gains of the people in the name of correcting the mistake of abandoning the ideological struggle inside the united front." At the same time, the CPI(M) could not betray the revolutionary working-class movement; the "bourgeois-petty-bourgeois ideology" of the CPI and other left groups made it all the more necessary for the Marxists to "expose" the dangers inherent in the ideology of the non-Marxist left. The most important conflict within the united front concerned the two Communist factions; "their [CPI's] principle that administration and agitation cannot go together, their insistence that only after the Kerala government has accomplished certain specific things can the struggle against the Centre be launched, their approach to food, industrial, and labor policies—it is all this that forces them to take a stand against the CPI(M). Their attacks on the CPI(M) is only a part of this basic conflict in ideology."

The Marxists had to perform the difficult talk of carrying on the ideological struggle within the united front without exposing it to disruption. "This means not only that no party either on its own leaves the front or others oust any party from it. The Party is emphatic that the method of discussion and struggle should be such as to help the united front as a whole to reach a commonly acceptable position." The tone of the Namboodiripad articles suggested, however, that while the Marxists would go a long way to maintain the united front, they were not to compromise "struggle" for the sake of "unity."

The most important aspect of "struggle" was the conflict between the bourgois–landlord-dominated central government and the states controlled by coalitions in which the Marxists had a dominant position. "The position today is that in a fully centralized state, as a result of the policies evolved and pursued by the bourgeois-feudal ruling classes, it is impossible for the government of any state to find solutions to the basic problems confronting that state."

It was therefore essential that the state governments exerted pressure on the central government to change its policies. "But there are elements inside the united front who, the moment they hear about struggle against the central government, become afraid or get worked up and abuse the CPI(M) for stating this truth." These elements, when they were compelled by circumstances to stand up to the central government, were unwilling to support "struggles organized by the CPI(M) alone." Inherent in this attitude were two political and psychological factors: their fear of the central government or their basic community of interests with those who rule at the national level and, second, their fear of the CPI(M). The Marxist party was therefore forced by circumstances and by its own ideology to lead and constantly feed the "revolutionary" struggle against central government policies.[53]

The new parliamentary tactical line was put into operation by the CPI(M) during the "mass struggle" in Bengal in 1968, and later, in 1969–70, when the party was the dominant group in the second united front government. The CPI(M)'s strategic-tactical line was sharpened and polished in 1968 at the Burdwan plenum of the central committee, at the central committee's meeting later

[53] *People's Democracy* printed English translations of Namboodiripad's article in three instalments, August 18, 25, and September 8, 1968.

at Madurai and, finally, at the eighth congress at Cochin. In between, all of the state committees also met to take stock of the situation in their respective areas, to elect delegates to the congress as well as new state committees, and to examine the draft resolutions prepared for the eighth congress by the party leadership.

Both Communist parties projected themselves in 1968 as true defenders of Indian democracy and parliamentary rule. Real threats to democracy, parliamentary rule, and even the constitution came not from the Communists, but from the bourgeoisie when its rule over the masses was challenged. Thus, Hiren Mukherji, CPI member of Lok Sabha, in assailing Dharam Vira's dismissal of the united front government, declared: "The masks are falling off the faces of those people who talk about the sanctity of the Constitution. It has been proved again and again that the bourgeois concept and practice of democracy are thrown overboard whenever the going gets tough." [54]

During the "mass struggle" against President's rule, *New Age* editorialized: "In embattled West Bengal one of the major battles of Indian democracy is now being fought. The issue is not merely one of restoration of the constitutional rights of the people of a particular state. The issue unmistakably is whether parliamentary democracy in this country will at all survive and be made safe. This imports to West Bengal's struggle and resistance a wider national significance." For the CPI(M), Harekrishna Konar wrote in the same vein in *People's Democracy:* "The reactionaries trampled under foot the constitution and threw away any pretence to parliamentary democracy." [55] West Bengal party boss Promode Das Gupta wrote to the Speaker of Lok Sabha denying a report attributed to him by a Calcutta daily that he had advocated a "bloody revolution." [56] The Indian Communists appeared to be

[54] *New Age,* December 10, 1967.
[55] *New Age,* December 24, 1967; *People's Democracy,* December 24, 1967.
[56] The letter to the Speaker was occasioned by the fact that Das Gupta's alleged remarks had been raised in Lok Sabha during a discussion. What Das Gupta claimed that he had actually said was that "the present Indian constitution is

anxious to demonstrate the legitimacy of their struggle to the elite, who had been shaken by the political developments in West Bengal.

PARTY "INDEPENDENCE"

On the question of independence also, the Communists, especially the Marxists, gained more ground. Peking, by supporting the Naxalbari uprising and by denouncing the CPI(M) leadership as "neo-revisionist" made it easier for the Marxists in 1968 to reject the Chinese revolution as the model for India, and to protest Chinese interference in Indian Communist party affairs. Ramamurti declared in Lok Sabha in December 1967: "Our party has adopted its program and political line on the basis of its own independent study of conditions in India and it refused to be guided . . . by the other Communist parties, however large and influential they may be. The whole world knows that our party differed on fundamental issues with such large parties as those of the Soviet Union and China." He faced a more responsive crowd when he articulated the same theme in Calcutta in April 1968, and affirmed that CPI(M) "has to carve its own way for leading the Indian revolution." [57]

The experience of 1967 taught the CPI(M) that its future lay in a firm identification with the interests of the rural and urban poor. Konar apparently played a significant part in bringing the rural poor to the forefront of the Marxists' tactical line. He was convinced that the united front government had been ousted in 1967 by a coup of *jotedars* and food-grain hoarders; this game had been "nakedly exposed" by the "unusual haste with which the

---

framed in such a way and it has had so many limitations that if the people really want to win their basic demands and take the country towards socialism, the whole constitution will have to be reframed. . . . To do this the mass of people will have to build a powerful movement so as to have a revolutionary popular front government at the Center and to bring about a radically new constitution in favor of the toiling people." *People's Democracy*, April 3, 1969.

[57] *Ibid.*, December 24, 1967; April 28, 1968.

united front ministry has been dismissed before the harvesting."
If the united front government had survived until the end of December, "the *jotedars* would have had no opportunity to rob the
peasants and sharecroppers." Since the dismissal of the ministry,
"the police have intensified their attack on the peasants, thus
proving their class loyalty to *jotedars*."

In such a situation, "the most important tasks of the democratic
movement is to strengthen the resistance movement of the peasants and to support their legitimate demands wholeheartedly." In
concrete terms this meant helping the peasants to defend their
crops and their lands "even with their own blood." It was, however, no longer enough to organize peasant resistance on reformist
lines. "It is necessary for the toiling people and the democratic
forces to understand that their struggle has reached a new phase.
The struggle for defense of democracy will have to be intensified
and spread to wider areas and should be linked with day-to-day
struggles of workers and peasants. Just now the peasants are faced
with a direct attack. Hence the democratic forces will have to
stand by the peasants and the struggle for democracy will have to
be taken deep into the villages." [58]

The party's perspective of the united front as well as of its constituents progressively hardened. "The united front never advances smoothly in a straight line, it advances through unity and
struggle." [59] Just any group willing to play anti-Congress politics
was no longer acceptable to the Marxists as a partner in a coalition. "Those who agree to remain in the united front must solemnly pledge before the people that they will protect popular
unity, loyally implement the program, and ceaselessly fight the
Congress." [60]

The CPI(M) looked upon the united front "as a weapon of

[58] *Ibid.*, December 24, 1967. Konar suggested that the struggle of the poor peasantry should get priority over the struggle of the urban proletariat. This line for
the Bengal CPI(M) was approved by the party leadership. It was a significant departure from Indian Communism's traditional preference for the urban proletariat.
[59] *Ibid.*, December 22, 1967.   [60] *Ibid.*, May 19, 1968.

mass struggle" and wanted to use it as such. It was imperative to "root out the wrong conceptions of the people about the power of the united front ministry." Within the crippling limitations of the prevailing Indian political system, "no fundamental solution of people's problems can be made"; it was not even possible to arrest the economic crisis. "The ruling classes have assigned to the state governments the role of carrying out their dictates and of suppressing the people on their behalf. It was the task of the united front ministry to fight against this attempt of the ruling classes and expose them before the people." [61]

THE SECOND UNITED FRONT

The results of the mid-term election in West Bengal in February 1969 radically altered the political balance within the second united front ministry. The CPI(M) took the position that it was the dominant group in Bengal's political life and demanded not only chief ministership in the new government but also control of the police and internal administration. Other partners in the front, however, refused to accept Marxist leadership. Negotiations ended in a deadlock which was broken by the intervention of the national leadership of the CPI. The Bengal unit was directed to

[61] *Ibid.*, December 22, 1967. The CPI stand on the role of the Bengal and Kerala united front ministries was basically different. It wanted the ministries to select from common programs a list of priorities and work, even within the limitations of the political system and the constitution, to ameliorate the distress of the toiling people. The CPI wanted the "fixation of priorities on the twin yardstick of some relief to the people and attack on positions of vested interests." There was a tendency in the united front ministry "not to utilize the powers of the state government within the limitations in the interest of the people and in some respects to compromise with the present socioeconomic structure and to avoid struggle in regard to the working class and in relation to the central government." The united front failed also to develop united struggle against obstacles. "Instead of a united movement developing, clashes are taking place among the front partners and attempts are being made to utilize governmental power to increase the strength of individual parties. The CPM is the main culprit in this respect." *New Age,* June 29, 1969.

accept the CPI(M)'s compromise solution which would give the chief and finance ministerships to Ajoy K. Mukherji, but police and administration to Basu, who was to be once again designated deputy chief minister.

The CPI(M) made no secret of its vantage point in the new setup. The second united front ministry, to the Marxists, was not just a replica of the first. The election had assumed "the character of a far more bitter political battle in the background, of further deepening of the crisis, and of further intensification of class struggle." The Marxists' strength in the front and in the assembly was "not an accident, it is a reflection of the popular support it has."

Stunned by the results of the poll, the central government, and even organized industry in Calcutta, offered cooperation to the new regime. This gesture, however, was deceptive, for reaction's "game is clear—drive a wedge between the CPI(M) and other parties of the united front and thus try to disrupt the united front itself." [62] This had happened once, and could happen again, unless the Marxists could build up a strong mass movement against all "conspiracies." This was now the first task of the united front, and certainly of the Marxists and their allies.

The objective conditions were more favorable for struggle after the mid-term election: reports received by the CPI(M) state secretariat from all of the districts "revealed one common feature— that the agricultural labor and poor peasants, non-Bengali workers, and Muslim masses have in a big way swung toward the united front, especially to the CPI(M)." The party now determined to make the best use of the opportunities available for large-scale mass mobilization, and directed the district committees "to simultaneously launch struggles of the workers and middle-class employees . . . to conduct immediately the struggles of the *kisans* against the hoarders, profiteers and *mahajans* (money-

[62] *People's Democracy,* July 21, 1968; March 2, 1969.

lenders)." The party was convinced that "the class struggles of the landless and poor peasants, agricultural workers, and workers have to be organized in rural and industrial areas with a view to helping the united front government implement its 32-point program."

In any case, the party needed mass support, for it was already anticipating, on the morrow of the mid-term victory, a polarization within the united front between the Marxists on the one hand and all the other groups, including the CPI, on the other. "As the class struggles become sharper and sharper, the anti-Communist forces of all shades will try to attack the CPI(M) more and more." It noted "with grave concern that certain forces inside the united front, such as the revisionists, SUC, and the like—have begun campaigning against the CPI(M)." [63]

The united front's second term in office coincided with the crisis in the Congress party leading to its split into two rival factions. To some extent the split in the Congress party was a result of the radical shift in the politics of Bengal. The united front took office in March 1969 with some advantages. The Congress party's effort to disrupt the non-Congress coalitions had proved to be a failure. In West Bengal, it seemed that any attempt to split the united front led to a split in the camp of the splitters themselves. The elimination of the Ghoshes and the Kabirs had a sobering effect on potential defectors. Reflecting the polarization that had occurred in West Bengal politics, the second united front ministry began with a more radical program, particularly in the three vital areas of food, land, and labor. The Marxists held the important portfolios of police, internal administration, land, labor, education, and relief and rehabilitation. Although Basu

---

[63] *Ibid.*, March 23, 1969. The delegation of the task of organizing the struggles to the district committees indicated the growing organizational strength of the party at the grass-root level. It is noteworthy that among the eight CPI(M) representatives on the second united front ministry, four were peasant leaders, of whom two had been functioning at the district *kisan sabha* level. Only two were trade-union leaders, including Basu.

was deputy chief minister, he began to function from the beginning as if he were the leader of the government. Konar was by this time armed with a land program which he began to put through with single-mindedness.

The ministry's list of achievements was not unimpressive. It stopped the eviction of sharecroppers in all districts, recovered 300,000 acres of land illegally appropriated by landlords, distributed 230,000 acres to poor peasants and landless laborers, gave small homestead plots to a large number of landless laborer-families free of cost, granted remission of land revenue on holdings of 3 acres and less, enabled 800,000 workers of the tea plantations, jute, textile, engineering, and other industries to wrest from their employers concrete benefits like cost-of-living allowances, higher salaries, bonuses, stopping of retrenchments, reinstatement of dismissed workers, and unionization—all these benefits amounting to Rs 200,000,000 (or $27,000,000). Other achievements included raises for teachers and government employees; a proposal for free schooling for girls up to the eighth grade; distribution of textbooks free to students of the first and second grades; and bringing within the purview of one or the other form of food rationing 30.8 million out of a total of 42.4 million people in the state. Alone of all the deficit states in India, it succeeded in fulfilling its target of grain procurement from the peasants.[64] For the first time in about three years, the price of rice registered a slight decrease in Calcutta, and rice was freely available for purchase, at a higher price of course, outside the ration shops.

In cold print these may look like measures long overdue in a society that was supposed to have been molded into a socialistic

[64] *Economic and Political Weekly,* March 28, 1970; *Pashchimbanga* (Bengali journal of the West Bengal government), March 6, 1970. Of particular significance is the recovery of *benami* land (land registered under false ownership). It involved considerable litigation, often against tea plantation owners and joint landholding families. There is much more *benami* land in Uttar Pradesh and Bihar than in Bengal. The impact of the recovery of such land and its distribution among the landless could not but have an impact on agrarian relations in Uttar Pradesh and Bihar also.

pattern for a decade and a half. In reality, however, almost every one of these measures met with strong resistance from the entrenched interests and their political defenders; each reacted on a stratified society like a corroding chemical.

The second united front regime launched itself with a rhetoric and a style that was distinctly militant on behalf of the poor and the underprivileged; moreover, its promises were backed by concrete action. Articulations by ministers, especially the Marxists, were a mixture of ideology and concrete action. The Marxist labor minister, for example, reported to the legislative assembly on the first four months' work of his department:

The united front government has taken only the first small step in meeting the legitimate grievances of workers and in giving them their legitimate rights. Behind these workers lie a tragic story of long suffering and a glorious tradition of struggle to achieve human rights.

Within twenty-four hours of the installation of the ministry, we started making efforts to settle industrial disputes in favor of the workers. As a result, several major factories which had closed down in 1968, reopened and began to function again. Within three months 298 disputes were settled, involving 111,839 workers.

This, however, is only a beginning. It is much less than what needs to be done.[65]

LABOR TACTICS

The labor tactics of the new regime in 1969 were a pattern of struggle-settlement-struggle. It made no secret of its bias for the workers, but it also to some extent took a realistic attitude to industry's genuine problems. The three areas where major and prolonged strikes occurred in 1969 were the jute, engineering, and plantation industries. The government claimed that it did not encourage *gheraos*. However, there were 281 cases of *gherao* in the first five months of the ministry's life in industry, 34 in education, and 48 in the "social sphere." [66] Each strike or *gherao* was fol-

[65] *Paschimbanga,* September 12, 1969 (translated from Bengali).
[66] The figures were given by Jyoti Basu to the state assembly. *The Statesman,* July 26, 1969.

lowed by negotiations among workers, employers, and government; the main emphasis from the government side was on an agreement favorable to the workers, but not beyond the means of industry.

One of the major successes of this tactic was the agreement signed between workers and employers of the engineering industry. A. K. Basak, then president of the Indian Engineering Industries' Association (now on the staff of the World Bank), who took part in these negotiations which often continued into the small hours of the night, told me that he was highly impressed by the Marxist labor minister's negotiating skill and ability and, above all, his firm hold on the trade unions. "This was a new experience for us," he said. "We are generally used to meeting with labor ministers who have little control over the trade unions. As a result, you do not quite know where you stand in negotiations. An understanding arrived at today may not be there tomorrow. But with Mr. Krishnapada Ghosh it was different. We knew where we stood. Every understanding was firmly maintained. I remember, at the end of an all-night session, I complimented the minister on his excellent physical stamina. 'It seems you enjoy very good health,' I said. He smiled wearily and replied, 'Used to.' "

The ministry's handling of industrial relations elicited praise even from leaders of the Indian National Trade Union Congress. Several pieces of legislation passed by the Bengal assembly, conferring benefits on the workers or improving upon existing laws, were now approved by the central government without much resistance.

LAND AND PEASANT MILITANCY

Of much greater consequence was the new regime's land policy formulated and implemented by Konar. It is necessary to examine this policy and the style of its execution in some detail for herein lies much of the future of Indian Communism—whether it can bring about structural changes in agrarian relations without pushing the rural poor and the rural rich into a civil war.

Social scientists know that it is not possible to bring about structural social change by legislation unless each piece of legislation is purposefully backed by executive action. In the 1950s, the Indian landowning gentry was usually able to thwart the objectives of the land "reforms" by keeping most of the land through fraudulant means; little executive action was taken to dispossess them of what did not belong to them legally. Konar's primary effort was to bring out the *benami* land and distribute it to the poor and the landless. He wished to move within the confines of existing legislation, but also to bring about new legislation to further limit the maximum holdings so that he would have more surplus land for the landless.

What distinguished him from the Congress ministers in charge of land and land revenue was that he was prepared to implement new legislations by using the coercive power of the state, the police, which was controlled by Jyoti Basu. It was this combined thrust of the law and the law-enforcing machinery working for the first time on behalf of the rural poor against the entrenched interests of the rural rich that created panic among the rural gentry. Moreover, Konar needed the active help of the rural poor to search out much of the *benami* land, for the poor and landless peasant knew how much land a particular landlord had kept illegally and what land he had converted into "fisheries" in order to escape the provisions of the land "reform" laws.

Konar utilized the machinery of the Marxist-controlled *kisan sabha* to activate the rural poor and thus kill two birds with a single stone. As a Marxist his objective could not be just to give each poor peasant an acre of land, even if he had that much land to distribute. In activizing the rural proletariat for a limited immediate objective, Konar was also trying to build the CPI(M) base among the village poor for the purpose of a future revolution. In the latter thrust of his policy, he ran into conflict with the other political parties and groups, especially those whose political base was in the countryside, such as the Congress party, Bangla Congress, the CPI and the Forward Bloc.

Within ninety days after the second united front ministry took office, Konar circulated a draft legislation lifting land revenue on three acres or less in single possession, and increasing the revenue on land above seven acres. False declarations were made cognizable offense punishable with three months' simple imprisonment or a fine up to Rs 1,000 ($140.00).[67]

In July Konar reported to the assembly on the progress made in reclaiming *benami* land. The program, he disclosed, had been delayed by a spate of litigations: in Burdwan district alone, 3,209 court cases had been instituted between February 1967 and March 1968 for a mere 138 acres of land. The worst culprits were the owners of tea plantations and "fisheries" and the *jotedars*. The law as well as the practices of the Bengal courts, including the high court, often went against the government; nor was the government's own machinery particularly efficient in conducting these land cases. Konar gave a list of cases pending in the law courts. The four largest allegedly illegal possessions were: 256 square acres and 25,000 acres (both owned by powerful landlord families); "several thousand acres" (owned by a religious endowment); and 1,004 acres (owned by a former Congress minister).[68]

The political problems created by the drive to recover *benami* land came up for discussion at a united front committee in July. These problems stemmed from the emergence of a "powerful peasant movement to recover *benami* land and land belonging to government but illegally possessed by landlords." The committee declared that without a strong peasant movement it would not be possible to recover from the wealthy landlords and "fishery"-owners the land they could not legally retain—the front therefore "welcomed" and pledged its support to the peasant movement. At the same time, the committee took note of "excesses" committed by peasants in several cases, and the "mistakes" they had made, as a result of which a number of lawful fisheries had suffered. It appealed to the peasants not to be carried away by their enthusiasm

---

[67] *Pashchimbanga*, April 10, 1969.   [68] *Ibid.*, July 25, 1968.

and to take every care to avoid such "excesses." A few days later an official journal of the Bengal government portrayed the changed rural landscape:

The unknown village became well-known on June 22. Chaitanyapur hit the newspaper headlines. It's a village in the Mangalkote police station in Burdwan district. Here two poor peasants were killed by *jotedars'* bullets and 85 others were injured.

The killing of poor peasants is nothing new in this country. Immediately after independence, killing of peasants began at Kakdwip, Bada-kamalpur, Midnapore, and Gajol; the killing went on during the rule of the Congress. . . . However, these killings used to be done by the police who always defended the interests of the *jotedars*. All this has changed now, under united front rule. The united front government has resolved to employ the police to serve the general public, not to kill the poor. The *jotedars* have therefore been compelled to come out with their own guns. These incidents have happened in a number of villages in several districts. . . .

The peasants know where the stolen land is. They told us, "You see that land there? Out of 5,000 acres, almost 2,000 acres are *benami*." . . . They said, "Those who possess *benami* land are lawbreakers. . . . They are enemies not only of the peasants, but also of the government, of the city-dwellers, of the whole country."

It is against these enemies that the peasantry is rising today. They are spearheading a statewide movement: to restore government land, to search out *benami* land. They believe they are helping to enforce the rule of law. The lawbreakers will at last be punished.

The statewide awakening of the peasantry has made the *jotedars* nervous. They have panicked. They cried out in a chorus, "Everything's lost!" But the peasants of Chaitanyapur were inspired. They tried to bring under their own plough land that belongs to the government.

The *jotedars* protested. "What's government land? There's no government land. All this land is ours. Who are the peasants to till this land?" The peasants replied, "This land belongs to the government, not to you."

The *jotedars* were outraged by the awakening of the lowly. They met, organized, and formed their own association. They resolved to teach the peasants a proper lesson. The shooting occurred a few days later. It was an organized armed attack by the *jotedar*-moneylender, on the poor peasantry.

The news spread like wild fire. . . . Peasants in the adjoining villages took over nearly 700 acres of government land. This land was distributed among 2,000 landless peasants (each getting one-third of an acre).

Under united front rule, the landless peasant and the agricultural worker have begun to get land of their own. . . . Land is the mother. The peasant is her first child. At Chaitanyapur and other villages, "they" reddened the mother's bosom with her children's blood. And so the green fields are swelling in anger, the earth roars, there are stirrings of new life.

With a single message: "Let's march ahead." [69]

This is how a left-wing weekly reported the land-seizure movement in 24-Parganas district:

The land-seizure movement at Mechhogheri in 24-Parganas has created a great deal of commotion. Thousands of landless peasants, armed with red flags, have taken possession of land in large parts of the district. Most of the wealthy landlords at Mechhogheri are Congressmen; they have complained to Delhi that Communists are looting their property. However, West Bengal's land revenue minister, Konar, says that there has been no looting; the peasants are only trying to stop the loot and plunder of the landlords over the years. According to the revenue department, 24 -Parganas has 33,000 acres of "fisheries". . . .

The present struggle will change the face of this district. Government has found thousands of acres of illegally possessed land in 24-Parganas, but could not take it over and bring it under the plough because of litigation. Now the peasants have refused to wait any longer for the courts to decide. They have taken over land vested in government in the first instance. . . . The 33,000 acres of "fisheries" are "owned" by only ten families; they bring in an annual income of Rs 33 crore and a net profit of Rs 15,000 ($2,000).[70]

[69] *Ibid.* The report was by the journal's own correspondent who quoted Konar as saying, "We are witnessing reestablishment of natural relationship between mother and her children." If correctly reported, this remark of Konar throws interesting light on the socialization of Marxism. Konar, a militant Marxist revolutionary, invokes the mother cult that is so deeply rooted in Bengali (and Indian) culture, to influence the minds of the rural proletariat.

[70] *Darpan* (Mirror), Bengali weekly, April 25, 1969 (translated from Bengali).

It is evident in these two sympathetic reports that the land-seizure drive, which spread rapidly from district to district, was creating an agrarian conflict of several dimensions. Once activized by the *kisan sabhas,* the rural poor were not always under control, but they were even less under control in areas where *kisan sabhas* were either new or did not exist.

In supporting the peasant militancy, local *kisan sabhas* at times became more militant than their leaders in Calcutta wanted. The movement was the first organized grass-root level assault after 1957 (in Kerala) on the rural foundation of the political system —the rich and middle-level peasantry, or the rural gentry, much of whose wealth and prosperity was based on fraudulant possession of land. The rural gentry were the political base not merely of the Congress party, but also of Bangla Congress and several other groups within the united front. These took up the cudgels on behalf of the wrongfully injured landlords, whose number apparently was not negligible. According to the CPI(M), the CPI too did the same.

In any case, the leftist groups in Bengal, all of whom had for many years neglected the rural poor, refused to permit the Marxists a free hand in mobilizing the landless peasant and agricultural worker. Clashes between activists of these competing leftist groups began to occur as soon as the land-seizure movement began. Yet the movement produced a momentum which the united front government could not but try to help. Thus in May the government issued an ordinance to bring under cultivation lands left fallow by their owners. The cultivation was to be done by peasants (sharecroppers) for three years. Twenty percent of the produce was to go to the landlord, 10 percent to the government, and the rest to the cultivator.[71] This was a powerful added incentive to land seizure by sharecroppers. *People's Democracy* reported within a month of the issuance of the ordinance:

[71] *People's Democracy,* May 18, 1969.

Inspired by the land policy of the united front government, agricultural laborers and poor peasants are rallying under the banner of the Kisan Sabha and recovering *benami* and vested land from *jotedars* and distributing it among themselves. The movement has spread to areas where there was no peasant organization. The movement is reported in 24-Parganas, Burdwan, Midnapore, Hooghly, Murshidabad, Bankura, Birdhum, Malda, and other districts, and is gaining momentum in 24-Parganas.

In Midnapore district, the movement for land took a turn toward racial tension between Hindus and Santhals, who constitute the bulk of the landless peasants.[72]

The movement soon led to an interparty crisis in the united front. Clashes began to escalate between activists of different parties. The first serious clash was reported in June between activists of the CPI(M) and the RSP at Alipurduar in north Bengal in which three Marxists were killed. The conflict arose over competition for grass-root bases; apparently the Marxists were threatening a base of the other group.[73] This was followed by a clash between CPI(M) and SSP workers at Beru Bari, also in north Bengal; the rivalry in this case seemed to be over a trade union. Also in June the CPI state council in a political resolution accused the CPI(M) of "using governmental machinery to further its own organizational interests." [74]

Clashes multiplied in July. The most violent incident was reported in a village in Burdwan district where "the clashes and

[72] *The Statesman,* July 8, 1969.

[73] *People's Democracy,* June 1, 1969. The paper wrote: "As CPI(M) is in the forefront of people's struggles, it is only natural that more people are coming into its fold and its strength is growing. Because of this, some constituent parties of the united front take a factional attitude in the matter of carrying forward their struggles, instead of forging a joint front. . . . Within some of the democratic parties of the united front, there are elements with a strong anti-Communist bias and except for CPI(M) which has laid down rigid standards for party membership, the doors of many of the other parties are open to antisocial elements who until yesterday were with the Congress and are today flocking to the united front with ulterior motives."

[74] *The Statesman,* June 24, 1969. The meeting was marked by a bitter debate on the CPI's organizational work in Bengal. Some members complained that the party had almost been defunct organizationally.

conflicts revolved around the recovery of vested land and the collisions were between the rural gentry, supporters of and supported by Congress, on the one hand, and the village dispossessed,
belonging to the low caste of Bauris, supporters of and supported
by CPI(M), on the other." The clash led to three deaths—the
headmaster of the local school, an old and retired teacher, and a
student. This incident had its own chain reaction. A student wing
of the Congress party called for a statewide students' strike, which
led to further clashes and to the death of another student, in another village of Burdwan. On the following day the student adjunct of the CPI(M) raided some newspaper offices in Calcutta.

At a meeting of the united front committee in Calcutta on July
9, Industries Minister Sushil Dhara, a Bangla Congress leader, expressed his party's "grave concern" at the disturbances that were
taking place over recovery of *benami* and vested land and its distribution. The land should be distributed, he said, through a government machinery in consultation with the united front partners
and *kisan* organizations.[75] Tension between the Marxists and the
other members of the united front continued to grow through the
summer.

Early in October, Bangla Congress adopted a political resolution which read like a bill of indictment suggesting that almost
every sphere of life in West Bengal had been disturbed during
the seven months of united front rule. The resolution said that
interparty struggles, *gheraos,* forcible occupation of land, a general deterioration of the law-and-order situation, and other unsavory developments had "combined to create a deep sense of insecurity and uncertainty among the people." Giving a grim picture
of the state of affairs in West Bengal, the resolution warned that
"if such clashes and lawlessness were not stopped immediately,
the Bangla Congress would be compelled to build up a resistance
movement on Gandhian lines to end this intolerable situation."

Ajoy Mukherji, who presided over the meeting, tried to mini

[75] *Economic and Political Weekly: Special Number,* July 1969.

mize the seriousness of the resolution by insisting that the united front was *not* disintegrating, and that the coalition would continue. However, the CPI(M) reacted sharply to the resolution and looked upon it as an implicit move by Bangla Congress to form a non-Communist or at least non-CPI(M) coalition in the state. The Politbureau of CPI(M) condemned the Bangla Congress resolution as "slanderous," and saw in it an attempt to return to the "path of 1967." [76]

The Marxists' assessment of Bangla Congress was presumably influenced by the crisis that was developing within the Congress party. Mukherji had only recently returned to Calcutta from New Delhi, where he had met with Mrs. Gandhi. For the Marxists, a split in the Congress party was fraught with the possibility of the non-CPI(M) partners of the Kerala and Bengal coalitions trying to set up alternative governments in the two states with the help of a "progressive" Congress party. This possibility was apparently discussed by the politbureau, although there was no mention of it in the resolution released for public information.

Meanwhile, the tempo of peasant activism in the Bengal countryside increased, and the non-Marxist constituents of the united front seemed to be unable to bring it under control. They could only keep step with it. In Calcutta and other urban areas, the breakdown of law and order assumed serious proportions. The most dramatic incident occured on July 31, when a force of uniformed policemen stormed into the West Bengal assembly, then in session, and started an uproar by smashing furniture. Their objective, some said, was to attack Basu and several other ministers. Several top police officials reportedly connived at the demonstration, if they did not actually instigate it. While Basu won public praise by his personal courage

[he] scornfully disregarded all advice to follow others . . . to the side exit and waited in his chamber in the Assembly House for the onrush of the angry mob. . . . As soon as the crowd burst in . . . he pounded

[76] *The Statesman,* October 8, 1969.

on his table and bluntly told the attackers what he thought about them. It had almost a hypnotic impact, and Jyoti Basu was not deviating from the literal truth when he said in his statement in the Assembly the next day: "They were cowards, every single one of them . . . I told them exactly what I thought of them; the cringing of the cowards then became pitiable" [77]

the attack raised questions about the political impartiality of the police, and its instrumentality in working out politics of radical social change.

This "counterrevolution in khaki," as one columnist described the police demonstration, led immediately to a massive demonstration of the Calcutta public in support of the Marxist leader. The law-and-order situation in Bengal, however, was never restored to normal after this incident, and isolated acts of violence, feeding on wild rumors, created a climate of insecurity in Calcutta. Antisocial elements apparently took advantage of it to create a psychology of fear, which the police department was unable or unwilling to bring under control. Rivalries among the partners of the coalition, sometimes leading to murder, aggravated the situation until a crisis of law and order overtook most of the urban areas in the state.

FOOD POLICIES

As the harvesting season approached, the united front government announced a food procurement policy that was a distinct victory for Konar. A graded system of levy was announced on the production of paddy, exempting only those with up to seven acres of land. Local food committees, now in most districts controlled by the *kisan sabhas,* were asked to help the police in ensuring that the rich peasants did not avoid the levy. At the same time, the government announced that the "crop belongs to those who till the fields" and not to the landowners. This policy was designed to protect the rights of the sharecroppers, who were often

[77] *Economic and Political Weekly,* August 9, 1969.

deprived of their due share of the harvest. Konar made the announcement in a rhetoric that reflected the polarization that had taken place in much of the Bengal countryside:

It has been the policy of the united front government to initiate land reforms by distributing, with the help of the organized movement of the toiling peasantry, vested land to the landless, and by recovering *benami* land and stopping evictions. Hundreds of thousands of poor and landless peasants have come forward in each district to make this policy a success. The government later acknowledged the right of the peasants to search out, recover, and distribute among themselves *benami* and vested land as well as land illegally converted into fisheries. . . .

The toiling peasants have recovered more than 250,000 acres of land from the illegal possession of *jotedars.* All of this land has been ploughed. . . . This huge new harvest must go to the poor peasants who have tilled the land. The *jotedars,* however, are not likely to submit to this just claim of the peasants easily. They are already very angry. They have been infuriated by the sight of hundreds of thousands of acres of land cultivated by the sweat of the poor peasants, and they will adopt every foul means at their disposal to deprive the peasants of what rightfully belongs to them. . . . The question of enabling the peasant to enjoy the harvest of his toil has therefore assumed great importance. And with this question is also related the other important question of maintaining law and order in the countryside.

When a mass of peasants embark upon movement to recover *benami* and vested land, certain mistakes and excesses are bound to occur. It is quite possible that in certain cases the legal possessions of individuals or families have been encroached upon. At some places poor peasants have clashed even among themselves. While these limited incidents are nothing in comparison with the vast success of the entire movement, we cannot ignore them. . . . The poor peasants and sharecroppers must avoid these mistakes at the time of harvesting; they must also correct such mistakes as they may have already committed. . . .

While no injustice should be done to anyone, the peasants will not be deprived of the harvest of their toil. Whatever be the state of the land in documents filed with the government, whatever the *jotedars* may do to frustrate the peasants' victory, the peasants will harvest the

crops in accordance to their legal right, and they will protect the crop.
. . . The united front government will stand by them. This is the
unanimous decision of the government, and has been explained to the
district officers.

These officers have been instructed to protect the right of the peasants to harvest the crops they have grown in recovered *benami* and
vested land. The district officers will help the peasants against any ob-
structions that may be coming from the *jotedars*. If necessary the police will intervene. If there are disputes as to who have tilled which
plots of land, government officials will give their decisions in consultation with representatives of *kisan sabhas* and political parties. *Jotedars*
may sometimes claim to have cultivated the land themselves or with
false tenants. In such cases, officials will make on-the-spot inquiries. I
have no doubt that the peasants' organizations will extend every help
and cooperation to the officials. . . .

I appeal to all the poor and toiling peasants for their cooperation in
making the government's policy a complete success. You have gained
from experience, and are now much stronger. You must avoid mistakes, correct past ones, protect your own harvest and the peace in the
villages. You have every right to defend yourselves from the attack of
jotedars. The government is with you against the *jotedars'* conspiracy.
You must, however, take every care to see that the peace is not disturbed and no poor or middle peasant is harmed.[78]

The "protect-the-toiling-peasant's-harvest" movement spread
rapidly from district to district. It enabled the CPI(M) to further
consolidate and expand its political base among the rural proletariat. It also brought the CPI(M) into many clashes with the political groups in the united front. In fact, the "unity" of the
united front, never very strong, collapsed in the turbulent fields
of West Bengal. As one reporter put it:

After all, the dozen Leftist parties of West Bengal are hardly divided
on ideological grounds. It is old personal loyalties and animosities that
alone have created the division, have been perpetuating it, and are
now endangering the very base of the Left in the state. For the leaders
of these parties, politics is a way of making a living, their daily bread

[78] *Pashchimbanga,* November 21, 1968.

and butter. In order to retain their identity and their means of living, they have to do everything possible to keep alive their respective parties. If it is not possible for these parties to retain their identity in joining in a common fight against capitalists and *jotedars,* their vested interest in their survival would force them into the arms of their very class enemies. That this embrace would be a kiss of death, that no Left party can survive in the state after having entered the camp of the bourgeoisie, is understood on all sides. The CPI(M) is trying to achieve precisely that, and it is precisely because of this understanding that the CPI and other parties allied with Bangla Congress are not insincere in saying that they do not want a minifront government, even while supporting the Bangla Congress in its deliberate moves for forming such a government.[79]

In certain respects, then, the predicament of the non-Communist left in Bengal at the beginning of 1970 resembled that of the non-Communist left in China during the mid-1940s. Its members could not join forces with the Marxists without risking the loss of their separate identity, nor could they join the bourgeoisie without facing political suicide. Confusion appeared to seize each of the leftist groups. The CPI, while ideologically agreeing with the Marxists on most major issues, actually lined up behind Bangla Congress protesting the CPI(M)'s attempt to establish its "hegemony." At the same time, it could not, without risking an internal revolt, subscribe to Bangla Congress' entirely negative evaluation of the work of the united front government. A minority in Bangla Congress left the party, protesting the leadership's anti-Communist stand. The Forward Bloc also broke into two units, one of them siding with the CPI(M). The RSP leadership, despite close ideological affinity with the CPI(M), faced a revolt of the rank-and-file who were indignant about the encroachments of the Marxists.[80]

The Ides of March brought about the end of the second united

[79] Ashok Rudra, "Who's Afraid of the Big Bad Wolf?" *Economic and Political Weekly,* February 21, 1970.
[80] *Economic and Political Weekly: Annual Number,* January 1970, p. 95.

front government in West Bengal. Mukherji tendered his resignation to the governor, who kept the assembly alive for a few weeks and finally dissolved it when it was clear that no alternative government was possible.

7

COMMUNISTS IN POWER:
KERALA

The chief difference between united front political tactics of the Communists in West Bengal and in Kerala during 1967–70 was that while in Bengal the emphasis was on political mobilization, in Kerala it was on polarization. The difference is easy to explain. While in West Bengal, the Communists got their first taste of power in an atmosphere of deepening economic distress and internal disruption of the Congress party, in Kerala they had already tasted power for more than two years (in the late 1950s), and the Marxists had established a dominant position among the electorate in the 1965 election. In Kerala, therefore, the Marxist bid in 1967 was to bring the coalition under its control.

However, the built-in mechanisms of parliamentary democracy enables minority groups to thwart the power-thrusts of the majority. This is exactly what happened in Kerala. What the Kerala model proved in late 1969 was that all alternatives to Marxist rule had not been exhausted. The parliamentary belligerency of the CPI(M) cost it popular support in urban areas, particularly in the numerous industrial-urban complexes that sprung up in Kerala during the 1960s. The rural poor apparently stood firmly by the CPI(M)—in appreciation of the Communists' land reforms in 1958. But the emergence of a new class of farm entrepreneurs among the rich and middle-level peasantry acted against the Marxist bid to win over the middle-level peasants. In short, the hectic run of Keralan politics in 1967–70 proved, first, that the non-Communist forces could not rule by themselves any longer and, second, that the non-Marxist forces were able to contain the CPI(M) within its existing support base, and even to nibble at that base while the Marxists were trying hard to penetrate the social base of the non-Communist parties.

In the united front government that took office in Kerala in February 1967, Chief Minister Namboodiripad held the portfolio of home and services, while his three other Marxist colleagues were placed in charge of revenue and general administration (Mrs. Gowri), forests and Harijan (untouchables) welfare (M. K. Krishnan), and transport and penal institutions (Imbichi Bawa). The CPI was given the portfolios of agriculture (M. N. Govindan Nair) and industries (T. V. Thomas). In charge of labor was Mathai Manjooran of the Kerala Socialist Party, a small group which allegedly had the support of the CPI(M). The Muslim League got the education portfolio; SSP, that of finance. Almost from the inception of the coalition, conflict arose between the two Communist factions which, between them, were in control of the entire economic structure of the state.

The two factions had two entirely different approaches to the working of the united front. The CPI's conception of the united front

is that it should prove in actual practice to be a real alternative to the discredited Congress rule, in the sense that the administration should be clean, more alive to the grievances and needs of the people, more efficient and quick in the redress of such of the grievances as are capable of being redressed within the limits of its resources, more democratic and responsive to the demands and representations made by various sections of the population, in short, a real contrast to the Congress. Of course, the power and resources of a state government functioning under our constitution are limited, and we should certainly not be a party to foster unwarranted illusions among the people that everything that they desire will be done for them. But within all these limitations, it is possible to give some relief to our much-suffering people and give them a better administration than the Congress had given. Only in this way can the united front government be made to act as a potent instrument of struggle against the rule of the Congress, a point of attraction around which all the democratic and revolutionary forces which are out to overthrow Congress rule in this country can be mobilized.[1]

The CPI(M), on the other hand, viewed the united front as an instrument of twin struggles: first and foremost against the central government, amounting to an assault on the political system from within and, second, against the antiworking class and antipoor-peasant policies of the non-Marxist partners of the coalition. Namboodiripad made this quite clear in answering five questions posed by a Washington *Post* correspondent, Bernard Nossiter, in December 1967. The united front governments, he said, could "effectively fight for changes in the policies pursued by the central government." At the state level, it could do only "small things by way of giving relief to the people." Even in doing small things

we come up against various obstacles arising out of the provisions of the Constitution, the rules and regulations framed by the central government and the interpretations of the law made by the Supreme and High Courts, all of them heavily weighted against the working people and in favor of the landlord-capitalist classes.

Whatever the united front government did, it could not expect to bring about a perceptible change in the living conditions of the people.

[1] C. Achutha Menon, *What Happened in Kerala* (New Delhi, PPH, 1969), pp. 2–3.

People today have . . . even less food (and that at higher cost) than ten months ago. The problem of unemployment and lack of all-round economic development has also become worse during the last ten months. But, despite all difficulties which they are facing, our people are still giving us their general support precisely because they find that we are doing our best and that it is the Center's policies that are preventing any worthwhile measure of improving their living conditions.[2]

Food was the first issue over which the two factions clashed. Kerala produces only 50 percent of its food grain requirements, even though its productivity is the highest in India. It is therefore helplessly dependent on food imports from outside. In normal years, it used to buy rice from Andhra Pradesh. Since 1965, however, scarcity of grains made the central government's help in grain distribution necessary. One of the measures taken to pool the country's grain production was the creation of food zones and the prohibition of free movement of grain from one state to another. The net result of this policy for Kerala was that it could not buy grain from Andhra Pradesh, but had to depend upon the central government to make supplies available. New Delhi's failure to meet Kerala's food needs created an acute rice shortage there in the difficult years of 1966–67; the meager rice ration had to be cut a number of times.

When the united front government came into being, it had no more than a week's supply of rice in stock, and immediately a battle began between Trivandrum and New Delhi. While all constituents of the coalition blamed the central government for Kerala's hunger (all the more so because Kerala earns a substantial amount of foreign exchange for India and gets very little in return in terms of national investment in industry), differences soon cropped up between the Marxists' and the CPI's approach to the food issue. Namboodiripad insisted on accelerating confrontation with the central government, while the CPI wanted the state government to apply itself to augmenting Kerala's own

---

[2] *People's Democracy*, January 14, 1968.

production without giving up the struggle against New Delhi. The actual difference between the two factions was not over whether Kerala should make an effort to increase its food output and grain procurement, but over *how* this program was to be carried out.

There were clashes fairly early between the food minister, Mrs. Gowri, and the agriculture minister, Govindan Nair, each faction blaming the other for helping the wealthy peasants. Conflict soon spread to cover the questions of distributing land to the landless, further land reforms, industrial policy, the role of the police in dealing with "legitimate" trade union and *kisan sabha* activity, jobs, education—almost anything. It became evident that among the partners of the coalition an acute struggle was developing over encroachments on one another's political bases. Each group was anxious, first, to protect and reinforce its existing political base and, second, to jog others out of their bases. The struggle mainly involved the four major groups in the coalition: the CPI(M), the CPI, the Muslim League, and the SSP. The smaller groups, however, found themselves in a strategic position to exploit these conflicts to their own advantage or at least to prevent any infringement on their own little political acres. The Marxists found themselves in a predicament because they were obliged to fight "revisionism" on the one hand and "ultra-leftism" on the other.[3]

[3] "There are reports, not all of which are suspect, that the CPI(M) leadership is under heavy pressure from the ultras in their ranks. It fears that without public anti-revisionist postures and pronouncements it may suffer the same fate as its counterpart in Andhra. When the Communist party was split the reasons given by Namboodiripad and Gopalan were that international revisionism had to be uprooted under the leadership of the Communist party of China and that national revisionism had to be uprooted through a revolutionary upheaval against the Congress. Now the Chinese Communist leadership is accusing Namboodiripad and Gopalan of revisionism and they are forced to counterattack by accusing the Chinese leadership of sectarianism and Big Brotherism. As for the revolutionary upheaval within the country, they now say that conditions have not yet matured. Naturally, many of the rank and file as well as the younger middle cadre are asking how the stand of Namboodiripad and Gopalan differs from that of the revisionist CPI." "Nemesis in Kerala?" *Economic and Political Weekly*, July 8, 1968.

INTERPARTY DUELS

The CPI(M) judged each constituent unit's loyalty to the united front by its willingness to fight New Delhi, and found most, if not all, of the units deficient. The Marxists' principal targets of attack were, however, the Congress party and the CPI, a liaison between the two being what they feared most. A cruel irony of the Kerala political situation could not have escaped the Marxists—had the two Communist factions been able to work together, they could have brought the state under stable Communist rule for five years, without having to share power with noncommited socialists and wavering bourgeois partners. What seemed to be hurting the Marxists most was that the CPI should have made revisionist Communism "respectable" to the bourgeoisie, who were now anxious to placate the CPI and whose chief enemy was now the CPI(M). In these circumstances the Marxists could be expected to make a bid to oust the CPI as a political force in Kerala. This is precisely what they sought to do immediately after the united front government came into being. It was not, however, a conflict between two entirely unequal antagonists, for each Communist faction suffered from severe weaknesses in its mass base and organizational machinery.

The CPI had some eminent leaders like M. N. Govindan Nair and T. V. Thomas, both of whom were in the united front government, as well as several others; each of them can be said to have been a builder of Communism in Kerala. When the Communist party split in 1964, most of the top leaders, except Namboodiripad and Gopalan, remained with the parent group. The portion of higher caste leaders is far greater in the CPI than in the CPI(M) The CPI in Kerala is a party "with a large number of leaders and few followers. In the urban centers and in the trade unions these leaders count as respectable people and as trade union leaders—but not as political leaders. And in the rural areas their influence is almost nil." The CPI leaders, however, "displayed tremendous capacity to maneuver in the assembly and to get the support of the press in their attempts to isolate the CPI(M) from other parties in the united front. But the party is not unified in its opposition to the CPI(M). A large number of CPI members feel that the party's political future is doomed if it breaks with the CPI(M). In the short run, the CPI's political survival depends on the support it can get from Congress, but in the long run Congress support will be a liability and, moreover, the all-India leadership of the party has not adjusted itself to an alliance with Congress." [4]

The source of CPI(M) strength is its rural base from whence comes most of its electoral support. The party "exercises relatively little influence in the social and economic fields, in the press and in the professions. A significant section of the rural masses solidly support it and its votes cannot be split by others. But these votes do not constitute a majority though they are the largest single block. In other words, if all the other parties unite and oppose CPI(M) the party will be defeated in a majority of the constituencies. But if there is no such alliance among the non-Marxists, CPI(M) will emerge as the largest single party in a fresh poll." However, the CPI(M) "is the only party in the united front that can afford to go into political wilderness and still survive. This is the source of its dynamism and aggressiveness." [5]

The Marxists did not show much of their "dynamism and aggressiveness" during the first months of the united front ministry although, as noted, conflicts with the CPI and the SSP began fairly early. Dynamism and aggressiveness grew with time, as a result of deliberations at the Burdwan plenum of the CPI(M) cen-

---

[4] "Kerala: Moving Towards a Poll," *Economic and Political Weekly*, July 8, 1969. This assessment, by a CPI intellectual who is the journal's correspondent in Kerala, was made when the Congress party was facing the crisis that soon afterward led to its split.
[5] *Ibid.*

tral committee and the Madurai meeting of that committee, and also as a result of what was happening in West Bengal. Thus, although the CPI complained within three months of the ministry's life that the Marxists were trying to dislodge it from some of its trade unions by setting up rival trade unions and by "making use of the government machinery to wreck well-established industrial relations committees," the Marxists took time to oppose certain "pro-capitalist" aspects of the industrial policy devised by CPI Minister Thomas.[6] However, they bitterly fought aspects of the agricultural policy of Govindan Nair.

The CPI, on the other hand, vehemently opposed the land, internal administration, services, forests, and Harijan welfare policies of the Marxist ministers. The cabinet was not functioning as a team except on a very limited number of issues like the paucity of the national government's assistance to Kerala in terms of food grains and agricultural development. Here too, as E.M.S. pointed out in his articles on the united front in *Deshabhimani* (see chapter 6), none of the non-Marxist groups was apparently prepared to carry the fight against New Delhi as far as the Marxists were prepared to do. Conflicts within the united front ministry were rationalized by Namboodiripad as inevitable, given the state of political affairs in Kerala and given the strength and position of the political parties; in fact conflicts, he claimed, lent the ministry a certain stability.

It is a fact that the government is composed of seven different political parties. They are different parties precisely because they do not see eye to eye on many questions of national policy. None of these parties conceals its views on any of these vital questions. Despite these differences, however, they have a common viewpoint with regard to questions of current policy.[7]

[6] *New Age*, October 20, 1967. E.M.S. told the Washington *Post* correspondent that it was the fault of Marxist ministers in the government, especially of his own, that they did not publicly verbalize their opposition to the "pro-capitalist" aspects of the CPI industrial policy.

[7] Interview with Washington *Post* correspondent, in *People's Democracy*, January 14, 1968.

The Marxist chief minister cited conflicts over industrial policy and their "resolution" as an example of the operational behavior of the united front. When the CPI minister's statement of industrial policy was published, it was "acclaimed" by industrialists inside and outside Kerala but was criticized by the trade-union movement. The CPI(M) politbureau was "the first to make a systematic critique of the policy statement and in suggesting that those parts of the statement which have anti-labor and pro-monopoly implications should be removed." After a few weeks of bitter controversy

It was possible to have a dispassionate exchange of views leading to a clarity of ideas and a broadly common approach. . . . Even now there is a fundamental difference of approach to the objective and program of industrialization. Our Party, for instance, is of the opinion that collaboration between Indian and foreign private monopolies will not help the process of rapid industrialization. Nor do we think that the incentives that are offered to industrialize should be extended to big monopoly capitalists. There are, however, certain other constituents in the United Front who disagree and hold that industrialization is impossible without collaboration between Indian and foreign monopoly capitalists. EMS mentioned the Right Communists as inclined to this point of view and added that this basic conflict of approach undoubtedly continued.

Industries Minister Thomas came in for severe attack by the Marxists for his alleged reluctance to fight central government "indifference" to Kerala's miseries and for his alleged planning with the Congress faction to topple the united front ministry. The Marxists strongly objected to Thomas' reported soliciting of Japanese collaboration in Kerala's industrial field.[8] E.M.S. him-

[8] Thomas explored prospects of Japanese collaboration during a visit to Japan in the autumn of 1967. The Marxists charged that in doing so he had exceeded his brief. Thomas, however, maintained that he had never acted in the belief that Japanese collaboration alone would solve Kerala's industrialization problems. His talks in Japan, he said, had been motivated by the desire to bring in Japanese capital and skills as a supplement to an intensive drive within the state. The Marxists apparently did not object to limited Japanese collaboration in the field of industry. E.M.S. himself praised a joint Indo-Japanese venture at Anakamaly. What the

self conducted negotiations with several East European governments for socialist participation in Kerala's industrialization.[9]
Neither effort, in effect, meant much more than a symbolic political gesture, for foreign participation in Indian industry is
decided not by the states but by New Delhi. What the Marxists were anxious to prove was that the CPI preferred foreign
monopoly-capital rather than the socialist countries, to help
India's industrialization.[10]

The CPI agriculture minister, Govindan Nair, faced Marxist
opposition when he wanted to introduce tractors on a large scale.
The united front ministry had set up an Agro-Industries Corporation. One of its objectives was to popularize agricultural machinery among the peasants. Among the Corporation's functions
was the hiring and selling of tractors. About 500 tractors were
already in operation in the state; rich peasants who owned them
made a lot of money by renting them to middle-level and even
poor peasants. Nair wanted the Agro-Industries Corporation to
acquire a large number of tractors which were to be sold to
"smaller farmers" on "easy hire-purchase terms," or rented out to
small farmers at reasonable rates. The Marxists opposed this policy
because the tractors would create more unemployment among the
sharecroppers and agricultural laborers.[11]

CONFLICT OVER LAND POLICY

In Kerala, as in West Bengal, it was conflict over land policy
that finally broke up the united front. The difference between
the two states was that while in Bengal, the two Communist factions, largely because of the newness of the peasant struggle, were

---

Marxists did not want to see was the entry of largescale Japanese capital into Kerala. A Communist-dominated government, they argued, must prefer collaboration
with the socialist countries to that with Japan or other capitalist nations. See
"Trouble in Kerala," *Economic and Political Weekly,* November 11, 1967, for a
statement of Thomas's position.

[9] E.M.S. spoke of his discussions with ambassadors of East European countries
in the course of his interview with the Washington *Post* correspondent.

[10] E.M.S. made this allegation in *ibid.*   [11] Achutha Menon, pp. 24–26.

locked in a relationship of conflict-cooperation-conflict, in Kerala they were in conflict from the beginning to the end. In Bengal, cooperation at the grass-root level sometimes obliged the state leaders of the two factions to act in unison; in Kerala, rivalry and conflict was as strong at the grass-root level as at the state level.

In charge of land revenue was Mrs. Gowri, CPI(M), who also looked after general administration; she was thus in a position to work out the Marxist land policy, and she had the powerful backing of the chief minister in the government and of A. K. Gopalan outside. She had piloted the land reforms bill of the first Communist government in Kerala in 1957–58, which had given her a thorough grasp of the state's complicated agrarian relations and of the differentiations that had occurred among the peasantry during the intervening years.

It was the differentiations that made her task in 1967 difficult. The Marxists had already a strong base among the poor peasants, landless workers, and sharecroppers; Mrs. Gowri's first task was to protect and legalize the gains secured by the landless and the poor peasant in occupying waste, forest, and other land since 1957. In 1967–68, the non-Marxist partners of the united front demanded that unauthorized land seizures be annulled, and that land be distributed through all-party committees. The CPI supported this demand for obvious reasons. Mrs. Gowri had no intention of doing anything of the sort. On the contrary, she distributed titles for several thousand acres of land to peasants the bulk of whom were CPI(M) supporters. Not every one of them qualified for the title.[12] The CPI and other coalition partners charged the Marxist minister with partisanship and corruption, but she was defended by her party with a certain measure of aggressiveness.

It is difficult to understand what the Rightists mean by partisanship in land distribution. Is it their contention that the available govern-

[12] Achutha Menon, pp. 12–17.

ment waste land should be distributed among the various political parties in the state instead of to the landless agricultural laborers and poor peasants? Will they demand that a party like the Swantantra among whose followers none are landless should also be given a share in the land if they are to consider the land distribution genuinely non-partisan? Or is it the contention of the Rightists that because the landless and poor in a particular place owe allegiance to the CPI(M) they should be deprived of their right to have the land distributed in that area?

Even the Rightists after the election debacle of 1965 will not challenge the fact that the CPI(M) commands the support of a much larger percentage of the rural poor than any other party in the state. It is only natural that they will form a good proportion of the beneficiaries of the government's land distribution scheme.[13]

The controversy that raged within the united front over land policy was related to the political factions' linkages with the disturbed and at times turbulent agrarian pattern in Kerala. The non-Marxists were united in trying to dislodge the CPI(M) from its commanding position among the rural poor; the Marxists were anxious to extend land reforms to the plantations, whose owners in 1958 had been granted a ten-year exemption from the ceiling provided in the first land reforms act. The CPI(M) also wanted to build up a constituency among the middle-level and rich peasants and thus penetrate the social base of its coalition partners as well as that of the Congress party.

In these circumstances, it was not entirely unexpected that Mrs. Gowri would bide her time to finalize new land reforms. She took eighteen months to prepare legislation to amend the Agrarian Reforms Act of 1958 and bring it before the legislature. A select committee of the assembly, over which she presided, took another year to study the legislation; its sessions were marked by the hardest possible bargaining. The united front broke up as soon as the legislation was approved by the government.

The coalition partners were apparently apprehensive that the

[13] *People's Democracy*, March 17, 1968.

Marxists would arouse the poor peasantry to *implement* the legislation themselves without waiting for the government to act. That would have brought about a new agrarian turmoil in the Kerala countryside, comparable to what happened in Bengal in 1969, but deeper in structural dimensions. Sundarayya was not entirely incorrect when he told the central council of the All-India Kisan Sabha in December 1970: "When the Kerala government passed the Agrarian Reform law and the Kisan Sabha declared for implementation from 1 January 1970, the ministry was broken." [14]

It is indeed the most radical land reform measure devised in any Indian state so far. It enlarged the definition of the tenant by including the term "deemed tenancies," which meant that the landlord could not evict a tenant if "actual cultivation exists." This provision went a long way to ensure that the benefit of the law reached the tiller and was not lost in a welter of legal formalities. The right of resumption was drastically restricted. Even the restricted resumption rights had to be exercised within six months of the Act's coming into force; there could be no resumption at all if the tenant belonged to the untouchable castes or the Scheduled tribes.

Each subtenant or sharecropper automatically became a tenant; the government had to find him and give him his land title; he could be owner-tenant by paying a "reasonable rent" in installments. No family or individual could own more than 20 standard acres of land, including nonarable land. The normal ceiling for an adult person or a family consisting of a sole surviving member was placed at 5 standard acres. A family, or a company, or an association could own 10 acres, with one additional acre for every member in excess of 5 (in the case of a family), subject to the overall limit of 20 standard acres. Exemptions allowed were very limited, and these did not cover religious institutions. Hutment

[14] *Millions Fighting for Land and Wages* (Calcutta, All-India Kisan Sabha, 1970), pp. 6–7.

dwellers, of whom there are hundreds of thousands in the towns and villages, could now buy the right of title to their homestead land by paying 25 percent of the market value, but only 12 percent if the landowner was in possession of land in excess of the ceiling.

Another major benefit conferred on sharecroppers was that they were not required to prove any specific permission of tenancy from the landowner. Permission would be assumed to exist if a sharecropper could prove that he had been in possession of the land from August 1968 to January 1970. The CPI minister for land revenue in the non-CPI(M) Kerala government described this as a "real Magna Carta for the *kudikidappukara* (sharecroppers)," a claim that was not unjustified in the context of the miserable condition of these people elsewhere in India.[15]

CONFRONTATION WITH NEW DELHI

The Marxists' principal tactical line, as already noted, was to build up a continuous confrontation with New Delhi. In the first place this was the CPI(M)'s psychological reaction to its memory of what happened in the late 1950s; the Marxists were genuinely apprehensive of a Congress "plot" to overthrow the united front regime. Their apprehensions were confirmed by the dismissal of Bengal's united front government in the autumn of 1967.

In the following February, the Marxists saw "all indications" that "the conspirators have already finalized their plan" to overthrow the Kerala government. "The diabolical plan is to continue

[15] K. T. Jacob, *Tiller Gets Land in Kerala* (New Delhi, PPH, 1970), pp. 3–7. The CPI-led government rushed the legislation through the legislature, and it received presidential assent and became operative in January 1970. The CPI(M) immediately induced its *kisan sabhas* to implement the Act without waiting for governmental implementation. Thus ensued the first major confrontation between the Marxists and the "minifront" ministry. According to the CPI(M), 32 peasants were killed and 50,000 arrested, but "in spite of brutal repression this struggle achieved great success." See Konar's report to the extended meeting of the Central Kisan Council at Bhagalpur, Bihar, in December 1970, in *Millions Fighting For Land and Wages*.

to starve Kerala . . . and simultaneously to raise a hue and cry about the breakdown of 'law and order'—shades of the 1959 'liberation struggle'—and prepare for the Center to dismiss the Government which enjoys not only overwhelming majority in the legislature but complete confidence of the state's people." [16]

In March, *People's Democracy* printed extracts from a "secret memorandum" from the Kerala Congress committee to the Congress high command accusing the Marxists of trying to build their party strength in Kerala at the cost of good government, and even of preparing for an "armed struggle." [17] The politbureau, meeting in Calcutta, came out with the "opinion" that "our Party together with its allies in the united front government in Kerala will have to confront the central government irrespective of the consequences." [18]

In May the CPI(M) started a campaign against the CPI for the latter's unwillingness to concentrate on the struggle against the central government. At the same time, it called "for a mobilization and struggle of the entire people against the discriminatory policies of the central government. The immediate task in Kerala is to mobilize people for the struggle against the Center. . . . Every party in the state will be judged by the people by the attitude it takes to this crucial struggle of the people for their food." [19]

In June, the politbureau directed all party units to "intensify the mass explanatory campaign and overcome the hesitations and vacillations of the democratic parties and groups and win them over for a joint and united mass struggle against central government policies. The entire energies of the party should be directed to this supreme task." This was an implicit confession that the struggles organized so far—in the form of strikes and moratoriums—had not been very successful because of noncollaboration of the constituent units of the united front. The Marxists

[16] *People's Democracy*, February 11, 1967. [17] *Ibid.*, March 31, 1967.
[18] *Ibid.*, March 24, 1968. [19] *Ibid.*, May 26, 1968.

began to accuse the CPI of hatching a plot to form an alternative united front with the Congress party, without the CPI(M).[20]

THE COLLAPSE OF THE UNITED FRONT

Tensions and conflicts within the united front exploded in the spring of 1969 into a barrage of allegations. The Marxists bore the brunt of the attack, but gave no quarter. The CPI was the first to bring to public notice certain serious lapses in the functioning of the ministry, particularly problems of corruption and the "hegemonistic aspirations" of the CPI(M). From then on the Marxists tried to isolate the CPI from the other constituents and to ease it out of the united front.

Corruption became a mass issue until eventually not a single member of the ministry remained uncharged. All charges and countercharges fell into three categories: personal graft, funds and benefits for the party and, particularly, the award of jobs. Ministers belonging to the minor factions of the front were suspected of personal corruption. Charges against the CPI(M) ranged from raising money for the party fund to favoritism in the grant of land titles and in land distribution.[21] Two ministers against whom serious charges of corruption were brought were Minister of Health Wellingdon and Finance Minister Kunju.

Evidently three principal reasons could be found for widespread corruption. First, the ministry functioned without leadership, each group operating by itself, each minister somewhat autonomous in his portfolio, responsible not so much to the chief

---

[20] *Ibid.*, June 2, 1968. T. V. Thomas told a news conference on May 22 that the CPI wanted the struggle against the central government to be conducted unitedly by all parties of the united front, but the present attitude and stand of the CPI(M) was not one of helping such unity. He denied that the constituents of the united front were isolating the CPI(M). "The fact is that they are isolating themselves. But so far as our party is concerned, there is no plan to form a front eliminating the CPI(M) from it; such a thing had never entered our thoughts." *New Age*, June 2, 1968.

[21] Among those who received titles to land was one Abu who, it was discovered, owned many acres of land and was a close relative of Mrs. Gowri. "Abu's Tribe," *Economic and Political Weekly*, April 13, 1968.

minister as to his own party. This created ample scope for the offering and receiving of rewards. Second, there was no drive or idealism behind the ministry; the coalition was a marriage of convenience, a poor papering-over underneath which conflicts raged
among the constituents. These conflicts often paralyzed the ministry and made it slow-moving. Conflicts between ministers sometimes made them use civil servants for their own personal or
party purposes making an ideal climate for corruption. The category of corruption which probably prevailed on a large scale was
raising contributions for party funds. This kind of corruption
apparently created a problem for the CPI(M). As one reporter
put it:

There are any number of instances to make the point that corruption
flourishes in a scandalous manner. It is corruption on a vast scale even
though the sums involved may be quite small. It may start off as "corruption for the party" or securing donations for the party through getting some favors done. Soon enough, however, this slides into personal
corruption, into sharing the largesse. Those who are on the donating
side are shrewd enough to do so in such a way that not only imper-
sonal entities but living persons become beholden to them. Taking
care of the education of the children of the party leader to whom the
"party donation" is to be made and through whom the favor is to be
secured; arranging for a car to facilitate trips to Trivandrum; "small
improvements" in the house of the party leader concerned, if not a
"small house"—this is the manner by which the erosion process takes
shape. Indeed, this is the manner by which the very class character of
the party is transformed. "Sugar-coated bullets" would kill the party
more effectively than any amount of repression: this is the warning
that Mao had given his party in 1949 on the eve of the nationwide victory of the Chinese revolution. The warning is quite relevant for the
CPI(M) in Kerala today.[22]

Yet it was not corruption that pulled down the united front
ministry. What was at stake was the concept of the united front.
In 1969 Namboodiripad resolved to establish his own and his par-

---

[22] "Compromise in Kerala," *Economic and Political Weekly*, August 2, 1969.

ty's leadership. This raised the question: is the united front a coalition of equals or is it under the hegemony of the CPI(M)? The group that put up the strongest resistance to Marxist hegemony was the CPI. The executive of the Kerala State Council of the CPI adopted a resolution in April 1969 "demanding" solution of thirteen issues "within three months"; otherwise, the party's "attitude towards the united front government in Kerala will have to be reconsidered." The thirteen issues charged the CPI(M) with interfering in the working of other ministries, disrupting agricultural development, serious irregularities in land assignment, non-implementation of major decisions taken by the coordination committee, and favoritism in the matter of appointments.

The first minister against whom serious charges of corruption were leveled was Kunju, a Muslim leader of the ISP, a group that leaned heavily on the CPI(M). The decision to investigate the charges was apparently made by the chief minister, without referring the issue either to the coordinating committee or to the ISP leadership. Namboodiripad asked Kunju to resign, and the latter did so under protest in May; the "storm" blew over temporarily, and the ISP remained in the united front.[23]

However, the major non-Marxist parties were not prepared to concede the power to make preliminary inquiries into corruption charges on the floor of the assembly to the chief minister; they wanted the entire process of inquiry, from the preliminary to the final stage, to be conducted by a high court judge. The CPI actually made a motion for a resolution that a high court justice be appointed to look into corruption charges against Health Minister Wellingdon; this was an overt move to deprive the chief minister of the right he claimed to make a preliminary investigation and order a judicial probe only if he thought a prima facie case existed. Nor would the CPI and others agree to Namboodiripad's suggestion that an assembly committee decide if a prima facie case

[23] *The Hindu,* May 13, 1969.

were there. The non-Marxist units of the coalition were determined to resist Marxist hegemony over the united front government.[24]

The Marxists interpreted this opposition as stemming from the groups' basic unwillingness to make a bona fide attack on corruption, and to their desire to use charges of corruption to discredit and finally disrupt the united front. The Marxists also were now determined to establish their supremacy in the united front; if the front was a coalition of equals, they were more equal than the others. *People's Democracy* argued that the parties to the united front had accepted the leadership of the chief minister by submitting details of the ministers' assets to him rather than to the coordination committee. "After accepting this position of the chief minister, when these parties today try to reduce the chief minister to the position of any one of the ministers belonging to any one of the constituent parties, their questionable motives have to be challenged." [25] To the Marxists, the crisis in the united front was not due to the problem of corruption; the basic question was "relations within the united front." As Namboodiripad saw it:

The question is to reach agreement on how the constituents of the united front should function . . . how they should behave toward one another. The question of machinery for probing into corruption charges against ministers is only a part of this basic question. It is a part for which a solution can easily be found if the other questions are resolved.[26]

The "basic question," however, remained unresolved. The crisis therefore deepened, and by the fall of 1969 the cabinet rarely met. On October 3, the CPI(M) suffered its first defeat in the assembly when a nonofficial motion demanding an inquiry into the charges of corruption against Wellingdon was declared adopted

[24] *People's Democracy*, June 8, 1969, printed a long statement by E.M.S. on the political problems created by the issue of corruption.
[25] *Ibid.*, May 11, 1969.
[26] *Ibid.*, June 8, 1969.

by the Speaker. Adoption of the resolution, which was presented by a CPI member, marked the Marxists' "complete isolation" from the other major partners of the coalition.[27]

Three days later, Gopalan declared that the united front ministry was "on the verge of breaking up." He charged the CPI and Muslim League with a "conspiracy" to form an alternative coalition and, as if to confrim this charge, the anti-Marxist parties— the CPI, the Muslim League, the SSP, and the RSP—met in Trivandrum on October 6 "to finalize the strategy of their final confrontation with the Marxists." [28]

Another meeting was held on October 11, at which seven demands were made on the chief minister which were, in effect, a repetition of the earlier thirteen demands of the CPI. The four groups declared: "If no satisfactory and clear decisions are arrived at quickly, the continued existence of the united front will be a violation of the promises made to the people and, therefore, we will be compelled in that event to withdraw the support our parties gave to E.M.S. Namboodiripad for the formation of a ministry under his leadership." [29]

In the meantime, the CPI(M) politbureau met in Calcutta to take stock of the Kerala developments, and apparently decided to accept the challenge. E.M.S.'s response to their seven-point demand was that he was unable to discuss them unless the four groups admitted beforehand that the method they used to bring the October 3 resolution into the assembly and get it passed with opposition support was wrong. The national leadership of the two Communist factions now fruitlessly intervened to resolve the deadlock between the two Kerala factions.[30]

---

[27] *The Statesman,* October 4, 1969.   [28] *Ibid.,* October 8, 1969.
[29] Achutha Menon, pp. 62–66.
[30] Two CPI leaders, Bhupesh Gupta and N. K. Krishnan, met with three CPI(M) leaders, Namboodiripad, Gopalan, and Sundarayya, but could not find a way to resolve the deadlock. *The Statesman* correspondent reported earlier that while the Kerala CPI was willing to form a coalition without the Marxists, the national leadership did not believe that it would be wise to do so. However, the national leadership had to approve the decision of the Kerala CPI to form a new coalition without the Marxists. *The Statesman,* October 5, 1969.

On October 17, E.M.S. struck the blow that felled the united front ministry. He announced his decision to order inquiries into charges of corruption made not merely against Wellingdon, but also against the two CPI ministers and a minister belonging to a local group. That same evening these three ministers as well as three others (two of them belonging to the Muslim League) resigned. E.M.S. first wrote to each one, pleading with him to withdraw his resignation. When none complied, he refused to tender the resignation of the ministry unless the assembly voted "no confidence" in him as chief minister. He challenged the four groups to bring forth a motion of "no confidence" which, he knew, could be carried only with the Congress party's support. His tactic obviously was to provoke the CPI to bring down the united front ministry with the active support of the Congress party.

The four groups, in their turn, introduced a resolution on October 24 calling for an inquiry into charges of corruption made against three Marxist ministers; the name of E.M.S. was kept off the list lest he should construe this as a motion of "no confidence" in his leadership. Namboodiripad, however, declared that he would consider passage of the resolution as amounting to a vote of "no confidence" in himself. The resolution was adopted by a margin of nine votes, all of the nine Congress members voting in favor. E.M.S. drove straight from the assembly hall to the governor's office and tendered his resignation. Thus ended thirty-two months of hectic government in Kerala under CPI(M) leadership.[31]

ISOLATION OF THE CPI(M)

The Marxists had evidently resolved to travel alone for a time. Their main purpose presumably was to demonstrate to the political parties and people of Kerala that without the CPI(M), the state could not have a stable government. It was only by breaking

[31] Achutha Menon, pp. 60–67.

the unity of the non-Marxist groups that the CPI(M) could rees-
tablish, more effectively, its leadership of a new united front.
E.M.S.'s tactic to disrupt the unity of the four groups failed, because until the last moment there was a shared belief among them
that he would not scuttle the ministry, and somehow a way out of
the impasse would be found.

If E.M.S. somewhat surprised them by his resignation, they in
turn disappointed the Marxists by putting together a "minifront"
government under CPI leadership. The new ministry included
Kerala Congress, an avowedly anti-Communist group, and was
supported by the Congress party in the assembly. The deepening
crisis in the Congress party awakened CPI hopes of a coalition between Communists, socialists, and the progressive elements in
Congress; the experiment in Kerala was thus regarded by the CPI
as pregnant with possibilities. The greatest benefactor from the
new alliance was, however, the Muslim League, which now was
given the coveted home (internal administration) portfolio, a phenomenon that would be unthinkable in any other Indian state.
Led by Govindan Nair, the "minifront" ministry applied itself
with some vigor to implement the former united front's program,
especially the measures that the Marxists had stalled—
amendments to the land reforms act, for example.

The Marxists from the very beginning bent their energies to
make it impossible for the new regime to govern. But their calls
for strike and demonstrations did not apparently arouse much enthusiasm among the urban middle classes. Nair's promise to give
the state a clean and honest administration, more issue- than ide-
ology-oriented, perhaps found favor with the urban population
that had grown somewhat tired of the feverish stagnation of the
past two and a half years.

The CPI(M) then turned to its traditional constituency. Gopalan, perhaps the shrewdest mass tactician in the CPI(M), asked
peasants not to wait for implementation of the Agrarian Reforms
Amendment Bill but to act immediately to seize lands.[32] In some

cases the peasants did so, but the ministry was cautious in handling peasant militancy; in fact, it seemed unwilling to provoke the Marxists more than was absolutely necessary.

Its programmatic zeal and issue-orientation brought in some immediate dividends. In two by-elections, both in predominantly urban constituencies, the "minifront" won with comfortable majorities over its Marxist rivals. Chief Minister Achutha Menon defeated his CPI(M) rival by a margin of 26,000 votes in a constituency where the latter had had very little following in 1967. The Marxist candidate, however, polled 16,000 votes, which was indicative of the influence the CPI(M) had acquired in three years.

What altered the political situation in Kerala, as in the rest of the country, was the split in the Congress party. The nine Congress legislators divided into two groups, five supporting the "Syndicate," and four Mrs. Gandhi's faction; the Kerala Congress Committee also split into two rival bodies.

The CPI identified the ruling Congress faction as a progressive force, and bent its efforts to work out a Congress-Communist alliance. As a modest beginning, the CPI supported a ruling Congress party candidate in the second by-election, and hailed his victory over the CPI(M) as a welcome wind of change. A CPI leader saw in this victory a change in the political outlook of the electorate. The voter, he hazarded, did not care any longer for anti-Communism or anti-Congressism. "What can be called a program-orientation has gripped large sections of the masses. They would exercise their choice against the background of what parties offer and what their record has been. Tactical lines will have notoriously short lives in the present transitional phase in Indian politicism." [33]

[33] Mohit Sen, "Kerala's Changing Politics," *ibid.*, May 16, 1970.

8

COMMUNISM AND
THE PEASANTRY

"The Indian village," says Gunnar Myrdal in *Asian Drama,* "is
like a complex molecule among whose parts extreme tensions
have been built up. Although the tensions crisscross in a manner
that maintains equilibrium, it is conceivable that they may reorganize in a way that would explode the molecule. This would
perhaps not happen spontaneously but as a result of forceful onslaught from outside."

The molecule of the Indian village, claim three agrarian ex-
perts of the CPI, has "started exploding." [1] While this would appear to be an overstatement if one took an overview of the rural
universe, it is true that peasant militancy under Communist leadership has shaken the traditional equilibrium in the rural areas of
certain portions of the country, notably West Bengal and Kerala.
Of greater moment than what has already happened is what *can*
happen in rural India if the long-prevailing objective conditions

---

[1] C. Rajeshawara Rao, Bhowani Sen, and Y. V. Krishna Rao, *Problems of India's Agrarian Sector* (New Delhi, PPH, 1970), p. 1.

meet with the proper kind of subjective stimulus in the years to come.

It is significant that during the last three or four years, the agrarian question has pushed itself into the forefront of Indian politics. For the first time in India, the Communists have turned their faces toward the rural proletariat, recognizing it as the largest single potential revolutionary element in Indian society. Peasant struggles have not only spread rapidly during this period in comparison to the preceding fifteen years, they have tended to take militant forms in several areas.

It is somewhat remarkable that the question of violence in the context of agrarian struggles has proved to be academic. Experience has shown that agrarian tensions almost automatically tend to lead to violence, for there is a tremendous amount of violence, hatred, and bitterness hidden beneath the superficially quiescent caste-cum-agrarian relations in India. Traditionally, the poor peasant and the landless agricultural laborer who are also, in most cases, untouchables, have borne with their famous docility and resignation the inhumanities inflicted by the landlords and their numerous rent-collecting agents. It is not generally recognized that life in the Indian village has been regulated for hundreds of years by one-sided violence and cruelty on the part of the landlord.

Nearly every significant peasant struggle in India has therefore tended to be violent. Gandhi discovered the potentially explosive molecule in the village during his first national nonviolent campaign against British rule; violence broke out not in the cities, nor among the working classes, but in a village in Bihar, whereupon Gandhi called off the entire *Satyagraha,* and never again dared to bring the peasantry actively into his struggles. Compared to China, India has had few significant peasant uprisings, but those that have occurred have hardly been entirely peaceful.[2] The

[2] Gandhi did not expect structural changes in agrarian relations in India to take place without violence. He expected some violence from the landless, and took an

landed "haves" have seldom hesitated to use force, and they have almost always been aided by authority. The question now is whether the land-based "have-nots," too, will have to use force to acquire the rights which have been long denied them.

Since 1967, there have been several major changes in agrarian relations, each of them pregnant with not entirely foreseeable possibilities. If the events of these years have lent some clarity to the realities of Indian politics, the phenomenon that has become most clear is that land relationships happen to be the strongest determinant in political alignments at the state level. In other words, the social alignments on which the Indian political system rests are predominantly determined by agrarian relations. It is mostly at the level of national politics that other factors exert powerful pulls—such as organized industry, unionized workers, the bureaucracy, the military, and the intellectual and technological elites. A radical realignment of agrarian relations will dis-

---

indulgent view of it. See his two interviews with Louis Fischer in 1942 in Nirmal K. Bose, *Selections from Gandhi,* (Ahmedabad, 1948).

There is unfortunately no comprehensive, documented history of peasant struggles in India. L. Natarajan's *Peasant Uprisings in India* (Bombay, 1953), covers the period 1850–1900, but actually collects information about four major series of uprisings—the Santal uprising of 1855–1856, the indigo cultivators' strike of 1860, the Maratha rebellions of 1875 and the Moplah uprisings in Kerala between 1836 and 1896. S. B. Choudhuri's *Civil Disturbances during the British Rule in India* (Calcutta, 1957), has information about peasant revolts up to 1857. In recent years, Abdullah Rasul, a CPI(M) peasant front leader, has done some useful work in Bengali, and his *Krishaksabhar Itihas* (History of the Kisan Sabha) (Calcutta, 1970), contains information about the major peasant struggles of this century. His accounts, however, are taken from records kept at the offices of the AIKS, and from personal memory; some of the records may well have been exaggerated. In spite of this and other defects, the volume is indispensable for a study of the Indian peasant movement. Rasul himself has said in the preface that many of the AIKS files have been destroyed—some by the police, others by the office holders themselves. There are particular gaps for the period 1936–43, when the peasant movement assumed a certain amount of militancy.

Of all the state committees of the AIKS, only the Bengal branch seems to have maintained a certain continuity of records and files. Neither in Malayalam nor in Telugu has any attempt been made so far to publish a comprehensive history of the peasant movement in Kerala or Andhra Pradesh. Such accounts as are available are sketchy and propagandist. The compilation of a documented and comprehensive history of the peasant movement in India during this century awaits Indian and foreign scholarly enterprise.

mantle the social base of the political system. If the molecule explodes, will the system explode too?

The two most notable changes that have taken place in the agrarian sector since 1967 are the "green revolution" and organized peasant militancy under Communist leadership. The two have occurred simultaneously. The "green revolution" is the result of the first large-scale application of science and technology to agriculture, opening up prospects of capitalist development of farming. At the political level, the "green revolution" has persuaded the majority of political leaders that technology would make structural changes in existing land relationships avoidable and could work as a substitue for land reforms.

The Communists, on the other hand, have been trying to exploit the tensions created by capitalist development of agriculture to organize the rural proletariat in demands for tenure and land reforms and for the amelioration of other hardships, like the burden of indebtedness. Capitalist development of farming has begun in earnest only in a number of states; in the rest, the agricultural pattern is still predominantly feudal and archaic.

Like the highly uneven pattern of Indian agriculture, the peasant movement also is extremely uneven; over the larger portion of India, it has hardly begun. But the tensions within both are already felt all over the country. This is but natural, for there are actually only two majorities in India, the young and the poor, both dominating the rural universe. What happens to these two majorities is bound to shake the Indian polity, although from reading the daily press in India one would get the impression that the peasant and the village hardly exist.

Among the many paradoxes of Indian life, nothing is probably more striking than the mutual exclusiveness of the city and the village. Indian intellectualism has been, and continues to be, predominantly urban. It is probably the urban intellectual or middle-class orientation of Indian Communism that made the undivided CPI indifferent to the peasantry as a revolutionary force.

Students of Indian Communism have often attributed this phenomenon to Moscow's domination of the CPI.

While it is true that the predominantly urban character of the Bolshevik revolution made it difficult for the CPSU and the Comintern to help the CPI develop creative tactical lines for mobilizing the peasantry, the fault lay primarily with the Indian Communists themselves. A relatively small group of atomized intellectuals, they had to function, during the 1930s and 1940s, within the Congress "system," which was itself basically an urban middle-class movement; the Communist leaders had neither the resources nor the mental equipment to seek pastures unexplored by the Congress party. In the early 1950s, the Chinese revolution made a brief impact on a few Indian Communists, and there was a short-lived attempt to borrow a Maoist orientation. This attempt collapsed not merely because there was no creative application of Maoist tactics to Indian conditions, but also because in the deceptive name of neo-Maoism, the CPSU tried successfully to keep the CPI under its own control (see chapter 10).

As the CPI opted for constitutional Communism and adopted the parliamentary line, it lost sight of the peasantry as a revolutionary element. This was inevitable. India's parliamentary politics is essentially urban politics, although elections are won or lost in the villages. Between 1957 and 1967, Indian Communists lived with a huge paradox. Their experience in Kerala and Andhra Pradesh showed them that only by mobilizing the peasantry could they build a strong and stable support base. But their tactical lines continued to be predominantly urban-oriented.

The change in tactical lines stemmed from several directions. The CPI(M), in rejecting the placid parliamentarianism of the CPI, was obliged to evolve a more militant tactical line. The search for a more revolutionary strategy than the CPI's made it look to the rural poor. The Marxists were helped by the serious depression of 1965–67, which hit the peasantry more than the urban proletariat. The severe drought brought about famine-like conditions in large portions of India and the Marxists, in organizing demands for food, found a responsive constituency among the rural poor.

Competition with the CPI induced the Marxists to launch mobilization programs in Kerala and West Bengal, their two traditional strongholds. Mobilization could be effective only among the poor peasants and landless workers, a constituency unexplored by the other political parties including the Congress one. The Moscow-Peking split, and the CPI(M)'s effort to chalk out an independent strategic-tactical line acted as a motivation for a reappraisal of the Chinese revolution and its relevance to the Indian situation. The outbreak of the peasant rebellion at Naxalbari worked as a catalyst.

The collapse of the Congress party's monopoly of power, the worsening economic situation, the formation of non-Congress coalitions in a number of states, all these factors introduced radicalism in the ranks of the CPI(M) and in some of its leaders. Many of the "extremists" broke away from the party to set up "Maoist" factions which rapidly sprang up in Bengal, Kerala, Andhra Pradesh, Bihar, Uttar Pradesh, Punjab, Jammu, and Kashmir. Some of the Bengal factions launched the CPI(ML) while, on an interstate level, there was set up a committee to coordinate the activities of "Communist revolutionaries." The Chinese began to extol the CPI(ML) as the "true party" of Indian Communists, and to project the philosophy of armed peasant guerrilla protest. The impact of all this on the CPI(M) was predictable. It had to defend and demonstrate its radicalism, even if it was determined to reject the Peking path.

While each of these factors upgraded the value of the rural proletariat for the CPI(M), it was during the united front regimes in Bengal and Kerala that the Marxists actually discovered the poor peasantry as a revolutionary element. The CPI(M)'s worker-peasant–alliance tactical line was born to political competition within the united front governments in the two states.

Although Communist mobilization of peasants is still limited, localized, and extremely uneven, the organized struggles have covered a wide spectrum, from symbolic protest (individual *satyagraha,* the "lowest" form of struggle) to armed guerrilla war (the "highest" form). Armed guerrilla endeavors have been organized on a very limited scale by the "Maoists" in the Srikakulam region of Andhra Pradesh and in isolated pockets in Bengal, Bihar, Uttar Pradesh, Punjab, and Kerala; these have been more or less flushed out by the police and the military. The CPI on its own initiative has organized some impressive marches, petitions, and a widespread symbolic "land-grab" movement that resulted in little actual acquisition of land by peasants but gained quite a bit of publicity for the agrarian problem.

The CPI(M) alone appears to be trying to work out a sustained militant struggle for the poor peasant, the sharecropper, and the landless worker. We have already seen how this movement worked in West Bengal and Kerala during 1967–69. In many of these struggles, as well as in Bihar, Rajasthan, Madras, and Punjab, cadres of the CPI have worked with the Marxists. The protests have not been peaceful. Peasants and sharecroppers have taken over *benami* land and "protected" their crops, resisting the landlords' organized attempts to prevent them from doing so. "Armed resistance" has therefore become a norm of peasant struggle where mobilization has been strong and effective.

The fundamental difference between the CPI(M) tactical line for peasant struggles and that of the "Maoists" is therefore not over *violence.* It is over *armed resistance* and peasant *guerrilla warfare.* The Marxists do not consider the agrarian situation or the political climate suitable for armed peasant guerrilla warfare —*not yet.* They consider such tactics to be not only adventurist but also self-defeating—these can only expose the peasants to the onslaught of the much superior forces of the state. They claim that the feasibility of their own tactical line has been proved not merely by the success of the peasant struggles in Bengal, Kerala, and parts of Bihar, but also by the collapse of the armed guerrilla activities organized by the "Maoists."

"LAND REFORMS" AND
THE AGRARIAN SITUATION

In order to examine the tactical lines of the Communist groups, we must have some basic idea of the Indian agrarian situation. It is a situation composed of two principal elements at the present moment: the results of the "land reforms" of the 1950s, and the beginning of capitalist farming or the "green revolution."

The British (we have already noted) introduced, over a period of sixty years, two major land-tenure systems: the so-called *zamindari* tenure in eastern and most of northern India, and the *rayiatari* tenure in southern and western India. The *zamindari* (or *malguzari*) tenure enabled the British raj to determine the total revenue payable for certain tracts used for agriculture; the settlement was made with particular persons called *zamindars* (or *malguzars*), either on a permanent basis (permanent settlement) or on the basis of periodical revision (temporarily settled estates). Quite clearly and explicitly, the settlements were not with the actual cultivators, but with a group of master holders who were, in effect, revenue farmers.

In the course of time, whole layers of middlemen emerged between the actual cultivators and the state, sharing the rent or revenue paid by the cultivator and ultimately meant for the state. The land "reform" measures adopted in India during the 1950s (in some cases the 1960s) practically abolished all these intermediary tenures. Nearly 20 million tenants under the intermediaries were brought into direct contact with the state. Although this was a major achievement, the abolition of intermediaries was "basically a reform of revenue administration rather than a measure of land reform." [3]

The gains of the tenancy reform included demolition of the feudal structure of the rural society and elimination of many forms of oppression and injustice. In most of the states, particularly West Bengal, legislation placed a ceiling on personal ownership of land. As a result, the state governments came into possession of several million acres of cultivable land, in addition to the sizable holdings they already owned. According to the surveys undertaken to locate such land, the state governments have in their possession 1.2 million acres in blocks of more than 250 acres each, and 4.6 million acres in smaller blocks. All this land was to be distributed principally to landless workers. It is "doubtful whether any considerable number of landless families have been settled in viable agriculture."

While fragmentation, litigation, indebtedness, and many other factors have added to the number of "dwarf" holders and landless cultivators, the worst feature of the tenure reforms is that they provided no protection to sharecroppers. Implementation of tenure reforms has also varied from state to state. For example, while in Maharashtra, ownership of land was transferred during the 1950s and early 1960s to the cultivating tenants and for all practical purposes tenancy was abolished, in most parts of Bihar the Tenancy Act of 1885 is still the rule. Nonoccupancy under-*raiyats* and sharecroppers remain completely unprotected. Most of these tenancies are unrecorded, and recent efforts to record them led to thousands of litigations in Purnea district. In Assam, under-*raiyats* in the former permanently settled estates are still governed by the Act of 1929, which lays down conditions for termination of tenancies. Sharecroppers have no security of tenancy. The situation is more or less the same in most of the other states. Even the problem of tenancy reform, then, has been neglected or attended

[3] V. M. Dandekar and Nilakantha Rath, "Poverty in India: Policies and Programmes," *Economic and Political Weekly*, January 9, 1971, p. 109.

to very indifferently in most of the states. "The reasons," as Dandekar has concluded, "cannot be other than political. It is obvious that some people will not move until it is too late." [4]

Radical land reform is no longer on the agenda of Indian political parties with the exception of the Communists. In 1969, Mrs. Gandhi tried in vain to induce the chief ministers to introduce structural changes in land relationship, but they categorically opposed a lowering of the ceiling on land. Instead they asked the prime minister to introduce a ceiling on urban property.[5] Myrdal has rightly observed that India has long passed the opportune moment for a radical reshaping of the agrarian structure by legislation.

Sweeping changes might perhaps have been accomplished in the revolutionary environment of the immediate postwar independence years. But if consent for a fundamental change in property and tenancy rights might have been won then, it is not possible now. The piecemeal reforms that have been accomplished have bolstered the political, social, and economic position of the upper rural strata on which the present governments depend for crucial support. Not only has the political influence of this group increased, but its interest in perpetuation of the status quo has been enhanced. Its stake in the existing order is,

[4] *Ibid.* The Fourth Five-Year Plan document says "Even the legislation as it exists has not been pursued and implemented [in some states] effectively. As a result only about 964,800 hectares have been taken possession of by the state governments. . . . . The program of distribution of surplus land has been taken up in recent years in a number of states. But there is still a large gap in most of the states between the area which has been taken possession of and the area distributed." *Fourth Five-Year Plan, 1969–1974* (New Delhi, Planning Commission), pp. 179–80.

"According to the latest figures, 42.5 million acres of cultivable waste and 32.8 million acres of current fallows is available for colonization. But nothing is being done for its distribution." H. S. Surjeet, "Report on The Agrarian Crisis," in *Millions Fighting For Land and Wages* (Calcutta, All-Indian Kisan Sabha, 1970), p. 46.

[5] A Planning Commission report in 1959 found that even some "politicians of liberal views" did not recognize the rights and privileges of the actual cultivator. Revenue officers exhibited "an unconscious resistance to liberal ideas," and in any conflict between landlord and peasant, "there is a greater tendency" among the administrative personnel "to believe the landlord rather than the tenant, the presumption being that a poor man is likely to speak untruth with a view to obtain some land." *Report of the Panel on Land Reforms* (New Delhi, Planning Commission, 1959), p. 38. See also *Report of the Committee on Tenancy Reforms* (New Delhi, Government of India, 1956).

of course, shared by the middle and upper strata of the urban population, whose members often own land. In combination, these forces exert a strong pressure for conservation in regard to the agrarian structure, however radical the tone of policy resolutions and certain laws, and however radical and behavior of some governments toward industry, particularly when foreign-owned. Piecemeal reforms have thus dimmed the prospects of radical reforms in agriculture, despite the deterioration of the status of the weaker members of the rural hierarchy and the rapid increase in their numbers, both absolutely and relatively.[6]

CAPITALIST FARMING

What has come to be known as "the new strategy of agricultural development" has led, during the last three years, to the "green revolution." The Planning Commission declared in 1969 that the success of the Fourth Five-Year Plan would be judged "above all, by performance in agriculture." [7] This change of priority stemmed not merely from the bitter experience of 1966–67, but from the realization that derelict agriculture impeded the growth of industry and threatened economic and social stability. The Commission, reflecting the new political mood in the country, has chosen the new strategy rather than structural land reforms as the principal instrument for achieving a 5 percent rate of annual growth in agricultural production. A combination of scientific inputs—high-yielding varieties, fertilizer, ground water, better

[6] Gunnar Myrdal, *Asian Drama* (New York, Pantheon, 1968), II, 1367. The Indian agrarian situation is comparable to that in southern Italy. "Ownership of land remains a primary sign of social status in the Mezzogiorno. This is true not only among the peasantry and the rural proletariat, but among middle-class city dwellers as well. In some regions of the south, every shopkeeper and clerk owns a small piece of land which he either farms himself or rents out to a peasant sharecropper or renter. So important is ownership of land as an index of social evaluation in the south that the PCI quickly made it the center of its program under the general rubric of 'bourgeois democratic revolution.' " Sidney G. Tarrow, *Peasant Communism in Southern Italy* (New Haven, Yale University Press, 1967), pp. 259–60.
[7] *Fourth Plan*, pp. 113–15.

seeds, expanding use of tractors—is expected to achieve this desired rate of growth, and even take it to a higher level of food production.

The new strategy has already succeeded in creating a certain buoyancy in agriculture; not only have there been successive "record" crops in several states, but the prospect of agriculture becoming a profitable commercial enterprise has drawn capital as well as entrepreneurship to farming. Although (record crops notwithstanding) India has been importing 6 to 8 million tons of food grains a year (mostly from the United States under PL 480), the hope is growing that imports will become unnecessary by 1982. Perhaps as a symbolic proclamation of that hope, Mrs. Gandhi, in April 1971, renamed the Central Food and Agriculture Ministry, calling it simply the Ministry of Agriculture.

Myrdal's study of Indian agriculture persuaded him to recommend a "genuinely capitalist path" of farm development, since structural changes in agrarian relations did not seem to be practicable without a major change in the configuration of social and economic power. Myrdal made it clear, however, that genuine capitalist development of agriculture "cannot tolerate passive and parasitic land ownership on the part of persons who sap the surplus of the agricultural sector but contribute nothing to its productive performance." [8] This warning is echoed in the Fourth Plan. It places greater emphasis on tenure reform rather than on land reform.

It has been observed that under the present arrangement of informal tenancy and sharecropping, the landlord considers it unwise to invest in improving his land; likewise, the sharecropper or the tenant is either unable or reluctant to invest in inputs like fertilizers. The insecurity of tenancy has not only impeded the widespread adoption of the high-yielding varieties but in some cases led to social and agrarian tensions. In the present context, therefore, it is essential that a cultivating tenant or a sharecropper should have effective security of tenure of the

[8] Myrdal, I, 1380.

land he cultivates and the existing tenancies declared nonresumable and permanent. [9]

Large-scale introduction of science and technology, or modernization of agriculture, has been accomplished in the world in two diametrically opposite ways—one is capitalist construction, the other socialist. Both have been expensive in terms of social dislocation, human misery, and coercion of the cultivating class, especially the poor and the middle-level farmer. In Western Europe the industrial revolution broke up feudal agrarian relations; the mass of surplus farm labor was, over a long period, absorbed in the rapidly growing industries. The problems of capitalist development of Indian agriculture are enormous. Slow industrial growth, paucity of investment capital, feudal relationships in the agrarian sector which still prevail in numerous ways on a large scale, and the great numbers of "dwarf" farmers, sharecroppers, and landless laborers are only some of the major ones. Even if capitalist construction of farming becomes an eventual success, the short-term consequences of such development are likely to add to social and political tensions. Such tensions are already visible in states where capitalist agriculture has shown promise.

The first tension that is visible almost everywhere stems from the insecure tenure of the large army of sharecroppers. Wolf Ladejinsky, of the World Bank, has shown in several studies that the sharecroppers have become "worse off than before because as ownership of improved land is priced very highly, there is mounting determination among owners not to permit tenants to share in the rights of land they cultivate. Their preference is to get rid of them." [10] The solution of the problem of the multitudes of tenants, he says, is even more difficult than tackling the problem of the small farmer, of whom there are 185 million in India each owning no more than 5 acres per family.

[9] *Fourth Plan,* p. 177. The document does not use the word "essential" while dealing with land reforms.
[10] Wolf Ladejinsky, "Green Revolution in Bihar," *Economic and Political Weekly: Review of Agriculture,* September 1969.

In areas where the agricultural transformation is a potent force—Punjab and Purnea district of Bihar—the accomplishment is marred by its adverse effects on the already troublesome tenurial conditions. Where the new farm practices are involved, land values have risen three-, four-, or even fivefold, and unrestricted landcontrol has never been more prized. As a consequence, not only have rents risen (though illegal under the reform) from the traditional 50/50 to as high as 70 percent of the crop, but the security of tenure and other rights in land a tenant might claim have also been perceptibly weakened. Now that "green revolution" land is practically invaluable, the owners would like to get rid of tenants altogether and resume the land for cultivation; making use of the plentiful supply of hired labor which has no claims on the land whatsoever. There are too many tenants or sharecroppers to deal with summarily without courting a good deal of trouble when the old squeeze, whereby tenants are reduced to sharecroppers and eventually to landless workers, is being accelerated as more of the bigger owners become involved with the new technology. The basic provisions of tenure reforms are less attainable than before the advent of the green revolution.[11]

Thus the "green revolution" is creating a situation in India somewhat similar to the Enclosures in Britain, but in a very different domestic and international milieu. In the words of Harekrishna Konar, the "green revolution" has "helped to further strengthen the position of the big landowners and rich peasants in the rural economy causing further intensification of the social and class contradictions." [12]

Dandekar has pointed out some of the other adverse consequences of the "green revolution." First is the vast difference that the new technology has made between irrigated and unirrigated agriculture.

The new inequalities thus created are far more glaring than the previous ones stemming entirely from unequal distribution of landholdings. Even more important is the fact that these inequalities are being created in the main at the cost of the community. All major and me-

[11] Quoted in *Millions Fighting For Land and Wages,* pp. 46–47.
[12] *Ibid.,* p. 10.

dium irrigation works are constructed at the cost of the community and their benefits are being monopolized by a few whose lands happen to be irrigated. All attempts to recover even part of the development cost from those who benefit therefrom are not likely to succeed in the near future. The new technology has placed the entire agricultural production at the mercy of those who own irrigated lands and the country cannot afford to invite their displeasure.[13]

The new technology, Dandekar adds, will act as a strong motivation for the rich farmers to expand their farms. "A ceiling on holdings does not prevent this process, for there is much room for many farms to expand below the ceiling." As farms are mechanized, there will be attempts to make greater use of labor-saving equipment and machinery. "Judging by the experience of capitalist agriculture in the developed countries, it seems certain that on balance the new technological advances will reduce and not increase the employment potential of agriculture." Nor can the new technology be expected to help the vast numbers of small uneconomic farmers with little existing or potential irrigation. "Indeed, if under the impetus of the new technology, Indian agriculture develops along capitalist lines . . . the small nonviable farmers will gradually be squeezed out of land and will perforce join the ranks of the landless laborer."

PEASANT PROTESTS: AN ANALYSIS

Objective conditions in rural India are, then, eminently suitable for peasant unrest and protest, and these conditions are being further sharpened by the immediate and short-term consequences of the "green revolution." The Communists have, as noted, turned their attention to the peasantry. Except in West Bengal and Kerala, the main thrust of the protest movement at the moment is against eviction, for a better share of the crop, for tenancy rights,

[13] Dandekar, pp. 114–15.

and for relief from debt, and for credit facilities. That most of the struggles are still relatively on a "low level" is borne out by the following:

Out of 100 protests analyzed, 52 were resisting eviction, 27 demanded land reforms (in 17 of these cases, peasants occupied government land, fallow land, forest land, and land wrongfully belonging to landlords), 9 asked for abolition of taxes, and most of the remaining 12 were related to a fairer share of harvested crops or improvement of the method of harvesting and crop-sharing. As to the prevalence of the protests, in two states (Bengal and Kerala) more than half the districts were involved, in four states (Uttar Pradesh, Bihar, Punjab, and Andhra Pradesh) less than a half but more than a third districts were involved, and in ten states (all the other states with the exception of Kashmir and Nagaland, where no protests were reported) one to three districts were involved. Of 88 protests, 27 involved "several thousands" of people, 14 were characterized by "huge demonstrations and rallies," and 22 were described as "sustained" protests.[14] "Sustained" protests often led to a redress of some of the grievances or promise of official action.

Konar gave the following account of the extent and intensity of peasant struggles in India at the extended meeting of the Central Kisan Council in December 1970:

WEST BENGAL: "The peasant movement has come to occupy a very important place in the democratic movement." The main slogans of the movement were: 1) defend the gains and advance them, "even at the cost of blood, if necessary"; 2) do not succumb to police attacks and false criminal cases; 3) foil the game of forming any "mini-front" (that is, anti-CPI [M]) government. By June 1970, "unprecedented mobilization" had taken place, unity of the rural poor strengthened and successful attempts were made to build rural peasant and democratic unity to isolate the *jotedars* and the police. Volunteer organizations are being developed. Large cadres'

[14] *People's Democracy* and *New Age*, 1968.

meetings are being held in every district. "Mischievous" *jotedars* have been boycotted in many places and forced to surrender. "The movement led by the Kisan Sabha became a part and parcel of the general democratic movement." In struggles against the *jotedars* and the police, fifty peasants and Kisan Sabha workers were killed. "In spite of the fact that the police wanted to arrest 70,000 peasants, they could arrest only about 9,000." "Harvesting has become a joint struggle. Volunteers are standing guard. Agricultural workers' movement is being coordinated with it. The most significant thing is that the peasant struggle has already been raised to the plane of an all-people's democratic struggle."

KERALA: By April 1970, one phase of the struggle of hutmen dwellers and sharecroppers and small peasants for implementation of the Agrarian Reforms Law was over. Now efforts are being made to consolidate the advance, strengthen the organizations, and prepare for further advance. About 250,000 peasants took part in a mass rally in May 1970. "In those areas and districts where powerful peasant and agricultural workers' struggles took place, the democratic movement registered significant advances in spite of heavy odds."

PUNJAB: Tenants have fought against eviction with some success in the districts of Ferozpur, Jullundur, Amritsar, and Sangrur. A significant victory has been won in the Sutlej riverbed area where "government has been forced permanently to allot 5 acres of land per family where it intended to set up a seed farm." 352 delegates attended the state Kisan Sabha conference. The movement had hitherto been confined to middle-level and rich peasants. Now it is being built around the poor peasants, sharecroppers and farm laborers.

RAJASTHAN: Struggles against eviction and for land are continuing in the districts of Sikar, Churu, Barmer, Pali, Bundi, and Alwar. A big struggle took place at Ganganagar in which the CPI also cooperated. In Bundi, peasants occupied 1,000 acres of fallow land.

MAHARASHTRA: "The powerful struggle of the peasants of Thana district forced the government to retreat from its attempt to evict peasants from about 48,000 acres of land they occupied. Though the government has not yet taken any final decision on 44,000 acres, it is clear that it can never evict the peasants." Struggles for relief from debt have been going in the districts of Wardha, Chandrapur, Yeotmal. Peasants occupied 5,000 acres in Wardha and 1,500 acres in Chandrapur.

ANDHRA PRADESH: The movement for tenancy rights, land, relief from debt, better wages and against eviction is "particularly strong" in the districts of Guntur, Nalgoda, Khammam, Warangal, and Hyderabad. The peasants have been able to defend their land against attacks by the police and landlords. In Khammam district, peasants occupied more than 700 acres illegally possessed by landlords. Title deeds were secured for about 42,000 acres of land.

UTTAR PRADESH: The peasant and agricultural labor movement is developing "step by step." It has spread to 15 districts. Peasants have successfully resisted eviction and, through their struggles, got 5,000 acres in Faizabad, 1,900 in Muzaffarnagar, and 450 acres in Meerut. 800 peasants were arrested, of whom 431 were sent to jail.

BIHAR: The *kisan* movement has "notably advanced." In the districts of Purnea, Saharsa, Bhagalpur, and Monghyr, it has assumed a mass militant character. . . . The struggle for share and land spread to *lakhs* (one *lakh*=100,000) of acres of land, owned by very wealthy landlords. Eviction has been successfully resisted in more than one *lakh* acres." More than 15,000 peasants are involved in "false" criminal cases in six districts.

TRIPURA: The peasant movement for land, against eviction, against high rent and debt burden and for the right of tribals to *zoom* cultivation is gaining strength. One weakness of the movement was that participation of Bengali peasants used to be "negligible." This is now being overcome.

TAMILNAD (MADRAS): Peasant struggles confined to East Tanjore, Coimbatore, Madurai, and South Arcot districts. In Madurai, peasants are successfully fighting eviction from 40,000 acres of forest land.

ASSAM: *"Kisan* movement is still weak, but it is advancing."

ORISSA: "Organized *kisan* movement is very weak."

HARYANA, HIMACHAL PRADESH, KARNATAK, MADHYA PRADESH: "Some

organized efforts to develop the *kisan* movement are going on, but there are no concrete reports." [15]

The anatomy of the peasant movement, outlined by Konar, does not suggest that the rural proletariat has been roused on a large scale to fight for its rights. The movement is extremely uneven and very weak in most of India. In the sprawling Hindi-speaking region, it is not gaining strength except in the districts of Bihar adjacent to West Bengal. Only in Bengal can the movement be said to have risen to a high political level; this is not so even in Kerala. A peasant struggle does not gain militancy except when land in illegal possession of landlords is occupied and protected against the police and the landlords' hired hoodlums. Only in Bengal and Kerala have peasants taken organized initiative to "implement" land reform legislations. However, resistance against evictions may develop into militant peasant protests in the context of the "green revolution," if these protests are successfully led by the Communists.

WEAKNESSES OF THE PEASANT MOVEMENT

The peasant movement suffers from great organizational weaknesses. The CPI(M)-led All-India Kisan Sabha, far stronger than its rival of the same name led by the CPI, has hardly a central organization. In December 1970 it had 1,636,007 primary members, but the majority come from "one state only," presumably West Bengal. The leaders who man the all-India center are too busy to give the required amount of attention to AIKS activity. Konar confessed that "with the present limited capacity of our functionaries, the scope of physical contacts is bound to be limited." [16] In

[15] *Millions Fighting for Land and Wages,* pp. 12–23. See also *Struggle for Land Surges Forward,* proceedings and resolutions of the Central Kisan Council, CPI(M) (Calcutta 1970). For an account of peasant struggles organized by the CPI, see *Resolutions of the National Council of the CPI* (New Delhi, PPH, 1970) and *The Land-Grab Movement* (New Delhi, 1970). Either party may have claimed credit for struggles organized and successes achieved by the other. The main point is that in peasant struggle the two parties have often been forced to work together.

[16] *Millions Fighting for Land and Wages,* pp. 26–27.

other words, peasant movements in the various states have to develop more or less on their own steam, with little systematic central direction. This development may in the course of time prove
to be of tremendous consequence for Indian Communism. The
great diversity of agriculture adds verisimilitude to the greater diversity of Indian society. It is quite likely that cadres springing
out of peasant movements in the different states will have different approaches to the strategy and tactics of the Communist
movement. Most of these leaders will be men and women of the
soil, and communication among the various linguistic cadres may
prove to be a difficult problem. Lack of central direction and control may also encourage localism and autonomous attitudes, lead
to a proliferation of militant or revolutionary peasant organizations, and impede the growth of a well-disciplined body under
the leadership of one Communist party.

WHICH PEASANTS? HOW MUCH MILITANCY?

The three Communist factions in India, as already noted, have
three different tactical lines for peasant struggles.

The CPI seems to be still predominantly influenced by Marx's
own concept of the peasantry's role. Marx pointed out the importance of organizing the peasantry for revolution as well as the *dif-
ficulty* in peasant mobilization. Marx's approach was dialectical:
the small-holding peasant is a Napoleonic class in its youth, but
an anti-Napoleonic class when the small-holding has been outdated. "Hence the peasants find their natural ally and leader in
the urban proletariat, whose task is the overthrow of the
bourgeoisie." [17] The CPI believes in the importance of mobilizing the small-holding and poor peasantry, but firmly stands by
the classical concept of the working class leading the struggle for a
proletarian society. Its current strategic concept of a National

[17] Karl Marx, *The Eighteenth Brumaire of Louis Bonaparte,* pp. 120–30. Also see
Tarrow, ch. 10.

Democratic State, however, leads it to make an inclusive and additive approach to the peasantry.

The CPI(M), on the other hand, can be said to have developed a Leninist approach to the role of the peasantry, with a readiness to learn from Maoism such tactical lessons as may be applicable to the Indian situation. Lenin systematized the relationship between the rural and urban proletariat, and conceived of an "alliance" between the two if the Russian revolution were to be speeded forward to a socialist victory. He divided the peasantry into three groups: rich peasants, agricultural proletarians, and a middle group that was being gradually proletarianized. He brought about a *tactical alliance* between the urban proletariat and the poor peasantry, and sought to neutralize the middle-level peasant, thus marking out the rich peasant as the enemy of revolution.[18]

In Lenin's concept, leadership of this alliance belonged to the working class. This seems to be the strategic concept of the CPI(M) also, although one can trace in current Indian Marxist writings on the peasantry traces of Togliatti's concept of an "equal partnership" between the working class and the poor peasantry. The CPI(M) is probably abandoning theoretical distinctions between urban and rural proletariats in the context of Indian society; there is a tendency to use the two terms with an equal relevance to revolutionary struggle. At the same time, the CPI(M) thinking on the peasantry points to a Gramsci-like concentration upon the land-hungry and landless proletariat and the poor peasant, although there is also an attempt, after Togliatti, to bring the middle-level peasant into the worker-peasant alliance, rather than to neutralize him, which was part of the Leninist tactics.[19] In short, the CPI(M) is in the process of developing a strategy of revolution in which the rural proletariat is emerging to a status of equal importance with the urban working class. Whether

[18] V. I. Lenin, "The Agrarian Question in Russia," *Selected Works* (New York, 1951), Vol. I.
[19] Tarrow, pp. 115–20.

the realities of Indian revolution will push the rural proletariat to a position of leadership in the alliance is a question that can at this stage be asked rather than answered.

The CPI(ML) espouses the strategic concept of a Maoist revolution with the armed rural proletariat in the vanguard. Both the CPI(M) and the CPI(ML) stand for a people's democratic revolution, and both consider the agrarian crisis to be the foundation of the general crisis in the Indian polity. The CPI(M) would agree with the CPI(ML)'s contention that rightist as well as leftist deviations in the Indian Communist movement have occurred mainly because its leaders have never given serious consideration to the role of the peasantry in a revolution. What the CPI(M) does not accept is the CPI(ML)'s thesis that the main content of the Indian revolution is agrarian, in which only the peasantry can play the determining role.[20] The "Maoist" party, like Mao Tse-tung himself, concedes leadership of the socialist revolution to the working class, but this leadership makes it obligatory for the working class to unite with the peasantry, which is "the main force of the revolution," and to "advance toward seizure of power through armed struggle."

Perhaps the crucial difference between the Marxist and the "Maoist" lines lies not so much on the role of the peasants as on the strategy of seizure of power. If power is to be seized first in the countryside, with the building of rural guerrilla bases, and with liberated rural areas finally encircling and taking over the cities, the rural proletariat inevitably occupies the vanguard position in the revolution. It is this strategic concept of seizure of power that is rejected by the CPI(M) as thoroughly adventurist and totally inapplicable to the Indian situation *at this stage*.

The CPI's general tactical line seems to be to build a mass movement of the landless farm worker and the poor peasant, but not to alienate other sections of the peasantry (except the wealthy

[20] Charu Mazumdar, "Fight Against the Concrete Manifestations of Revisionism," *Liberation* (monthly journal in English of CPI [ML], now banned) September 1969.

landlords), and to use it as an instrument to bring about a national democratic coalition in the central government. In other words, the CPI is not particularly anxious, at this time, to wage a class war in the countryside. Its strategic adherence to the parliamentary line and to peaceful transition obliges it to take a mainly incremental view of rectifying the grave ills in India's agrarian relations.

The CPI(M), in contrast, adopts a militant, class-struggle tactical line of mobilizing the rural proletariat in order to advance toward a people's democratic state. Basically, it is the tactic of mixing parliamentary and extraparliamentary struggles to create a climate of controlled militancy in the rural areas. Landless farm workers and poor peasants are to be mobilized around a program of immediate land reforms, but the rural proletariat cannot wait for land reforms to be brought about through the legislative process. They must themselves take the initiative to seize land and defend themselves against evictions.

Experience has proved that the efforts to solve the problem of redistribution of land through legislation fixing ceilings on land-holding are totally ineffective. . . . Our Party should ceaselessly educate the peasants and agricultural labor masses that the basic slogan of abolition of landlordism without compensation and the giving of land to agricultural laborers and poor peasants free of cost is to be realized through the mass action of the entire peasantry. In fact, these struggles for the realization of their basic demands are a part of the main revolutionary struggle of a People's Democratic State.[21]

The Marxists do not look upon land reforms as the ultimate goal of peasant mobilization, but only as a means—that goal is, of course, the people's democratic revolution. In fact, the Marxists have identified reformism as a major obstacle to peasant militancy, and they have gone forward, wherever possible, to make the militant struggle of the peasantry political. In the CPI(M) tactical line on the peasantry, one can discover explicit strains of

[21] *Tasks on the Kisan Front* (Calcutta, CPI [M], 1967), p. 20.

thinking in terms of an extensive *agrarian* base of the Indian revolution, not a guerrilla base—a base that, in certain circumstances, could function as a "parallel" democratic organization of
the rural masses.

The day-to-day agitations and struggles of every stratum of the peasantry, including the rural wage laborer, should, therefore, be combined with systematic educational and organizational work of recruiting, educating, and organizing the mass of militants drawn from the
rural poor into active organizers of the agrarian revolutionary movement. Such a process of raising the level of consciousness of the vanguard of the rural people should be based on democratic functioning
of *kisan sabhas* and agricultural labor organizations on the one hand,
and the further development and strengthening of the Communist
Party among the mass of rural people on the other. Such a parallel development of democratically functioning broad organizations of the
rural masses . . . and the development of the consciously organized
Communist vanguard would be the best guarantee that the slogan
"turn your face to the peasantry" will, in fact, be realized.[22]

In turning to the peasantry, the CPI(M) emphasizes a sharp
class differentiation between the poor and the nonpoor peasant,
the importance of the village as the basic unit of peasant organizations, and the building up of extensive, contiguous bases. Thus,
A. K. Gopalan, presiding over an AIKS session at Madurai in
January 1968, declared: "Agricultural laborers now constitute 25
to 40 percent of the population in most of the states and we have

[22] *Ibid.,* p. 25. "Simultaneously, efforts are being made to set up bases and parallel administration in the rural areas. It is reported that in some parts of Burdwan
district the (Marxist) party's influence is so overwhelming that it has started col-
lecting taxes. It has also set up an organization of sorts in certain areas in Sundar-
bans under the police stations of Hingalgunj, Gosaba, Sandeshkhali, Harora, and
Basanti of 24-Parganas district. Access to these areas is only through ferry and it is
practically impossible for any outsider or 'undesirable' person to reach there without detection by the CPM's supporters. Armed men guard these villages, especially
at night; dacoity and looting are frequent, and to keep the villagers on the right
side, booty is distributed among them. The police have been terrorized into inac-
tion and the writ of the government has practically ceased to run." Shankar Ghosh,
"A Strike That Failed: Setback For CPM," *Times of India,* August 31, 1970. Ghosh
is one of the most knowledgeable reporters on Indian Communism, particularly the
CPI(M). See also his *The Disinherited State* (Calcutta, Orient Longmans, 1971).

to make them *the hub of all our activity*. Reluctance to take up their demands, fearing that this will drive the rich and middle-level peasant away will have to be given up." Only the rural proletariat, Gopalan pointed out, will enable the party to build a militant mass movement in the villages.

In going toward such a movement, the first tactical need is to merge the struggles for land and struggles for higher wages for farm labor. This will concretely treat the poor peasant and the agricultural worker as belonging to a single class of exploited peasantry. The peasant movement has to be organized "with the village as unit, under its own local leadership, duly elected by members enrolled in the village itself. These organized villages must form parts of compact areas chosen in every district, concentrated work round which must expand in a planned manner. In every such village we must have a volunteer corps to defend our movement and save our active workers from attacks by the class enemies." [23]

PROBLEMS OF PEASANT MOBILIZATION

The Marxists appear to be aware of the tremendous problems inherent in organizing the peasantry for revolutionary militancy. Although there is no evidence that they have undertaken a serious study of the cultural and economic factors that have made the Indian peasant traditionally docile and quiescent, they are sobered by the fact that the democratic and socialist movement "is not yet firmly rooted in the working class of the advanced industries or the multi-million rural proletariat and semi-proletariat in the countryside." The aspirations, urges, immediate and long-term interests, moods, and tempers of the urban and rural proletariat are therefore not adequately reflected in party decisions.[24]

The peasant movement has been more lacking in proletarian content than has the working-class movement. Whatever peasant

[23] *People's Democracy*, February 11, 1968.
[24] *Why the Ultra-'Left' Deviation?* (Calcutta, CPI [M], 1969), p. 12.

movement was organized in the 1950s "was mainly oriented to the middle-level and well-to-do peasant sector, instead of the growing numbers of agricultural labor and poor peasant sections. The relative new opportunities for well-being that presented themselves to the middle-level and rich peasant sections in no small way influenced the Communist party in the rural areas and, in particular, a good part of the middle-level and rich peasants occupying leading positions in the rural party committees." (A great many of these Communists now belong to the CPI.)

The CPI(M) is thus faced with the task of not only extending the peasant movement to the rural poor, but also of recruiting a sufficient number of cadres from among the poor peasants and agricultural laborers. While this means long, sustained effort in the countryside, there are elements in the CPI(M) susceptible to impatient adventurism.

These comrades pick out stray, scattered, and tiny islands of militant peasant and tribal people's struggles in the vast ocean of our country's peasantry and then proceed to make the thesis of a matured peasant revolution and give armed struggle, people's war, national liberation war, and similar other grossly exaggerated and highly inflated slogans of the day; and as a result of this totally un-Marxian outlook, contempt is shown for patient, painstaking and sustained work among the basic revolutionary classes of the proletariat and the peasantry, while directing their appeal to the emotions of the petty bourgeois student and youth sections who are yet to be schooled, tempered, and trained in Marxism-Leninism and its revolutionary theory and practice.[25]

The Marxists have attempted a reconstruction of the Telengana uprising of the late 1940s in order to solve the complex problems of mobilizing peasant militancy for revolution. This exercise has, of course, been partly prompted by Peking's elevation of the Telengana rebellion as the true path of revolution in India, and by large-scale leftist-deviationist defections from the CPI(M) in Andhra Pradesh. What is of greater interest, however

[25] *Letter to Andhra Comrades* (Calcutta, CPI [M], 1969), p. 27.

is the anatomy of Telengana that has emerged from the recent CPI(M) post-mortem of the uprising of nearly thirty years ago.

The illegal Communist nucleus that was set up in the princely state of Hyderabad in 1933–34 was, according to this post-mortem, a group of leftist petty-bourgeois intellectuals and some radicals of liberal landlord origin who were connected with the nationalist movement in Hyderabad and were inspired by the Congress-led freedom struggle in British India. The agrarian program on the basis of which the Telengana Communists sought to organize the peasantry in the mid-1940s, was not "conspicuously radical or revolutionary." The mass peasant upheaval in Telengana was an "inseparable part of the postwar upsurge in the country," in other words, of the national liberation movement. The Telengana peasant struggle started as a movement against large-scale eviction of poor peasants and other injustices and gained rapid momentum because it was able to combine agrarian demands and the political demand for the overthrow of the Nizam's power. The armed struggle of the peasantry was basically a response to the armed attacks by the Nizam's forces.

Despite its achievements, the Telengana struggle had several built-in weaknesses as a model. First, there was the contradiction between the acute crisis in agrarian relations in the Telengana area and the absence of any such crisis in the Andhra Pradesh area where the peasant struggle received its political guidance and direction. Second, while the Communists succeeded in capturing the leadership of the national liberation movement in Telengana, they failed to secure a leading position in the national liberation movement in Andhra (that is, in British India). However, the deadlock between the Nizam of Hyderabad and the Indian government provided the CPI "with elbow room to maneuver, develop, and expand the struggle" in Telengana. The CPI was also helped by the complete isolation of the Nizam from the democratic and nationalist forces in India. Yet the Telengana struggle was doomed to failure as soon as Indian "police action" liquidated the Nizam's rule and integrated Hyderabad with the Indian Union.

The formation of Andhra Pradesh sharpened the contradictions between the Telengana peasant base and the CPI: while there was in Telengana a powerful agrarian movement, it was without a strong Communist party unit, whereas Andhra Pradesh had a strong CPI branch without a solid mass working-class and peasant revolutionary base. These contradictions led to the twin deviations of revisionism and left-wing adventurism among a strong section of Andhra Communists. The greatest mistake made by the Communists was that they neglected "the independent mobilization and consolidation of the working class base in the urban areas and the agricultural labor and poor peasant base in the rural areas," and failed to build the Communist party "on correct theoretical, ideological, and political lines." [26]

The meaning of this post-mortem of the Telengana peasant uprising is clear. It was possible for Communists to build up an extensive armed peasant protest movement in Telengana primarily because they were also able to lead the movement of national liberation from the Nizam's reactionary rule. The weakness of the movement stemmed from the fact that it was not anchored on a tested, strong, and disciplined unit of the CPI. The Andhra Communists who provided ideological leadership wrongly elevated it to the level of an armed peasant insurrection against the newly born Indian state. Pitted against resurgent bourgeois nationalism, this left-wing adventurism was bound to fail. The failure, however, does not write off Telengana as a non-event; indeed the Marxists look upon Telengana as a "golden chapter in modern Indian revolutionary movement," rich with practical experience and revolutionary traditions. It was an experience from which the Indian revolution must draw the proper lessons.

The first proper lesson to be drawn is realism. Communists must learn to judge accurately whether a situation is revolution-

[26] *Why the Ultra-'Left' Deviation?* pp. 23 –30.

ary or not. They must not try to substitute the "tested Marxist-Leninist yardstick" of judgment with their own dogmatic formulas. They must make an objective assessment of how the proletariat is organized in any state or in the country as a whole, of the level of its class and political consciousness, of its "mood." They must know whether the peasantry is organized or not and whether the Communist party has so far succeeded to any appreciable extent in popularizing its revolutionary agrarian program, let alone organizing mass struggles on the widest scale. Communists must also be able to realistically evaluate the existing stage of the "much-needed worker-peasant alliance." [27]

The CPI(M) agrarian program calls for a dynamic mixture of realism and boldness—realism in the large parts of India where Communist organization is weak and the peasantry's discontent remains politically unmobilized. In these areas the CPI(M) is now trying to foster peasant protest movements as soon as opportunities occur. The first need is to build *kisan sabha* units in states, districts, and villages; simultaneously, primary membership drive and recruitment of peasant activities have to be taken up in earnest. For tactical reasons, peasant bases are to be built in contiguous districts rather than in isolated areas throughout a state, and as often as possible peasant demands have to be linked with the demands of urban workers and the lower middle classes. The protests are intended to be "peaceful" though militant—for instance, the landless peasants are to be organized to seize lands vested in government or owned by landlords in excess of the ceilings. If, however, landlords and/or the police attack the protesters, they have to be taught to resist attacks and defend themselves. It is out of this kind of organized controlled militancy, firmly led by the CPI(M), that a strong, united, independent, revolutionary peasant movement could be built.

In those states where the Marxists may be in power, peasant militancy is to be built up more rapidly with the kind of boldness

[27] *Letter to Andhra Comrades,* pp. 25–26.

which we have seen being used in Bengal by Konar. The example of the police helping the poor peasant to get his legitimate share of land and crops in states ruled by the CPI(M) would hopefully inspire the rural proletariat in other states to opt for greater militancy in pressing their demands for radical agrarian reforms, and thus create a climate of polarization in the countryside, a confrontation between the rural rich and the rural poor. It is this confrontation on a nationwide scale that seems to be the CPI(M) objective during the next few years.

For the Marxists, this confrontation is necessary for undermining the mass base of the Congress party, without which the CPI(M) does not consider the effective building up of united fronts from below practicable. The CPI(M) makes a distinction between the monopoly of state power by the bourgeois-landlord alliance and the monopoly of that power by *one political party*.

By distributing the enormous patronage of development aid, the ruling Congress party has built a strong rural political base with the rich and middle-level peasants, but its influence goes deep into the ranks of the rural proletariat, a fact confirmed by the popular votes it won in all of the states. It is only by dislodging the Congress party from the countryside that the Communists can expect to bring about a radical change in agrarian relations. The only way to effect this dislodgment is to lure the rural poor away from the Congress fold, and the only way to lure them away is to mobilize them around struggles against eviction, for land, and for an equitable share of harvested crops. It is hardly within the means of the revolutionary elements in India to launch a frontal assault on the bourgeois-landlord monopoly of state power without first striking effectively at the monopoly of that power by the Congress party.

They (the left-deviationists) are anxious to teach the "ignorant" CPM the elementary truth that the present Indian state is a bourgeois-landlord state led by the big bourgeoisie, and that state power essentially lies in the military, police, courts, judiciary and bureaucracy. Since the state power is not in any way broken or weakened due to the electoral defeats of the Congress party, it is "atrocious" on the part of CPM to speak about "breaking the Congress monopoly of power!"

. . . May we, first of all, tell our critics that they do not understand the difference between the *concept of breaking state power* and the *concept of breaking the monopoly of that power by one political party,* namely the Congress party.

The bourgeois-landlord state power can never be broken except through a people's democratic revolution or socialist revolution. But before that . . . breaking up the one-party monopoly of power is considered as an important step forward, and thus the slogan of breaking the Congress monopoly is advanced. If anyone is to understand it as a substitute to the people's democratic revolution which alone can break the bourgeois-landlord state power, he should blame his colossal political ignorance in the matter.[28]

Essentially, the peasant activization programs of the two Communist groups differ as much in their class approach to the peasantry as in their approach to political power at the state and national levels. The Marxists concentrate on the poor peasant and landless agricultural worker as revolutionary allies of the industrial proletariat. The CPI, in contrast, regards all but the affluent landholder as a partner of the national democratic front and, in its agrarian program, it underlines "the basic unity of interests of the great mass of peasants with those of agricultural workers as a class." [29] The CPI therefore encompasses the great mass of peasantry as well as farm labor "in the new alignment of class forces that is developing in our countryside." The CPI would, by inference, be reluctant to wage class war between the poor peasant and agricultural labor on the one hand, and the rich and middle-level peasant on the other. At the same time, it has been trying to organize agricultural laborers as a distinct class on an all-India basis. In April 1968 it claimed to have brought to-

[28] *Ideological Debate Summed Up by Politbureau* (Calcutta, CPI [M], 1968), pp. 163–64. Italics added.

[29] Z. A. Ahmed, "For a Breakthrough in Agriculture," *New Age,* February 4, 1968.

gether 60,000 agricultural workers of Andhra Pradesh in a march to the state assembly in Hyderabad to present a petition to the legislators.

A CPI peasant leader wrote that about 50 percent of Andhra's population consisted of agricultural workers and poor peasants; 500,000 children went to the fields to work instead of to schools; in some parts of Telengana, women got 50 to 75 *paise* (less than 10 cents) as daily wages; men got almost no work for 230 days a year. At the same time, there were 3 million acres of cultivable waste land in Andhra, which had not been distributed to the landless peasants. The writer's emphasis was on the distinct class character of the farm worker of Andhra who, in his march to the state capital, reportedly was helped by the urban worker as well as by the party machinery of the CPI. The march was "the fore-runner of mighty, united class battles against the oppression and exploitation of the landlords and their power," and "the herald of the coming storm in Andhra's villages." [30]

However, in conducting peasant struggles under its own leader-ship, the CPI apparently played down land seizures by landless peasants, and preferred to bring pressure on the government to stop evictions and distribute land to the landless. Thus, the All-India Kisan committee, the policy-making body of CPI's AIKS, meeting in Rajasthan in June 1968, gave the "highest national importance" to the distribution of waste and fallow land to poor peasants and agricultural workers and not to the peasants taking over land in illegal possession of landlords. It welcomed "the struggles that the landless and land-hungry peasants are carrying on in various parts of the country for bringing fallow and waste land under the plough," without openly calling on the peasants to seize land. However, the committee "directed the *kisan sabha* units to organize mass resistance to the eviction of sharecroppers, which is taking place on a large scale in several states." [31]

[30] G. Yellamanda Reddi, "Cooli Dandu—Mighty March of Andhra Agricultural Labour," *New Age,* April 7, 1968.

[31] *New Age,* June 2, 1968.

From this brief account of the CPI's agrarian activism, it seems reasonable to surmise that the party's peasant-front workers are becoming increasingly radicalized while leading the poorest sections of the population to fight for their rights, and a distance is growing between them and the national leaders. Efforts to compete with the CPI(M) for the loyalty of the rural proletariat are probably compelling the CPI at the grass-roots level to adopt a sharper class posture than its strategy of national democracy would normally permit. In the fall of 1968, the CPI organized the first all-India conference of agricultural workers as "the starting point for the spreading of the agricultural workers' movement to all the states and for coordinated statewide and all-India mass action and struggles." The national council of the party explicitly bestowed on the landless farm labor a crucial role in bringing about an agrarian revolution in India.

This class is to be the spearhead of the struggle against landlordism and for land, if the revolution for agrarian reforms has to gather momentum. This class, because of its social position, because of its being economically and socially the most oppressed section, and also because of its numbers constituting more than 30 percent of the rural population, plays a very important role in the successful conclusion of the national-democratic revolution and the advance towards socialism. It is the most important ally of the proletariat in the rural areas. Unless this class is organized, its militant movement is built up on the basis of the struggles over pressing and basic demands, and it is politically made conscious of its role in the national-democratic revolution and advance toward socialism, it is foolish to expect the development of the revolutionary-democratic movement to any appreciable extent.[32]

Both Communist parties, then, now perceive in the 120 million agricultural workers—one-third of India's 360 million rural population—a major force for the desired social revolution. Both parties see this mass of humanity as the most powerful ally of the working class, although the two parties differ on the meaning, im-

[32] C. Rajeshwara Rao, "Agricultural Workers Must Organize on All-India Basis," *New Age*, September 29, 1968.

plications, and dimensions of the worker-peasant alliance. Neither Communist faction, unlike the third Communist party, would like to usher in peasant Communism in India. Both factions' perspective of the peasant role in revolution is governed primarily by their respective strategic objectives. The CPI, in its bid to bring about a national democratic state, in which the Communists would not be in control of state power but would share it with other democratic forces, spearheads mass peasant movements in order to strengthen its own position in the coveted national democratic coalition. The CPI(M), with its strategic objective of a people's democratic state, in which the Communists would control the commanding heights of a coalition of democratic forces, is anxious to radicalize the rural proletariat and use it as an active, even creative, agent of social change.

However, peasant radicalism, once started, may gather its own momentum which neither Communist party may be able to keep under control. In other words, peasant radicalism may radicalize each Communist party more than its leaders at present may wish, and this may well affect the form, content, style, mood, and temper of Indian Communism in ways and directions at present not easily predictable.

9

MAOISM OR
LEFT-WING COMMUNISM?

In 1969, when the Communist movement in India split for a second time, it was partly in response to a call from the Chinese Communist party. The CCP first became dissatisfied with some of the CPI(M) leaders in 1965; the dissatisfaction turned into a strong and vocal disapproval in the following year when the CPI(M) decided to participate in the fourth general election despite a sizable minority's opposition to parliamentarianism. Throughout 1966 the CCP perceived in India the rising waves of mass revolutionary discontent and a qualitative realignment of social forces, thus creating an excellent objective condition for revolutionary struggle. When the CPI(M) joined with the CPI and other non-Communist elements to set up united front governments in Kerala and West Bengal, the CCP apparently saw in this action a victory for the revisionist elements in the party and a surrender of revolutionary militancy. There were also probably other reasons for the CCP's direct intervention in 1967 to set up a Maoist party in India, which we shall explore in the next chapter.

As soon as the peasant rebellion broke out at Naxalbari in West Bengal in the spring of 1967, Peking hailed it as the "Spring Thunder Over India." Naxalbari, in Chinese perception, "blazed a Maoist trail" in India, and the Marxists, by their determination to suppress the rebellion, proved that they were no different from the "Dange renegade revisionist clique." [1] In August 1967, when the rebellion of the Girijan tribals in the Srikakulam region of Andhra Pradesh took on aspects of armed guerrilla resistance, when several "Naxalbaries" sprouted in Bengal, Bihar, Uttar Pradesh, Kerala, and Punjab, and when the CPI(M) set itself firmly against such peasant insurgencies, the CCP explicity called for the formation of a Maoist Communist party in India:

The revolutionaries in the Indian Communist Party and the revolutionary people of India should draw on the profound historical lessons of Telengana, drawing a distinct line of demarcation with the revisionist line politically, ideologically, and organizationally, and wage a resolute struggle against modern revisionism with the Soviet revisionist ruling clique at the centre. The revolutionaries in the Indian Communist Party will surely close their ranks in the struggle and build a genuinely revolutionary party of Marxism-Leninism and Mao Tse-tung's Thought.[2]

It was not quite explicit in this *People's Daily* formulation whether the CCP preferred a vertical split in the CPI(M) or wanted the Communist revolutionaries to work together within the party "resolutely" trying to convert it to a truly revolutionary, antirevisionist organization. However, the Marxist cadres who had led the short-lived Naxalbari peasant rebellion and who had refused to recant had already been expelled from the CPI(M). These revolutionaries set up a coordinating committee to mobilize the radical elements in the CPI(M) in West Bengal and began the publication of a Bengali weekly, *Deshabrati* (Servants of the Nation).

[1] See my "A Maoist Line for India," *China Quarterly*, January–March, 1968.
[2] Observer, "Historical Lessons of Telengana Uprising, *Peking Review*, August 11, 1967; *People's Daily*, August 3, 1967.

CRISIS IN THE CPI(M)

In the fall of 1967 a serious ideological-political-organizational crisis developed in the CPI(M). For three years the party had put off taking a stand on the ideological issues that divided the CPSU and the CCP; linked with these issues were the strategic-tactical lines most suitable for the CPI(M) itself. As already noted, the party leadership during this period had moved considerably toward the right, with equivocation on the question of peaceful or nonpeaceful struggle and, finally, with a return to parliamentarianism. Dissatisfaction was growing within the ranks over the leadership's apparent nonradicalism. After the Naxalbari peasant rebellion and its projection by the CCP as the "front paw" of the Indian revolution, the leadership was obliged to come out with a thesis on ideological issues. The central committee adopted a draft thesis in August 1967 and released it for discussion.[3] It was principally an examination of the CPSU positions on the major ideological issues. The draft rejected all of these positions except one that called for "unity in action" despite ideological differences between Moscow and Peking. The Chinese positions were not examined at all, except on the question of unity in action.[4] Thus, the CPI(M) leadership was prepared to reject the revisionism of the CPSU leadership without accepting the alternative line of the CCP.

[3] *Central Committee's Draft for the Ideological Discussion* (Calcutta, CPI [M], 1967). The central committee made it clear that while all units and members were free to criticize the draft during intraparty discussion, the "Program of the Party and its tactical line enunciated in various resolutions are not open to discussion," p. 1.

[4] "However, our party cannot subscribe to the view that the slogan of unity of action in principle is wrong, since it advocates unity in action between the revisionist leaders of the CPSU and the Marxist-Leninist leaders of the CPC, since the contradictions between revisionism and Marxism-Leninism is by nature antagonistic, and such unity is impermissible. The very concepts of united front, sanctions united action against a common enemy, at a particular stage of development, together with several other classes and parties with whom the proletariat has contradictions, including antagonistic contradictions at times," pp. 47–48.

While the draft was thus antirevisionist without being Maoist, it was critical of the CCP's intervention in the affairs of the CPI(M), and it condemned in no uncertain terms the Communist revolutionaries who had already received the blessing of the CCP.

It should be emphasized that if certain individual contingents of the international Communist movement prove immature or weak in discharging (their) tasks . . . they can get over these weaknesses by learning from their mistakes and through their own experience, in the main, and no outside party, however big and experienced, can substitute itself for this task, and hence it is extremely harmful to try to dictate and guide the work of another party . . . Such interference may be permissible in extraordinary circumstances, when a party and its political line gets completely on the wrong track, when friendly fraternal criticism is rejected, and when there is no other alternative left except to openly express criticism. However, this should be an exception.

Our party notes with extreme regret that this sound proletarian internationalist principle which should guide the relations between parties is violated by major parties, of course, either under the pretext of some creative Marxism of theirs or under the totally erroneous notion that they alone can think, not only for themselves, but for all other parties of the world. The glaring example is the leadership of the CPSU, after its 20th congress, which began to assert that its thesis is the program for the entire world Communist movement, and used and is using all its might to force it on every other Party in the world. Another major Communist party, the CPC, which correctly pointed out and fought against this dangerous tendency on the part of the CPSU leaders and is bearing the main brunt of fighting modern revisionism, is also, sometimes, found to disregard this principle. Our party, while modest enough to learn from the achievements and mistakes of all other fraternal parties of the world, should guard itself against any such outside interference and jealously defend its independence and its independent political line." [5]

The draft was equally critical of revisionist trends within the CPI(M) and of "sectarian, dogmatic, and adventurist tendencies." The latter "expresses [itself] in the form of challenging the Party

[5] *Ibid.*, p. 51.

Program, in opposing the political-tactical line of the party, in advancing infantile and adventurist forms of struggle and, finally, in the open defiance of party norms and forms, its discipline and democratic centralism." [6]

The draft met with strong opposition in several CPI(M) state committees, notably in Andhra Pradesh, Kerala, Madras, Jammu and Kashmir, and Uttar Pradesh. The greatest protest came from Andhra Pradesh. The state plenum rejected the draft and, going further, declared its opposition to "a whole series of basic questions concerning the Indian revolutionary movement." [7] It asked the central committee to prepare a new draft based on the two major theses exchanged between the CPSU and the CCP in June-July 1963 as well as two resolutions placed before the state plenum by T. Nagi Reddy, C. Pulla Reddy, and Kolla Venkiah.[8] The thrust of these resolutions was that there could be no unity of action between revisionism and Marxism-Leninism, two antagonistic contradictions, and that the CPI(M) leaders were directly compromising with Soviet revisionism and its Indian agent, the CPI. The Andhra plenum "tended to agree with the Chinese assessment of the Indian situation, including the need for armed struggle." [9]

ANDHRA PRADESH AND WEST BENGAL

The Andhra dissenters carried the fight to the CPI(M)'s Burdwan plenum in May 1968. They rejected the leadership's preference for parliamentarianism when a "large peasant uprising" was taking place in Srikakulam and other areas. The CPI(M), as a partner of the united front regimes in Kerala and

---

[6] *Ibid.*, p. 53.   [7] *Letter to Andhra Comrades* (Calcutta, CPI [M], 1969), p. 1.

[8] These are the CPC letters to the CPSU dated June 14, 1963, and the CPSU's reply of July 14. For texts, see Alexander Dallin, ed, *Diversity in International Communism* (New York, Columbia University Press, 1963).

[9] Mohan Ram, *Maoism in India* (New Delhi, Vikas, 1971), p. 80. For documents of the Andhra plenum, see *Andhra Plenum Rejects Neo-Revisionist Draft* (Vijaywada, 1968).

Bengal, was suppressing the "rising tide of mass struggle" against the capitalist-landlord ruling alliance, and was anxious to "preserve the legality of the party." One of their leaders told the plenum: "We have not raised the perspective of the path of struggle from the point of academic discussion. Our movements in Srikakulam, Nalgonda, Warangal, Khammam are being subjected to intensified repression from landlord-*goonda*-police combine. . . . The question of resistance in this repression has come to the forefront. Because of lack of clear perspective of the path of struggle, the leadership is not able to gear the party and the masses for resisting this repression, and to take the movement to a higher level." [10] The Burdwan plenum passed the central committee draft with minor changes. This was followed by large-scale defections from the CPI(M). Altogether 7,000 left the party, the bulk of them from Andhra Pradesh, where the party lost 60 percent of its membership.[11]

The Andhra revolutionaries set up a state-level coordination committee in September, by which time similar committees had come to be formed in Jammu and Kashmir, Uttar Pradesh, Punjab, and Bihar. In November the West Bengal committee took the initiative to link all of these bodies together in an All-India Coordination Committee of Revolutionaries in the CPI(M). At first the Andhra revolutionaries were reluctant to join the all-India body. Much less were they inclined to join in the setting up of a separate Communist party. However, the all-India coordination body changed its name after the CPI(M) Burdwan plenum to All-India Coordination Committee of Communist Revolutionaries (AICCCR). This new body, after reviewing the year following the Naxalbari rebellion, called for the building of a "true" party through Naxalbari-type struggles, "for revolution cannot be victorious without a revolutionary party." It also called for boy-

[10] Quoted in Mohan Ram, p. 81. See also *Liberation*, May 1968.
[11] For a detailed report on defections, see *Political-Organizational Report*, pp. 287–89 and Appendix I.

cott of elections and for "revolutionary class battles under the banner of Chairman Mao's Thought" leading to a people's democratic revolution.[12]

The theoretical arguments for a new party came from Charu Mazumdar, the principal ideologue of the Naxalbari struggle, and now of the AICCCR. The main contradiction in the countryside, wrote Mazumdar, is between the feudal landlords and peasants, and only by setting up liberated zones through peasant armed forces under working-class leadership can this contradiction be resolved. All of the Indian parties have turned out to be enemies of the revolution. While the "new democratic" revolution can succeed only by following the Maoist path, a revolutionary party cannot be built merely with the defectors from the two Communist parties. Basically "such a party will be formed with the youth of the working class, the peasantry, and the toiling middle class, who not only accept the thought of Chairman Mao but also apply the same in their own lives, spread and propagate it among the broad masses, and build bases for armed struggle in the countryside. Such a party will not only be a revolutionary party, but it will be at the same time the people's armed force and the people's State power." [13]

Mazumdar, meanwhile, elevated the Naxalbari struggle to a higher plane; he declared in June 1968, when nothing was left of the peasant armed struggle there, that the Naxalbari struggle was not for land or crops but for the seizure of political power.[14] When the AICCCR met in October, the peasant struggle was perceived to have already entered the second stage, "the stage of guerrilla warfare," in various parts of India. The revolutionaries

---

[12] *Liberation,* June 1968; Moham Ram, pp. 81–84.

[13] "Mazumdar, like the CPC, was placing a premium on new entrants to the ranks of revolution and minifying the role of those who had revolted against the CPI(M). Second, he was making the dangerous formulation that the revolutionary party will also be the people's armed force and the people's State power which implied all the three were co-extensive synonyms." Mohan Ram, p. 84.

[14] *Liberation,* June 1968. Mazumdar appeared to be quite confused about the lower and higher forms of struggle. See Mohan Ram, pp. 84–88.

decided to plunge into work among the peasant masses and set up as many revolutionary bases as they could. They apparently decided that party-building as well as the building of a mass base must await this "basic task" to be completed.[15]

About this time Mazumdar further sharpened his own concept of party building. The revolutionary cadres, he wrote, must work secretly among the peasants, avoiding open propaganda and demonstrations. The secret organization of these cadres is to become the party of the future. The cadres can build revolutionary bases among the peasants through successful application of four weapons: class analysis, investigation, study, and class struggle. The "class analysis" theme was picked up with approval in a *Peking Review* comment whose main purpose apparently was to warn the revolutionaries not to be carried away by the romanticism of armed peasant struggles. Ignoring Mazumdar's claim that the Naxalbari-type struggles were for the seizure of political power, the Chinese commentary pointed out that the peasants were fighting in Srikakulam, and in parts of Uttar Pradesh and Bihar, with arms "against brutal repression" and "to seize land." [16]

Peking began to glorify the Srikakulam armed struggle, pointing out that the struggle was being led by revolutionaries of the CPI(M).[17] This struggle covered the 800-square-mile tribal agency tract inhabited mostly by the Girijan tribe. Since 1959, the Girijans had been mobilized by the district committee of the CPI(M) around a militant program that included learning the lessons of the Telengana armed struggle and the raising of a politically conscious militant tribal cadre. The organizational base of the district committee was the Girijan Sangham. The objective situation was favorable for tribal militancy since the Girijans had been subjected to a very severe form of feudal exploitation that

---

[15] *Liberation*, November 1968.

[16] "Revolutionary Struggle of the Indian People Grows in Depth," *Peking Review*, January 31, 1969.

[17] NCNA report, Peking Radio, March 7, 1968.

included some of the worst features of serfdom and bonded labor together with systematic alienation of tribal land by nontribal landlords and their agents. Encouraged by the progress of mobilization, the district committee had started implementing a 10-point agrarian program in 1967. It included occupation of land held by the landlords and the seizing of their crops. It was customary for the Girijans to carry weapons like axes, bows and arrows, and even handmade guns whenever they held processions. The tribals began to clash with landlords and police in the spring of 1968, and the police set up special armed camps in the Srikakulam area. The first major exchange of fire was reported on March 4. Two Girijans were killed "causing great demoralization in the movement." [18]

FACTIONALISM AND THE BIRTH OF THE CPI(ML)

About this time, serious differences arose between the district committee and the state committee of the CPI(M) over the basic question of armed struggle as well as the related questions of what form it should take and how to train the Girijans for it. Apparently, the district leaders were for carrying armed struggle to the next stage—armed guerrilla warfare—while the state leaders thought that the struggle should be built around armed resistance. After the majority of the Andhra state committee members rebelled against the CPI(M) leadership, the district committee decided to establish links with the AICCCR, thus creating a further difference between themselves and the state-level rebels.

In September, the district committee unanimously decided on armed struggle for Srikakulam. "Some district leaders said that the state leadership (that is, the rebel revolutionaries) were neo-revisionists, and saw political motives for the delay in starting

[18] Mohan Ram, pp. 89–90. "On the one hand there is the fact to be reckoned with that the present (Andhra) government is sympathetic to, and draws its support from the better-off sections of the rural population; on the other hand, the rural landless, and the tribals especially, are abysmally poor and suffer from multiple social disabilities." *Economic and Political Weekly*, October 22, 1970.

armed struggle and for not joining the AICCCR." The committee also decided to formally join the AICCCR. In October, the state coordination committee also joined the AICCCR and attended its meeting in Calcutta. However, differences soon broke out between the AICCCR and the state coordination committee over the political content of the Srikakulam struggle. Differences continued between the state committee and the district leaders also. According to one report, the district committee continued functioning as a rival state center with direct encouragement from the AICCCR, and when armed struggle was about to begin in Srikakulam, "the AICCCR wanted to deprive the state committee of any credit for leading it and claim the credit for itself." [19]

Armed struggle began in Srikakulam toward the end of 1968. The locals who were now affiliated with the AICCCR immediately claimed that it had reached a "high level," that the peasants, led by the Communist revolutionaries, were setting up their own revolutionary organization which was "in embryo the organ of the people's political power in villages." [20] In February 1969, the AICCCR disaffiliated itself from the state coordination committee and decided to launch a new Communist party. It declared that the revolutionary situation in India was excellent, but "without a revolutionary party there can be no revolutionary discipline and without revolutionary discipline the struggles cannot be raised to a higher level." Struggles among the Communist revolutionaries now had to be waged within the new party. "Idealist deviation on the question of party-building arises as a result of the refusal to recognize the struggle that must be waged within the party. The idea that the party should be formed only after all opportunistic tendencies, alien class trends, and undesirable elements have been purged through class struggles is nothing but subjective idealism. To conceive of a party without contradictions, without struggle

[19] Mohan Ram, pp. 92–94.
[20] *Liberation,* March 1969. The organization was named Royotanga Sangrama Samithi (Council of Peasant Struggle).

between the opposites, that is, to think of a pure factionless party is indulging in mere idealistic fantasy." [21]

The AICCCR went ahead and converted itself into the Communist Party of India (Marxist-Leninist) on April 22, 1969, and the party was formally launched on May 1 at a rally in Calcutta. Several Maoist factions, including those of Andhra Pradesh, Kerala, and Maharashtra, remained outside of it. The Andhra revolutionaries met in a plenary session in April and reconstituted their coordination committee as the Revolutionary Communist Committee of Andhra Pradesh with an "immediate program" to prepare the ground for the formation of a revolutionary party.[22] In July, the CCP conferred legitimacy on the CPI(ML) by publishing a summary of its political resolution in *People's Daily,* July 2, 1969.

The political resolution bore a distinct imprint of Mao's concept of the Chinese revolution and his analysis of class alignments in China in the late 1930s. The principal contradiction in Indian society, said the resolution, is between feudalism and the peasant masses. The strategic goal is a people's democratic revolution, "the main content of which is the agrarian revolution, the abolition of feudalism in the countryside." The revolution is to be won through an alliance of the working class with the poor and landless peasants as well as the middle-level peasants. The working class is to lead the alliance toward seizure of power through armed struggle. A revolutionary front of all revolutionaries and revolutionary classes is to be built on the basis of the worker-peasant alliance.

Only through a people's war can a weak revolutionary force win over an apparently powerful enemy, said the resolution. The basic tactic of the peasant struggle is to be guerrilla warfare; the party's main task is to rally all revolutionary classes around the

---

[21] *Liberation,* March 1969.

[22] Mohan Ram, p. 103. Ram has discussed in some detail the differences between the Andhra revolutionaries and the Bengali leadership of the AICCCR as well as between the Srikakulam locals and the Andhra revolutionaries. See chs. 3 and 4.

basic program of agrarian reforms. The Indian revolution will have to fight both American imperialism and Soviet social imperialism. The party will firmly reject parliamentarianism and adhere to armed revolution. It will be rural-based so that it can rouse the peasantry to wage guerrilla war, unfold the agrarian revolution, build liberated rural bases, use the countryside to encircle the cities, and finally capture the cities. It will be a secret and underground party, keeping its main cadre underground; it will utilize all possible legal opportunities for struggle, but under no circumstances function openly. The party will try to integrate revolutionary theory and practice, forge close links with the masses, and practice criticism and self-criticism.[23]

GUERRILLA WARFARE
AND REVOLUTIONARY TERRORISM

Differences arose within the CPI(ML) leadership almost immediately over a number of tactical issues. The main point of difference was over secret versus mass activity. In Mazumdar's own language, the "debate" centered around three questions: Was guerrilla warfare to be the only form of struggle? Was there any need for mass organization? Should the party function secretly? Mazumdar's own tactical line, which eventually prevailed, was that only an underground party could organize an agrarian revolution —a mass organization would inevitably be dominated by middle-level and rich peasants and would thus be revisionist. Guerrilla warfare alone could mobilize the poor peasants and establish their leadership of the party.[24] Mazumdar's hostility toward mass mobilization and his preference for a secret underground party led him to formulate the concept of "annihilation of class enemies." In 1969, apart from Srikakulam, peasant guerrilla warfare under CPI(ML) leadership was taking place on a very limited scale

[23] *Liberation*, May 1969.   [24] *Liberation*, July 1969.

along the Bengal-Orissa-Bihar border (Debra-Gopiballavpur), in parts of southern Bihar, and along the Uttar Pradesh-Nepal border in the *terai* region, in addition to smaller isolated incidents in Punjab, Assam, Madras, and Kerala. Peking media publicized the following "major successes" of this struggle:

In West Bengal, "the peasant revolutionary armed struggle has spread from the Tarai (that is, Naxalbari) in the northern part of the state to Midnapore and other coastal regions, in the south. In Srikakulam, Andhra Pradesh, "the peasant guerrillas turned 300 villages into red areas for launching struggle, and more than 100 guerrillas were active in an area of about 500 square miles in the Srikakulam mountains. One hundred square miles of mountain area deep in the interior of Parvathipuram Agency came under the control of the peasant forces. The current peasant armed struggle in Andhra Pradesh has spread from the remote mountain area of Srikakulam district to more than nineteen rural areas in ten districts on the spacious plains of Telengana in the northern part of Andhra Pradesh." In Bihar, peasants took up arms and organized "small guerrilla squads" to conduct operations at Mushahari, in Muzzaffarpur district. Similar armed struggle was also "developing in areas close to the jungle areas of Gunupur in Koraput district of Orissa, in areas close to Lakhimpur in Uttar Pradesh, in Bhatinda and some other districts in Punjab, and in Kerala state." [25]

All of these "revolutionary peasant bases" have certain geographic and ethnic features in common, said Peking. They are in "remote" areas, either in the mountains or in deep jungles, either along interstate borders (Bengal-Orissa, and Orissa-Andhra Pradesh, where coordination between the police forces of neighboring states is generally poor), or along international borders (between India and East Pakistan, India and Nepal, India and West Pakistan, India and Tibet). Some of these areas are politically

[25] *Peking Review,* February 13, 1970.

"soft"—such as the region bordering Azad Kashmir and the five districts of Assam (Kamrup, Cachar, Golpara, Lakhimpur and Chiier) linked by road with Bhutan and Sikkim. Most of these areas have strong segments of tribal people that are either traditionally militant (Girijans of Srikakulam, Santhals of Chhotanagpur, the hill tribes of Uttar Pradesh) or are freer from the tyranny of caste. All of these areas are inhabited by large numbers of landless farm workers and poor peasants.

Reports in CPI(ML) journals stressed the insurgencies along the India-Nepal border, and in Srikakulam. *Lok Yudh* (People's War), the Hindi weekly of the party, carried 124.24 columns of reports of "peasant guerrilla war" in thirty-five issues published between August 8, 1968 and May 8, 1969, of which 82 columns carried reports of activities in Bihar, Uttar Pradesh, and Bengal. The bulk of these activities were located in areas close to the India-Nepal border.

The party's English language monthly, *Liberation,* devoted 88.50 columns in eleven out of the fifteen issues published between March 1968 and April 1969, of which 31.50 columns continued to report the armed struggle in Srikakulam, 9.75 events in Bihar, 14 those in Uttar Pradesh, and 10.5 those in West Bengal.

By the end of 1969, the armed struggle took the form of "annihilation." The following "successes" were among those reported in *Deshabrati* (December 18, 1969; January 1, February 12 and 19, 1970):

NOVEMBER 9, 1969: Four peasant guerrillas killed a *jotedar* named Elphus Mian while the latter was returning home at night.

DECEMBER 25, 1969 to January 8, 1970: Two guerrillas disguised as patients killed a *jotedar*-physician named Dr. Amulya Patra at Debra in Midnapur district.

DECEMBER 29, 1969: A notorious *jotedar* named Madhav Mandal was slain by three guerrillas in the Sundarban forests near Hemnagar village in 24-Parganas district.

JANUARY 3, 1970: A *jotedar* named Nandalal Ghosh was slain by three guerrillas, all peasants, in broad daylight in a village near Howrah town.

ON JANUARY 16, 1970, a group of thirty guerrillas attacked the house of a landlord in a village in Muzzaffarnagar district. The landlord escaped but the guerrillas looted almost everything that belonged to him.

ON FEBRUARY 1, 1970, peasant guerrillas killed a notorious class enemy in a village in Muzzaffarnagar district of Bihar.

ON FEBRUARY 13 at about 7 p.m., at Sakrile *thana* near Gopiballavpur, on Bengal-Orissa border, a notorious *jotedar* and moneylender named Mohini Shau was killed by a group of five armed peasant guerrillas. . . . Mohini Shau had 250 acres of land and he used to exploit the poor landless workers.

ON FEBRUARY 15, 1970, in a village named Ambadikambram on the Andhra-Orissa border, peasant guerrillas murdered a landlord and looted his estate.

Only at Srikakulam did the armed struggle acquire a certain organization and depth, as shown in reports appearing in the *Peking Review* on August 6, 1969, and January 2, 1970.

Since the beginning of 1969, the revolutionary peasants of Srikakulam district have scored many victories in countering the "combing" operations of the reactionary landlord armed bands and the reactionary police. The people's forces have been growing stronger day by day. Adopting flexible strategy and tactics, they skilfully pounded the enemy out on "combing" operations. They fought heroically and skillfully and armed themselves with weapons seized from the enemy. According to the Indian bourgeois press, the Girijan armed forces in Srikakulam District have in their possession large quantities of explosives and many guns in addition to spears, bows and arrows, and axes.

It was reported that recently the guerrilla units in Srikakulam District made frequent, successful attacks on the reactionary police. Within two days in early June, the guerrillas in Sompeta and Parvathipuram areas of the district launched four comparatively large-scale attacks on the reactionary police, dealing them telling blows. On June 5, using homemade weapons, a guerrilla unit in Parvathipuram made a surprise attack on the reactionary police sent there on "combing" operations.

A phenomenal expansion of the red area of revolutionary armed struggle is taking place in Srikakulam and various other districts of Andhra, according to a report in the July (1969) issue of the Indian monthly *Liberation*. Despite vicious enemy suppression campaigns, more than 300 villages have been turned into red areas. Panic-stricken landlords have fled for their lives, it adds.

The report says: "Here no machinery of the reactionary government operates. Here no forest or revenue official of the reactionary government, no *panchayat samiti* [village council] man can enter. The guerrillas and members of the village self-defense squads try their best to protect the villages from police marauders. The administration is run, production is looked after, and disputes are settled by the *ryotanga sangrama samithi*—the revolutionary mass organization of the peasants." It goes on to say that this organization has 8,000 members in the special area alone. Here the *ryotanga sangrama samithi*—the new power structure—is carrying on investigations of the land whose owners have escaped or have been wiped out by the guerrillas, and investigations of the land handed over by the landlords. The *samithi* is expected soon to distribute all this land among the poor and landless peasants. Here, in every village, justice is meted out to the enemies of the people by people's courts.

Members of the Srikakulam District Committee of the CPI(ML) went deep into the countryside, established guerrilla units and propagated the truth pointed out by Chairman Mao that political power grows out of the barrel of the gun. . . . The CPI(ML) has now more than 100 guerrilla squads under its leadership and the areas of armed struggle have rapidly extended from the mountains to the plains and coasts. . . .

Srikakulam's revolutionary peasants scorn the ferocious enemy. Fighting with homemade guns, hand grenades, swords, spears, and bows and arrows they have badly battered the "Central Reserve Corps" and the state police forces equipped with modern weapons. In 1969, they fought 65 engagements with the police and smashed the reactionaries' armed "encirclement and suppression" operations one after another. The peasant masses and the guerrilla squads fought side by side, raiding landlords' estates, seizing enemy weapons, suppressing local despots, burning land and loan contracts and distributing the landlords' grain and land.[26]

Differences within the CPI(ML) leadership widened as the weaknesses of the peasant struggle became apparent after late 1969. The West Bengal united front government had flushed out the Naxalbari peasant rebellion with relative ease, although not without considerable political furor raised by non-Communist elements within the front as well as by the central government. The Srikakulam rebellion was a much greater affair than Naxalabari, and it also was hailed by Peking as a significant victory for Maoist tactics. However, in view of the fact that Andhra Pradesh was ruled by the Congress party with its support base among the well-to-do peasantry, the central government underplayed the Srikakulam rebellion, at the same time urging upon the state authorities the need to initiate reforms and to take strong security measures to suppress the uprising. Throughout 1969 the attention of the Andhra government was riveted mainly on the agitation by the elite of Telengana for a separate state. Toward the end of 1969, as this agitation was brought under control, the state authorities began to deal with the Srikakulam trouble in earnest. By January 1970, it was all but finished and the police drive was succeeding. The local leadership began to blame the CPI(ML) leaders of Bengal for the debacle. "The guerrilla squads dispersed over a wide area to escape encirclement and suppression by police forces and the people had to bear the brunt of the police repression, with no guerrilla squads to protect them." [27] Belatedly, the Andhra government, prodded by New Delhi, introduced certain tenancy reforms in the Srikakulam area, the most important of which was forbidding the purchase of tribal land by non-tribals.

---

[26] For more reports of the peasant insurgency in India, see *Peking Review*, October 31, 1969 and January 30 and February 13, 1970.

[27] Mohan Ram, pp. 116–25.

The other pockets of armed guerrilla warfare also began to disintegrate rapidly. The crisis this created within the CPI(ML) had three major manifestations in 1970. At the party's first congress it brought into the open major differences regarding tactics between Mazumdar and some other leaders, notably Kanu Sanyal, who occupied the second rank in the party, and Sushital Roy Choudhuri, a theoretician. Mazumdar had already established his personal hegemony over the party, and his followers had been trying to build a personality cult around him.[28] Others opposed his annihilation tactics as petty-bourgois terrorism and denounced his rejection of mass organization and mass activity as psychopathic. The congress, however, adopted a political-organizational report upholding the tactic of annihilation and generally endorsing the line of clandestine functioning. The report maintained that only class war—liquidation of class enemies—could solve the problems before the party and carry the struggle to a higher stage. "The liquidation movement liberates the man not only from the oppression of the landlord class and the State but also from reactionary outdated ideas, selfishness, parochialism, regionalism, casteism, and religious superstition." The liquidation movement "can therefore elevate man to his full glory and nobility." Mazumdar introduced two important changes in his tactics of liquidation. First, the revolutionaries should eschew the use of firearms and depend mostly on conventional weapons, even "bare hands." "If guerrilla groups start their liquidation campaign with conventional weapons then the landless and poor peasants will come forward to participate in the liquidation program with bare hands. They will then avenge themselves on their class enemy and develop unbounded revolutionary zeal." The second change was a contraction of the guerrilla squad's operational base. The annihi-

[28] "Observer" wrote in *Liberation*, February 1970, that the task before the party was to "establish firmly the authority of leadership of Comrade Charu Mazumdar at all levels." Mazumdar was likened with Mao and Lin Piao." We must be loyal to Chairman Mao, Vice-Chairman Lin Piao, and the Communist Party of China and must fully accept the revolutionary leadership of Comrade Charu Mazumdar."

lation program should be carried out on the basis of "one area, one unit, one squad." [29]

FROM LIQUIDATION TACTICS TO TERRORISM

How the liquidation tactic dissipated into sheer terrorism was brought out in a series of special reports in the *Hindustan Times* in June. The newspaper's special correspondent, D. Sen, toured the Debra-Gopiballavpur region on the Bengal-Orissa-Bihar border and found that twenty-one murders had been commited in the two villages since December. "Quite a few of these had nothing to do with 'class struggle' but were committed purely on grounds of personal malice." While "scores of students and other young people" from Calcutta and the district towns continued to visit rural areas to "de-class" themselves and educate the villagers, "a substantial section of them found the villages difficult places to work in and complained that they would be misfits at working among peasants." Sen reported the existence of a CPI(ML) "nucleus" in each of the seventeen districts of West Bengal. [30]

Two months later a *Times of India* report said that there were 700 squads in Bengal, concentrated in eight districts, and about 90 of them in the industrial belt around Calcutta. This was probably the first clear indication that the annihilation program was being changed into urban terrorism. At the beginning of August, the CPI(ML)'s clandestine Bengali journal reported that the program was now to be extended to Calcutta. [31]

[29] The CPI(ML) publications were banned by this time. For reports of the congress, see *Times of India* June 1 and July 19, 1970; also *Liberation*, June–July 1970, issued clandestinely. The congress was held on May 15–16 in a Bihar village. For Mazumdar's admission of differences over the tactical line, see *Hindustan Times*, July 20, 1970.

[30] D. Sen, "Naxalites on the Move—II," *Hindustan Times*, June 16, 1970.

[31] *Times of India*, August 4 and 7, 1970. The latter report said that the squads were small, each consisting of five or six persons, raised locality-wise, and each functioning more or less autonomously. Annihilation would now include the police, military, and paramilitary personnel located in the Calcutta area. See also *Deshabrati*, July 24, 1970. This weekly reported that three paramilitary personnel had been liquidated on July 14.

In October the differences over annihilation reached "a break-ing point"; Mazumdar himself admitted the existence of "wide differences" in a letter written to an unnamed comrade. Members defected and some of the defectors were mercilessly beaten, even murdered.[32] A number of dissident leaders, some of them from Andhra Pradesh and others from Bengal, were rounded up by the police on information believed to have been supplied by Mazum-dar's followers.[33] Several of the leaders who disagreed with Ma-zumdar let themselves be arrested by the police. In November Mazumdar came out with the grandoise plan of a "long march" of the revolutionaries from Debra to somewhere in the district of Purulia, nearer Bihar; [34] this apparently reflected an admission that the annihilation campaign in the Debra area had been flushed out by the police.

YOUTH AND TERRORISM

What now remained of the movement was urban terrorism in the Calcutta area and in some isolated parts of Bengal and other states. How urban terrorism flourished in Calcutta and other parts of Bengal before and during the mid-term election of March 1971 we have already noted briefly in chapter 8. It easily became a much tougher and more complex sociocultural problem than armed guerrilla warfare in the countryside. In the countryside, the CPI(ML) revolutionaries were either liquidated by the police or neutralized by the militant peasant struggle of the CPI(M). Toward the end of 1970, the CPI(M) claimed that the "Naxal-ites" had been "almost extinct" in the Naxalbari area and "they are seen nowhere in rural West Bengal." [35] This claim was more

[32] *Times of India,* October 22 and 25, 1970; see also *Deshabrati,* October 20, 1970. One defector was beheaded. *Times of India,* November 6, 1970.

[33] Interview with a prominent dissident leader who broke with the party in De-cember. See also editorial in *Times of India,* August 5, 1970.

[34] *Times of India,* November 7, 1970. The August issue of *Liberation* claimed; "Our party and revolution have received and are receiving the personal care and guidance of Chairman Mao." Quoted in *Times of India,* August 8, 1970.

[35] *People's Democracy,* December 27, 1970.

or less confirmed by the CPI(M) successes in the rural areas in the mid-term poll.

On the other hand, the "Naxalites" made their presence felt in Calcutta in a big way. "Naxalism" flourished in the deprivation and squalor of Calcutta and meshed with interparty conflicts, especially conflicts between the CPI(M) and the others. Mazumdar found his most responsive constituency among the youth of Calcutta, who enthusiastically took up his call to boycott examinations, destroy books, beat up teachers and proctors, raid schools, colleges, and universities, defile and even pull down portraits and statues of national heroes like Gandhi, Vidyasagar, and Vivekananda, smash science laboratories, harass motorists, and generally defy all symbols of the establishment. They wrote threatening letters to doctors who charged patients high fees, they warned moneylenders, blackmarketeers, and profiteers and sometimes waylaid and murdered them. A good deal of their revolutionary wrath spent itself in maiming and killing cadres of the CPI(M), and not infrequently they themselves were killed in political violence. The "hard core" of "Naxalites" observed a strict code of ethics, but hundreds of hoodlums and antisocial elements carried on their own vandalism under the omnibus banner of "Naxalism."

It was reported in August 1970 that there were 25,000 "Naxalites" in India, the bulk of them "frustrated, educated, unemployed youth." [36] A scholar from Delhi University who made a study of "Naxalite" youths, wrote that each of his cases was "reacting, though from different angles, to the general socioeconomic stagnation, especially to the problems of poverty and unemployment." [37] Sen, of *Hindustan Times,* was told that nine

[36] *National Herald,* editorial, August 27, 1970. *The Hindu,* however, wrote in an editorial on November 20, "The naxalite following has been estimated at between 13,000 and 20,000 including 'sympathizers' in colleges, and even after the arrest of 4,000 of them, quite a few are still free to organize their trained assaults."

[37] Nayan R. Chanda, "Roots of Student Violence," *Times of India,* August 8, 1970.

of the twelve national scholarship holders in Calcutta in 1969 had turned "Naxalite." Many brilliant boys and girls, he reported, had deliberately become "Naxalites" out of an idealism that could not find a more fruitful and constructive expression. "These are boys and girls, most of whom can confidently look forward to getting jobs after they come out of the university. But many of them have rejected good jobs or have deliberately taken minor jobs which, in the language of such a Naxalite, will not corrupt them to developing a vested interest in the bourgois system which they want to overthrow." [38]

Scores of boys and girls of well-to-do families left their colleges and universities in Delhi, Lucknow, Allahabad, Banaras, and Patna to join the peasants in their armed struggle. Many of them straggled back to the cities and their institutions, frustrated and wounded spiritually, sometimes physically. In Calcutta, urban terrorism even cast a spell over teen-agers, who joined in annihilation campaigns and sometimes got killed or more often found themselves in prison. In the Calcutta area alone some 1,500 murders were placed at the door of "Naxalism" in 1970. By September 9, 12 policemen were killed and 325 injured.[39] Sometimes police violence and repression evoked the pent-up wrath of the

[38] D. Sen, "Naxalites on the Move—III," *Hindustan Times*, June 17, 1970. See also R. N. Sinha, "Naxalites Not Yet Vanquished," *Mail*, October 16, 1970; "Wasted Idealism," *Hindustan Times* editorial, June 19, 1970. "There is little doubt that the Naxalite movement has captured the imagination of a section of youth in this country. In West Bengal, a very considerable portion of the urban youth, especially the student youth, has been drawn into this movement one way or another. Besides, while the number of active participants may be small, those who sympathize with the movement are fairly numerous. It has also been noted that in their ranks are many brilliant students. The causes that have given rise to this phenomenon would make an interesting subject for sociological study. Were such a study to be made, it is very likely that it would find among the causes of the movement inadequacy and corruption of our present educational system, the frustration of youth arising out of the lengthening queues of the unemployed, the disgust and the hatred roused by the degeneration in standards of political behavior by leaders of the established political parties, not excluding the leaders of Left parties, and lastly the absence of any worthwhile national perspective." J. Mohan, "Naxalites, the New Left," *Economic and Political Weekly: Special Number*, 1970, p. 1122.

[39] "Ludicrous Priorities" *The Statesman*, November 7, 1970; see also "Mythology of Naxalism," *ibid.*, October 18, 1970.

people. In Krishnagar town of Nadia district in Bengal, policemen beat up not only innocent citizens but also a senior police of-
ficer. "So sharp was the reaction of the local people to the police
misbehavior that the policing of the town had to be transferred to
the CRP (central reserve police, a para-military force controlled
by the central government) and the Border Security Force." Extensive searches conducted by the police led to public estrange-
ment in several places, and added fuel to the fire of violent protests.[40]

COLLAPSE IN ANDHRA PRADESH

In Andhra Pradesh, the Communist revolutionary movement
collapsed in 1970. As noted, the two main factions were the locals
of Srikakulam led by the district committee which was affiliated
with the CPI(ML), and the district coordination committee that
functioned independently. Factionalism and rivalries between the
two, and within either, weakened the movement from the very
beginning.

The leader of the state committee was T. Nagi Reddy who, in
the early 1950s, had been a prominent member of the "Maoist
faction" within the united CPI. Nagi Reddy was opposed to the
tactic of armed guerrilla warfare by the Girijans of Srikakulam
without first preparing a mass base for such tactical action; the
revolutionism of the locals, however, forced him to adopt parallel
revolutionary tactics without adequate preparation. The cadres of
the district committee were mostly drawn from middle-class
farmer families who were said to be opposed to "wanton
killing." [41]

Nagi Reddy was expelled from the CPI(M) in 1968 for "leftist
adventurism"; thereupon he denounced parliamentarianism and
in the following year resigned from the Andhra legislative assem-

---

[40] Sankar Ghosh, "Naxalite Attacks on Police," *Times of India*, September 22,
1970.
[41] S. Dharmarajan, "Naxalites in Disarray," *Times of India*, June 23, 1970.

bly. In June 1969, he and his followers assembled in a secret conclave in Madras to chalk out a plan "to liberate villages, encircle towns and gradually the urban areas"; the campaign was to begin in the Warangal, Khammam, East Godavari, Godavari Nalgonda, and Mehboobnagar districts. The police surprised the conclave and arrested Reddy and forty-three of his close associates.[42]

By June the police had built up a massive "anti-Naxalite" operation in the depths of the hilly Srikakulam area. A prominent leader of the locals, M. V. Ramanamurthy, who was said to be the second in command of the annihilation campaign, was killed by the police. By this time, the police had arrested 1,400 revolutionaries in Andhra Pradesh; the police operations, claimed an official spokesman on June 18, had broken the mass base of the "Naxalites," and brought the movement under control.[43]

Then came the big disaster. In an encounter with the police on July 10, two top leaders of the tribal rebellion, Vempatapu Satyanarayana and Adibhatla Kailasam, were killed. Satyanarayana, a former school teacher who had identified himself with the trib-

[42] "The organized, theoretical opposition to the CPI(ML) line has come mainly from the Nagi Reddy group in Andhra and the Promode San Gupta group in West Bengal. Nagi Reddy, in a document circulated to the rank and file of his party in Andhra Pradesh, states that the only program of the CPI(ML) for mobilizing the rural masses is guerrilla actions directed against the class enemies in the countryside. 'For them,' he says, 'the agrarian program has no role to play in mobilizing the masses.' As against this, 'for the Communist revolutionaries agrarian revolution, that is abolition of feudalism, distribution of land to the tiller, and abolition of all kinds of feudal exploitation is the immediate program for mobilizing, organizing, and leading the vast masses of rural people into struggles—the struggles that would develop into armed struggle." Accusing the CPI(ML) of robbing 'the People's War of its main content by preaching the postponement of agrarian revolution,' Nagi Reddy affirmed that 'for us today there is no People's War without agrarian revolution' . . .
"Even more far-reaching is the criticism by the Promode Sen Gupta group of Maoists. In an article published in their monthly *Forward,* they charge the CPI(ML) with violating all fundamental principles of Marxist-Leninist teachings and, in the name of Mao, beginning 'to preach a patently anti-Mao ideology.' In support of this, the *Forward* article points out that 'while Marx, Engels, Lenin, Stalin and Mao—all have taught that Communists must work in all mass organizations of workers and peasants and must take part in the day-to-day struggles of the toiling people . . . the party (CPI-ML) began to advocate boycott of all mass organizations." J. Mohan, p. 1122.
[43] *Times of India,* June 18, 1970.

als and married a tribal woman, was a charismatic leader whose word was said to be the law for the tribals and was the "brains" of the revolutionary movement. The death of these two leaders was so important that the state's home minister himself announced the news to the press, claiming at the same time that the rebellion had been "almost liquidated." [44]

Police sources disclosed that of the sixty-odd *dalams* (bands) of rebels operating at one time, only two remained, and that also under tribal leadership. These two *dalams* were reported to have sent feelers to the police for surrender. The remaining leaders gave themselves up, while the rank-and-file revolutionaries returned to their middle-class life.[45] In editorial obituaries, the *Times of India* remarked that "only textbook revolutionaries and romantics believe that the (Srikakulam) area could be converted into a kind of Yenan from where the revolution could spread to neighboring areas to cover the whole of Andhra and the adjoining Orissa. The region is easily accessible to the forces of law and order. The state police has in fact been able to clean it up without any help from the army." The *Hindu* hoped that the collapse of the Andhra campaign would teach the "Maoists" how difficult it was to organize the poor peasant and the landless in India for a violent revolution.[46]

[44] K. P. Rao, "Govt. Steps, Group Rivalries Cripple Andhra Naxalites," *Hindustan Times*, July 22, 1970.

[45] *Indian Express*, July 14, 1970. "Today the Naxalite ideology commands the support of quite a few intellectuals and educated young men (in Andhra Pradesh). Some of them are in detention under the preventive detention act . . . and many others have been arrested and are awaiting trial. But nothing, it seems, will deter them from pursuing their objective of mobilizing the landless peasantry, tribals and scheduled castes." *Economic and Political Weekly*, February 21, 1970.

[46] "In Disarray," *Times of India*, July 14, 1970; "Naxalite Activity in Andhra," *Hindu*, July 14, 1970.

In December, a Vishakhapatnam court sentenced five Andhra revolutionaries, including two peasants, to death, and eight others, including three peasants, to life imprisonment. The prisoners shouted Maoist slogans as they entered the court to hear the sentences. *Times of India*, December 2, 1970.

"Naxalite" activity in Kerala remained more or less under control. There were a few noteworthy incidents of violence and murder such as the killing of a family of five in Trivandrum district on November 14, 1970. Incidents were limited to the

IMPLICATIONS OF PEASANT ARMED STRUGGLE

Were the peasant armed struggles in Srikakulam and other isolated parts of India genuine attempts to organize the peasantry
along Maoist lines, or were they manifestations of left-wing Communism or revolutionism? That the CPI(ML), in building the
third Communist party as well as in directing the guerrilla struggles, deviated seriously from essential features of the Chinese revolution was apparent even to the CCP; as we note in the next
chapter, the CCP did try to point out the deviations if only by
stressing time and again how peasant armed struggle was to be developed in the countryside. The question remains, however,
whether Maoism, transplanted to India, will not tend to deviate
into left-adventurism; in other words, whether India is suitable
for the kind of sustained, protracted peasant guerrilla war that
the CCP waged for more than two decades in China before it
could overthrow the Kuomintang. The two senior Communist
groups in India both regarded "Naxalism" as left-wing adventurism and sectarianism, although the CPI put the blame for the deviation squarely at the door of the Marxists and, at times, took a
somewhat indulgent view of the "Naxalites" if only because of the
antagonistic relationship between the "Naxalites" and the Marxists.

Left-wing deviations have plagued all Communist movements
and parties in the world. In fact, the dominant leadership of al-

Malabar region mostly. Home Minister Koya reported to the state assembly in November that "Naxalites" had committed six murders in Kerala. *Times of India,* November 2, 1970.

  In Punjab, the "hard core of Naxalites" in August 1970 was said to consist of
about thirty-six, "mostly students." The police had already killed thirteen. *Hindustan Times,* August 10, 1970. See also *Times of India,* November 30, 1970. There
were five "known" cells in the rural areas of Sangrur, Jullundur, Ludhiana, Hosh-
iarpur, and Rupar districts. *Hindustan Times,* August 13, 1970. For a somewhat
alarmist "map" of "Naxalite" activity in India in 1970, see Satindra Singh, "Naxalism: The 20-year Itch, "*Illustrated Weekly of India,* October 4, 1971.

most every Communist party has used charges of left- or right-wing deviation against competing factions and their leaders. Lenin, however, conceptualized left-wing Communism and offered a sociology of Communist revolutionism. According to Lenin, left-wing Communism stems from the individual's "sense of horror" at the "incredibly acute and rapid deterioration in conditions of his life" under capitalism, and his inability or unwillingness to fight capitalism with "perseverence, organization, discipline, and steadfastness." Lenin wrote: "The petty-bourgeois, driven to frenzy by the horrors of capitalism, is a social phenomenon which, like anarchy, is characteristic of all capitalist countries." Revolutionary extremism "crops up at unexpected moments in a somewhat new form in hitherto unknown vestments or surroundings in peculiar—more or less peculiar—circumstances." The revolutionist refuses to make a "strictly objective estimate of the class forces and their interrelations."

Lenin drew a clear line between left-wing extremism and the Communist struggle for revolutionary social change. A revolutionary party must have behind it long and varied experience; it is obligated to learn from its own and others' mistakes; it cannot ignore any form of struggle, nor even compromise, as long as it is certain that it is on the right track; and, above all, it must "imperatively work wherever the masses are to be found." "Left doctrinairism persists in the unconditional repudiation of certain old forms and fails to see that the new content is forcing its way through all and sundry forms, that it is our duty as Communists to master all forms, to learn how, with the maximum rapidity, to supplement one form with another, to substitute one for the other, and to adapt our tactics to every such change not called forth by our class, or by our efforts." Lenin saw in individual terrorism and assassination one of the fundamental dividing lines between left-wing Communism and the revolutionary party of the proletariat.[47]

[47] Lenin, 'Left'-wing Communism, an Infantile Disorder, in Selected Works (2 vols.; Moscow, 1942), II, 629–35, 580.

To be successful, peasant guerrilla warfare is more in need of a mass base than is urban working-class insurrection or a revolutionary coup d'etat. For, the purpose of guerrilla war is to show that a rebel party can make a revolution against a regime protected by a professional sophisticated army. A revolutionary party will be foolhardy to take to guerrilla warfare before it has gained the cooperation and support of the broad masses of people. In Peter Paret's language, it must first conquer the people before it can wage insurrectional war.[48] In the words of Mao, "Because guerrilla warfare basically derives from the masses and is supported by them, it can neither exist nor flourish if it separates itself from their sympathies and cooperation." [49]

Revolutionism appears to manifest particularly in social situations of acute contradictions which the existing political parties are incapable of mobilizing for gradual or radical change. It breaks out unexpectedly because the contradictions remain hidden behind a facade of stale and flabby politics, but reveal themselves to individuals or groups who, however, have neither the organizational base nor the perseverence and tenacity to wage a systematic, disciplined struggle to win over the broad masses. Revolutionism also breaks out in societies which deny normal outlets for organized protests, or in which impatient groups, stung by an acute and painful awareness of deprivation, find avenues of desired change blocked by the lethargic functioning of the political process.

In a highly stratified and long-stagnant society like India's, revolutionism should normally find a fertile soil, especially when the process of development begins to stir social classes long subjected to gross inequities. The tradition of nonviolence may itself encourage violence by groups that reject the philosophy of reconciliation but are unable to change the existing norms of organized political behavior. Terrorism flourished during the Gandhian

[48] Peter Paret, "The French Army and *La Guerre Revolutionnaire*," *Journal of the Royal United Service Institution* (February 1959), p. 59.

[49] *Mao Tse-tung on Guerrilla Warfare* (New York, Praeger, 1961), p. 44.

phase of the freedom struggle, and its appeal to the urban middle classes was much greater than its actual manifestation in Bengal, Punjab, and Maharashtra. The traditions of terrorism, however, prove to be a strong handicap for organizing effective peasant insurgencies, as became evident in the case of the CPI(ML), and particularly its leader, Charu Mazumdar. Under his leadership, "Naxalism" acquired cultural traces of Dostoevsky, Che Guevara, the Indian mother cult, the tantrik cult in Indian spiritualism, and the terrorism of the 1930s.[50] However, both within the CPI(ML) and without, there exist groups of Communists who seem genuinely to believe that creative application of Maoism to Indian conditions alone can lead to a successful social revolution in India. Many of these groups left the CPI(ML) since 1970 because they could not agree with Mazumdar's tactics of annihilation of the class enemy. The Bihar group broke with the party in late 1970 and has since been functioning as an independent "Maoist" unit. Similar groups exist in Andhra Pradesh, Uttar Pradesh, Punjab, Maharashtra, and Kerala. According to Mohan Ram, there are mainly "two shades of Maoism" in India, one represented by the CPI(ML) and the other by the Andhra Pradesh Revolutionary Communist Committee and "the various formations agreeing with it." [51] Conversations with some of the anti-Mazumdar Maoist groups in Calcutta did not, however, persuade me that compelling ideological or programmatic factors exist to bring the various anti-CPI(ML) groups together in a united party in the near future.

All of these groups believe in the tactic of armed peasant struggle. Each feels strongly against parliamentarianism. They seem to agree that objective conditions exist to mobilize the exploited sections of the peasantry for armed struggle. They find confirmation

---

[50] Mohit Sen, "The Naxalites and Marxism," *Economic and Political Weekly: Annual Number,* 1971, pp. 195–98. Sen compares the "Naxalite" rebels with the "primitive rebels" of Eric Hobsbaron.

[51] Mohan Ram, p. 163.

of this belief in the fact that armed struggles did occur, however limited or short-lived these might have been, in widely dispersed areas with peasants never mobilized for such struggles before. While it may be premature to draw such a conclusion from so weak a cluster of premises, it is undeniable that peasant militancy has occurred during the last three years in areas where agrarian stratification has been the most acute. In Andhra Pradesh, 42 percent of the rural population are landless workers, while the land ceiling is the highest in India—27 to 324 acres. No surplus land has been distributed to the landless.[52]

Musahari, in Bihar, suffers from the heaviest pressure on land. A survey of the area found that 118,757 people depended on 43,983 acres of cultivable land. The land/man ratio worked out at 30 cents per capita. Forty percent of the people were landless laborers; adding those who came from outside, it was 45 percent. "This fact, taken together with the land/man ratio accounts, among other things, for the uncommon dominance of the landowning families, the exceptionally low wages, particularly of the 'attached' laborers, the high degree of unemployment, the extreme poverty of the agricultural laborers, and of the general climate of discontentment."[53] No wonder, then, that Musahari would be a "Naxalite" base.

In Surajgunj, another "Naxalite" base in Bihar, there are only two classes of people: rich farmers with holdings of 33 acres or more and the poor who have no land. It has no middle class to act as a buffer between the extreme rich and the extreme poor.[54] A survey undertaken by the Orissa government in 1970 showed that

[52] C. Rajeshawara Rao, Bhowani Sen, and Y. V. Krishna Rao, *Problems of India's Agrarian Sector* (New Delhi, PPH, 1970), pp. 13–14.

[53] Jaya Prakash Narayan, "Politics of Violence: The Roots," *Amrita Bazar Patrika,* November 28, 1970.

[54] *Times of India,* November 17, 1970. "The number of well-to-do farmers is roughly 100. A dozen among them possess 1,000 to 4,000 *bighas* of land (3 *bighas* = 1 acre). The rest of the people live a miserable existence." *Ibid.,* June 27, 1970. In Purnea district in Bihar there are landlords owning as much as 22,000 acres of land. See table in Rao, Sen, and Rao, p. 16.

nearly one-sixth of the state's territory of 60,000 square miles was "threatened" by "ultra-left activities." [55] The worst-affected areas were Koraput and Ganjam districts bordering Andhra Pradesh. An overwhelming percentage of the population of Koraput and Mayurbhanj are tribals whose conditions are no better than those of the Girijans of Srikakulam. In certain areas, Monghyr in Bihar, and several places in Punjab, for instance, the "green revolution" aggravated the agrarian disparities which the "Naxalities" came forth to exploit.

In such conditions of acute agrarian inequities, Maoist or "Naxalite" groups will not find it difficult to lead or mislead deprived sections of the peasantry to armed struggle. They may succeed more easily with the tribals of the various states, who have a war-like tradition and who are not bound down by caste loyalties. Whether or not Maoism spreads in India on a wider organized scale will probably be determined by the success or failure of the peasant mobilization tactics of the two elder Communist parties, and the urgency and purposefulness with which the governments in New Delhi and in the states can redress the grievances of the rural poor. Mohan Ram views the sprouting of Maoism in India in the late 1960s primarily as a crisis in the CPI(M).

The chances of a strong, centralized Maoist movement emerging on a national scale depend largely on the luck of the CPI(M) with the parliamentary system. . . . In the absence of a credible Maoist rallying point, thousands of CPI(M) militants are still in the party functioning as pressure groups. The party is facing slow erosion at both the ends. Those who believe in the parliamentary system and peaceful transition would profitably turn to the CPI and those who believe in armed struggle would naturally look to the Maoist groups. The consolidation of the Maoist groups into a viable party would depend on two developments—accord among these groups on a tactical line and a large-scale exodus of the Maoist elements from the CPI(M).[56]

The Marxists, however, believe that the bulk of the Maoists outside their party will either slowly return to it or act in unison

[55] *Hindustan Times*, November 25, 1970.   [56] Mohun Ram, pp. 161–62.

with its cadres as the CPI(M) agrarian struggles gather greater momentum and spread beyond West Bengal and Kerala.

Meanwhile, the "Naxalite" rebellions have not been without an impact on Indian politics. They have dramatized the agrarian problem and brought it to the forefront of national issues. They have compelled the two CPIs to turn their face to the rural poor. In this, "Naxalism" has acted as a catalyst.

"Naxalite" revolutionism can be said to have introduced the concept of armed peasant guerrilla warfare in India's operational political vocabulary. It has shown how urban guerrilla terrorism by a relatively small number of people can create difficult, complicated, and stubborn problems for the Indian political and social system. By organized defiance of the state apparatus of force by peasants and middle-class youth, it has sought to reduce the image of the coercive power of government to that of a "paper tiger." The sum total of the three "contributions" to Indian politics can be noticed in the changed psychological and cultural attitude of large sections of people, especially the youth and the peasantry, toward the question of violence as a political tool.

The fact that thousands of poor peasants over widely dispersed areas could be mobilized for guerrilla war for even a brief period of time would seem to have shaken the foundation of the belief that the Indian peasant is too passive and too resigned to his fate to seek redress through violent action. One has only to travel in the countryside and talk to peasants to realize that the psychology of rural society has begun to change from one of resigned acceptance of gross inequities and massive distress to that of a certain defiance of the "arrangement" (*bandobast*) that has made these inequities and distress possible. Among the youth, urban and rural, the change is more pronounced. This is not to suggest that widespread social and class violence will break out in India in the immediate or near future. However, the masses of people are unlikely to bear passively much longer the sufferings that have been their lot. This is realized and admitted by leaders of the Union government, especially by Indira Gandhi.

10

THE ROLE OF CHINA
IN INDIAN
COMMUNIST POLITICS

Unlike the Bolshevik revolution, the Chinese revolution had lit-tle impact on the Indian bourgeoisie. The liberation of the Rus-sian working class from the oppression of tsarism had stirred the minds of many leaders of the Indian nationalist movement, in-cluding Jawaharlal Nehru.[1] The liberation of the masses of peas-antry from the shackles of feudalism in China had no such stir-ring impact. The CPI leadership hailed the second Chinese rev-olution as an epoch-making event, but continued to regard the Soviet Union as the fountainhead of doctrinal as well as tactical directives and to relegate the People's Republic of China to second place.

[1] For impact of the Soviet revolution on Indian nationalism, see Jayantuja Ban-dyopadhyaya, *Indian Nationalism versus International Communism* (Calcutta, Mu-khopadhyaya, 1966), chs. 5–6.

THE CPI AND THE CCP

Three factors appear to explain the CPI's resistance to the agrarian dimensions of the Chinese revolution. First, the city-oriented CPI had made no particular attempt to study the special characteristics of the Chinese revolution; the tendency was to regard it as an extension of the Bolshevik revolution.

Second, and this is rather important for an insight of Indian Communism, the middle-class leaders of the CPI showed a striking affinity with the intellectual orientation of the progressive bourgeoisie. It was an urban and Europe-centric orientation. Intellectual affinity with the bourgeoisie made the Communists accept the parliamentary system without much debate, without a serious attempt to think in terms of an alternative. Nehru and others had conferred a certain "legitimacy" on Marxism-Leninism by making "socialism" part of the ethos of the nationalist movement; the anti-Communism of the Congress party did not reject the "good and beneficial" aspects of Marxian socialism.[2] A trade-union movement had grown in the "suburbs" of the nationalist movement before the CPI was born. Even when the CPI, at the Comintern's behest, pitted itself against the Congress party, it functioned within the Congress "system" of politics, which was

---

[2] There had been little indigenous political thinking in India for a thousand years before the British conquest. Since the nineteenth century, Indian political thinking has centered round the British-type parliamentary democracy. Marxism-Leninism entered this mainstream of political thinking mainly through British socialism. Emotional responses to the Soviet revolution by men like Nehru and Tagore made the Soviet experiment, minus the principal institutions of the Soviet state like dictatorship of the proletariat and use of regimentation and terror, a part of the liberal-socialist, Indian democratic ethos. See Dr. Sankar Ghosh, *Indian Communism and Socialism* (Calcutta, 1970); also Nehru's writings, especially his *Discovery of India* (New York, Doubleday, 1968), and *An Autobiography* (London, Bodley Head, 1938). For Nehru's views on the Soviet revolution, see his *Soviet Russia* (Allahabad, 1928). For an interesting class-oriented analysis of the social background of Indian liberal-socialist thinking, see A. R. Desai, *Social Background of Indian Nationalism* (Bombay, 1954).

urban-oriented. Moscow showed no particular propensity to send Indian Communists to the villages to arouse the peasantry to work for an agrarian revolution.

The third reason was Moscow's determination not to allow the Chinese Communist party to persuade Communists in countries newly emerged from colonial status—countries in Asia, Africa, and Latin America—that the Chinese revolution was more relevant to their backward, agrarian societies than the Bolshevik revolution. Nor were the Chinese in a position (and a mood) in the 1940s and 1950s to defy the Soviet Union and claim that Maoism alone could guide these societies to emancipation. The Chinese did attempt in 1949–50 to claim that their revolution was different from the Russian one, but in doing so, they immediately came up against Soviet opposition. Soviet ideologues refused to concede that the Chinese revolution and Mao Tse-tung had made any momentous contribution to the theory and methodology of Communist revolution not already contained in Soviet strategic and tactical thinking. The CPI was perhaps not more than marginally aware of the ideological rivalry between Moscow and Peking during 1949–51; in any case, its loyalties were firmly fixed on Moscow.[3]

Liu Shao-chi's well-known formulation, at the Peking conference of the WFTU in November 1949, that the "path of Mao Tse-tung" could also be the "main path of the people's of other colonial and semi-colonial countries for winning their emancipation" was a somewhat muted version of his articles in *Pravda* earlier in that year and much milder in tone and content than the claims made by other CCP leaders.[4] For instance, Chen Po-ta as-

[3] For documented accounts of this rivalry, see John H. Kautsky, *Moscow and the Communist Party of India* (Cambridge, M.I.T. Press, 1956), chs. 2 and 3; Charles B. McLane, *Soviet Strategies in Southeast Asia* (Princeton, Princeton University Press, 1966), chapter 6; Bhabani Sen Gupta, *The Fulcrum of Asia: Relations Among China, India, Pakistan and the USSR* (New York, Pegasus, 1970), chs. 2 and 3.

[4] Liu's speech, or the relevant portions of it, can be found in Kautsky as well as McLane; for a lengthier quotation, see V. B. Sinha, *The Red Rebel in India* (New Delhi, Associated Publishing House, 1968), pp. 46–47. Liu, in his Peking speech,

serted Mao's intellectual independence of Stalin, while Lu Ting-yi drew a geographical line dividing the "spheres of influence" of the Soviet and Chinese revolutions.[5] However, Moscow did not concede these Chinese claims, particularly those regarding the Indian revolution. Some scholars have suggested that the Cominform journal, *For a Lasting Peace, For a People's Democracy*, in an editorial of January 27, 1950, recommended the Maoist (or a neo-Maoist) path to Communist parties in countries newly emerged or emerging from colonial status—the "third world" countries.[6] This suggestion, however, claims too much. The article presented the following two main "lessons" of the Chinese revolution:

1. The working class must unite with all classes, parties, groups, and organizations willing to fight the imperialists and their hirelings and to form a broad, nationwide front headed by the working class and its vanguard, the Communist party, the party equipped with the theory of Marxism-Leninism, the party that has mastered the art of revolutionary strategy and tactics, that breathes the spirit of revolutionary irreconcilability to enemies of the people, the spirit of

---

listed four pillars of success for the Chinese revolution: rural bases, broad national front, people's revolutionary army, and armed struggle. In a long article printed in *Pravda* of June 7–9, 1949, Liu had stressed the need to mobilize the peasantry for protracted armed struggle in the colonies and semicolonies, and recommended for the Communist parties there, including India by name, the strategy of the broadest united front *from below*. See Sen Gupta, p. 335n.

[5] Chen Po-ta claimed in 1949 that Mao had reached conclusions similar to Stalin's "on many fundamental problems through his independent thinking." "Stalin and the Chinese Revolution," *Sino-Soviet Friendship* (Peking, December 15, 1949). In so doing Chen was, in fact, asserting that Mao led the Chinese revolution *independently* of Moscow, and that in creative Marxist-Leninist thinking, he was at par with Stalin. Two years later, Chen Po-ta claimed with further clarity the distinctiveness of the Chinese revolution from the Soviet revolution, especially with its rural base area and guerrilla warfare. "Mao Tse-tung's Theory of the Chinese Revolution is the Integration of Marxism-Leninism with the Chinese Revolution," *People's Daily*, June 28, 1951.

Lu Ting-yi, in an article in the Cominform journal in 1951, said that the classical model of revolution, the Soviet, held good for the imperialist (capitalist) countries, while the Chinese revolution was the model for the colonies and semicolonies. *LPPD*, June 29, 1951.

[6] Kautsky, p. 87. This is also suggested by Gene D. Overstreet and Marshall Windmiller, *Communism in India* (Berkeley, University of California Press, 1959), and Mohan Ram, *Indian Communism: Split Within a Split* (Delhi, Vikas, 1969).

proletarian organization and discipline in the mass movement of all peoples.

2. A decisive condition for the victorious outcome of the national liberation struggle is the formation, when the necessary internal conditions allow for it, of people's liberation armies under the leadership of the Communist party.[7]

Both "lessons" were distortions of the principal methodology of the Chinese revolution, the second more so than the first.

In his *Pravda* articles, Liu Shao-chi recommended the tactics of a united front *from below* on the basis of a clear differentiation between the reactionary and progressive sections of the bourgeoisie. Communists "must for the sake of their national interests . . . adopt a firm and irreconcilable policy against national betrayal by the section of the bourgeoisie, especially the upper bourgeoisie, which has surrendered to imperialism. . . . On the other hand, Communists . . . should enter into an anti-imperialist alliance with that section of the national bourgeoisie which is still opposing imperialism and which does not oppose the anti-imperialist struggle of the masses of people."

The Cominform article made no such differentiation, nor did it specifically recommend a united front *from below*. In the second "lesson," there was no mention of rural bases, of protracted insurrection by peasant guerrillas. The Cominform article did ask the Communists to strengthen the "alliance of the working class with *all* the peasantry in order to fight for the introduction of the urgently needed land reforms." This, however, was very different from mobilizing the peasantry around a revolutionary and militant program of land reform. The Cominform article directed the CPI to forge an alliance between the working class and *all* the peasantry, and this was projected as "the experience of the national liberation movement in China and other countries." However, it took no account of the fact that the CCP had been able to

---

[7] Quoted in a statement by the editorial board of *Communist*, the monthly theoretical journal of the CPI, February–March 1950.

mobilize the general mass of peasantry only because of the Japanese imperialist invasion of China, and that there was not only no such objective condition in India; on the contrary, the newly established Indian national government had already forged political links with the great landholders and rich peasantry. Predictably, the CPI interpreted the Cominform directive as a guide that it should lower its ideological sights of activity among the peasants, and soon the peasant movement lost whatever limited militancy it had gained during the 1940s in isolated areas in the country.[8]

THE FIRST "DEBATE" ON THE "CHINESE PATH"

It is probably more accurate to suggest that the Cominform directive was meant *not* to allow Indian Communism to tread the Chinese path, but to bring it back to the Soviet path after its brief and traumatic diversion toward a peasant-oriented strategic tactical line during 1949–50. Inspired by the impressive exploits of the armed peasant struggle in Telengana, a group of Andhra Communists, led by Rajeshwar Rao, had in June 1948 submitted the famous "Anthra thesis" to the central executive committee of the CPI. These Communists were reported to have eagerly studied the theoretical works of Mao Tse-tung and Liu Shao-chi and other prominent leaders of the CCP, and they argued that "the only way to victory for Communism in India was through applying the strategy of the agrarian revolutionary war, which had been developed and tested in China." [9] Ranadive, who was gen-

[8] Abdullah Rasul, *Krishaksabhar Itihas* (Calcutta, 1970), chs. 10–14. According to the author, the Bengal branch of the Kisan Sabha, perhaps the strongest peasant front under CPI leadership, held no annual conference between 1947 and 1951. The Bengal unit had only 30,000 primary members in 1952 (pp. 179–80). Primary membership rose to 104,000 in 1953, but there was practically no peasant struggle except two mass rallies in August–September (pp. 187–89). It was not before 1959 that the peasant protests against shortage of food grains assumed some mass proportions (p. 212). In 1960 the Kisan Sabha for the first time formulated demands for land reforms rather than tenancy reforms (pp. 207–12).

[9] For a fairly detailed summary of the main formulations of the Andhra Communists, see Mohan Ram, pp. 23–29.

eral secretary of the CPI, doggedly resisted the Andhra thesis, and at one time even denounced Mao's claim to be a creative Marxist thinker.[10]

While the CPI leadership was torn between the Ranadive and the Andhra groups, a debate had been going on among Soviet ideologues on how much of the Chinese model could be adopted by the CPSU for guiding the Communist movements in "third world" countries. During this debate (briefly referred to in chapter 1), some Soviet scholars for a while inclined toward the Maoist path, and the Telengana peasant struggle was glorified in a number of Soviet formulations.[11]

There is, however, absolutely no evidence to confirm the suggestion that during Mao's visit to Moscow in 1949–50, Stalin agreed to place the Communist parties of South and Southeast Asia under the strategic direction of the CCP.[12] It is doubtful if Mao made such a claim. In fact, even during 1949–50, when Stalin was anxious to placate Mao without making more than the minimum concessions either on ideological or national interest issues,[13] Soviet ideological writings, while acknowledging the Chinese revolution's significance for the "third world" countries, did *not* admit that Mao had accomplished anything in the realm of strategic and tactical thinking not already achieved by Stalin.

---

[10] Ranadive wrote about Mao: "First, we must state emphatically that the Communist Party of India has accepted Marx, Engels, Lenin, and Stalin as the authoritative sources of Marxism. It has not discovered new sources of Marxism beyond these. Nor for that matter is there any Communist Party which declares adherence to the so-called theory of new democracy alleged to be pronounced by Mao and declares it to be a new addition to Marxism." *Ibid.,* p. 31.

"While there is no evidence to suggest that the Andhra leadership had any communication with the Chinese party, it is quite possible that Ranadive had Soviet backing when he denounced Mao." *Ibid.,* p. 32.

[11] For accounts of the debate, see Kautsky, pp. 88–91, McLane, ch. 6, and Sen Gupta, ch. 2. Also, Overstreet and Windmiller, pp. 259–74.

[12] This suggestion is made in Victor M. Fic, *Peaceful Transition to Communism in India* (Bombay, Nachiketa, 1969), pp. 22–23.

[13] For the hard bargaining that took place between Stalin and Mao over Soviet interests in Sinkiang and Manchuria, see Allen S. Whiting, *China Crosses the Yalu* (New York, Macmillan, 1960), pp. 27–30 and 179–80.

This was a major difference between the writings of those years in Chinese and in Soviet newspapers and journals.

It may be useful to look briefly at the main trends of Soviet thinking on the Chinese path during 1948–1952. In 1948, the economist A. Kheifets made a distinction between "the new democracy" and "people's democracy," and said that while the former was applicable to countries where the revolution had to fight the predominant survivals of imperialism tied to imperialist interests, the latter held good for the countries with varying degrees of feudal survivals.[14] This amounted to conceding leadership of the revolutions in the East to the CCP, and Kheifets' proposal was quickly rebutted by E. M. Zhukov, who asserted that "people's democracy" was equally applicable to all countries of the world. "The general pattern of social development," Zhukov declared, "is identical for both Eastern and Western countries. One can talk of differences in tempo and in concrete forms of this development. In this case, people's democracy in the East is no different from People's Democracy in the West." "People's democracy," Zhukov pointed out, was a "special form of regime" made possible by the victory of socialism in the USSR and the strengthening of the democratic forces throughout the world.[15]

In the latter half of 1949, Soviet thinkers appeared to have moved somewhat closer to the Maoist strategy. At the June 1949

[14] A. Kheifets, "The National Liberation Movement in the Colonial and Dependent Countries," *Molodoi bol'shevik*, No. 7 (1948), pp. 43–52. "The new democracy, the struggle for which goes on now in colonial and dependent countries is not identical with people's democracy, which is victorious in the countries of Central and Southeastern Europe. The states of Central and Southeastern Europe—these in the past were capitalist countries—had in a greater or lesser measure significant feudal survivals. People's democracy in these countries is a suitable form of transition from capitalism to socialism. In the East, the situation stands otherwise. Imperialist subjugation caused survival of feudalism as a rule to predominate in the economy of the colonial and dependent countries and the imperialist subjugation interlaced with the feudal. Even for such countries as India and China, more developed in industrial relations, the central question is the liquidation of feudal landholding in the countryside. New democracy in the East rises from the anti-imperialist and antifeudal struggle."

[15] *Voprosy economiki*, No. 9, 1949; *Current Digest of the Soviet Press*, 16 (January 3, 1950), pp. 5–6.

meeting of the USSR Academy of Sciences, Zhukov's thesis supported a broad-based united front in the "third world" countries
and a differentiation of the bourgoisie. Only the prosperous bourgeoisie, he said, had "finally gone over into the camp of imperialist reaction." [16] Maslennikov, in a general report, had much to say
in favor of the four-class strategy of the CCP, although he maintained that the revolutionary experience of the Soviet Union "was
and still is of tremendous significance for the national liberation
movement." At a special session the Academy held on India, Bala-
bushevich read a paper the significant point of which was his emphasis on the peasantry, agrarian reforms, and armed struggle in
the countryside. Summing up the discussion, Zhukov said that the
"controversy as to at what stage the colonial bourgeoisie begins to
play a reactionary role can be solved only when an answer is
given to the main question of its attitude toward the Soviet
Union." [17]

By November 1951, however, the Soviets firmly rejected the
claim that the Chinese revolution was *the* model for "third
world" countries. At a meeting of the USSR Academy of Sciences,
Zhukov now recognized the "immense significance" of the
Chinese revolution, but ruled that it could happen only in China
and that its essential component, armed struggle, was not an
obligatory element for all socialist revolutions. Zhukov observed
that it would be "risky to regard the Chinese revolution as some
kind of 'stereotype' for people's revolutions in other countries of
Asia," and he particularly mentioned India and Indonesia as
countries that would "require consideration of the concrete experience of the Chinese revolution or of the experience of the Soviet
revolution." [18]

Zhukov's downgrading of the Chinese revolution was followed
by A. Sobolev's restoration of the supremacy of the Bolshevik rev-

[16] Kautsky, pp. 88–91.   [17] Sen Gupta, pp. 55 –62, 335–37.
[18] E. M. Zhukov, "On the Character and Attributes of People's Democracy in
Countries of the Orient," *CDSP,* IV (June 28, 1952), 3.

olution as the universal model. In a major thesis in 1951, Sobolev described the people's democratic revolution as a special type of two-stage revolution, a bourgois-democratic revolution succeeded by a socialist revolution. The East European revolutions had passed through both stages. The Chinese revolution, on the other hand, was a manifestation of the Soviet doctrine of "people's democracy"; however, it lagged behind revolutions in East Europe because it had not proceeded beyond the first stage.[19]

The controversy went on until 1952 when the Chinese, evidently in pursuit of a newly contrived "soft" Asian policy and under the strains and pressures caused by the Korean war, muted their claim to lead the colonial liberation movement. In the meantime, the Russians made a terminal concession to the Chinese point of view. Zhukov generously conceded that China had provided an "example" that could "stimulate" and "inspire" other Asian peoples in their struggle for emancipation.[20] By that time the CPI had discarded the neo-Maoist line of the Andhra leaders and taken the crucial decision to function within the Indian parliamentary democratic system.

It is therefore hard to conceive that in 1950 the Cominform asked the CPI to adopt the Chinese or Maoist path. The main purpose of the Cominform article was to indulge the ideological preferences of the Andhra Maoists to some extent, and at the same time bring the CPI back firmly under Moscow's direction. This was confirmed in the interview the British Communist party leader, Rajni Palme Dutt, gave to two CPI leaders at the beginning of 1951. The "Chinese interlude" in Indian Communism, said Dutt, had served a useful purpose.

After the slanderous attack on Comrade Mao Tse-tung, the refusal to recognize the difference between the Russian and the Chinese way and

---

[19] A. Sobolev, "People's Democracy as a Form of Political Organization of Society," *Bol'shevik*, 19 (1951), 25–28.

[20] Donald S. Zagoria, "Strains in the Sino-Soviet Alliance," *Problems of Communism*, May–June, 1960.

the great lesson of the Chinese Revolution for India, it is correct and necessary to break with this past and assert that India must adopt the China way. . . . But having once recognized this, we should guard against drawing a mechanical parallel with China and try to evolve a correct policy for India on the basis of the concrete situation in India, bearing in mind the broad lessons of China. The Indian situation presents some essential differences from China.[21]

"AN INDIAN PATH"

It appears that the task of evolving a "correct policy for India" was taken up by some CPI leaders in 1951. In that year, the CPI resolved to discover an "Indian path to Communism," a path which would be "neither only the Soviet path nor the Chinese path, but a path of Leninism applied to Indian conditions." [22]

A creative contribution to Indian Communism stemmed from the combined efforts of Dange, Ajoy Ghosh, Rajeshwar Rao, and Basavapunniah to apply the Soviet and Chinese experience to India. The four leaders went to Moscow where they had discussions with various Soviet leaders. A "highly secret" document jointly prepared by them was circulated to the central committee members during the third congress of the CPI at Madurai in December 1953.[23] It attempted some concrete and comparative analysis of objective conditions in China and India, and came to the conclusion that it was a "wrong understanding of the experience of the Chinese revolution" to assert that "the Indian revolution would develop exactly the same way as the revolution in China and that partisan war would be the main or almost the only weapon to ensure its victory."

What was needed in India was the building of a "genuine mass peasant movement" and an "alliance between the working class and the peasantry." Conditions in China that had made large-

[21] For the text of R. P. Dutt's interview, see *Indian Communist Party Documents, 1930–56* (Bombay, Democratic Research Service, 1957), pp. 61–70.

[22] Sen Gupta, p. 337.

[23] For the text, see *Indian Communist Party Documents*, pp. 71–85. The report, entitled "Tactical Line," was not circulated to the delegates of the congress.

scale partisan warfare possible did not exist in India. While premature peasant uprisings in isolated areas must be avoided, "in
the course of development of the movement a situation will arise
in several areas which will demand armed struggle in the form of
partisan warfare. . . . The party is of the opinion that partisan
warfare in such a situation, undertaken on the basis of a genuine
mass peasant movement, especially the most oppressed and exploited strata, combined with other forms of struggle, such as social boycott of landlords, mass no-rent struggles, agricultural
workers' strikes, can, if correctly constructed and led, have a rous-
ing and galvanizing effect on the peasant masses in all areas and
raise their own struggles to a higher level." In the initial stages,
partisan struggle could only be "defensive"—"the objective of
partisan struggle is above all to defend the peasants from the attack of the government and its punitive organs." The document
firmly rejected individual terrorism; the "objective of partisan
struggle is not to destroy particular individuals, but to destroy the
hated regime in a prolonged struggle of the popular masses."

This document was only mildly reflected in the political resolution adopted by the Madurai congress.[24] The resolution raised
the strategic slogan of a "Government of Democratic Unity,"
which "demands organization and unleasing of mass struggles on
the widest scale" to defeat the economic and political policies of
the ruling classes. It spoke of democratic unity from below, to be
forged on the anvil of struggle, and it warned against "top negotiations and maneuvers and weakening of the mass movement." It
called for the building up of an extensive peasant movement and
categorized agricultural workers and poor peasants as "the foundation for the broader unity" of this movement. While these mili-

---

[24] Editors of the *Indian Communist Party Documents* say "The Statement
adopted by the Madurai Congress was entirely on the lines of this document received from Moscow." This, however, is not borne out by a comparison of the two
documents. The fact is that the policy statement contained very little of the major
formulations of the four CPI leaders. For the text of the Madurai congress political
resolutions, see pp. 93–124.

tant formulations fell far short of the tactical content of the "Indian path" document, the most significant point of the political resolution was its admission that Nehru's foreign policy in recent years was "helpful to peace" and appreciated by "all peace-loving people." As we have seen in chapter 1, once the "peace-loving" peoples—meaning socialist countries—had begun to appreciate the foreign policy of the Indian government, it was only a matter of time for the CPI also to rally to its support.

CCP–CPI CLASH AND CONFLICT

During the 1950s, Chinese efforts to influence the national liberation movement and to offer the Chinese path as the only model for revolution in the "third world" countries were made within the approved formalities of fraternal relations between the various Communist parties. For the CPI, there was no particular compulsion to pay any special attention to the lessons of the Chinese revolution. Having adopted the strategic line of the CPSU twentieth congress, and the tactical line of peaceful transition and the parliamentary path, the CPI progressively shifted away from the strategy and tactics of the Chinese revolution. After the 1957 Moscow conference, where Mao himself opposed the major planks of the 20th congress line on the national liberation movement and peaceful coexistence, the CCP position appeared to the majority of the CPI leadership to be antithetical to their own strategic and tactical preferences. The "Indian path" was now very different from the Chinese; it had the blessing of Moscow, and by and large also the approval of progressive sections of the Indian bourgeoisie.

The next period of Indian Communism's interaction with China and Chinese Communism was 1959–64, which we have examined in chapter 1. We saw how the dominant faction in the CPI progressively identified itself with the Indian nationalist ethos and came to look upon Communist China as an aggressive, expansionist power guilty of serious and unpardonable deviance from Marxism-Leninism. We noted that the majority faction in the CPI supported the CPSU position in the Sino-Soviet ideological conflict not so much on the merits of the disputes—these were hardly debated beyond a small coterie of top-level Communists— as because the Chinese formulations appeared to undermine the strategy and tactics which had, since 1952, gained the CPI legitimacy within the Indian political system. Also, in the conflict between the Chinese and Indian nation-states, the CPI, which had developed a vested interest in the prevailing political system thanks to its parliamentary preoccupations of nearly a decade, sided with Indian nationalism rather than with Chinese Communism.

True, the CPSU was anxious to keep the CPI under its wing, and in 1963 was even prepared to see a split in the party lest the revolt of the left-wing lead to a mass exodus of state-level cadres.[25] However, the majority faction's uncritical, complete alignment with the CPSU was largely self-willed. Like the CPSU and the Indian bourgeoisie, the majority faction in the CPI saw more China than Communism in the CCP; this China was perceived to be an arrogant and powerful threat to an India allegedly treading the non-capitalist path, to the beating of which the CPI believed it had made a significant contribution.[26]

---

[25] Mohan Ram says the majority faction in the CPI had explicit encouragement from the CPSU to have a showdown with the dissidents (pp. 185–88). CPSU accused the dissidents of attempts to split the CPI even in 1959. *Partinya Zhizh,* Moscow, No 11, Part I. At the Vijayawada congress, Sulsov was surprised at the minority group's strength, and he reportedly remarked to a CPI leader, "There is a lot of Chinese influence in your party." Ram, p. 209. The author of this book writes: "The CPSU leadership raised the bogey of a split in the CPI long before the dominant right group of the CPI came across any evidence of it. It was in the Soviet interest to avert a split at the Vijayawada Congress in 1961, and Suslov worked for a compromise. But, in 1964, the CPSU seems to have felt that if a split was not forced immediately, there was every chance of the whole party going over to the left group at the next party congress" (p. 208).

[26] A noted Indian intellectual believes that the friendship between India and the Soviet Union rests partly on the fact that Russia is the "least occidental" of the Western countries and India the "least oriental" of the Eastern societies. Sisir Gupta in *Seminar,* January 1965.

THE CPI(M) AND THE CCP: 1964–67

After the split of the CPI in 1964, the parent party as well as the Indian government (supported by Moscow for a while and the Indian press for a long time) joined together to dub the CPI(M) "pro-China." [27] The new Communist party, however, was at best a limited ally of the CCP in its conflict with the CPSU, never a partisan. Even this partial alliance was one-sided and short-lived. The Chinese press welcomed the formation of the CPI(M) but refrained from reporting its strategic and tactical formulations. In fact, no ideological unity bound the CPI(M) leaders together; the party was formed on the basis of an agreed program, not an agreed ideology.

Namboodiripad made this clear in August 1965 when he pointed out that the party had taken no stand on the ideological issues that divided the international Communist movement; whatever views were expressed by individual leaders and members were their own. At that time the CPI(M) was caught in a crisis of revolutionary conscience. India was fighting Pakistani infiltrators in Kashmir. This shadow war led in September to the India-Pakistan war, in which the Chinese firmly stood by Pakistan, condemned India as the aggressor, supported the Kashmiri people's right to national self-determination, and served India with an "ultimatum" threatening to intervene along the Sikkim-

[27] In a broadcast from Delhi on January 1, 1965, Union Home Minister Nanda said, "There is reason to believe that the new party (CPI [M]) was formed under Peking's inspiration. It was to serve as Peking's instrument to create conditions of instability in the country and to facilitate the promotion of Chinese designs against India in furtherance of her grand strategy of establishing hegemony over Asia and her declared aim of world revolution. There is reason to believe that the Left Communist Party has close links with the Chinese from whom it draws ideological inspiration and receives support in other forms." Nanda's attempt to denounce the CPI(M) is of some interest in the context of this study, for he tried to make Indians suspect the party's legitimacy and independence of external control. See V. B. Sinha, pp. 186–89.

Tibet-Indian border. During the India-Pakistan war, the CPI(M) politbureau condemned Chinese intervention along the Sikkim border and the "ultimatum"; it rejected the Chinese interpretation of the Kashmir problem. It did not concede that the Nagas and Mizos were fighting for their "national liberation," nor that Pakistan was a progressive anti-imperialist country.

The only difference between the two Communist factions was that while the CPI echoed all of Moscow's charges against Peking and shared "nationalist" anti-China sentiments, the CPI(M) tempered its criticism of China and was anxious not to contribute to "nationalist" hostility toward the Chinese. Thus, the CPI had denounced, while the CPI(M) had not, the first Chinese nuclear explosion in October 1964, but the Marxists had not sent greetings to the CCP as did the pro-China Communist groups in Nepal and Ceylon.

For more than two years, the CPI(M) postponed taking sides on the major ideological issues between Moscow and Peking. This remarkable passivity on the part of its leaders allowed various ideological "pools" to be formed within the party.[28] In 1965 several leaders then in prison reacted sharply to some of the ideological formulations by individuals or groups within the party and asked the leaders still at large to deliberate on the major ideological issues and come out with an authorized party position. The politibureau prepared a draft that met with strong opposition from some of the leaders. The matter was dropped at that stage. It was, however, decided that while party journals could publish formulations of the fraternal parties on various issues, including the Indian situation, party members were strictly to follow the CPI(M)'s own line and reject all views that deviated from its official program.

At the beginning of 1966, Peking made a fresh appraisal of the Indian situation, and perceived a revolutionary political crisis

[28] *Why the Ultra-'left' Deviation?* (Calcutta, CPI [M], 1968), p. 44.

rapidly arising from a deepening economic crisis. In February, Radio Peking began to speak of a "determined revolt" of the Indian masses against the policies of the Congress government. In March, it reported "frequent peasant struggles in the country-side" against the landlords and the government.[29] Soon after the official launching of the great proletarian cultural revolution in August 1966, Peking saw Indian political forces as going through a revolutionary upheaval and realignment.

Excellent is the Indian people's struggle since the beginning of this year. This struggle is spreading to the whole country on an unprecedented scale, in which more than ten million people have taken part. It is evident that the struggle is extending in scope from the field of economics to the field of politics. The surging waves of the Indian people's struggle show that the various political forces of India are undergoing a great political upheaval, a great division and a great reorganization.[30]

Peking media now began to unfold to India the Maoist strategy of the broadest possible united front against the "reactionary authorities"—landlords, capitalists, and their imperialist masters. Peking presumably expected that the true Indian Communists of the CPI(M) would accept this strategy and provide the subjective requirements of revolution. The Marxists, however, adopted an election strategy that was a compromise between the parliamentary and nonparliamentary elements in the leadership. The CPI(M) refused to form a single united front of all leftist parties, including the CPI, except on the basis of recognition of its dominant position in the partnership, and said that it would use the parliamentary system for the purpose of revolution. It was this reversal of strategy and return to the revisionist parliamentary line that apparently led the CCP to believe that the CPI(M) leadership was not revolutionary. In April 1967, Peking Radio de-

[29] Bhabani Sen Gupta, "Moscow, Peking, and the Indian Political Scene," *Orbis*, Summer 1968, p. 546. See also Sen Gupta, "A Maoist Line for India," *China Quarterly*, January–March, 1968.

[30] Sen Gupta, "Moscow, Peking, and the Indian Political Scene."

clared: "There is no Communist party of India. There are only certain individual Communists." [31]

These "individual Communists" functioned from within the CPI(M); they were strong in West Bengal and Andhra alone, but they existed in almost all the state committees. They had opposed the party's adherence to the parliamentary line. They were afraid that once the leadership found itself in power in Bengal and Kerala, it would tend to settle for static, revisionist parliamentary politics. Some of these "individual Communists" in Bengal glorified the spontaneous tribal-peasant uprising in the Naxalbari area to a revolutionary event, and they were taken by surprise, as were the leaders of the CPI(M), by Chinese support for their position. The Chinese saw great revolutionary significance in the Naxalbari rebellion, and in hailing it as the first spark of an on-coming Maoist revolution in India, they put forward, for the first time, a well-constructed strategic-tactical line for Indian revolutionaries within and outside the Communist movement.

MAOIST STRATEGY AND TACTICS FOR INDIA [32]

Mao's line for India covered all three of the major issues in Marxist-Leninist evaluation of an objective situation: the class character of the Indian state and government and the role and character of different sections of the bourgeoisie; an analysis of the objective political-economic situation, the nature of contradictions, and the tactics relevant to these contradictions; and the strategy and tactics of the Marxist-Leninist-Maoist party of the proletariat. The Chinese considered the Indian bourgeoisie to be a parasitic class fostered by the British; they represented the comprador or bureaucratic capitalist in India. The Congress government was the chief instrument and mouthpiece of this comprador

---

[31] Quoted in *Link*, April 23, 1967.

[32] This analysis of Maoist strategy for India is based on Sen Gupta, "Moscow, Peking, and the Indian Political Scene" and "A Maoist Line for India." See also Ram, *Maoism in India* (New Delhi, Vikas, 1971), ch. 1.

or bureaucratic, monopolistic, capitalistic class. For a time after independence, Nehru had acted on behalf on the progressive sections of the bourgeoisie. However, in the latter years of his life, he had completely gone over to the imperialist camp as a result of the sharpening of internal class contradictions as Chiang Kai-shek had done in China in 1927. To the Chinese, the Congress government in 1967 represented the antinational upper bourgeoisie and landholders; its foreign policy served the interests of imperialism as its domestic policies served those of comprador monopoly capital.

The fourth general election, in Chinese eyes, further sharpened Indian class contradictions. It brought about, at the head, a government "more reactionary than ever" and "still more subservient to U.S. imperialism and Soviet revisionism." In several states, however, the "one-party monopoly of local political power" was broken, and the Congress party became "ineffective in the face of people's resistance." The elections had left India "littered with dry faggots," but there were also dangerous possibilities of the rising Indian revolution being betrayed and brutally suppressed. To the Chinese, the greatest danger came from the revisionists in the Indian Communist movement, not merely those in the "Dange clique." Dangerous, too, was Indian thinking (to which even the CPI(M) leadership had been contributing) that the formation of non-Congress governments in a number of states was, in itself, a step forward to the revolution. On the contrary, said the Chinese, the two leftist-oriented governments in Kerala and Bengal were being used by the reactionary central government to contain the oncoming revolution.

So in June 1967 Peking called on the Indian people to wage "relentless armed struggle" in order to "overthrow" the government and "forcibly seize power." Encouraged by the outbreak of the Naxalbari peasant revolt, the Chinese laid down the Maoist tactical line for India in clear, unmistakable terms.

Naxalbari should be the "prelude to the violent revolution by hundreds of millions of people throughout India"; but to make it possible, the Indian revolution must "take the road of relying on the peasants, establishing base areas in the countryside, persisting in protracted armed struggle and using the countryside to encircle and finally capture the cities." Indian Communists must give up their city-orientation, and make the peasants "the invincible force of the Indian revolution." The proletariat must therefore integrate with the peasants. Since the reactionary forces were "temporarily stronger" than the revolutionary forces, Communists must use "the whole set of flexible strategy and tactics of people's war," and "persevere in protracted armed struggle." The armed struggle must begin in the countryside "where the reactionary rule is weak, and where "the revolutionaries can maneuver freely."

It will not matter if the beginning is small, and if the peasants have to fight with bows and arrows, advised Peking. So long as the Indian proletarian revolution adheres to the revolutionary line of Marxism-Leninism-Mao Tse-tung Thought, and relies on its great ally, the peasants, it is entirely possible for the revolutionaries to advance from one rural base to another in the huge backward rural areas and build a people's army of a new type." There will of course, be "twists and turns" and "difficulties"; but it will be possible eventually to develop "from isolated areas into a vast expanse."

The Chinese recommended the strategic concept of a "new democratic" revolution in India. Its basic task is an agrarian revolution, and "this revolution will inevitably be a peasant armed revolution." Obstacles to the revolution come not merely from its class enemies, but also from the Communists, many of whom are mistakenly under the spell of parliamentarianism. The Chinese therefore called for a sustained systematic campaign against revisionism. They saw little difference between Dange and Namboodiripad; both belong to the same class of revisionists who preached that India is an "exception" to the scientific laws of class

struggle and who insist that India should follow the line of peaceful transition through the parliamentary way. The revisionists of
the CPI(M) had "babbled much about the parliamentary road"
and "peaceful transition" but, in fact, they "stand firm against
peasant armed struggle," and, worse, "they hanker after office . . .
and seek to have themselves elected."

PEKING'S INTERPRETATION OF EVENTS

Peking asked the revolutionaries in the Communist movement
and the revolutionary people of India to draw a clear-cut line of
demarcation between themselves and the revisionists "politically,
ideologically and organizationally." We have seen how this advice
was taken literally by the rebel group of "Naxalites" in West Bengal to launch the CPI(ML) in 1969 as the CCP-blessed true Communist party in India. Chinese media welcomed the formation of
the new party and listed it as part of the Peking brand of the international Communist movement. Major formulations of the
party, notably of its leaders, Charu Mazumdar and Kanu Sanyal,
as well as reports of armed peasant struggles conducted under its
leadership in several parts of India, particularly the Girijans of
Srikakulam, were reported for more than two years.

Peking could not have been unaware of the existence of several
Maoist groups in India, which had serious differences with the
Bengal Maoists over the launching of a separate Communist
party. None of these groups, not even that led by Nagi Reddy in
Andhra, were discussed in Chinese media. However, the Chinese
frequently used the phrase "Communist revolutionaries" presumably to deny the CPI(ML) the exclusive credit of introducing
Maoism in Indian Communism. None of the important formulations of Nagi Reddy found their way to the Chinese press. Differences within the CPI(ML) also went unreported, nor did Peking
take public notice of the desertions from the Maoist party following the adoption of Mazumdar's tactic of annihilation of the
class enemy.

In reproducing the CPI(ML) formulations and reporting the events taking place in Srikakulam and elsewhere, the Chinese persistently tried to keep before the revolutionaries the essential features of Maoism, without which it would be impossible to mobilize the peasantry. It was repeatedly stressed, for example, that there could be no guerrilla war without the active support of the rural masses; that the revolutionary Communist party must firmly rely on the poor peasants and the mass of rural proletariat; that the party's task was to carry out an agrarian revolution for which it must have a revolutionary agrarian program and toward which its cadres must integrate themselves with the peasants, sharing their thoughts and living as they lived; that there were clearly definable stages in a rapidly escalating peasant armed struggle—it had to progress from self-defense in rural bases to attacks on feudal forces after the peasantry had set up its own armed organizations; that the guerrillas could frustrate the encirclement and mopping up operations of the enemy only when they were closely united with the peasant masses; and that peasant armed struggle in the countryside must be supplemented by struggles of the broad masses of people.[33]

Some of these essentials of Maoism were noticeable in Srikakulam and a few other much smaller areas for a while in 1969. But the "revolutionist" impatience of Charu Mazumdar, his refusal to organize broad mass struggles, his insistence that the CPI(ML) must function as a secret party and that the guerrillas operate in small, self-sufficient squads, his neglect of building up broad peasant support, the absence of any agrarian program of the party,

[33] In summarizing the political resolution of the CPI(ML), Chinese media selected mainly those portions which reflected Maoist strategy and tactics. See *Peking Review*, July 11, 1969. In reporting armed peasant struggles, Maoist tactics and the Maoist essentials of such struggle were carefully put forward. See reports in *Peking Review*, August 6, September 19, and October 31, 1969, and January 2, January 30, and February 13, 1970. See also, Shao Yung-hung, "Rising Revolutionary Storm of the Indian Peasants," *Peking Review*, September 9, 1969. Shao's article was clearly designed to tell the Indian Communist revolutionaries how to organize peasant armed struggles on Maoist lines.

and, finally, Mazumdar's drift toward urban terrorism led to the failure of the armed peasant struggles in all of the CPI(ML) "bases." The Chinese suspended publicizing the CPI(ML) formulations and exploits in the fall of 1970.

THE CPI(M) REJECTS THE CHINESE PATH

The persistence of Chinese intervention dogged both the CPI(M) and the CPI. Its presence was emphasised by the Indian government and other non-Communist political parties and forces, who predictably utilized Chinese intervention to arouse nationalist sentiments against the CPI(M). However, behind this political game, there was an uneasy awareness that Communist mobilization of rural proletarian militancy would pose a formidable challenge to the Indian political system.

The CPI borrowed, and then made its own, the Soviet stance on the CCP and Mao Tse-tung. It had no theoretical problem in meeting the Chinese challenge. Maoism, for the CPI, was no Marxism-Leninism but a *narodnik* deviance fortified by petty-bourgeois chauvinism. The CPI adopted the entire spectrum of Soviet assessment of the CCP and its Maoist leadership. The CPI's assessment of the Indian and world objective situation and of the major contradictions within India and in the international community ran parallel to that of the CPSU.

For the CPI(M) the problem was very different and difficult. Among its cadres was a substantial number that would prefer to abandon the parliamentary line and use militant mobilization of the masses. The party had been born of a protest against, and rejection of, revisionism, Soviet as well as Indian. It could not afford to have its radical image tarnished. It had rejected the anti-CCP "bourgeois-nationalist" stance of the CPI. The Marxists owed it to their genesis to have at least an open mind toward the CCP.[34]

[34] For ideological perspectives of some of the prominent CPI(M) leaders in 1964, see *A Contribution to Ideological Issues* (New Delhi, 1964). This publication was

We have noted that the CPI(M) postponed for some two years making any decisions on the main ideological issues that divided Moscow and Peking, and that when it did finally take a position on these issues, it accepted most of the Chinese charges against Soviet revisionism without accepting any of the Chinese alternatives. The CPI(M), then, decided to be antirevisionist without being a Maoist party. On two crucial claims of the CCP, however, the Marxists adopted a negative stand. They were not prepared to recognize that the Soviet Union had become a country of capitalist restoration or that it had forged a collusive relationship with U.S. imperialism against China. Nor were they prepared to accept the Chinese formulation that contradictions between revisionism and Marxist-Leninism, that is between the USSR and China, had become antagonistic, ruling out unity of action against imperialism. The effect of rejecting these two post-1965 major aspects of Maoism was that the CPI(M) was able to wrest recognition from the CPSU that it was "the rival Indian Communist party." The Chinese, however, were less indulgent. The CPI(M)'s acceptance of most of the CCP position on the international Communist movement and on the revisionist character of the CPSU leadership was not enough for it to be recognized by the Chinese as a true Communist party.

The Marxist leadership came out with its formulation on ideological issues *after* the Chinese had condemned it as revisionist and had acclaimed the Naxalbari peasant revolt as the herald of the Indian revolution. Naturally, the leadership defended its own strategic-tactical line and rejected the Maoist alternative put forward by Peking. The CPI(M), in fact, rejected the entire CCP assessment of the objective Indian situation as "highly exaggerated and extremely subjective," and running counter to the Marxists' own understanding of Indian realities. India, according to the CPI(M), was going through a "deepening economic crisis and the

---

not issued on behalf of the party evidently because the party at that time had no official ideological line.

initial stages of a political crisis," whereas the CCP perceived it already plunged into a political crisis of revolutionary magnitude.[35]

To the CPI(M), the Indian government was a bourgeois-landlord government led by the upper bourgeoisie which was compromising and collaborating with foreign monopoly capital, and not a "puppet government led by comprador bureaucratic capitalism, run principally in the interests of imperialism." On the contrary, the Indian government, according to the CPI(M), had "a wider social base when compared to most of its counterparts in several countries," and it does not face the imminent danger of class revolution at home. It had therefore no need to play the role of a puppet, a stooge, or lackey of imperialism.

Our own experience teaches that the Congress party still holds considerable political influence among the people, that several bourgeois-landlord reactionary parties still command a certain mass following, that the character of many petty-bourgeois parties and groups still is not exposed to any appreciable extent, and that the proletariat and its revolutionary party are far from properly organized and built. In the face of such reality it would be a grave error to exaggerate this aspect of sharpening class contradictions to the point of suggesting that class revolution on the part of the masses has already become (so) immediate and acute and menacing to the bourgeoisie as to make its capitulation to imperialism final and irrevocable.[36]

The CPI(M) believed that contemporary Indian capitalism and the Indian bourgeoisie were very different from their counterparts in China before liberation. The place and role of the comprador bourgeoisie and its bureaucratic capital in preliberation China was also different from the role and place of the upper bourgeoisie in contemporary India. Bureaucratic capital was a

---

[35] Political resolution adopted at the Madurai session of the CPI(M) central committee. *People's Democracy: Supplement:* September 10, 1967. Earlier, in July, the politbureau issued a statement declaring that the "entire assessment" of "Peking Radio" of the Naxalbari struggle was "at complete variance with that made by our party." *The Statesman,* July 2, 1967.

[36] *People's Democracy: Supplement,* September 10, 1967.

special feature of the Chiang Kai-shek regime. Though bureaucratic capitalist tendencies were present in India, these were by no means the principal characteristic of the situation. However, the CPI(M) did not consider the Indian bourgeoisie, because of its "natural" counterrevolutionary character, to be deserving of a place in the people's democratic front despite its occasional contradictions with foreign monopolies.[37]

The CPI(M) took a much more inflexible stance on the Chinese ideological position after the ninth congress of the CCP. The politbureau rejected some of the principal strategic formulations as "highly incorrect" and as violating the basic principles of Marxism-Leninism.[38] Among these are, first, the "completely novel and absurd class division" of the imperialist and social-imperialist countries, "reducing the contradictions between the Soviet Union and the imperialist countries to one of inner-imperialist contradictions." Second, the CPI(M) rejected the Chinese term "revisionist countries" as applied to those socialist states whose leaders had taken to various norms of reformism and revisionism. The Chinese concept implied that all countries of the socialist camp, with the sole exception of China and Albania, had become "revisionist states and countries," and had ceased to be socialist; this to the CPI(M) was an attempt to define these states not on the "essential criterion" of productive relations, but on the basis of "ideological errors and deviations of the leadership." Third, the CCP at the ninth congress had so formulated and presented the contradictions as to "arbitrarily elevate" all the ideological-political differences in the world Communist movement to the "level of social contradictions." Revisionism and rightist opportunism was no doubt a bourgeois trend of thought and as such alien to Marxism-Leninism, but "it is highly incorrect to equate it with, and transform it into, one of the antagonistic and funda-

---

[37] *Ibid.*
[38] *Politbureau Statement on the Ninth National Congress of the CPC* (Calcutta, CPI [M], May 1969).

mental world social contradictions." The CPI(M), then, refused to recognize Maoism as the only manifestation of correct and pure Marxism-Leninism, and rejected the Chinese claim that the USSR and the East European countries had ceased to be socialist.

Even less acceptable to the CPI(M) was the claim that Mao Tse-tung Thought was the Marxism-Leninism "of the era in which imperialism is heading for total collapse and socialism is advancing to worldwide victory." The politbureau statement said, "It is elementary that no individual, or for that matter, no Communist Party and its leading committee can be considered as infallible." Marxism-Leninism had come to be used "to convey the complete meaning" of the "science" of socialist transformation of capitalism, and although Mao had made a great contribution in guiding the "new democratic" revolution to victory in China, the politbureau "neither sees the justification to add the word 'Mao Tse-tung Thought' to Marxism-Leninism . . . nor does it deem to be correct that all that is being thought by Mao Tse-tung shall necessarily be infallible Marxism-Leninism." The CPI(M) also took serious objection to the nomination of Lin Piao as the successor to Mao; this was building a Communist party "on faith," and not on the sound foundation of democratic centralism. It was "really strange and monstrous" to replace the principle of democratic centralism by the "principle of succession."

The CPI(M) thus came close to the Italian Communist party in exercising its right to publicly criticize the CPSU as well as the CCP. In so doing, it projected itself as one of the few really independent Communist parties in the non-Communist world. Unlike the Italian party, however, the CPI(M) was kept officially outside both factions of the world Communist movement, and of either of the two premier Communist parties.

Neither the CPI nor the CPI(M) visualized the Indian revolution traveling the Chinese path. The CPI, because of its close ties with the CPSU, took a much dimmer view than the CPI(M) of the relevance of the Chinese revolutionary model for India. The CPI was categoric in its conviction that

There is not a ghost of a chance for that type of a long drawn-out armed guerrilla warfare which went on in China for 22 years to succeed in India. Here and there some type of armed resistance might go on for some time. But it cannot take you to final victory as in China. In India any revolution can succeed only under the direct leadership of the proletariat with cities as the leading center of revolution.[39]

This conclusion came from the once-Maoist Rajeshwar Rao. In 1969 Rao took a very different view of the role of the peasantry in the Indian revolution. Considerable capitalist development had taken place in India, argued Rao, to make it very unlike the China of the 1930s and 1940s. A "big, modern proletariat" had arisen, making the Chinese model of armed guerrilla warfare in the countryside out of date.

Experience of the last decade and a half in our country shows that it is always the working class, apart from its strike actions, which is at the head of the mass movements like *bandhs* (moratoriums), *hartals* (closures), etc., that have taken place against the Congress regime. The peasantry is yet unable to come forward in a big way into the general mass movement.[40]

The CPI(M) saw for the rural proletariat a much bigger role in the revolution than did the CPI; its experience of peasant mobilization in West Bengal since 1969 enabled it to take a more hopeful view of the part the peasantry could play in the general mass movement. However, the Marxist party's thinking on the role of the peasantry appeared in 1971 to be still in the process of development. At the theoretical level, the Marxists had already given the rural proletariat an equal position with the urban working

[39] Rajeshwar Rao, "Naxalite Movement: Origin and Harmful Consequences," *New Age*, June 29, 1969.
[40] Rajeshwar Rao, "Militant Mass Movement Only Answer to Naxalbari," *New Age*, January 5, 1969.

class as a motor force of revolution: the two were equal allies, rather than leader and follower. Tactically, a certain priority had been given since 1969 to mobilization of the rural poor and to the building of party bases in the countryside. However, the CPI(M) was not prepared to place the peasantry in the vanguard; in other words, it was not ready to advocate "peasant Communism" in India. Nor did the Marxists believe that India was *yet* ready for protracted peasant guerrilla warfare. Without formally rejecting the relevance of the Chinese model for India, the Marxists appeared in 1971 to be willing to adopt certain aspects of the Chinese revolution to Indian conditions.

Creative thinking in this regard came primarily from Harekrishna Konar, who appears to be emerging as the principal CPI(M) tactician on the agrarian question. What distinguishes Konar from the Maoists of the early 1950s is that his tactical thinking stems not from preconceived ideological preferences, but from the actual experience of peasant mobilization in the changing Indian environment. In two articles in *People's Democracy* in 1968, Konar rejected the Maoist slogan of "armed revolution here and now," and perceived considerable revolutionary possibility in mass struggles within the confines of parliamentarianism. His arguments run as follows:

Even the limited rights of parliamentary democracy, a form of bourgeois class rule, threatens the control held by the bourgeoisie-landlord ruling classes. This is indicative of the crisis brewing in the political system. The working class and the poor are intensifying their class struggles by utilizing the very limited rights of parliamentary democracy. In this situation, the struggle for the defense of democracy is infused with revolutionary significance. It is a struggle which, by uniting the widest scope of people to face the attack from reaction, can defend their democratic rights and take their struggle forward. This struggle will not bring about revolution, said Konar; indeed, revolution is not even the immediate objective. This struggle, though remaining within the confines of the present social system, can, however, help the development of revolutionary forces necessary for affecting radical changes in the social system. This is well understood by the ruling classes; they know that success in this struggle will enhance the strength of the revolutionary forces and their vanguard, the CPI(M). As the ruling classes continue to suppress this struggle with the help of the police and the army, the power of resistance of the people will be greater, and the struggle will reach a higher form.

Revolution is not made by a few leaders, said Konar, but by the people when they are compelled by the ruling classes to make revolution. The Indian revolution must proceed step by step, through its own experience, learning from the accumulated experience of the Soviet, Chinese, Vietnamese, and other revolutions, and also from the failures of other revolutionary attempts, especially those in Indonesia. The objective conditions in Bengal and in India are far from ripe for armed peasant struggle. What went wrong at Naxalbari was that a healthy peasant struggle for land was declared to be "an armed struggle for the capture of political power" and, moreover, this struggle, instead of being concentrated against the big *jotedar,* was directed against all owners, large and small. The "Naxalite" concept was not of militant mass struggle; it was a hotchpotch of extremely irresponsible adventurism and sectarianism.

It is necessary to clearly understand the Marxist theory of revolutionary violence and armed struggle, Konar thought. The main question for the Indian revolution is whether the bourgeoisie and the landlords will allow any basic social change peacefully. If they do not, and attack the toiling classes with all the repressive machinery at their command, only two ways are open to the working people: surrender, or armed struggle against armed attack. Marxists must be able to make an objective, dispassionate appraisal of the configuration of social forces in a given society. Indian Marxists must clearly understand what the present objective situation

in India is and how it is likely to change. Class struggle is growing. But it has not reached the revolutionary stage. The economic
crisis is deepening; the initial stage of a political crisis has begun.
But it has a long way to go to mature to the revolutionary stage.

What is the condition of revolutionary forces in Bengal and in
India? Konar asked. In a majority of places in India, Communist
presence is weak. Even in Bengal, the majority of the working
class are either under bourgeois influence or under the influence
of economism. The adventurists might argue that the working class
is not needed in a revolution; the poor peasantry alone can be in
the vanguard. This is nothing but a prostitution of the lessons of
the Chinese and Vietnamese revolutions. However, the political
consciousness and organization of the poor peasants in India is
very weak. Efforts have just begun to overcome these weaknesses.
The bourgeois and petty-bourgeois parties still wield great influence in the countryside. Marxists must also consider the state of
consciousness of the people who support the Communist party. It
would be a serious mistake to think that they are prepared for
revolutionary action simply because they support the party.[41]

Konar, then, rejected the slogan of "armed struggle here and
now" because objective conditions in India did not permit such a
struggle to succeed. Armed struggle might, however, be necessary,
he pointed out, if the bourgeoisie refused to allow for peaceful
transformation of society. Armed struggle is, then, the Communists' response to the ruling class's behavior. In India, Konar implied, the ruling class behavior has not yet reached that stage
when armed resistance is obligatory. This is the time for the revolutionary forces to gather strength.

Konar explicitly made a difference between the "Naxalite"
leadership and the "heroic spirit" of the Naxalbari peasants. This
implied that the CPI(M) welcomed peasant militancy, and was

[41] Harekrishna Konar, "What Does It Really Mean?" *People's Democracy*, March
31 and April 7, 1968. In summarizing, Konar's language has been kept as far as possible.

ready to identify itself with it, but this militancy must be kept under the party's control. Once militant peasant movements are established in large contiguous areas embracing hundreds of thousands of poor peasants and agricultural workers, it will be easier to offer armed resistance to the armed attacks of the ruling class.

Konar himself slightly changed the accent of his articulations a year and a half later, when the peasant movement in Bengal had arrived at a certain consolidated strength. Presiding over the twentieth session of the All-India Kisan Sabha at Burdwan in October 1969, Konar declared: "Now the task is to carry forward the struggle. The peasants will have to be made more *politically* conscious. Their organization has to be strengthened. Their volunteers and other organizations will have to be prepared for any eventuality." [42]

WHY DID THE CCP INTERVENE?

We can only speculate on the motivation of the CCP's determined effort in 1967 to build a Maoist revolutionary movement in India. The CCP seldom agreed with the CPSU's assessment of the Indian situation since 1949. As I have tried to show elsewhere, India has been a major bone of contention between the world's two most powerful Communist parties since the late 1940s.[43] In 1949, Liu Shao-chi pointed out where the CPSU had gone wrong in India. The two main points he made were that there had to be a differentiation between the reactionary and progressive sections of the Indian bougeoisie, and that India was not suitable for a Chinese-type armed peasant struggle.[44] Liu made the second point probably not only because objective conditions in India were different, but also because the subjective conditions were entirely lacking.

[42] *People's Democracy*, January 18, 1970.
[43] Bhabani Sen Gupta, *The Fulcrum of Asia.*   [44] Kautsky, ch. 2.

It was only during the very brief period of 1953–55, when the CPSU too made a differentiation between the two main sections of the Indian bourgeoisie, that it did not clash with the CCP over its Indian strategy. However, the CCP did not accept the twentieth congress strategic and tactical formulations, and as soon as these began to be applied to India, friction intensified between Moscow and Peking. The drift and scale of Soviet tactics in India since the late 1950s successfully pitted not only the Indian bourgeoisie but also the majority of Indian Communists against China and the CCP. It would therefore be entirely natural for Peking to strike at the Indian "base" of the CPSU's worldwide revisionist operations.

The CCP rejected unity-in-action with the CPSU in early 1966, and gave Moscow's India policy as one of the major reasons. Having finally parted company with the Soviet leadership, it was not unexpected of the CCP to build, if it could, an international Communist movement parallel to the one that was still, by and large, loyal to the CPSU. Efforts toward that end began around 1965. Since the CCP claimed that the Chinese model was more relevant than the Soviet one for the developing societies in Asia, Africa, and Latin America, it was somewhat obligatory for Peking to demonstrate to the CPSU that it had considerable following in the Communist parties and among the Communist revolutionaries of the "third world." In 1965 the CCP drew much comfort from the Indonesian Communist party's rejection of Soviet revisionism, and the close relationship that had grown between Peking and Jakarta. A majority of Asian Communist parties appeared to be more responsive to the CCP than to the CPSU.

Early in September, the famous Lin Piao thesis on people's war was published. This important document has been interpreted by different scholars in different ways. It should perhaps be seen as a major theoretical attempt to bring home to the national liberation movements in the former colonies, as well as to Communists operating there, the essence of the Chinese revolution in the context of the prevailing international situation.

The Lin Piao thesis is a marriage of national liberation and peasant-oriented proletarian struggles, a marriage of anti-imperialism and Communism of the Maoist brand. It holds up U.S. imperialism as the enemy of all national liberation movements, and tells the leaders of these movements how they can defeat the powerful United States by waging simultaneous attacks on American imperialism on multiple "fronts." These attacks can be successful only if they pursue the Maoist flexible tactics of people's war. However, they must wage people's war largely relying on their own strength, and not on external assistance, guidance and leadership.

In projecting this self-reliance aspect of people's war, the CCP apparently had three main considerations before it: the limited ability of China to befriend individual revolutionary movements; China's reluctance to get overly involved in other people's wars with the United States (including the Vietnam war); and a warning to the Communist and national liberation movements in the "third world" that dependence on the Soviet Union would not merely frustrate their liberation wars, but also make them satellites of the USSR. In short, the Lin Piao thesis was the most organized of Chinese attempts to export the strategic and tactical contents of the Chinese revolution, without promising active Chinese assistance in making revolution in countries formerly of colonial status.

The collapse of the PKI only a few weeks after the publication of the Lin Piao thesis must have come as a tremendous shock to the CCP. The Chinese Communists were not unaware of the fundamental weakness of the PKI, which was its lack of strong rural bases and its failure to mobilize the peasantry around a revolutionary agrarian struggle. How costly this weakness proved became evident in the first days of October when the Indonesian

army and people massacred hundreds of thousands of Communists, and practically liquidated the world's largest Communist
party outside the socialist bloc.

During the cultural revolution in China, Liu Shao-chi and his
cohorts were blamed for the debacle of the PKI; in actual reality,
however, the PKI's weakness stemmed from its long apprenticeship with the Soviet revolution. It is probable that after analyzing
the causes of the PKI's downfall, the CCP came to the conclusion
in 1966 that it must do whatever it could to do more than warn
Communist parties and movements in Asia, Africa, and Latin
America of the dangers inherent in copying the Soviet revolution
as well as in pursuing the twentieth congress strategy and tactics.
It was probably with this objective in view that the decision was
made to encourage the formation of Maoist parties in Asia, Africa, and Latin America. Rivalry with the USSR was, of course,
an additional motivation.

It so happened that this attempt on the part of the CCP to en-
ergetically promote Maoist parties in the "third world," coincided
with the proletarian cultural revolution of which the CCP "establishment" became one of the first victims. The tested, battle-hard-
ened leaders were either under persistent (and often cruel) attack
from the Maoist revolutionaries or were anxious to demonstrate
that their own revolutionary fervor equaled or even surpassed
that of the Red Guard. It is inconceivable that the projection of
the Maoist line to Asian Communist movements was preceded in
1966–67 by careful objective assessment of actual social, economic, and political situations obtaining in individual countries.
Revolutionary fervor apparently got the better of Marxist-Leninist homework. This seems to be borne out by the Chinese assessment of the Indian situation in 1966–67: evidently, the CCP saw
a revolutionary political upheaval in India because it *wished* to
see it. It was the same with the 1966–67 CCP stance of objective
situations in several other countries, notably Burma.

It is not suggested that but for the cultural revolution, the CCP would not have sought in 1967 to encourage the formation of a Maoist party in India. What is suggested is that the general disruption of the CCP leadership might have resulted in a subjective appraisal of the Indian situation and in premature upgrading of the Naxalbari peasant rebellion. The acute economic crisis in India after 1965 that led to the beginning of a political crisis in 1967–68 would probably have induced the CCP to project the Maoist model to India in any case, but the style and dimension of this projection might have been different if the party had been firmly in control of the leadership. This speculation seems to be confirmed by the fact that almost as soon as the CCP was brought under firm control of the leadership elected at the ninth congress, Chinese media suspended publicizing the exploits of the CPI(ML), which, by the middle of 1970, came down to little more than killing and mutilation of individuals in the urban complex of Calcutta. Toward the end of 1970, the CCP might have learned from experience what it had often professed in the past: no revolution can be exported. However, if one of the CCP's objectives was to promote militant peasant movements as the motor force of revolution in India, its adventure in the late 1960s to build a Maoist movement in the neighboring country did not prove to be entirely fruitless.

11

PROBLEMS AND PROMISES
FOR THE 1970s

What are the prospects for Communism in India in the coming decade and what are the problems it faces in its bid for power and its stride toward a revolutionary transformation of Indian society? If Communism succeeds in dramatically expanding its social and political base in India, along which strategic-tactical lines is it likely to act and how will these interact on the other political forces and major institutions of the social system? Will the Indian revolution, if it comes, follow any external "model," or will it have to charter its own independent course? What *kind* of Communism is likely to emerge in India and how will it be different from other Communisms? These are some of the questions I propose to explore in this concluding chapter.

A RETROSPECT

On the face of it, Communism in India, despite its stunted progress, has not done too badly. In fact, Indian Communists would seem to have done better than their counterparts in any other country in Asia outside the socialist states. While in the Philippines, Malayasia, Thailand, and Burma, Communist-led insurgencies have been more or less contained, and in Indonesia the once-powerful PKI has been humbled to almost nothing, in India Communism, though until now more of a regional than a national element, would seem to have emerged as the political force second only to the Congress party.

Rajani Kothari, the political scientist who has, probably more than anyone else, tried to discover the hidden dynamics of Indian democracy, observes: "It is . . . significant that the two Communist parties have been the most successful of all the non-Congress parties." [1] In the 1971 mid-term parliamentary poll, one out of every ten of the electorate voted Communist. The Communists are the strongest political element in two states, Kerala and West Bengal, where they have successfully deprived the Congress party of its traditional hold on the electorate.

Although sections of the bourgeoisie still dub the Communists agents of foreign powers, Indian Communists would seem to have largely resolved the problems of legitimacy and acceptance.[2] In fact, the stronger of the two CPIs, the Marxist party, is the only significant Communist group in Asia which has adopted a stance independent of Moscow and Peking and which has no organizational links with either.

Identification may still be a problem for the Communists as a whole, but strategic exercises of the past four years appear to have clarified the situation. The Marxists have identified themselves with the urban and rural poor, and the CPI with broad sections of the class spectrum that may qualify for the National Demo-

---

[1] Rajani Kothari, *Politics in India* (Delhi, Orient Longman, 1970), p. 215.

[2] "Talking about acceptance and respectability, the silliest charge that continues to be leveled against the Communists is that of 'extra-territorial loyalty.' The grounds for such an allegation are flimsy and full of bad taste. No doubt, by their futile and endless controversies on abstract issues of ideology, the Communists have themselves contributed to such criticism." Kothari, p. 215n.

cratic Front. If one looks at Indian Communists as a single collectivity, despite their many schisms and differences, one sees that they have succeeded in forging strong links with segments of the urban-rural proletariat as well as with the national bourgeoisie.

Again, if the two parties are taken as a single Communist collectivity, their tactical lines would seem to be designed to attack the entrenched system from above as well as from below. While the CPI(M) attack is being launched from its bases in Bengal and Kerala, the CPI has been trying to mingle with the progressive bourgeoisie at the national level. Either tactic influences the other. Depending upon the direction of Indian politics, one may progressively yield to the other or, what is more likely, both may be employed to achieve the common end.

The more or less rigid conformation to a single tactical line, which characterized Indian Communism between 1953 and 1966 has ended. There is now a choice of a variety of tactics ranging from *satyagraha* to parliamentarianism to armed peasant insurgency and the Communists have, in the last four years, engaged in all forms.

By building a strong and well-entrenched political base in West Bengal, the Communists were able to threaten "capture" of one of the most strategic crossings of Indian lifelines. Not only does Calcutta hold a commanding position in the economy of the mineral-rich hinterland extending from Assam to Madhya Pradesh, it has been the historical and traditional communicator of radicalism to Indian politics, and its impact on the idea-milieu of the Indian elite cannot be ignored.[3] If the Congress party is unable to stage a substantial political comeback in Bengal, the Communists, particularly the CPI(M), will succeed in further extending and consolidating their base, and push it into Bihar, Orissa, and Uttar Pradesh.

---

[3] "It [Calcutta] cannot be written off; for the direction Calcutta takes now will be inevitably followed by the rest of India in the coming years." Ajit Bhattacharjea in *Hindustan Times*, November 18, 1970.

The agrarian policy of the CPI(M) in West Bengal has reaped a rich political harvest. A peasant movement has rapidly grown in the countryside. It has quickly acquired a *political* dimension. Unlike the limited, low-level peasant movements organized by the united CPI during the 1950s and early 1960s, the current CPI(M)-led peasant movement in Bengal and in parts of southern Bihar is militant and oriented toward "armed defense" and organized defiance of the state apparatus of force.[4] It is being built over large contiguous areas covering millions of peasant population. Its strategic-tactical guidelines include, albeit in an embryonic form, the concept of a parallel government (Indian "soviets"?) in a certain cluster of circumstances. The CPI(M), then, seems to be moving toward building its own brand of "rural bases." These, however, are very different from the bases built by the Chinese Communists in Hunan, Hopeh, Kiangsi, and Kwangtun provinces of southern China during the period 1927–1934.[5]

The CPI(M) peasant struggles since 1967 have been tactically designed to combine economism with political mobilization of the poor peasantry. While struggles are organized around the peasants' immediate problems such as land and tenancy security and equitable sharing of crops, simultaneous efforts are made to educate and organize the peasants politically. The result is an unprecedented political mobilization of the poorer sections of the peasantry in West Bengal during the last four years.[6] The

[4] The three contiguous districts in Bihar where the CPI(M) has been trying to build a militant peasant movement are Champaran, Purnea, and Muzaffarpur. An interesting point to note is that the CPI has joined some of the peasant struggles for land and against eviction. From these districts a large number of peasants migrate to the Calcutta industrial area for unskilled jobs, and many of them return to their villages after a term of employment. They are actual or potential communicators of CPI(M) politics to the peasants of Bihar. Many of them voted for the Marxist party in the Bengal elections of 1969 and 1971. *Economic and Political Weekly,* February 22, 1969.

[5] In China, the CCP also began with peasant self-defense units in some of the southern provinces.

[6] Calcutta's chief Bengali daily, reported in 1969: "The poor in the village now discuss political issues. Until recently, even the village rich did not show much interest in politics. Political issues did not bother even those in the villages who read newspapers, listened to the radio, and kept direct contacts with the towns and cit-

CPI(M) appears to have come to the conclusion that only by organizing peasant militancy can the Communists build up a militant, revolutionary, trade-union movement. The Marxists have tried, not without success, to coordinate working-class and peasant protest movements in Bengal, where the two have begun to feed one another to some extent.

THE PARTY TODAY:
BASIC PROBLEMS AND CHALLENGES

PARTY EXPANSION: BIHAR AND ANDHRA PRADESH

In Kerala and West Bengal, expansion of the Communist support base has been achieved primarily by a long period of continuous struggle and the opportunity to use governmental power to build a strong party base among the poor peasantry. In the Indian political system, the government has been deliberately given the commanding role in political and social reconstruction. This role has mingled easily with the hierarchical social values.

---

ies. Politics became an issue only in election time. In normal times, the villager was bothered only by his many daily wants, for which he blamed the government.

"The picture has changed in the last year or so. The common man in the Bengal village today talks and thinks politics more than the nonpolitical man in the town. The villager does not talk about Delhi. But villagers often engage in heated discussion about the village "party," the district "party," and the *babus* who come to the village from the town "party." The poorest villager knows which party stands for whom, what the party spokesmen say, and what they do. The village poor make every attempt to attend meetings. Sometimes they walk ten to twelve miles to a meeting. If they cannot go themselves, they hear reports from those who do. The villager is now clearly anxious to comprehend what the party *babus* tell them.

"Whenever an issue concerning the village poor comes up, one or the other political parties is now seen to defend the interests of the 'have-nots.' This has brought about a major psychological change in the countryside. The poor still have many fears of the rich, but they are more fearless than ever before. They have acquired the courage to take the first step forward.

"This is an entirely new phenomenon. It never happened in the villages before. No government party stood for the defense of the right of the poor against the rich. This awakening of the poor has upset not only the village rich, but the rural middle class also. For them, this is a kind of anarchy." *Ananda Bazar Patrika*, December 2, 1969: translated from the Bengali, slightly condensed.

Political power has thus become more important than social and economic power. In fact, political and social power have been linked together through politically organizing the most important social institution—the caste.

The party that has benefited most from this combination is the Congress party because of its "adoption" of the dominant castes in the rural areas. Thus, Congress power in Maharashtra now rests on the loyalty of the dominant Maratha caste, in Bihar on the Kayasthas, and in Andhra Pradesh on the Reddys. In Kerala, as noted, the CPI was able to work through the major caste organizations, and its support base rests on the numerically strong Ezhavas. In recent years, however, the CPI(M) appears to have cut deeply across caste alignments in Kerala, while in West Bengal, which has a looser caste complex, its support base can be said to rest on the economic classes of the urban and rural proletariat and the educated urban middle class. In acquiring this position of vantage, the Communists have used all the political power they could command in these two states.

The crucial problem for Indian Communism today is how to expand its support base beyond Kerala and West Bengal. As long as Communist strength remains confined to these two states, Communism in India is a regional force, in the geographical sense of the term, and its impact on national politics is bound to be limited. The picture, however, will be different if the Communists become strong in one or two more states. In most of India, Communist organization is weak; in some states, such as Madhya Pradesh, it is almost nonexistent. In two states, however, the Communists have a certain measure of following. These are Bihar in northern India and Andhra Pradesh in the south. These two appear to be the Communists' next target.

Bihar is one of the poorest states in India. Its economic structure is one of the weakest and its per capita income the lowest. Agrarian stratification is perhaps most solidified in Bihar, as already indicated. Bihar has been a stronghold of the Congress party, but from an early stage of the nationalist movement, its politics assumed a caste base. One result was factionalism within the Congress party, which became more and more acute with the passage of time. All the dominant caste groups functioned from within the Congress party. As long as the Congress leadership could maintain some kind of a consensus-cohesion among the dominant factions with an equitable distribution of patronage, Bihar enjoyed political stability despite a very slow rate of economic development.

The balance and consensus broke down in 1966 when Bihar was in the throes of a widespread famine. Two of the four caste groups that dominated the Bihar Congress party broke away in December 1966 to form a new party, Kranti Dal (Revolutionary party). Bihar thus earned the distinction of being the first state where the Congress party failed to maintain its consensus-balance role, and split. The split, however, did not restore cohesion either in the Congress faction or in the breakaway groups. The two remaining factions in the Congress party continued to be at loggerheads, while one of the breakaway groups left Kranti Dal to form still another party. Bihar faced the fourth general election in 1967 with a fragmented Congress party and with a famine rendering more than half of its fields barren and broken.[7]

The Communists had made no impressive showing in Bihar up to the 1962 election. They won a mere 12 seats in a house of 318.[8] In 1967, however, Communist seats in the legislative assembly more than doubled. The CPI which, after the split, was able to retain its Bihar apparatus more or less intact, won 24, and the CPI(M), which had to build from nothing, gained 4 seats. The CPI won 5 seats in Darbhanga district; 3 each in Champaran,

[7] Chetkar Jha, "Caste in Bihar Congress Politics," and Ramashray Roy, "Politics of Fragmentation," in Iqbal Narain, ed., State Politics in India (Meerut, 1967), pp. 575–87, 415–30. Also Subhas C. Kashyap, The Politics of Defection: A Study of State Politics in India (Delhi, 1968), ch. 5.

[8] Kashyap, p. 188.

Bhagalpur, and Gaya; 2 each in Santhal Parganas, Monghyr, and Patna; and 1 each in Sarab, Muzzafarpur, Purnea, Shahabad, Dhanbad, and Palamau. The Marxists' 4 seats came from Champaran, Saran, Hazaribagh, and Monghyr. The two Communist groups who opposed each other in thirteen constituencies were, nevertheless, able to increase the Communist electoral strength between 1962 and 1967, seatwise from 4 to 9 percent and votewise from 6 to 8 percent.[9] The Communist support was almost equal in north Bihar and Chotanagpur, with 7 percent of the votes; it was higher in south Bihar with 10 percent. In Chotanagpur, the Communists lost heavily to the Congress party because of the latter's alliance with the political organization of the tribals.

TABLE 11.1. BIHAR: PERCENTAGE OF VOTING (1967) FOR MAJOR PARTIES IN THREE REGIONS

Party	North Bihar	South Bihar	Chotanagpur
Congress	34	32	31
SSP+PSP (Socialist)	30	27	7
Jan Sangh	8.5	10	16
CPI+CPI(M) (Communist)	7	10	7

Source: *Economic and Political Weekly,* August 24, 1968.

The first non-Congress coalition in India after the fourth election took office in Bihar; it was a united front of five groups: the two Socialist parties, the Jan Sangh, the Kranti Dal, and the CPI. The CPI had three ministers in the coalition, two of them of cabinet rank, who were given the important portfolios of revenue, and irrigation and power. The minister of revenue, Indradeep Sinha, was also in charge of famine relief. The CPI ministers apparently failed to use government power to expand the party's po-

[9] Navneeth, "Congress Debacle in Bihar," *Economic and Political Weekly,* August 24, 1968.

litical base in the countryside. What was worse, the CPI was unable to forge a united front of the leftist parties. The CPI's involvement in Bihar's politics of defection (it had four coalitions in sixteen months between March 1967 and June 1968, when the assembly was dissolved and the state placed under President's rule) exposed it to the general sickness of Bihar politics—loose discipline and noncommited legislators.[10]

On the eve of the mid-term election in 1969, Indradeep Sinha saw the coming poll as "characterized by a sharp and bitter struggle between two opposing political trends, emanating from two opposing groups of political forces: On the one side stand the Congress party, the Jan Sangh, and the Janta party of the Raja of Ramgarh, who are conspiring to stage a comeback to power in alliance with certain middle of the road forces like the PSP and the Loktantric Congress. On the other side stand the CPI, the CPI(M), and other Left and progressive forces who want to install a democratic coalition government on the basis of a Left-democratic front." [11] Sinha reported a CPI initiative to form such a front, but apparently it fell through because of lack of support from the two socialist groups. In the poll, the CPI increased its strength by only 1 seat, while the Marxists lost 1 of their 4 seats in the dissolved house, and thus the total Communist strength remained the same. However, the CPI polled 10.30 percent of the total valid vote as against 6.91 percent in 1967. It came second in thirty-two constituencies as against nineteen constituencies two years earlier.

In a post-election review, the CPI state council blamed the party's relatively poor showing on lack of leftist unity: if the five leftist groups could stand together, it said, they could have secured 143 seats instead of 106, and they might even have succeeded in forming a leftist democratic coalition government. The council decided to launch "a powerful mass movement" in urban as well

---

[10] Kashyap, p. 188.
[11] Indradeep Sinha, "Struggle for Left Democratic Front," *New Age*, December 15, 1968.

as rural areas because parliamentary politics alone could not build a strong Communist movement.

The state council claimed that the mid-term poll had revealed that "the influence of the CPI had grown extremely among the agricultural laborers and poor peasants as a result of the agrarian policy pursued by the Party" during the period of the united front government. However, this policy had "intensified" the hostility of the well-to-do peasants, and even the middle-level peasants were "confused" by the hostile propaganda. "The rural poor, who were powerfully attracted by the CPI in most of the areas, lacked organizations strong enough to stand up against the oppression of the landlords and rich peasants. This naturally affected the prospects of the CPI in the countryside." [12]

For the 1971 mid-term parliamentary election, the CPI sought an electoral alliance with Mrs. Gandhi's Congress faction, but the best it could get was electoral arrangements at the local level in certain areas. In Bihar, even this was not possible because of the "tough" attitude adopted by the Congress president, Jagjivan Ram, a Bihari. All that could be arranged was to avoid Congress-CPI contests in a number of specific constituencies. The CPI was able to retain the 5 seats it had won in the Lok Sabha from Bihar in 1967, although its popular vote went up to 1.5 million. It came second in eight constituencies, losing in two of them by less than 1,000 votes. The CPI(M) contested 4 seats, secured none. [13]

[12] *New Age,* April 6, 1969.
[13] K. Gopalan, "CPI Holds Its Own Fighting All Alone," *New Age,* March 21, 1971.
Mrs. Gandhi's Congress party won 39 of the 53 seats it contested. However, its popular vote was 33.75 percent as compared with the 34.88 percent polled by the undivided Congress party in 1967 though it had won only 34 seats. All of the other parties suffered heavily in the mid-term election. The SSP paid the heaviest price, retaining only 1 of the 7 seats it had won in 1967. The "Syndicate" Congress party lost all the 8 seats it held in the dissolved house; the Jan Sangh won only 2 of the 28 seats it fought for. The small local parties were wiped out, and so were the independents. The tribal Jharkhand party won 2 seats. The four-party alliance of the "Syndicate" Congress, Swatantra, Jan Sangh, and SSP parties failed miserably in Bihar as in the rest of the country. The CPI drew comfort from the electorate's rejection of "right reaction" as shown in the poor performance of the alliance.

In Bihar, then, the CPI appears to have built up a fairly large support base which, however, lacks in depth. While the CPI has some support in both urban and rural areas among the working class as well as the poor peasantry and landless laborers, it is difficult to assess the stability of this support. The state leadership seems to be divided on the question of intensifying the "class struggle" in the countryside. While the CPI has worked together with the CPI(M) in south Bihar to organize peasant struggles against eviction, the dominant faction in the state committee as well as the national leadership seem not to favor an agrarian program that may alienate the middle-level and well-to-do peasant and thus push the party into conflict with the Congress party.

Bihar does not have a strong industrial proletariat. A new political element, however, is the student youth, mostly offspring of land-based rural families going through their first experience of alienation in the city. Of late a minority of the student-youth has shown an inclination toward Naxalism. None of the established political parties has much of a hold on these young people; the politically conscious among them seem to be looking for a radicalism the existing parties are unable or unwilling to supply.

In the next election of the Bihar legislative assembly, the CPI will probably increase its representation handsomely, though not spectacularly. Much will depend upon the electoral arrangement it can work out with the ruling Congress party and the leftist groups. If the ruling Congress faction regains enough confidence to "go it alone," it will not care to make adjustments with the CPI. If, on the other hand, it feels the need for allies, electoral arrangements will probably be worked out. Whether or not the CPI will be a major partner of a Congress-led (or supported) coalition will also be determined by the state of the ruling party in Bihar before and after the next election. Bihar is the one state in India where the concept of a national democratic front still has some chance. If this happens, the result of the experiment will be worth watching. The next phase of the Communist thrust for

Bihar will be determined by the success or failure of the national democratic front tactical line of the CPI.

In Andhra Pradesh, the Communists face a different set of problems. Unlike its situation in Bihar, the united CPI had built a strong support base in the Telugu-speaking regions of South India, even in the 1940s. In the feudal chieftaincy of Hyderabad, the armed uprising of the Telengana peasants in the late 1940s is still regarded as the high watermark of the CPI's exploits. Two factors helped the Communists build their impressive presence in the areas now comprising Andhra Pradesh. First, they were able to mobilize, albeit without durable success, peasant nationalism against the oppressive feudal antinational rule of the Nizam of Hyderabad. Second, they identified themselves with the linguistic nationalism of the middle-class elite. The Communists were at the forefront of the struggle for a separate Telugu-speaking province.

In the years immediately following independence, south India was seething with subnationalist discontent. The impressive gains of the CPI in the first general election (1952) in Travancore-Cochin, Madras, and Hyderabad were largely the result of its alliance with subnationalist groups. Through the tactics of a united front, the CPI secured 42 seats in the Madras assembly, as many in Hyderabad, and 32 in Travancore-Cochin.[14] So exhilarated was the CPI by this success that the central executive committee characterized the situation as "the general political instability of the ruling party" caused by "fundamental changes in the co-relation of forces" during the past few years. As a result of these "basic changes," the central executive claimed, the CPI had emerged as

[14] In Madras the Congress party, with 152 seats out of a total of 375, was reduced to a minority; so was the case in Travancore-Cochin, where the Congress party won 44 out of 108 seats. For the Communists, "these were small, but highly significant inroads into the monopoly of power of the Congress party, for it must not be forgotten that the CPI emerged from illegality and started operating as a constitutional force only a few months before the elections." Victor Fic, *Peaceful Transition to Communism in India* (Bombay, Nachiketa, 1969), p. 58.

the "major political force" in the three south Indian provinces. Going a step further, it saw the "instability of such dimensions" as the beginning of a "general and deep political crisis of the ruling classes."

The CPI, however, soon discovered that the Congress party was much better at "adopting" the linguistic elites than the Communists were. In the first Andhra assembly election in 1955, the CPI won only 15 seats in a house of 196.[15] It is generally assumed that the CPI debacle was caused by *Pravda,* which heaped lavish praise on the Nehru government's foreign and domestic policies only a few days before.[16] Even if Moscow planted the kiss of death on the CPI in Andhra Pradesh, in order to force the party to rally to the support of the national bourgeoisie, the real cause of the Communist debacle was its overwhelming reliance on the "good work" it had done among the middle-class intelligentsia, and its indifference to organizing working-class and peasant movements.

The middle-class intellectual orientation of the Andhra Communists pushed them in two opposite directions: parliamentarianism and extremism. When the CPI split, a majority of the Communist leaders and cadres joined the Marxist party. The failure of the CPI(M) leadership to correct the "mistakes" it realized only too late resulted in the extremist rebellion in 1968, noted in chapter 9. The Maoism of the Nagi Reddy group held a powerful spell over the youthful cadres. In fact, there was a two-way exodus from the CPI(M) in Andhra—the party's leader in the state assembly, P. Sanyasi Rao, was expelled for working with the CPI in the trade unions, while the mass exodus was in the direction of Maoism.[17]

[15] For evaluation of election results by the CPI leadership, see *Crossroads,* February 22, 1952; for the central executive resolution, *Crossroads,* April 4, 1952. See also, *For A Democratic Government in Madras State* (Bombay, PPH, 1952).

[16] The *Pravda* editorial came on January 26, 1955. For its impact on the CPI leadership, see Vic, pp. 126–40.

[17] The CPI(M) leadership made the following assessment of the Communist situation in Andhra in 1969: "However, the fact remains that the Communist movement

The Communists might have salvaged some of the losses if the two factions could have united to win the 1967 election. They failed to do so. The splitting of Communist votes reduced both parties to the status of an insignificant minority in the legislative assembly. The collapse of what was once a strong Communist base, however, compelled the state factions of the two parties to work together. There seems to exist a mutual openness between the CPI(M) and the CPI in Andhra not to be found anywhere else in India.[18]

PARADOX AND DILEMMA

Bihar and Andhra Pradesh are not the only problems Communism faces in India in its bid to expand its influence. They do,

---

in Andhra, as it stands at the present stage, is not yet able to firmly base itself either on a strong and organized working class movement or a powerful and solid agrarian revolutionary movement. The bourgeois-landlord classes through their political party, i.e., the Indian National Congress, utilizing the state and governmental power they secured, were able to capitalize on the democratic gains more than us, the democratic gains achieved mainly by our party's active participation and contribution. Thus, in the struggle that our party, as a working class party, is locked with the bourgeois-landlord classes during the last one and a half decades, we were thrown on the defensive, and our advance has been very tardy, halting and has been even reversed in some respects. For this state of affairs, apart from the temporary and short-lived political advantages our class enemies could secure for reasons beyond our control, the ascendancy of the right-reformist outlook and practice in the Andhra Pradesh party unit, which subsequently led to the serious revisionist disruption and split in the party and people's movements under its leadership, has its disastrous contribution, and in no way can it be minimized." *Letter to Andhra Comrades* (Calcutta, CPI [M], 1969), pp. 39–40.

[18] In 1968 the two parties came to an understanding to support each other's candidates in the forthcoming biennial election to Rajya Sabha, upper house of parliament. *New Age*, March 17, 1968. In the 1971 Lok Sabha poll, they avoided splitting the Communist vote. The CPI retained its Cuddapah seat, which was the only Communist victory in Andhra Pradesh. The CPI, however, polled 700,000 votes, which was 5.5 percent of the total valid poll.

In reporting the Communist performance, *New Age* wrote on March 21, 1971: "While the CPI polled as many votes as it polled in 1967 in Nalgonda, the CPM won Miryalguda with CPI support. The CPI's performance in Siddipet and the CPM's performance in Khammam were also reasonably good in the face of the (Telengana Praja) Samithi challenge." The places named were assembly constituencies within a parliamentary constituency. Since 1969 the Communists have been facing another subnationalist challenge: the demand of the Telengana elite for a separate Telengana state. Spearheading this demand is the Telengana Praja Samithi which is nothing but the local faction of the Congress. The two Communist groups started by opposing the "separatist" move, but adopted a somewhat supportive attitude after the widespread 1969 riots.

however, illustrate some of the major problems. These problems are inherent in India's historical experience, in the history of its freedom struggle, in the evolution of its political system, and in its social institutions, political culture, geography, and demographic structure. India, in short, presents a paradoxical phenomenon for Communism. On the one hand, the massive and increasing poverty of the bulk of its population, and the *awareness* of deprivation that is being created by the process of development, foster an objective situation in which Communism should flourish. On the other hand, there exists another (at the present moment more powerful) set of objective conditions which the Communists must overpower.

These conditions are created by the whole complex of the political system operating through institutions, interest groups, social structure, and political culture. The (at present) unequal combat between these two sets of objective conditions generally tend to militate against the Communists. Added to this are factors peculiar to Indian Communism: the intellectual orientation of its leadership, the weakness of its working-class and peasant base, the conflict between the various Communist groups, factionalism within each group, the regional character of the Communist support base and party leadership, and the general lack of creative thinking.

The fundamental dilemma of Communism in India can be stated in simple terms. The Communists are pitted against a state and a political system created, devised, and evolved by the bourgeoisie to which the Communists could make little positive contribution of their own. The choice that has baffled them all these years is whether they should work within the political system and use its institutions and instruments to gradually change its qualitative character, or whether they should try to overthrow the system and replace it with another based on a radical realignment of productive relationships. The united CPI began with the "overthrow" tactic, then swung to the opposite tactic of working within.

The split of the Communists into three factions, however, now enables them to try three different tactics at the same time. The CPI tactic is to work with the progressive bourgeoisie so that eventually it can take over the system. The CPI(M) tactic is to wreck it from within. The Maoist groups intend to overthrow the system by nibbling at it first in the countryside, and finally by leading an offensive front from liberated rural bases against the urban citadels of power. The splintering of the Communists, then, can be seen as performing two contradictory roles at the same time. It has weakened as well as strengthened the Communist movement. In terms of mobilization, fresh strategic and tactical thinking, and recruitment of new cadres, the movement has been strengthened rather than weakened.

This new strength has begun at a critical phase in Indian politics. The stability of the Indian political system, despite the country's relatively slow rate of economic development, has surprised some of the political scientists.[19] The stability has been, by and large, the result of the convergence of two systems—the system of parliamentary democracy and the system of the Congress party as the party of consensus and balance. The Congress party has been the brown umbrella under which the major factions of the Indian bourgeoisie have operated together in a broad consensus. Beneath the consensus, conflicts and cleavages have been at play without seriously upsetting the balance. The Congress party has been both a movement and a party even after independence; as a movement it directed the energies of the people to build a nation; as a party it ruled the nation. The one-party dominance in India, as Rajani Kothari has pointed out, is very different from single party regimes to be found elsewhere in Asia, Africa, and Latin America.

In 1947, the Congress party, which functioned as a broad-based nationalist movement before independence, transformed itself into the dominant political party of the nation. Although a number of opposition

[19] Samuel P. Huntington, *Political Order in Changing Societies* (New Haven, Yale University Press, 1969), p. 84.

parties came into existence, it was recognized that the Congress party was the chief party, representing a historical consensus and enjoying a continuing basis of support and trust. Under the circumstances, political competition was internalized and carried on within the Congress group. There developed an elaborate system of factions at every level of political and governmental activity, and a system of coordination between the various levels through vertical "faction chains." In the process, a system of patronage was worked out in the countryside, traditional institutions of kin and caste were gradually drawn and involved, and a structure of pressures and compromises was developed. . . . It was in the course of the working of this system that political competition was intensified, changes took place, new cadres of leadership drawn from a more diffuse social base come to power, and an intricate structure of conflict, mediation, bargaining, and consensus was developed within the framework of the Congress party.[20]

The Congress party thus played the role of the government party as well as the main opposition party within its one-party dominant system. The non-Congress opposition parties, because of their limited influence and their inability to offer a viable alternative to Congress rule, performed the role of pressure groups. The Congress leaders accommodated these parties as far as practicable, sometimes giving them more importance than they deserved, and thus persuading them to function in the "suburbs" of the Congress party, more or less as part of the Congress system.

It is a party system with a difference, oriented toward building an authoritative structure of political affiliations downward to the base, assimilating new and divergent interests upward to the center, and weaving all these into a framework of organization that was originally designed as an oppositional movement, rather an extension into the constituencies by two or more parliamentary groups in the wake of a widening franchise as happened in many of the Western countries. The consequence of directing political mobilization through the movement's organizational network (which now assumed the role of the rul-

[20] Rajani Kothari, "Congress System in India," in *Party System and Election Studies*, Occasional Papers No. 1, Center for the Study of Developing Societies, Delhi, Allied Publishers, 1967, p. 6. See also W. H. Morris-Jones, "Parliament and Dominant Party: Indian Experience," *Parliamentary Affairs*, Summer, 1964.

ing party while permitting dissenting elements to organize themselves into oppositional and factional pressures) gave rise to a pattern of dominance and dissent that gave considerable legitimacy and resources to the new inheritors of power, but subjected them to continuous criticism and scrutiny from a variety of social and political sites. The system was differentiated and crystallized through a confident implementation of universal adult franchise which, by allowing for an open confrontation between competing elements at various levels, made acceptance of the authority of the governing party legitimate and mandatory. The election confirmed the dominance of the Congress party at the national level, led to political consolidation at various other levels, provided substantial cushioning through the mobilization of rural support and, together with the penetration of planned programs, for the first time enabled a national government to reach out to the villages of India.[21]

THE STABILITY OF THE CONGRESS SYSTEM

The mobilization-recruitment-linkage drive of the Congress party enabled it to draw large segments of the emerging middle class, industrial workers, and the peasantry into the twin systems of party and government. Monopoly of government power made a wide distribution of patronage possible. At the state and district levels, the implements of power were shared among main factions, sometimes giving rise to acute but not uncontrollable conflicts.[22] Inevitably, the political system had to function through established social institutions. The castes were thus politically activated, lending strength to the functional structure of the system. The system proved remarkably "adoptive" of subnationalist elites. By creating linguistic states and by conferring statehood or semi-statehood on extramural nationalities like the Nagas and the hill people of the northeastern border, the system not only established institutional linkages with these groups but also helped the var-

---

[21] Kothari, *Politics in India*, p. 154.

[22] Paul R. Brass, "Patronage Is the Cement of the Congress Organization," in Brass, ed., *Factional Politics in an Indian State: The Congress Party in Uttar Pradesh* (Berkeley, California University Press, 1965).

ious linguistic and ethnic-cultural groups to develop a stake in the system.

Through its own trade-union organization and by means of patronage, the Congress party succeeded in keeping organized industrial workers relatively satisfied and the trade-union movement within the confines of economism. Its most impressive recruitment gains, however, came from the countryside, where the well-to-do sections of the peasantry rapidly became the mainstay of its power. Through these peasant leaders, who also in many cases happened to be leaders of the dominant castes, the Congress party was able not only to mobilize the electoral support of the large mass of peasantry but also maintain stability in the stratified villages. The success of the rural recruitment of the Congress party in the 1950s made an American political scientist predict that while electoral defeat of the Congress party is "ultimately inevitable, disintegration is not."[23]

If the stability of the Indian political system has been the product of the convergence of the twin systems of politics and party, the decay of one cannot but lead to the decay of the other. In other words, for the continued survival of the political system, continued survival of the Congress system of consensus and balance may also be essential. A political party of consensus and coalition of different factions, engaged in competition and conflict, can survive only as long as the strains remain tolerable and the pool of patronage does not fall too far short of minimum distributive demands. Also, such a party can afford to be only a center party—it cannot move either too far to the left or too far to the right. In the language of Duvergar, the center can be composed only of the "moderates of the Right and the moderates of the Left."

Herein lies the great danger to which a party of the center like the Congress party is exposed. "For, the Center is nothing more

[23] Myron Weiner, *Party Building in a New Nation: The Indian National Congress* (Chicago, Chicago University Press, 1967), p. 492.

than an artificial grouping of the right-wing of the Left and the left-wing of the Right. The fate of the Center is to be torn asunder, buffeted, and annihilated: torn asunder when one of its halves votes Right and the other Left, buffeted when it votes as a group first Right and then Left, annihilated when it abstains from voting. The dream of the Center is to achieve a synthesis of contradictory aspirations, but synthesis is a power only of the mind. Action involves choice and politics involves action." [24]

The Congress party was torn asunder in November 1969. The conflict that went beyond control and destroyed the consensus was at least given an ideological *appearance*—one part of the Center did at least *appear* to have voted left and the other part right. Pending a systematic analysis of the cleavages that caused the split in the Congress party, it may be tentatively suggested that the sudden shrinkage of the economy in 1964–65, a serious recession, followed by two years of severe drought and famine conditions in large parts of the country probably dried up the resources of reward at the command of the party and made factional competitions and conflicts highly attritional. The crisis in the economy became a political crisis. One section of the leadership wanted to move a little to the right and sought to remove Mrs. Gandhi. She, in turn, moved a little to the left and staged a coup against the rival group.

The defections from the party during 1967–69 were clearly attributable to unsatisfied demands for patronage and power from various factions in the states. Leaders of defecting groups became chief ministers while almost every defector claimed a ministership. The defeat of the Congress party changed the role of the opposition parties as pressure groups; they joined together in eight states to form non-Congress coalitions. Thus ended the first phase of post-independence Indian politics.

The new role of the opposition parties and the split in the

[24] Maurice Duvergar, *Political Parties: Their Organization and Activities in the Modern State* (London, Methuen, 1967), pp. 23, 215.

Congress party marked the start of a process of "reconstructing the party system." Rajani Kothari saw for the 1970s the emergence of two "competitive coalitions" of rightist and leftist parties, "both sharing in the larger consensus of the system, and providing the electorate with alternative teams to choose from." The task that faced the "elite at the center of the system" was to "turn the new opportunity of adopting the democratic consensus to a new institutional framework." If the elite failed in this task, it was likely to be swept away by the other tendency: "This is the tendency of a polarization of extremes around the appeal of a sectarian and revivalist right on the one hand and the doctrinaire militancy of the left on the other." The alternatives Kothari foresaw for India in the next decade were a polarization of the extremes and a "polarization of the center, which assimilates other divisions around a structure of alternatives while still sharing the basic consensus of the system." [25]

The turn of political events between 1967 and 1971 can be said partly to have confirmed Kothari's thesis. The opposition groups that banded together to rule in eight states had no socioeconomic programs different from the declared program of the Congress party; even in Bengal the difference was noticed not so much in program as in the *style* of politics. Most of the non-Congress governments, including the CPI-led coalition in Kerala, could only promise to implement the Congress programs better than the Congress governments could. In this, too, the majority of them failed, for leaders of these coalitions were kept busy maintaining themselves in power and found little time for constructive work.

Meanwhile, the split in the Congress party enabled the dominant faction of Mrs. Gandhi to establish vertical links with several new inheritors of power. The most notable among these was the DMK of Madras. In the mid-term parliamentary election in 1971, Mrs. Gandhi's Congress faction staged a spectacular come-

[25] Rajani Kothari, "Toward a Political Perspective for the Seventies," *Economic and Political Weekly: Annual Number,* January 1970, pp. 101–16.

back to the dominant party position at the national level. Among its new allies were the DMK in Madras and the CPI. Its impressive election victory was won mostly at the cost of the rightist parties like Swatantra, the "Syndicate" Congress group, and the Jan Sangh. The impact of defeat virtually scattered the "Syndicate" Congress faction. A mass exodus began toward the ruling Congress party. Efforts were made to restore Congress rule in the non-Congress states. Thus in mid-1971, the Congress faction of Mrs. Gandhi began to look very much like the Congress party before the split. The politics of consensus was restored, though it was more assimilative and broader and therefore looser and less stable than the consensus of the Nehru era. A mild polarization of the center arrested a polarization of the extremes.

Given the concept of two polarizations, the CPI tactical line is designed to polarize the center and that of the CPI(M) to polarize the extremes. In polarizing the center, the CPI has reconciled itself to, at best, a junior partnership of a broadly (and mildly) leftish national democratic consensus; it therefore prefers to operate at the national level of politics. The CPI(M), on the other hand, intends to polarize the antagonistic social and economic classes—the working class and the poor peasantry and the capitalists and feudal elements in the countryside. The CPI(M) therefore prefers to operate at the base of Indian politics—in the states. The Maoist groups entertain the same objective but prefer to operate from outside the political system.

The CPI(M), we have noted in chapter 10, regards the collapse of the Congress system as an essential precondition of a revolutionary political crisis in India—the collapse of the Congress system (the Marxists apparently believe) will create conditions necessary for the collapse of the political system. For revolution is impossible as long as the existing political system is viable and capable of commanding the loyalty of the elite groups.

The fundamental law of revolution, which has been confirmed by all revolutions . . . is as follows: it is not enough for revolution that the exploited and oppressed masses should understand the impossibility of living in the old way and demand changes, it is essential for revolution that the exploiters should not be able to live and rule in the old way. Only when the "lower classes" *do not want the old* and the "upper classes" cannot *carry on in the old way*—only then can revolution triumph. This truth can be expressed in other words: revolution is impossible without a nationwide crisis (affecting both the exploited and the exploiters.) It follows that for a revolution, it is essential, first, that a majority of workers (or at least a majority of the class-conscious, thinking, politically active workers) should fully understand that revolution is necessary and be ready to sacrifice their lives for it; second, that the ruling classes should be passing through a government crisis, which draws even the most backward masses into politics (a symptom of every real revolution is a rapid, tenfold and even hundredfold increase in the numbers of the toiling masses—hitherto apathetic—who are capable of waging the political struggle), weakens the government and makes it possible for the revolutionaries to overthrow it rapidly.[26]

The first essential condition of revolution, then, is a crisis in the *ancien regime*. The crisis must be of such dimension that the ruling elite find it impossible to rule and that vast segments of the population realize that this is so. A society undergoing modernization is always in a crisis, India all the more so because of its teeming humanity and unredeeming mass poverty. However, a developmental crisis does not easily become a political crisis. The test of a political system is how much tension and conflict it can tolerate and assimilate through change and adjustment. Few political societies possess what Chalmers Johnson calls a homeostatic equilibrium.[27] In India, there are forces which may repeatedly

[26] Lenin, *Left-Wing Communism, an Infantile Disorder,* in *Selected Works* (2 vols.; Moscow, 1947), II, 621. Italics in original.

[27] "On certain occasions, however, social systems which were previously functioning in equilibrium move out of equilibrium. These situations pose a threat, not necessarily immediately but still a threat, to the continuation of the system. Purposeful changes must be undertaken in order to recreate a homeostatic equilibrium, and if a new equilibrium is reached it will usually differ from the one that was destroyed." Chalmers Johnson, *Revolutionary Change* (Boston, Little Brown, 1966), p. 60. Johnson's "dialectical" model, however, differs fundamentally from Marxian dialectics, for he does not approach the social system from the vantage point of antagonistic classes, but from the point of elite operators of the system. "By 'elites'

buffet the political system. It faces ever-swelling demands for change. The politics of consensus aims at keeping these demands within control. When the demands go out of control, the politics of consensus is in danger.

Polarizing Factors. The biggest danger to the politics of consensus in India emanates from the demographic situation. There are two real majorities in India, the young and the poor: 250 million Indians are below the age of sixteen; about one-third of the population lives below the poverty line; a little over one-fifth live below the line of destitution. An inquiry conducted by the Indian Institute of Public Opinion (IIPO) finds among these poor "a major loss of confidence . . . in the prospects of economic justice within their generation." Poverty alone would not create serious disequilibrium in a society. Two factors which have in recent years tended to infuse mass poverty in India with a dangerous political content are the rapid mobilization of the poor caused by acute competition among political parties, and the process of economic development.

The IIPO report shows that the poor have been playing some part in the decline of the Congress party's electoral support since 1957. The decline has been rather sharp since 1962. "Of the erosion of the Congress popular vote of 3 percentage points between 1957 and 1962, practically all could be accounted for by the vote of the really poor and the destitute." Between 1957 and 1962, the poor and the destitute seem to have moved further away from the party of consensus, while the higher income groups have moved closer to it. "There appears to be a polarization of political effects caused by the factors of well-to-do-ness and poverty within the wide canvas of the political spectrum represented by India's multiparty system." The report says that even if the Marxist dogma that the poor and the destitute would be revolutionary is still to

we mean the group of actors who occupy the statuses of authority in a social system" (p. 93n). See also Karl Deutsch, *The Nerves of Government* (New York, Free Press, 1963), p. 40, for definitions of elite and nonelite groups.

be proven in India, it seems clear that "currently, the poor are more ready to change their political loyalties than the rich."[28]

Fragmentation of the political parties, sharpened in the 1960s, has tended to make the poor and the destitute participators in the political process. The bulk of the poor, of course, still live beyond the organizational reach of the Communists. However, the drift of politics since 1967 may close the gap more quickly than many are inclined to think.

The non-Congress parties which joined together to form coalition governments in the states after the fourth election succeeded in politically activating the poor to some extent. But they failed to meet the demands of the poor they had aroused during and after the election. This failure has underlined what is probably the greatest weakness of the Congress system of consensus and balance. Since most of the non-Congress parties function within the extended frontiers of this system, the viability of the united front experiments might have provided India with alternative governments without seriously upsetting the equilibrium of consensus. The only non-Congress governments that worked to some extent on behalf of the poor were those of West Bengal and Kerala and these were dominated by the CPI(M). The failure of the opposition groups to provide a credible alternative to Congress rule may have greatly reduced their appeal to the poor. If this happens, a polarization will take place between the Congress party and the Communists as the only two political forces that are capable of ruling in India.[29]

Neither Communist party believes that Mrs. Gandhi's faction, as it is now constituted, will be able to attack Indian poverty successfully. Since the real base of poverty is the countryside, and the

[28] IIPO, *The Anatomy of Indian Poverty* (New Delhi, 1968), p. 28.

[29] If the mid-term parliamentary election of 1971 is any measure of the mood of the poor, they would seem to have rejected the non-Communist opposition parties and registered their support in a large part of the country either for the ruling Congress party or the Communists.

agrarian structure the foundation of Indian politics, the CPI(M) tries to polarize the rural classes and thereby strike at the foundation of the political edifice. The CPI embraces the "progressive" Congress faction of Mrs. Gandhi with the belief that she will be obliged by the sheer weight of the politically activated poor either to move to the left or court political suicide. The CPI therefore concentrates its attack on the right-wing of the ruling Congress group and brings pressure upon the party, through nonmilitant mass action, to implement its "socialist" program.

The CPI's sights are fixed on how much toward the left the center will have to shift if it does not choose to abdicate its prerogative to govern. A steady leftward shift will enhance the CPI's own strength as a political force. The situation thus emerging would make possible a government of the National Democratic Front. If, on the other hand, the opposite happens, and the center shifts to the right, the CPI would exercise the option, never formally and conclusively abandoned, of revolutionary opposition to the ruling forces.

Economic Development and Revolution. The great challenge to the Indian political system comes not from poverty and the poor, but from poverty politically awakened and the poor who have begun to be less poor. Revolution is not caused by economic crisis until it turns into a major political crisis. The process of development and modernization is a potential ally of revolution, for it creates widespread dislocation and instability.

Herein lies the cruel paradox that faces India's politics of consensus. If Mrs. Gandhi and her colleagues (or their successors) find it possible to bring the resources of development within the reach of the poor through the parliamentary democratic process that rules out coercion as a means of resource mobilization, there will be *more* tension and conflict between the classes, not less. The level of economic development achieved in India, "far from enhancing political stability, has tended to be politically unstabilizing." [30] The Communists have no reason to fear the process of development and modernization; what they fear is the slowness of the process.

The Indian Census Commissioner has classified 323 districts into four groups in descending order of development on the basis of infrastructure, participation rates in economic activity (with special reference to the traditional economy), potential of human resources (including literacy and the extent of urbanization), and development of the distributive trades and of manufacturing and organized industry in the modern sector of the economy. In the first group of 84 districts, there has been 57.06 percent urbanization, the literacy rate is 31.15 percent, and there are 77,759 industrial establishments. For the second group of 76 villages, the figures are 23.29 percent urban population, 26.66 percent literacy, and 27,606 industrial establishments. "The Congress party is marginally better entrenched in the relatively more developed than in the less developed parts of the country. *The same appears to be the case with the Communists.* The PSP-SP, the Swatantra Party, and the Jan Sangh on the other hand have done better in the less developed areas." [31]

Rural Unrest. Stability in India has been very largely due to the comparative quiescence of the countryside. The quiescence was achieved mainly through the political linkages established be-

[30] Bert F. Hoselitz and Myron Weiner, "Economic Development and Political Stability in India," *Dissent* (Spring 1961), p. 173. Alexis de Tocqueville was the first to discover the link between the process of development and political instability leading sometimes to revolution. He observed: "It was precisely in those parts of France where there had been the most improvement that popular discontent ran highest. This may seem illogical—but history is full of such paradoxes. For it is not always when things are going from bad to worse that revolution breaks out. On the contrary, it more often happens that when a people which has put up without protest suddenly finds the government relaxing its pressure, it takes up arms against it." *The Old Regime and the French Revolution* (New York, Doubleday Anchor, 1955), p. 176. See also James C. Davis, "Toward a Theory of Revolution," *American Sociological Review*, February 1962; his *Human Nature in Politics* (New York, Wiley, 1963), p. 350; Johnson, ch. 4; Cyril E. Black, *The Dynamics of Modernization* (New York, Harper, 1966), pp. 90–94; and Huntington, ch. 1.

[31] Gopal Krishna, "One Party Dominance—Development and Trends", in *Party System and Election Studies*, pp. 19–75. Italics added.

tween the ruling Congress party and the landholding community; it has also been due to the slow pace of change in the agrarian sector. While no section of the rural population was entirely deprived of the benefits of development, the bulk of the new resources created by community development—irrigation, rural credit societies, industrial cooperations, and rural electrification —accrued to the new "kulaks." They manned the new institutions of political power in the villages ranging from the *panchayats* (village councils) to the *zila parishads* (district councils). It was among these rising village leaders that the ruling party sought new recruits.[32]

Development steadily began to widen the disparity between the rural rich and rural poor, but the political actors, including the Communists, did not polarize the rural scene by organizing the discontent of the poor. The rate of urbanization was relatively slow, barely 3.9 percent for the whole decade 1951–61.[33] Very few agriculturists were leaving the villages. One factor that kept the net urban flow so low was what an economist has called "turnover migration"—people going to towns and cities and then returning to the villages.[34] Caste institutions, fully organized politically, meshed with the newly created economic and political resources, and became the functional framework of party politics focused on elections.

All this has begun to change. The first major jolt came from the economic stagnation of the 1960s. The food riots in Bengal, we have seen, reached the countryside on a large scale in 1966. The second factor contributing to change is the acute competition among the political groups for electoral support. This has lead to an unprecedented mobilization of the rural population

[32] Hoselitz and Weiner, p. 173.

[33] Kothari, *Politics in India,* pp. 355–60. In 1951, 17.29 percent of the population was urban; in 1961, it was 17.97 percent. The net addition to the urban population was 16.5 million.

[34] Ashish Bose, "Six Decades of Urbanization in India, 1901–1961," *Indian Economic and Social History Review,* January, 1965.

since 1967. The third and most important cause of change is the "green revolution."

The "green revolution" promises to carry the process of development to the villages on a grand scale. It has already created some polarization in the countryside. The Union Home Ministry in a special report in 1969 drew attention to the widespread eviction of sharecroppers by landlords in the irrigated areas. The report warned that the problem of rural unemployment was becoming serious and was likely to cause increasing agrarian unrest. Rajani Kothari has said: "There seems to be a greater threat from class conflict within the rural sector . . . than from any general movement of protest against the 'system' as a whole." [35]

What Kothari seems to ignore is that the system rests mainly on the agrarian status quo. Moreover, class conflict in the countryside will not leave the urban areas peaceful, although the opposite may often happen. The rural strength of the regime enables it to survive the hostility of the city in the first stages of modernization.[36] If the system cannot politically mobilize the rural poor, they will be mobilized and organized *against* it.

MOBILIZING THE PEASANTRY

It is in this context of an emerging agrarian crisis that one has to look at the CPI(M)'s tactic of peasant mobilization and organization, and the Maoist groups' efforts to build up peasant guerrilla forces. Organized rebellions by the land-hungry, job-hungry rural proletariat may well be the catalyst that may make the politics of consensus and slowly incremental change irrelevant.[37] The

[35] *The Causes and Nature of Current Agrarian Tensions,* Research and Policy Division, Ministry of Home Affairs, 1969, unpublished monograph, pp. 12–15; Kothari, *Politics in India,* p. 365.

[36] Huntington, pp. 75–77. "Revolutions are thus unlikely to occur if the period of frustration of the urban middle class does not coincide with that of the peasantry" (p. 277). "The countryside . . . plays the crucial 'swing' role in modernizing politics" (p. 292).

[37] Johnson, p. 97. History of revolutions shows that a foreign invasion generally acts as the "accelerator." However, "accelerators" can also originate domestically.

Boxer Rebellion was caused by the promises of reforms made but never implemented by the Empress Dowager. As the Indian finance minister, Chavan, has said, "Unless the Green Revolution is accompanied by a revolution based on social justice, I am afraid the Green Revolution may not remain green." [38]

There is nothing peculiar to the rural society and rural culture of India that makes the peasant necessarily unreceptive to the doctrine of Marxism-Leninism. In fact, to posit that the peasant, because of his firm caste loyalties, his deeply religious inclination, and his famous passivity, will turn away from Communism in all circumstances is to confuse the effects of a series of historical and social circumstances as the cause of a culture that may be seemingly indifferent to the strongly activist determinism of the Marxian doctrine.[39]

It is true that the Indian peasant has been quiescent in comparison with the peasant in China; there have been few peasant rebellions in India of any magnitude. This has been a paradoxical phenomenon, for the Indian rural framework contains perhaps a greater potential for protest and violent class conflict than did the traditional Chinese village. Explanations of this phenomenon, however, are to be sought in the Indian peasant's historical experience, in the institutions and traditions that have governed his life and molded his psycho-cultural reflexes. Two factors would

---

The quickening of peasant restlessness in predominantly agrarian societies, caused by pressure of internal developments or external intervention, will probably act as an "accelerator" for revolution.

[38] *Link*, January 18, 1970.

[39] Inadequacies of the agrarian theory of Marx emanate from the fact that he regarded the agrarian problem from the angle of production rather than from that of social organization. His perspective was shaped by his observation of the English and Irish scene about the middle of the nineteenth century. Everything seemed to point to the concentration of land in the hands of a small group of large owners. He saw in "land grabbing on a great scale" the "first step in creating a field for the establishment of large-scale agriculture." He came to believe that in agriculture as in industry property was becoming increasingly concentrated. This, of course, was only partly true. Marx took a dim view of the small-holding cultivator as an ally of the revolution. The concept of worker-peasant alliance was fashioned by Lenin.

seem to have been mainly responsible for these "tranquil" land-lord-peasant relations.

First, there is the separation of the rural universe from the political universe, depriving the former of catalysts of change. For a thousand years and more, the villages lived at a great remove from government, ruled by the castes which provided a self-sufficient framework by regulating all human conduct from cradle to grave. Exploitation and expropriation were sanctioned by the castes, and therefore by religion; it was almost always carried out, on behalf of the remote raj, by the local landlords who, being *born* into the higher castes, were seen to be performing functions which carried the sanction of religion. The Brahmin, often himself a landlord, and the scriptures which he alone could read and interpret, were defenders of exploitation and expropriation. It was a milieu that taught the peasant neither that the injustices heaped upon him and the miseries of his life were wrong or unethical nor that he could unmake what had been ordained for him by the malevolent gods and their mortal spokesmen. Hence grew the third dimension of the milieu—the mythology of fate. This mythology rationalized deprivation as an inheritance from previous births, which could be gotten rid of in a future birth only by patient and meek submission to what life had to offer in the present.

The second reason lies in the nature of the Western impact on India. The British left the rural framework severely alone, carried out exploitation of the peasantry largely through native landlords and their agents, and even reinforced the authority of the exploiters by conferring on them permanent land settlements. Moreoever, they kept the peace in the countryside, and effected improvement in the lot of peasants. They knew that the quiescent village was the best assurance for imperial rule, and they made no effort to change the landscape.[40]

[40] A detailed examination of the history of agrarian relations in India and China is outside the scope of this volume. A few points may, however, be made. In both

The nationalist movement led by the Congress party was not merely city-oriented, but was heavily weighted, from the beginning, in favor of the landowning class. For the first twenty years of its existence, the Congress party was dominated by the city-oriented landed gentry. In 1893 the Congress party began to adopt resolutions championing the interests of the landlords as against the British raj. The famous Bordoloi resolution, adopted in the

---

countries a surplus of agricultural produce *did exist*. In India this surplus was expropriated in part by the British, the rest went to feed the culture of conspicuous consumption of the feudal classes. In China, the surplus went in refurbishing the imperial regimes and for the benefit of the landlords. Expropriation by foreigners was indirect, carried out through unfavorable terms of trade and repatriation of profits.

It is difficult to conclude which rural society was more cohesive. One distinguishing feature of the two societies was that while in China, the gentry were of the same clan as the poorer members, in India, the gentry belonged to the higher castes and had the Brahmin priests as their allies. Exploitation obtained a religious sanction in India, which was not the case in China; on the contrary, Confucianism sanctioned protests against injustice and even the overthrow of a ruler who could not rule wisely and benevolently.

While peace prevailed in India following the British conquest (with the one great exception of the rebellion of 1857), in China the Western impact brought in a long period of conflicts which had their inevitable effect on the social framework in the villages. From the Opium War onwards right up to the middle of this century, chaos and mismanagement continued, except for brief periods. The institution of warlords was unknown to India. With the rise and fall of these warlords land changed hands, and exploitation of peasants increased.

For India, see: Romesh Dutt, *Indian Famines: Their Causes and Prevention* (London, 1901), B. M. Bhatia, *Famines in India: A Study in Some Aspects of the Economic History of India* (Bombay, Asia Publishing House, 1963); Robert Wallace, *Lecture on Famine in India* (Edinburgh, 1900); Vera Anstey, *The Economic Development of India* (London, 1952); M. N. Srinivas, ed., *India's Villages* (Bombay, Asia Publishing House, 1960).

For China, see: R. H. Tawney, *Land and Labor in China* (London, Allen and Unwin, 1932); H. J. Forrest, *Report of China Famine Relief Fund* (Shanghai, 1879); Jack Belden, *China Shakes the World* (London, Gollanz, 1950); Edgar Snow, *Red Star Over China* (London, Gollanz, 1937); Franz Schurmann, *Ideology and Organization in Communist China* (Berkeley, University of California Press, 1966); C. F. Remer, *Foreign Investments in China* (New York, Macmillan, 1933); T. H. Shen, *Agricultural Resources of China* (Ithaca, Cornell University Press, 1951); W. W. Rostow and others, *The Prospects for Communist China* (Cambridge, M.I.T. Press, 1954); and C. P. Fitzgerald, *The Birth of Communist China* (Pelican, 1964).

For comparative studies, see: Barrington Moore Jr., *Social Origins of Democracy and Dictatorship* (Boston, Beacon Press, 1967); Rushikesh Maru and Rajani Kothari, eds., *India and China: Contrasts in Development* (New Delhi, 1969); and C. S. Thapa, "The Political Economy of India and China before 1945," *China Report* (New Delhi, January–February, 1970).

background of a "no-rent" campaign led by Vallabhai Patel, assured the *zamindars* that the Congress movement "is in no way intended to attack their legal interests." Gandhi, as already noted, knew that the countryside was potentially explosive, and though he gave the nationalist movement a universal dimension and took it to the villages, he was anxious not to mobilize the peasantry actively for the freedom struggle. He undertook the symbolic breaking of the Salt Laws but he did not ask peasants to stop paying rent to the government.

In conducting the only "no-rent" campaign under Congress leadership at Bordoloi, Patel took care to reassure the landlords that the Congress party was mindful of their interests. "The proprietorship of the land," declared Patel, "rests, not with the state, but in the landlords." Gandhi himself was in favor of agrarian relations being managed by a community of benign, benevolent, socially responsible landlords, though at times he also spoke vaguely about communal ownership of land. In all the resolutions adopted by the Congress faction on the agrarian problem prior to independence, there was hardly any bold, precisely defined program for rehabilitation of the rapidly increasing community of landless laborers.[41]

With the coming of independence, the rural scene began to change rather quickly. The peasantry began to be differentiated through the direct intervention of the government. The apathy of the peasant could no longer be taken for granted. "The rural depressed classes, largely landless laborers, have in many instances

---

[41] Jagdish S. Sharma, ed., *India's Struggle for Freedom: Select Documents and Sources* (Delhi, S. Chand, 1962), I, 1–55. In 1928 the Congress party organized a forest *satyagraha*. In the (then) Central Provinces, the man who was asked to organize it was Seth Govind Das, the wealthiest landlord of the province. "A silver sickle was generally presented on these occasions to the leaders, with which they inaugurated the symbolic cutting of grass in the closed area." *Communists Challenge Imperialism from the Dock* (Calcutta, National Book Agency, 1967), pp. 157–97. This volume, which comprises the statement made by the Communist accused in the Meerut Conspiracy Case, gives an interesting account of the agrarian base of the Congress party.

become articulate and active and insistent, remarkably enough under leadership drawn from themselves. There have been some local riots, some fairly serious." [42] As disparities grew, the moods of the "have-nots" began to change in response to the moods of the "haves." What was lacking was the induction of subjective conditions to explosive objective realities. No political party, the CPI among them, intervened to mobilize the rural masses.

When the Communists took up this task in the late 1960s, they were surprised by the response they got from the peasantry. CPI(M) peasant cadres told me in early 1970 that the peasants and landless laborers in Bengal "are so militant that we just do not know how to keep them from desperate acts." At peasant meetings in Burdwan district of West Bengal, the cadres found themselves almost always "behind the peasants in militancy." A CPI peasant leader in Bihar remarked: "The poor peasant is in a terrible mood. He is ready to rise. We are not ready at all." [43] This was the mood of the peasantry that the Maoist factions were able to exploit in widely scattered parts of India during 1968–70.

Interviews with Communist cadres working among peasants in Bengal and Bihar suggest that while the peasants do not care for the theoretical subtleties of Marxism-Leninism, "they are quick to understand the concept of class struggle once it is related to their own experience, to the realities of their life." The first generation of peasant youth, born shortly before or just after independence, was described by several Communist cadres as "very good material for recruitment." [44] "The problem is ours," said a CPI(M) peasant-front cadre in Burdwan, "for we are short of books on Marxism-Leninism which these men, with their little education,

[42] Albert Mayer et al., *Pilot Project India: The Story of Rural Development at Etawah, Uttar Pradesh* (Berkeley, University of California Press, 1958), p. 14.

[43] Interviews with Communist peasant-front cadres in West Bengal and Bihar. Most of the Marxist cadres belonged to district committees of the Kisan Sabha. They generally revealed contempt for the parliamentary wing of the CPI(M).

[44] Many of these rural youths had attended school for a few years and were literate. The CPI(M) in West Bengal and Kerala has concentrated on recruiting cadres from among this class.

can comprehend. We have been trying hard to speak in idioms that ring true in their ears."

The Communists seem to have grasped some of these idioms. In inducing the peasants and sharecroppers in Bengal to take over *benami* land and defend their crops, Konar described land as the "mother" to whose bosom her children were returning. This mother-cult idiom may have nothing Marxist about it, but it certainly stirred the land-hungry and the landless. The poverty and "blankness" of the Indian peasant may well make him a "superior revolutionary" in India as it is said to have done in China.[45]

Techniques of Mobilization. This is not to suggest that Communist mobilization of the peasantry in India will necessarily follow the Chinese model. Indications are that it will *not*. Revolutions, as Chalmers Johnson has rightly pointed out, are better studied in the context of the social system rather than in the techniques of seizing power.[46] Tactics emerge from a given set of social forces, their alignment and responses to one another, as well as from the accumulated political and cultural experience of the actors.

The two well-tested and successful techniques of Communist-led revolutions so far are Lenin's insurrection and Mao's protracted people's war. Huntington has categorized them as "western" and "eastern" revolutions.[47] The first stage in a "western" revolution, says Huntington, is the collapse of the *ancien regime*. The final step, according to Lenin, is the "insurrection," which Marx described as "an art quite as much as war."[48] In the "east-

---

[45] Mao Tse-tung first put forward his thesis that the Chinese people were possessed of superior revolutionary capacities because they were "poor and blank" in the first issue of *Red Flag* in January, 1958. See Stuart R. Schram, "The Party in Chinese Communist Ideology," *China Quarterly,* April–June, 1967.

Celso Furtado has remarked about the peasantry in Brazil that they are "much more susceptible to revolutionary influences of the Marxist-Leninist kind than the urban classes, although the latter, according to orthodox Marxism, should be the spearhead of the revolutionary movement." Cited in Huntington, p. 296.

[46] Johnson, p. 97.   [47] Huntington, pp. 267–74.

[48] "Insurrections must rely upon the *crucial moment* in the history of the growing revolution, when the activity of the advanced ranks of the people is at its height, and when the *vacillations* in the ranks of the enemy and *in the ranks of*

ern" revolutions, the revolutionary forces first establish a base area of control far away from urban centers, struggle to win the support of the peasantry through land reforms and other measures as well as through propaganda and terror, and steadily expand their authority and escalate the level of their military operations until they have stormed the urban citadels of power.

The technique of revolution hinges upon the crucial question: how do the revolutionary forces weaken and finally overpower the armed forces of the regime they wish to overthrow? Revolutionary guerrilla warfare is an attempt to demonstrate that a revolution *can* be made, even with a modest beginning, against the armed might of the regime. Between the two tested typologies of revolutionary techniques, however, the CPSU 20th Congress thesis has indicated the *potentiality* of the undefined and so far unsuccessful technique of "peaceful transition." [49]

The technique of Communist mobilization of the peasantry in India will be determined mainly by four factors: the response of the regime and the rural "haves" to such mobilization; the strategic-tactical perspectives of the Communist actors; Communist organization in the different states; and external intervention.

The crucial factor is the regime's ability to ameliorate the distress of the rural poor. If the regime proves to be unable to neutralize unrest in the countryside and, instead, employs punitive measures to bring it under control, organized peasant militancy will probably be inevitable. The degree of militancy will depend on the intensity of the class war. Guerrilla insurgencies on a limited local scale cannot be ruled out, but it is highly doubtful if that will be the general pattern of peasant struggles.

---

the weak, half-hearted and irresolute friends of the revolution are strongest." Lenin, "Marxism and Insurrection," *Selected Works*, II, 120–22. Italics in original.

[49] No Communist party has so far come to power as a result of peaceful transition, which actually means without civil war. However, a Communist-led coalition has been in power in Chile through constitutional means since 1970, and it is an experiment full of interest for students of politics and comparative Communism. The success or failure of the Italian Communist party's coalition tactics also compels close watching.

Unlike the CCP, the CPI was *not* born of guerrilla war.[50] Even in 1927, when the CCP organized the Autumn Harvest Insurrection in southern China, it had its own army, and it could easily, though not profitably, recruit from the ragtag armies of the warlords. The Indian Communists' experience has been entirely different. The middle-class intellectuals who have constituted the leadership of Indian Communism have shown little acumen about either insurrection or protracted peasant warfare techniques. The "insurrectionary" misadventure of 1948 proved to be as futile and expensive as the Telengana armed struggle. Also, the Communists cannot afford to ignore the lessons of the counter-productive peasant guerrilla wars in the Philippines, Malaya, and Burma.[51]

THE DIFFERENT SITUATION IN INDIA

The peculiar juxtaposition of internal and external factors which enabled Mao Tse-tung to mobilize the Chinese peasantry for protracted warfare and ultimate seizure of power does not exist in India. Between 1927 and 1934, Mao's protracted peasant guerrilla war was far from a success. The Autumn Harvest Uprising was a costly failure.[52] Chiang Kai-shek's successive annihila-

[50] Mao has written: "Apart from armed struggle, apart from guerrilla warfare, it is impossible to understand our political line and, consequently, to understand our party-building." Stuart Schram, ed., *The Political Thought of Mao Tse-tung* (New York, Praeger, 1966), p. 374.

[51] Ruth T. McVey sums up the lessons of these guerrilla uprisings thus: "In retrospect, it would appear that the insurrections . . . failed in good part because they were undertaken at the wrong time, from weakness rather than from strength. They were attempts to take advantage of situations that had begun to change, and to seize leaderships that were already consolidating in other hands. Time was against the rebels, but—by necessity or design—they pursued victory through protracted civil wars rather than through the lightening seizure of power. They assumed that their insurrections would thoroughly cripple the government and the economy, and that if outside aid came it would be for them and not for their opponents, and both suppositions proved fatally wrong. If the revolts contained a common lesson for the Communists, it was that the task of transforming the insurrection of a group into a full-blown civil war was no simple one to accomplish, and certainly not undertaken by movements whose position was on the wane." "The Southeast Asian Revolts," in Cyril E. Black and Thomas P. Thornton, eds., *Communism and Revolution* (Princeton, Princeton University Press), 1964.

[52] Roy Hofheinz Jr., "The Autumn Harvest Insurrection," *China Quarterly*, October–December, 1967.

tion campaigns, together with the promises made to the peasantry in the New Life Movement, forced Mao to evacuate southern China and take the remnants of his armed forces, through the Long March, to the deep north adjacent to the USSR.

What completely changed the fortunes of the CCP was the Japanese invasion of China. Mao was now able to mobilize the nationalism of the Chinese peasantry for the revolution because Chiang was more anxious to fight the Communists than the Japanese invaders. Mao's creative contribution as a Communist was that he succeeded in carrying out the "democratic" revolution in the liberated areas simultaneously with mobilizing the peasantry for the defense of the fatherland. The two factors firmly established Communist leadership of the peasantry which, in the aftermath of World War II, Mao could easily direct for the overthrow of the Kuomintang forces. Tito's success in Yugoslavia was due to similar reasons. The Greek Communists failed to transform the anti-fascist resistance into a war of liberation against the British mainly because they did not carry out the "democratic" revolution along with partisan war.[53]

In India, apart from the Communist leadership's lack of mili-

[53] For the crucial role played by foreign imperialist invasion in the expansion, consolidation, and triumph of the Communist movements in China and Yugoslavia, see Chalmers A. Johnson, *Peasant Nationalism and Communist Power* (Stanford, Stanford University Press, 1962); D. A. Tomasic, *National Communism and Soviet Strategy* (Washington D.C., Public Affairs Press, 1957); and Cyril E. Black, "Revolution, Mobilization, and Communism," in *Communism and Revolution*.

For the successes and failures of the Greek Communists during and after World War II, see Stavrianos, *Greece: American Dilemma and Opportunity* (Chicago, 1952). "It appears [Stavrianos writes] that the Communists were genuinely interested in organizing as effective a resistance movement as possible, but at the same time they were confident that their leadership in the resistance struggle would attract to them such a large proportion of the population that 'the will of the people' would mean a postwar regime in which they would have substantial or dominant influence. It should also be noted that the fifth plenum of the central committee of the Greek Communist party (January 30–31, 1949) adopted a resolution condemning 'right-wing opportunistic deviations' during the occupation period. Owing to these 'deviations,' according to the revolution, the EAM Army was organized as a purely resistance body rather than as a 'people's revolutionary army,' with the result that it was successful against the Axis but succumbed to British intervention in December 1944." Quoted in Hans Morgenthau, "We are Deluding Ourselves in Vietnam," *New York Times Magazine*, April 18, 1965. See also Vladimir Dejijar, *Tito* (New York, 1953), pp. 150–65.

tary training and experience, and their instinctive sharing in the national cultural mystique of pacifism and reconciliation, there are other powerful factors working against a general tactical line of peasant guerrilla warfare. The country is too highly developed in transport and communications to allow the Communists to build and protect liberated bases in remote isolated areas. Limited local insurgencies may, however, continue for a long time as has been the case with the Nagas and Mizos of the eastern frontier, but something on a larger and more durable scale would require, as a precondition, a general breakdown of the political order. Second, the armed forces of the country are strong enough, disciplined enough, and motivated enough to crush Communist peasant insurgencies. Third, no foreign imperialist invasion is likely to help the Communists as it did the Communists in China and Yugoslavia. The only "invasion" India has had after independence came from China, and it hardly proved to be of any advantage to the Communists.

Moreover, as long as the Indian government remains friendly with the USSR, there is every possibility that it will get Soviet military assistance in putting down Communist-led peasant warfare. Indeed, except in conditions of a global war, it would be foolish on the part of Indian Communists to expect overt Chinese or Soviet support and assistance in their thrusts for power.

THE COMBINING OF TACTICS

Since the Indian revolution, if it comes, would occur in the context of the country's political experience and institutions, it is most unlikely that the Communists will entirely abandon parliamentary tactics and opt for a direct assault on the regime from outside the constitutional framework. Only by demonstrating that political power is persistently used by the ruling class to keep the Communists out of power, even when they enjoy the electorate's support and confidence, can the revolutionaries effectively undermine the confidence the elite feel in the system. Every time the

Indian government dismisses a legally constituted Communist government in a state, or prevents the Communists from forming a government even if they enjoy the support of a majority of the voters, an erosion is made in this confidence, and the political forces are further polarized. It should therefore be in the interests of the Communists to challenge the national bourgeoisie on its own ground, and *prove* that Indian democracy does not permit the voters to choose their government.

Besides, the Communist experience in Bengal and Kerala has shown that it is far easier for the Communists to expand and consolidate their influence on the masses, especially in the countryside, by using governmental power than by acting in opposition to legally constituted governments. Parliamentarianism therefore has still a revolutionary role to play in India, if the Communists do not succumb to the bourgeoisie style of parliamentary activity.

In this context, the CPI(M) tactic of wrecking the system "from within" seems to be more relevant to the Indian social and political framework than either insurrection or protracted peasant guerrilla warfare. Of course, the "wrecking" is likely to be attempted both from within and without at the same time, by combining parliamentary and extraparliamentary struggles of increasing militancy. Street politics has earned legitimacy within the Indian system; [54] it has been resorted to by all sections of the bourgeoisie, including the Congress party. Some of the major political decisions, such as divisions of states along linguistic boundaries, have been forced by extraparliamentary agitations which were not always exactly peaceful.

The more radical among the Communists have, in recent years tried to *create* a nationalist instrument for mass mobilization, though without much success. The Maoist factions have accepted the Peking position that India has been reduced to a satellite of American imperialism and Soviet social-imperialism. The

---

[54] Kothari, *Politics in India*, p. 219.

CPI(M) in West Bengal has raised the cry that the central government has established a "colonial" hold on that state.[55] The Marxists have also been trying to use government-state relations as a weapon of class war, as we have already noted. Neither the Maoists nor the Marxists would seem to have so far succeeded to imprint these ideas on the minds of the ruling elite. The CPI(M) has found, to its dismay, that no non-Congress government in the states responded positively to its concept of a class war with the central government; on the contrary, the predominant tendency has been to establish links with the government in New Delhi.

The Marxists, on their part, have rejected the Maoist position that India is a satellite of the United States and the Soviet Union. As long as the Soviets regard India as an independent, progressive state, the Maoist stance is unlikely to prevail among a majority of the Communists. Their stance will, however, change if the Soviet outlook on India hardens. While this will not easily happen, it cannot be entirely ruled out. Much will depend on the drift and scale of India's internal policies and on the future of Sino-Soviet relations.

BUREAUCRATS, THE POLICE, AND THE ARMY

Among the subdivisions and institutions of the bourgeois state that the Communists have to contend with, the two most important, from the point of view of undermining the strength of the system from within and without, are the bureaucracy or civil services and the punitive forces or the police and army. The civil services have undoubtedly played a major role in the evolution of the Indian system, in making it how good and how bad it is. While the civil services can be said to be generally anti-Communist, their capacity to prevent a Communist takeover, constitu-

[55] "A new note of challenge in some speeches of the CPM leaders has also been noted. Mr. Jyoti Basu has said that West Bengal refuses to remain a colony of the central government for long. The state committee of the CPI(M) at its last meeting alleged that the 'despotic' Congress rulers of New Delhi are virtually treating West Bengal as an occupation area." Shankar Ghosh in *Times of India,* August 31, 1971.

tionally or otherwise, seems to be limited. Constitutionally, they are required to be apolitical, serving any government in power regardless of its ideological complexion. In practice, however, the civil services have been to some extent politically activated.[56] The cult of subservience and sychophancy is, in any case, widespread; the predominant tendency of the civil servant is to please the political boss.

Things turn out to be different, however, when a clear ideological divide exists between the political actor and the civil servant.[57] It seems that both in Kerala and West Bengal, civil service staffs were divided during CPI(M) rule between a majority of those who were reluctant, lukewarm, or resistant and a minority of those who were enthusiastic toward Communist strategies and tactics. Yet if the limited Communist experience in Bengal and Kerala is any indication, bureaucratic recalcitrance is not likely to be an insurmountable problem for the Communists' bid to employ governmental power to enhance their mass influence. A notable experiment tried by the Marxists in both states was to have important agrarian issues, such as distribution of land to the landless and division of crops between landlord and sharecropper, decided at joint party committees at the local level, in which the

[56] See C. P. Bhambri, *Bureaucracy and Politics in India* (Delhi Vikas, 1971). Bhambri deals only with the central bureaucracy and offers a number of case studies of conflict between civil servants and political leaders. "Bureaucracy and political parties are always competing for sharing political power in a developing society," observes Bhambri and adds, "Indian bureaucracy during Congress party rule has been in collusion with Congress party leaders, even factional leaders, and has actively worked for the personal or party interest of the Congress leaders. This is done in return for benefits of promotion and better jobs." A former central government minister, N. V. Gadgil, reports one particular instance of civil servants working for factional leaders. The All-India Congress Committee was meeting in Delhi in the background of a bitter feud between Nehru and the Congress president, P. D. Tandon. "The partisans of both camps had pitched their camps in Delhi two days before the session. Even government servants joined in discreet canvassing for votes." N. V. Gadgil, *Government from Inside* (Meerut, Meenakshi Prakashan, 1968), p. 192.

[57] This came particularly in evidence during Krishna Menon's tenure as defense minister. See Neville Maxwell, *India's China War* (Bombay, Jaico, 1970), pp. 170–200.

Communists had the major say. This proved to be a rather successful method of bringing "democracy" to the grass-roots and creating grass-root pressures on the bureaucracy at the state level.

The Marxists have been able to infiltrate the police forces in
West Bengal to some extent. Three or four major police protests
in Bengal during the last three years would at any rate indicate
that this punitive force is no longer apolitical.[58] In the most dramatic of these incidents, noted in chapter 4, a substantial number
of uniformed policemen raided the legislative assembly hall in
Calcutta, reportedly to kill Jyoti Basu. The Marxist deputy chief
minister made use of the incident to purge the police of "undesirable" elements, and to influence sections of the police force with
persuasion and patronage.

The broken state of law and order in Bengal since 1967 has
brought the police force, including the armed police sent out by
New Delhi, into almost daily confrontation with the people, the
vast majority of whom are law-abiding citizens who resent police
encroachment on their liberties and privacy. These kinds of en-
demic law-and-order crises tend to polarize relations between the
people and the coercive apparatus of the state.

The "Naxalite" annihilation campaign felled more than 30 policemen and injured more than 200.[59] In May 1971, three un-
armed constables escorting a group of "Naxalite" prisoners were
set upon in a police van and brutally murdered. When the bodies
arrived at Burdwan town, a large number of policemen and their
wives staged a noisy demonstration, and the entire police line had
to be disarmed and cordoned off by the military.[60] Such incidents
have so far been few and far between, but they indicate the kinds
of things that can happen if India or a part of it is thrown into a
continuing crisis of law and order because of a strong ascendence
in Communist strength.

[58] "Revolution in Khaki," *Economic and Political Weekly*, June 12, 1969.
[59] Dilip Mukerjee, "Danger in the Rear," *Times of India*, May 25, 1971.
[60] *Patriot*, May 30, 1971.

The armed forces present the Communists with a much greater problem, and it is somewhat curious that current CPI and CPI(M) literature is mostly silent on the subject. The Maoists alone have categorized the armed forces as a major enemy of the revolution. One of the objectives of "Naxalite" tactics of guerrilla war and annihilation of the class enemy is to undermine public fear of the state's apparatus of force. The Marxists have been trying to mobilize public opinion in Bengal against the stationing of several thousand troops before the mid-term parliamentary election, their continued presence since then, and their active participation in "combing" operations in Calcutta and elsewhere in search of "Naxalites." This has been a major theme in the CPI(M) political campaign since 1970.

Neither of the two Communist parties has articulated in recent years any fear of a military coup in India.[61] However, they have, on occasion, seen an undue amount of military influence on government policies and decisions. The thrust of their argument has been that the top brass of the military tend to pressure the government into aligning with the United States and generally following pro-Western foreign and pro-capitalist domestic policies. These apprehensions were articulated particularly in 1962–63, and also after the India-Pakistan war of 1965. Criticism of the military as a pro-Western pressure group has been muted following substantial Soviet collaboration in augmenting India's defense capability. The tendency of late seems to be to blame the government for using the military to suppress the democratic movement.

However, the CPI(M) has, on occasions, demanded reorganization of the army into a "patriotic people's army." It has accused the government of following British methods to build the army "around material incentives only." An article in the CPI(M) weekly in 1967 pointed out that officers were recruited only from the "upper classes." Privates were poorly paid and fed in compari-

[61] For reports and rumors of political ambitions harbored by individual senior officers of the army, see Welles Hangen, *After Nehru, Who?* (London, Hart-Davis, 1963), pp. 50–62; Maxwell, Part II.

son with officers. Worse, the soldiers were subjected to "rigorous political scrutiny and dismissed on political grounds. . . . Servicemen cannot be approached by political parties, nor can they contact their parliamentary representatives for redress of their grievances. Top officers, however, engage in much political activity." [62]

Communist influence in the armed forces seems to be nonexistent. Officers are still drawn largely from the "martial races" of Punjab, Rajasthan, Maharashtra, and the Deccan. The common soldier is mostly a peasant from these areas or from further south. Recruitment is made in rural areas that are politically quiescent. Measures are taken to protect land holdings of a soldier. While the combat forces come mostly from regions with a low level of political awareness and a high degree of stability, large sections of noncombatant elements are drawn from the Hindi-speaking states. As long as the homeland of the soldier is politically stable and agrarian relations remain tranquil, he is unlikely to be influenced by Communist propaganda even if much of it reaches him, which is not the case at present. His mood may, however, change if peasant unrest quickens in the countryside on a large scale, and if it is mobilized by the Communists.

Many of the Marathas in the army come from families of the rural poor, and the Maharashtraian countryside happens to be one of the most undisturbed in the country. Perhaps the first winds of peasant unrest to blow into the barracks will come from Bihar during this decade. It is, however, too early to speculate on the probable impact of serious, widespread peasant unrest on the army, except to suggest that a potential source of danger to the stability of the system lies in this direction, lending additional urgency to programs of radical reforms in agrarian relations.

If the Communists are seen as a single collectivity, one perceives outlines of three tactical approaches to the coercive forces of the system. Should the Maoists succeed in expanding and con-

[62] *People's Democracy*, June 22, 1967.

solidating their bases even in scattered portions of the country, they will engage the punitive forces in guerrilla combat. At the other end of the spectrum stands the CPI with its strategic objective of a government of the "Democratic front." If such a government were to be set up, the CPI would expect the armed forces to be transformed gradually into a people's army serving the interests of the masses. The Marxists have begun to engage the punitive forces in a different kind of confrontation. If they are in power in any state, they intend to deploy the police and, if they can, the army, to enforce, enhance, and protect the interests of the poor against the privileges of the rich, within the legal framework. The impact of such a government-generated revolution could not escape the policeman and the soldier. At the same time, the Marxists have been trying to organize their own paramilitary elements in the form of volunteers and peasant guards as a *defensive* force at present.

The CPI(M)'s parliamentary tactics can be seen to be partly dictated by the enormous punitive power at the disposal of the system. Working within the system, even with the objective of wrecking it, may not bring the party to a direct confrontation with the armed forces; there may be, on the contrary, some means of subverting the armed forces from within. Here one can see a possibility of the CPI and the CPI(M) supplementing each other's tactical line in a certain cluster of circumstances. Should the CPI be in power in the central government as a builder of the "national united front," the armed forces would be serving a government of which the Communists would be a partner. The Marxists may find such a situation somewhat to their advantage, for the CPI would be hard put to it to defend large-scale use of the army to suppress Communist-led struggles. In sum, Indian Communism, in the period of its growth, has begun to face, directly and indirectly, the state apparatus of force. The patterns of interaction that develop between the two will determine future tactics of the Communist groups and these, in turn, will influence and shape the style and content of the Communist bid for power.

A main thrust of this study has been to emphasize that Communism in India has entered a period of growth, facing problems peculiar to growth and development. We shall now try to list some of these problems.

THE PARTY OF THE FUTURE

It seems to be quite likely that there will be more than one Communist party in India, at least for a long time.[63] The CPI and the CPI(M) have quite different geographical bases, and it is unlikely that one will swallow up the other in the whole country. If the Marxists succeed in the coastal states, the CPI is likely to expand its influence in the northern Hindi-speaking region. The two will be locked in bitter, multiple conflict, but as they come to realize that neither can push the other out of existence, there may grow a basis for working together in rivalry and competition.

If this happens, the overall Communist strategy and tactics may be moderate rather than extremist. Rajani Kothari visualizes that, as the Communists increase their support base, they will steadily move toward the broad left-democratic consensus rather than away from it. "The main problem of the Communist parties," Kothari writes, "of course, is their narrow regional base, limited as they are to West Bengal, Kerala, and Andhra Pradesh, with some support in the industrial areas of Bihar. With growing industrialization, they may well pick up in a few other states, especially if

---

[63] Although minority factions exist almost in all Communist parties, and no Communist party is, strictly speaking, quite monolithic, there has been no case outside India so far where two near-equal Communist groups have been working side by side, often in conflict, sometimes in cooperation. Rivalries between the two groups are the bitterest in areas where Communism has registered substantial gains, such as Bengal and Kerala. Conflicts are less intense in areas where the movement is just building, as in Bihar and Andhra Pradesh. Moscow's recognition of the CPI(M) as the parallel Communist party seems to indicate that the Russians also expect to see two Communist parties function in India for quite a long time.

they manage to close their ranks, to gain wider acceptance and re-spectability, and to absorb large segments of other leftist parties. As they do this they are likely to move still closer to the Congress ideology and the emerging 'left of center' consensus." [64]

If Indian Communism tends to be milder and more moderate in the course of expansion, it will probably be due to the intellec-tual, middle-class leadership which is not expected to be rapidly replaced by working-class and peasant leadership. In the CPI, such new recruitment as has been taking place still comes mainly from the educated middle class. In the CPI(M), grass-root leader-ship is growing, and at the district level in Kerala and West Ben-gal, it is quite in evidence.[65] However, district cadres often com-plain that they are "kept down" for a long time, and that the leaders are reluctant to admit them to the higher echelons of the party apparatus.[66] The Communists are hardly immune to the in-fluence of the hierarchical values of Indian society. Any change will, of course, be judged by the Communists' social engineering, their style of mobilization for rapid development, and the use they make of the instruments of coercion. Neither Communist party has so far spoken in terms of proletarian dictatorship; the CPI, at its eighth congress in 1968, declared itself in favor of maintaining the institutions of representative government.

While these questions will be decided mainly by the style and momentum of Communist capture of power, the vast and com-plex diversities of India may dictate certain unavoidable choices. One of these might center round the question of how much coer-cion the Communists will be able to use once they are in power to restructure agriculture for maximum resource mobilization.

[64] Kothari, *Politics in India,* p. 215. Note that Kothari minimizes Communist in-fluence on the rural proletariat and considers reunion of the two parties to be nec-essary for an expansion of influence. This study takes a different view on either issue.

[65] This is based on my personal observation and inquiry in West Bengal, conver-sations with several CPI(M) leaders in Kerala, and discussion with five CPI leaders in Delhi.

[66] Interview with ten district-level cadres of the CPI(M).

Apart from the Communists' own preferences, the barriers—fourteen language groups, several linguistic-nationalist subcultures, and social institutions like the caste—to forcing through a collectivization program for the whole country seem to be formidable.[67]

The great diversities of the country and the likely process of expansion of Communist influence argue strongly against the growth of either Communist party as a highly disciplined, centrally controlled organization. The Communists are not likely to escape the factionalism inherent in India's geography and social institutions. Discipline was conspicuous by its absence in the united CPI; it has not been much better in either of the groups since the split.

It is difficult to foresee at this moment the emergence of a "monolithic" all-India Communist party dominated by a charismatic leader. Neither Communist group is at present in a position to discipline a strongly entrenched state leadership, and it is the powerful state units that control the central leadership. The problem will become greater as the parties expand their bases. National leaders are already finding it difficult to communicate effectively with the emerging grass-root cadres because of the language barrier; the communication distance will be wider as the two parties extend their organization to more linguistic areas. In short, the process of growth will probably build up pressures for a federal-type organization for either party. The state units will probably have to be given a good deal of autonomy within the framework of a *working* discipline.

This may, over time, raise another problem: the influence of regional cultures on Indian Communism. If Russian Communism is Marxism plus Slavic culture, and Chinese Communism is Marxism-Leninism plus Han culture, can Indian Communism be immune to the many cultures that go into the making of what can be loosely described as Indian culture? Put another way, will Ben-

[67] Barrington Moore Jr., pp. 409–10.

gali Communism and Malayali Communism and Telugu Communism be the same? As Communism becomes socialized in the various linguistic areas, all-India strategy and tactics will inevitably have to be worked out more in the form of a consensus of several Communisms rather than firm policies handed down by a unified leadership. The influence of a diverse culture may persuade the Communists to opt for mild and moderate doses of compulsion and coercion. It will probably be a strong factor in the Communists' choice of political institutions, at least in the first stages of their control of power.

Regional-nationalist sentiments appear to be stronger among the middle-class intelligentsia than among Communist groups. Neither Communist party seems to be thinking until now in terms of separatism; both would like to rule in all of India, not in a part cut off from the country as a whole. The nationalist uprising in East Pakistan in March 1971 has not generated any articulate thinking even among the Marxists and the Maoists in terms of seizing power in a united Bengal rather than in India. Both CPIs have welcomed the uprising and have been pressing the Indian government to recognize the "Bangla Desh" government.[68] However, at least one prominent CPI(M) leader is reported to have drawn an analogy between the colonial status of East Bengal in Pakistan, and the "colonial" position of West Bengal in India. More significant is the Marxist perspective of the long haul of political development in East Bengal. According to the secretary of the West Bengal Committee of the CPI(M), Promode Das Gupta:

Recent reports indicate that a National Liberation Front (NLF) and army have been formed in Bangla Desh. This front has taken upon itself the task of continuing the present struggle against the Pakistani

[68] This is yet another issue on which the CPI(M) has openly "differed" with the CCP. *People's Democracy*, May 16, 1971. The Marxist party, however, has denied CPI allegation that it equates the political situation in the two Bengals and that it believes that the frontier between them has "disappeared." For the CPI allegation, see *New Age*, May 9, and for the CPI(M) rebuttal, *People's Democracy*, May 23, 1971. The Communist party of East Pakistan is Moscow-oriented; it has fully supported the nationalist revolt. See *New Age*, April 18, 1971.

armed forces for liberating the people from the exploitation of monopoly capital, feudalism, and imperialism. They have already started training cadres in the various forms of war. It can now be hoped that with the emergence of the NLF, a qualitative difference will be imparted to the struggle going on in Bangla Desh.[69]

The CPI(M) therefore is looking with some hope to the emergence of a Vietnam-type liberation movement in East Bengal. Should this happen—there is no firm indication yet that it is going to happen—a Communist-ruled East Bengal may well introduce a qualitative change in the politics of India, especially of its eastern region. If the Marxists can once again form a government in West Bengal, they will probably try to foster the NLF in East Bengal. The uprising in East Bengal has thus introduced a new element in the politics of the subcontinent. Its future impact on Indian politics and on the fortunes of Communism in India will deserve careful watching.

International Communism has proved to be a help as well as a hindrance to the growth of Communism in India—it is difficult to judge precisely which. Until the Sino-Soviet split, Moscow kept Indian Communism firmly under control. While under Moscow's guidance, the CPI was able to establish its legitimacy within the Indian political system, but lost its independence and faced grave problems of identification. Since the split in the CPI, these problems would appear to have been more or less resolved. The CPI(M) is now independent of both Moscow and Peking, while the CPI's loyalty to Moscow is self-chosen. The former now attacks the system from below, the latter from above. These tactics determine their identification with the classes.

However, the existing state of relations between Moscow and Peking would suggest that external Communist powers may hinder rather than help the future growth of Communism in India. This is not to suggest that Communist victories in other Asian

---

[69] "The Movement in Bangla Desh," *People's Democracy*, May 9, 1971.

countries, the Indo-China States for example, will not be of any help to Communism in India. Such a major change in the balance of political forces in Southeast Asia will certainly have its impact on India. However, neither the USSR nor China can be expected to come to the aid of Indian Communism unless it is assured that Communism will more or less be of its own brand. It is even doubtful if the USSR would like to see Communism triumph in India as long as it can count on the friendship of the national bourgeoisie. So far, the Indian national bourgeoisie has proved to be of much greater importance to Moscow than has the party of the proletariat.

Neither Moscow nor Peking has hesitated to sacrifice the Communists of other countries for the sake of Soviet or Chinese national interests. Stalin kept his promise to Churchill that he would do nothing to help the Greek Communists seize power. The Chinese have come to the help of the Pakistan army to suppress the uprising in East Bengal in which the Communists have made common cause with the articulate nationalist elements. India is too vast and strategically too important to permit either Moscow or Peking to welcome the triumph of "any Communism" in that country. Thus, while Indian Communism will find strength in Communist successes in any part of the world, it will have to chart its own course toward revolution, not merely without counting on a Soviet or Chinese helping hand, but taking into account that the two great Communist neighbors may do positive harm to the revolution.

The history of international Communism bears the imprint of some spectacular successes, many tragic failures, and dogged persistence toward the desired objective. Communist revolutions have not succeeded in more than a dozen countries. In almost all of them, war—global, colonial, or local—has played the role of "accelerator." The capitalist system has proved to be more resilient and adaptive of pressures for change than either Marx or Lenin could foresee. The technological revolution, together with man's ability to learn from experience and draw upon the accumulated wealth of human wisdom (including the wisdom of Marxism-Leninism-Maoism), has injected new vitality, dynamism, and adaptibility to established political institutions.

The crucial factor for the new societies is time. Given time, India may well meet the destabilizing challenge of development and modernization. Communism offers a shorter road to development and stability. However, its acceptance by the majority of the Indian people will depend on the exhaustion of alternative methods. These have not yet been exhausted. At the same time, the Indian political system is under strain, and the pressures upon it from the rising waves of expectations will increase in the years to come. The survival and success of the political system cannot be predicted with certainty. Nor can one predict its failure and collapse. Even if the system gives in, there is no certainty that power will pass on to the Communists. But it may. And if it does, Communism will hold sway over the entire landmass of Asia. Its impact on the rest of Asia will be profound.

India has miles and miles to go within a relatively short time if its post-independence political experiment is to succeed. The challenge is taller than the men and women who have been trying to meet it—including the Communists.

INDEX

Adhikari, Gangadhar, 12, 19, 75-76, 85; quoted, 18, 23, 75, 76

Africa, Communism in, xv, 356, 386, 388, 405

Agrarian question, 288-321, 329-30, 351-52, 399, 400; peasant militancy, 289-92, 294, 295-302, 309, 314-21; "green revolution," 291, 298-302, 352, 418, 419; CPI role, 292, 293-94, 316-20; CPI(M) role, 292-93, 294, 320-21, 393; in India and China, compared, 420-21n41; *see also* Landlords and landowners; Land reform and seizures

Agro-Industries Corporation (Kerala), 274

Ahmad, Muzaffar, 64; quoted, 12

Akali Dal party (Punjab), 96, 107, 114-15, 116, 137

All-India Communist Convention (Tenali), 62, 65-66, 77, 93

All-India Coordination Committee of Communist Revolutionaries (AICCCR), CPI(ML), 327-28, 330-31

All-India Coordination Committee of Revolutionaries (AICCR), CPI(M), 327

All-India Kisan Sabha (AIKS), 29, 66, 97, 277, 297n4, 306, 319, 385; CP/CPI(M) struggle within, 98, 100; in West Bengal, 161-62, 306

All-India Trade Union Congress (AITUC), 29, 66, 97, 100, 288, 231; CP/CPI(M) struggle within, 98-100

Amrita Bazar Patrika, Calcutta daily: quoted, 351

Ananda Bazar Patriki, Bengali newspaper: quoted, 393-94n6

Andhra Pradesh: CPI in, 29, 37, 41, 42, 57, 64, 96, 98, 120, 121, 122 (*table*), 136-37, 176, 292, 314-15, 318-19, 401-3; peasants' movements in, 37, 294, 303, 305, 314-15, 318-19, 323, 334; guerrilla warfare in, 37, 294, 334, 336-38, 344-46 (*see also* Srikakulam uprising); CPI(M) in, 65, 81, 85, 96, 98, 120, 121, 122 (*table*), 127, 159, 294, 313, 326-27, 329-31, 332, 341, 344-46, 350, 371, 402-3; Congress Party in, 108, 136-37, 174, 338, 395, 402; Srikakulam uprising, 294, 323, 326, 327, 329-31, 333, 334, 335, 336-38, 344-46, 352, 374, 375; collapse of Communist revolutionary movement in, 344-46, 402; Revolutionary Com-